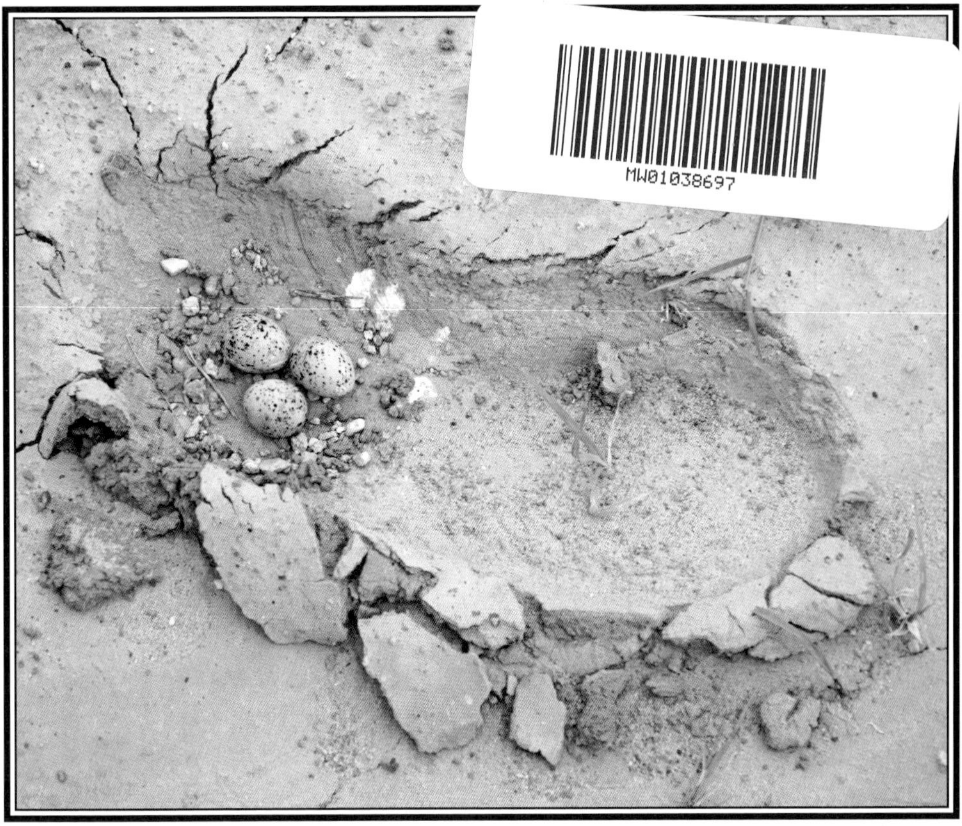

Tread gently through the wild

© Bob Gress, BirdsInFocus.com

This book belongs to:

____

Date

____

Wings across the water

Everglades Pinelands at Dusk

© Judd Patterson, JuddPatterson.com

First Light

THE LIVING GULF COAST

A Nature Guide to Southwest Florida

by Charles Sobczak

The Living Gulf Coast
A Nature Guide to Southwest Florida

Published by: Indigo Press LLC
2560 Sanibel Blvd.
Sanibel, FL 33957

Cover, Book design and layout by Maggie Rogers, MaggieMay Designs. **Cover photo** by Dick Fortune and Sara Lopez. Sunrise photo inside the lettering by Judd Patterson and both are used with the permission of the photographers.

ISBN: 9780982967478
Library of Congress Control Number: 2011920903
This is a work of nonfiction.

The Living Gulf Coast, along with all of the titles published by Indigo Press LLC, may be purchased for educational, business, or sales promotional use. For additional information and a discount schedule please write to: Indigo Press, 2560 Sanibel Blvd., Sanibel, FL, 33957 / E-mail at: livingsanibel@earthlink.net / Phone: 239-472-0491 / Fax: 239-472-1426.

This is a first edition printing, February 2011
Printed in the United States by United Graphics Inc., Mattoon, Illinois.

Table of Contents

The Living Gulf Coast

"In the end we will conserve only what we love.
Love only what we understand. Understand only what we are taught."
— *Baba Dioum*

Senegalese conservationist Baba Dioum is right. In the end we will preserve only what we love, and we who live here, or those of us who journey through Southwest Florida, have much to love. We have world-class aquariums and zoos, tropical botanical gardens and historical sites, beautiful state forests, and state and national parks—all there for us to roam and enjoy. There are countless creeks, rivers, and estuaries to paddle, and remote barrier islands upon which we can pitch a tent or, better still, sleep beneath the stars. There are miles of hiking trails and bike paths beckoning each and every one of us to get outside and experience the endless variety and beauty that is our natural world.

With all of that in mind, this book is divided into two sections. The second half focuses on the numerous parks, preserves, and eco-destinations found in Southwest Florida (162 total), while the first half describes and helps a nature lover identify the birds, mammals, reptiles, and amphibians they might discover there (419 total). The two are inexorably linked. Without vast tracts of land where the skies are free of power lines and buildings and the landscape unbroken by lawns and highways, there is no place for wildlife to flourish. Lacking sufficient habitat, species as diverse as the Florida scrub jay and the awe-inspiring panther cannot survive the onslaught of development that has overwhelmed much of Southwest Florida over the past 60 years.

Once we are out there, away from our computer screens and televisions, we can connect with the wildlife that still abounds in these natural places. We might catch a fleeting glimpse of a yellow-rumped warbler, corn snake, or white-tailed deer. There may well be a huge alligator basking on the bank of a stream we are canoeing or a pair of peninsula cooters sunning themselves on a fallen log. Once an animal is spotted, you can turn to the pages of this book and learn more about it. What is it, and what is its niche in the wild? How long does it live? What does it eat, and what might in turn eat it? In understanding these animals better, we come to love them. In loving them, we will strive to preserve their habitats, because without them they perish.

We must never take these wild places for granted. The laws that established these preserves were written by men and can just as easily be unwritten by them. As Florida's population approaches 33 million by 2050 there will be mounting political pressure to take back and develop these large tracts of land, whether state forests, preserves, or parks. Natural resources such as timber, phosphate, and clean water may tempt legislators in Tallahassee to revisit the thin sheets of paper and scrawls of ink that form the unfortified statutes that protect them. It will be up to all of us to ensure that this does not happen. The wildlife itself has no other voice in the marble hallways of human power.

There are other threats. While working on *The Living Gulf Coast* in the spring of 2010, an event happened that came perilously close to changing the title to

Oil covered Pelican
Courtesy Wikimedia Commons

The Dying Gulf Coast. On April 20, 2010, an oil rig, the infamous Deepwater Horizon, exploded off the coast of Louisiana and sank into the Gulf of Mexico. The blowout preventer, located a mile below the surface, failed to cap the well and for the next 86 days the wellhead spewed out an estimated 205.8 million gallons of crude oil, the largest accidental marine oil spill in the history of the petroleum industry. From Mote Marine to Rookery Bay contingency plans were being laid in the event this oil slick might approach Southwest Florida.

Had that oil come ashore, the results would have forever changed this region. Most, if not all, of the endangered manatees would die. Hundreds of bottle-nosed dolphins would likely succumb, and most of our mangrove forests would suffer irreparable harm. The tourism industry would collapse overnight, and tens of thousands of jobs that rely on the annual influx of beach lovers, naturalists, and snowbirds would be lost. The shorebirds and seabirds, like the pelican in the photo, would become mired in the oil slick and not survive. No matter what the spin by those who run the oil industry, or the politicians who do their bidding, the price of offshore drilling in Florida is too high. It must never happen.

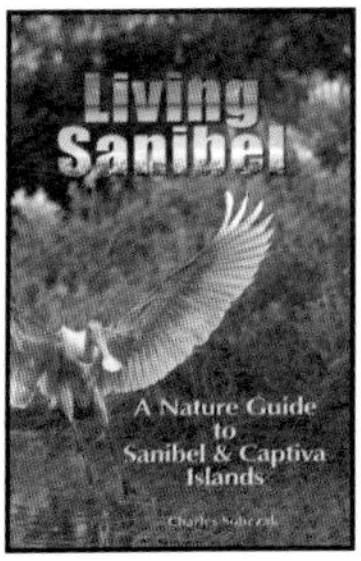

Finally, it is important to mention that this book is a companion to *Living Sanibel - A Nature Guide to Sanibel & Captiva Islands.* Whereas *The Living Gulf Coast* covers the megafauna no longer found on any of the barrier islands—creatures such as the Florida black bear, panther, white-tailed deer, and wild turkey—*Living Sanibel* contains chapters on saltwater and freshwater fishes, shellfish, plants, insects, and shorebirds. When combined they cover almost 1,000 living organisms, from fire ants to tarpon, and give the reader the ability to identify almost any creature, large or small, he or she might come across while voyaging through Southwest Florida. Both books combined are illustrated with more than 1,250 stunning photographs. These are not just field guides, but feel-good guides.

The future is up to us. We must be vigilant in protecting the Big Cypress National Preserve, Babcock/Webb Wildlife Management Area, the half-dozen preserves that create the Myakka Island, and all the others as well, because once lost, so too will be the warblers, kites, armadillos, and otters that live there. We must strive to keep species such as the snowy plover and red-cockaded woodpecker from joining the list we started with the passenger pigeon and the Caribbean monk seal. For their sake and the sake of our children, we must be committed to saving what's left. I hope you enjoy and, more importantly, use the book you are holding in your hands and use it lovingly.

Charles Sobczak
January 2011

Acknowledgments

There is not sufficient space here to thank the hundreds of people by name that helped make this book possible. It is challenging even to contemplate where to begin. That said, I have to start with my wife, Molly Heuer, and her adventurous spirit. When I first announced the concept of this book in the winter of 2010, and that it would require us to spend most of the following spring, summer, and fall visiting more than 60 regional parks, preserves, and eco-destinations, she didn't hesitate for a second. We found ourselves time and again jumping into the Prius, the cooler filled with water and Gatorade, our camera and binoculars in hand, mosquito repellent and sunscreen packed, to head north, south, or east toward all points natural. The most exciting adventure of all was when we found ourselves in mid-July wading through knee-deep water at Alligator Creek Preserve in Charlotte Harbor wondering if we were going to run into an errant alligator or cottonmouth along the waterlogged trail. We never did. Thank you, Molly, for all of your help and support in making this book, and all my writings, possible.

Secondly, my thanks and professional respect go to Maggie May Rogers of MaggieMay Designs. Although there are more than 600 photos in this book, there were literally three times as many shots to sort through, edit, and crop. Through it all, Maggie never once lost sight of the goal, which is to make all of us appreciate what a national treasure we have in the distinct flora, fauna, and wild places that are the heart and soul of Southwest Florida. She has done yet another outstanding job with this project.

My sympathies and admiration go out to Susie Holly, who in addition to being owner of MacIntosh Books & Paper on Sanibel is a copy editor who helped massage these words into print. She alone knows the depths of my dyslexic sense of the English language and manages to protect you, the readers, from the world's lousiest grammatician (which, by the way, isn't a word). Susie single-handedly makes my words readable. What more can I say?

Then there are the photographers. Wow! As they did in *Living Sanibel*, Dick Fortune and Sara Lopez came through with extraordinary and artful images. Their photograph of a great egret and its chicks graces the cover of *The Living Gulf Coast*. The trio of photographers who run the Website, www.Birdsinfocus.com, were also indispensable in making this book come alive. Judd Patterson, David Seibel, and Bob Gress all deserve my heartfelt praise.

I must not forget Alan S. Maltz, whose artistic talents never cease to amaze me. A true artist with a Nikon, he sees the world unlike any other photographer I have ever come across and captures that vision perfectly. I also have to single out Dr. Kenny Krysko of the University of Florida for supplying dozens of "herp" shots (reptiles and amphibians) from his personal collection. You can learn more about all of the photographers—Heather Greene, R.J. Wiley, Clair Postmus, Blake Sobczak, Jennifer Belton, Dr. Joe Blanda, Al Tuttle, and David Irving, among others—in the Contributors section near the end of this book.

I want to thank the many organizations and individuals who gave their time and shared their beautiful photos to help make this a better book. Erin Thomas

Duggan of the Sarasota County Visitors and Convention Bureau (VCB) and Jennifer Huber of the Charlotte County VCB provided some fabulous shots of these two fabulous counties. In Lee County not only did Nancy Hamilton of the Lee County VCB share her incredible photos of the Calusa Blueway, Edison-Ford Estates, and more, but also Kenneth Mills of Lee County Parks and Recreation sent me dozens of incredible shots of Lee County's scenic parks.

In Collier County I have to give thanks to the entire staff of the Conservancy of Southwest Florida, who helped design and create the county maps used in the destination section. Barbara Wilson, director of marketing, helped with some fantastic conservancy photos, and Troy Fensley, Education and Discovery Center manager, took Molly and me on a personal tour of the conservancy's ever improving, eco-friendly campus. Its next-door neighbor, the Naples Zoo, also came through with an informative tour by Tim Tetzaff, the youngest son of the original owners of the zoo, and a great cache of zoo photographs. The Naples VCB staff, especially JoNell Modys of the media center, supplied us with great shots and good suggestions about which preserves and parks to include. I must also thank Shannon Palmer of the Naples Botanical Garden for her lovely tour and stunning photographs of the newest and one of the friendliest destinations in this book. On a different note, I have to thank Dr. Meg (Canopy Meg) Lowman Ph.D., Andrew McElwaine and Don and Lillian Stokes for endorsing, as well as believing, in this work.

Not to forget Martha Robinson of Florida State Parks for supplying a huge selection of fantastic photos of all the state parks located in the six counties covered in this book, and the countless park rangers who were always there to answer my questions, take my calls, or correct a small but important detail of this book. In addition, there are many more helpful hands, hearts, and minds that went into making a work like this possible.

Finally, and most importantly, there is the wildlife itself to thank—the amazing diversity of birds, mammals, reptiles, and amphibians that make Southwest Florida a unique and special place in the world. I hope that I have honored each and every living creature covered in this book with my tales of who they are, how they live, reproduce and feed, and what they need to survive. What they ask from us is open space, the 10,000-acre parcels we are often so reluctant to let go of. I pray this book will help everyone understand the need to protect and preserve these precious landscapes and the wild things that roam them, because now, more than ever, we need them just as much as they need us. Without them we are nothing more than selfish fools living in an empty house. We can, and will, do much better than that if we care enough about the future of this wonderful world we live in.

Charles Sobczak

Burrowing Owl

*To all the organizations, great and small, and
all the environmentalists, young and old,
who work together toward saving what's left!*

Preening Roseate Spoonbills © Dick Fortune and Sara Lopez

The Birds of Southwest Florida

There are an estimated 10,000 species of birds in the world. New species are discovered every year in the remote forests of Borneo and jungles of South America and there is little doubt this number will continue to rise, albeit very slowly from this point foreword. Depending on the source, the continental United States has between 654 species (Audubon) and 925 species (American Ornithologists Union). The exact tally is blurred along both the Canadian and the Mexican boarders where many species ignore political boundaries in lieu of finding good habitat, regardless of who claims the territory it's located in. Accidentals, casuals and escaped avian pets make this tally an ongoing challenge.

Florida ranks in the top five states for bird bio-diversity, boasting 497 verified species. Of these 150 are permanent residents and the balance, some 347 species, are migratory. Because Southwest Florida borders the Carribean and is less than six-hundred miles from Mexico and Central America we have the distinction of being on the receiving end of two annual migrations. In the winter the Sunshine State swells with hundreds of species and tens of thousands of birds migrating south to avoid the inhospitable winters of the great plains and the northern boreal and deciduous forests. In the summer we become home to a surprising number of migrants that arrive here from South America to nest and raise their chicks in Florida. These include birds like the swallow-tailed kite and least tern. Depending on who you ask, there are between 300 and 400 bird species that frequent Southwest Florida.

Choosing which birds to include in this section proved difficult. Because The Living Gulf Coast is more of an overall field guide to flora and fauna as well as a destination guide, limiting the number of birds described herein was a necessity. There are plenty of excellent Florida birding guides available for those readers interested in pursuing this captivating aspect of the natural world. The companion book, Living Sanibel, has far more shorebirds included than does this work since it focused on barrier islands and not on mainland Florida.

Coming up with a list of approximately twenty percent of the total number of birds known to frequent Florida was a collaborative effort. Dedicated Audubon birders, naturalists and ornithologists all provided their input and helped cull the original list to a workable number. In choosing this selection I wanted to include the most commonly observed species while not ignoring certain birds that are unique to Florida, such as the Florida scrub jay and crested caracara. I also wanted to highlight species that were especially fascinating like the tiny ruby-throated hummingbird and the ungainly wood stork. While not all encompassing, I hope you will enjoy the birds I've chosen. An extended checklist of the species found here but not covered in detail is located at the end of this section.

Here is a synopsis of how this section is put together. Each bird species starts with a check box and a space to note the date the bird was first observed. Directly behind the birds common name is its Latin scientific name. Next comes a section called "Other names." These regional nicknames can speak volumes about the bird and its behavior and can also be quite amusing. That is followed by its current population status. The abbreviation FL stands for Florida, while the term IUCN stands for the International Union for Conservation of Nature, a worldwide organization that tracks species population trends across the globe. This organization is responsible for sounding the alarm when a species becomes seriously endangered. The abbreviations used are as follows: LC = Least Concern, NT = Near Threatened, VU = Vulnerable, EN = Endangered, CR = Critically Endangered, EW = Extinct in the wild, EX = Extinct.

The next three statistics are self explanatory; length, wingspan and weight, given in both American and metric units of measurement. The life spans are derived from data obtained by the Patuxent Wildlife Research Center operated by the U.S. Geological Survey located in Laurel, Maryland. The number given represents the longest known age of any given species and the reader should know that most of the birds in this section seldom make it to half that age in the wild. Where the birds nest is self explanatory.

The next section, "Found:", is followed by abbreviations of the six counties described in this work. They are as follows: AC = All Counties, SC = Sarasota County, ChC = Charlotte County, LC = Lee County, CC = Collier County, GC = Glades County and finally HC = Hendry County. Once again, these are only general guidelines. The following definition of where best to find each species is intentionally oversimplified. Coastal means the most likely place to spot this species is somewhere along the barrier islands and estuaries that line the Gulf coast of Southwest Florida. Near Coast means within fifteen to twenty miles of the actual coastline and Mainland means anywhere from fifteen miles from the coast all the way to the shores of Lake Okeechobee.

The final abbreviation is for months found. Obviously the capital letters used represent the months of the year, JFMAMJJASOND. When these are in black the bird is living in Florida. When they are in red the bird is breeding, nesting and raising its brood in Florida. A combination of red and black means the bird is a resident. Solid red means the bird breeds all year round in Florida. A blue color means the bird has migrated north and that usually means they are headed north to breed, nest and raise their chicks during the verdant summer months. A purple color means they are migrating south, returning to the Caribbean, South or Central America for the winter to either nest or overwinter there, only to return to Florida the following summer. Seeing either blue or purple in this abbreviated calender indicates the species is migratory. The individual birds are arranged in their taxonomic order as established by the American Ornithologists Union (AOU).

I hope you enjoy reading the bird section as much as I have enjoyed writing it. Birds are fascinating and it is easy to understand why birding is one of the most popular outdoor activities in North America. They are exquisitely designed creatures, weighing more than twenty pounds or as little as two-tenths of an ounce. Colorful, songful and fleeting, here are the birds of Southwest Florida.

❒ ______ **Fulvus Whistling Duck** (*Dendrocygna bicolor*) Other names: fulvus tree duck, Mexican squealer / Status: FL = stable, IUCN = LC / Length: 17.3-20.1 in. (44-51 cm) / Wingspan: 36 in. (91 cm) / Weight: 1.6-2.1 lb (595-964 g) / Life span: to 11 years / Nests: around Lake Okeechobee / Found: SC, ChC, GC, HC, CC, inland / Months found: **JFMAMJJASOND**.

Fulvus Whistling Ducks © David Seibel, BirdsInFocus.com

Although all eight species of whistling ducks are called ducks, they are actually more closely related to swans and geese than to members of the duck, or *Anas,* genus. Worldwide, the whistling duck is represented on every continent in the world. The fulvus whistling duck occurs in Central and South America, Africa, India, and the gulf coast of the U.S. Florida's population has been recently estimated at more than 20,000 birds statewide, with most of them centered on the southern shoreline of Lake Okeechobee, the headwaters of the St. John's River, and the Atlantic central coastline.

The whistling duck gets its name from the sound it makes, sometimes while in flight, which resembles a high-pitched two-toned whistle. Each of the eight members of the genus *Dendrocygna* has its own distinctive whistle; none vocalizes anything vaguely resembling a *quack.* One explanation for the expansion of this duck into Florida is that it thrives in agricultural areas such as the Everglades Agricultural Area, where it feeds on crops such as rice and vegetable farms.

Another reason the fulvus whistling duck is proliferating is that it has, on average, a clutch size of 12 to 17 eggs. This unusually high fecundity, coupled with manmade feeding grounds, bodes well for this medium-size bird. The fulvus whistling duck is rarely taken by alligators and is seldom preyed upon by owls and eagles. The largest source of mortality is the annual duck-hunting season, where one fulvus duck can be included in the six-duck daily bag limit.

Muscovy duck detail © Judd Patterson, BirdsInFocus.com

❐ ______ **Muscovy Duck** (*Cairina moschata*) Other names: royal duck, Barbary duck / Status: FL = expanding, IUCN = LC / Length: 28-34 in. (71-86 cm) / Wingspan: 3-4 ft (91-122 cm) / Weight: 5-15 lb (2.26-6.8 kg) / Life span: to 12 years / Nests: throughout SW Florida, mostly in urban settings / Found: AC, coastal, near coast, mainland / Months found: **JFMAMJJASOND.**

The Muscovy duck, a wild native of Central America and northern South America, is one of only two domesticated birds that have come out of the New World (the other being the Mexican wild turkey). In the wild this duck is a lustrous, iridescent green/black color. Most of Florida's population is from domestic stock and appears in a wide assortment of colors and patterns.

The Muscovy duck has patches of red bumpy flesh surrounding its beak, eyes, and face. Especially pronounced in the male, this warty, ungainly face looks as if the duck has just come out of a radioactive enclosure and is suffering from a bizarre mutation. This disfigurement is not abnormal, however, and is believed to pertain to attracting a mate. In Australia, where the Muscovy duck is domesticated for human consumption, this bird has been selectively bred to weigh as much as 20 pounds at harvest, nearly as large as a turkey.

In Florida, the Muscovy duck is considered a pest. It is rarely found in the wild but makes its home in urban or suburban lakes and ponds where it feeds mostly on vegetation, small fish, crustaceans, insects, and millipedes. Populations of this duck, which lays from 8 to 16 eggs and breeds throughout the year, can quickly overwhelm golf course ponds to the point where eradication companies are brought in to remove the over-abundant animals. The Florida Fish and Wildlife

Conservation Commission considers the Muscovy duck a nuisance animal. A permit is required to have it removed.

The Muscovy duck is not considered table fare in the United States, but it is a popular food source throughout much of the world. Its meat is less fatty than that of the domesticated mallard and has a flavor similar to beef or veal. This duck is extremely hardy, with feral populations able to withstand cold spells as low as 10 degrees Fahrenheit, despite its tropical roots. Considering the fact that the Muscovy duck is both flourishing and delicious, Florida should seriously consider a method of harvesting this large, strange-looking duck as a food source.

The Muscovy duck is taken by dogs, feral cats, alligators, bobcats, and raccoons. Its eggs are eaten by water snakes and invasive lizards such as Nile monitor lizards and black iguanas. The chicks, which are born precocial (able to stand up and feed themselves within hours of being hatched), are taken by a wide array of predators, from owls to rats.

❒ __________ **Wood Duck** (*Aix sponsa*) Other names: summer duck, woodie, squealer, swamp duck, acorn duck, Carolina duck / Status: FL = stable, IUCN = LC / Length: 18.5-21.3 in. (47-54 cm) / Wingspan: 26-28.7 in. (66-73 cm) / Weight: 16-30.4 oz (454-862 g) / Life span: to 22.5 years / Nests: a small, remnant population nests in Florida, most nest north of the Mason-Dixon Line / Found: AC, near coast, inland / Months found: **JFMAMJJASOND**.

Wood duck © David Seibel, BirdsInFocus.com

The male wood duck is considered by many birders and photographers to be one of the most beautifully adorned birds in North America. Its distinctive pattern, coupled with a multitude of colors such as its iridescent green head, white neck, red breast, and buff-colored belly make it an unmistakable sighting in the wild. The female, although also attractive, is nowhere near as flamboyant.

A combination of habitat loss and severe over-hunting brought the population of this bird to the edge of eradication around the turn of the 20th century, roughly the same time that the passenger pigeon and Carolina parakeet vanished.. The demise of the wood duck population helped push through the 1916 Migratory Bird Treaty, followed by the enactment of the Migratory Bird Act of 1918. These new regulations protected the remnant wood duck population, but the bird was given an additional boost in the 1930s with the development of the artificial nesting box. Today, wood-duck nesting boxes are ubiquitous across the U.S. and well up into Canada. In the winter months the resident Florida population swells with migrating flocks, making this an easy bird to add to your life list.

This small duck prefers hardwood swamps, especially flooded oak forests where it dines on acorns, seeds, insects, and berries. It is a cavity nester and can lay as many as 20 eggs per clutch. The newly born chicks jump out of the nest shortly after being hatched; because they are so light and down covered, they have been known to survive falls from as high as 290 feet without injury.

The wood duck has recovered from its brush with extinction and is now a game bird in Florida. The daily bag limit is six ducks per day, and three can be wood ducks. Slightly smaller than the mallard, the wood duck has a similar taste. The adult duck is taken by falcons, owls, and eagles, and the nestlings and eggs are subject to any number of tree-climbing predators.

❒ __________ **Mallard** (*Anas platyrhynchos*) Other names: greenhead (drake), gray mallard (hen), Susie (hen), wild duck / Status: FL = stable, IUCN = LC / Length: 19-7-25.6 in. (50-65 cm) / Wingspan: 32.3-37.4 in. (82-95 cm) / Weight: 2.2-2.8 lb (1-1.3 kg) / Life span: to 26 years / Nests: migratory birds nest across southern and northern Canada / Found: AC, coastal, near coast, inland / Months found: **JFMAMJJASOND.**

Mallard pair, female (left) male (right) © Bob Gress, BirdsInFocus.com

Without question the male and female mallard pair are what most people imagine when they think of wild ducks. The distinctive, iridescent green head, yellow bill, white necklace, and dark brown chest of the male mallard make it an easy bird to identify. The female mallard is easily mistaken for either sex of the Florida mottled duck. To make identification even easier, both sexes make an unmistakable *quack*, when flying or foraging. The old adage could easily be modified to read, "If it looks like a duck, quacks like a duck, and walks like a duck... it's probably a mallard."

The mallard and the Muscovy duck are the root of all domesticated ducks in the world. The mallard has been introduced into Asia, Europe, Africa, and Australia and is thriving. The mallard is considered an invasive species in New Zealand, where it displaces native birds.

It is easy to domesticate, and with feeding even wild flocks can settle in a backyard pond for their entire lives. In North America the mallard can be found from the Aleutian Islands of Alaska, east to Greenland, and south to Mexico. Most of the Florida population is migratory, but a fair number of resident birds are found across the state as well. All of the resident birds are semi-domesticated, as the true wild mallard returns north to nest every year.

Because of its ability to adapt readily to urbanization, the mallard is flourishing worldwide. It is a game bird in Florida, where hunters are allowed as many as four mallards in their six-duck daily bag limit, though only two can be hens. The mallard is a dipping feeder whose diet is almost exclusively duck weed, insect larvae, seeds, and aquatic vegetation. It is preyed upon by a wide array of predators, from coyotes to foxes and owls to falcons. The chicks and eggs are taken by everything from snapping turtles to water moccasins.

❐ ________ **Mottled Duck** (*Anas fulvigula*) Other names: Florida duck, summer mallard / Status: FL=stable, IUCN=LC / Life span: to 13 years / Length: 17-24 in. (44-61 cm) / Wingspan: 30-33 in. (76-83 cm) / Weight: 2.3 lb (1.04 kg) / Nests: throughout Florida / Found: AC, coastal, near coast, inland / Months found: **JFMAMJJASOND**.

Often seen in pairs, the mottled duck is readily observed in marshes, swamps, and wetlands in the early morning and evening. It tends to fly just above the treetops and can be heard making a distinctive *quack, quack, quack* as it travels. Both male and female mottled ducks bear a striking resemblance to a female mallard duck.

Mottled duck family © Judd Patterson, BirdsInFocus.com

The mottled duck is a game bird in Florida and is heavily hunted in the St. Johns River marshes in north central Florida, as well as other wetlands across the state. More than 13,000 mottled ducks are harvested annually. In hunting-free urban areas the mottled duck is far tamer than the migratory blue-winged teal and if approached slowly, will not fly away. It feeds primarily on small crustaceans, insects, and mollusks but will also filter-feed on vegetation. In shallow water it can be observed tipping, with its head buried in the muck and only its tail feathers sticking out of the water.

It is monogamous, mating very early in life, and it keeps solitary nests in dense vegetation. On the mainland the mottled duck has even been known to nest in tomato fields. It is in danger of losing its identity as a result of hybridization with feral mallards across the state. The offspring of these cross-breed pairings are fertile, which will eventually create an entirely new species. The chicks and eggs are preyed upon by snakes, alligators, snapping turtles, and hawks.

❐ ________ **Blue-winged Teal** (*Anas discors*) Other names: blue-wing, summer teal, white-faced teal / Status: FL=Stable, IUCN=LC / Life span: to 23 years / Length: 14-16 in. (35-40 cm) / Wingspan: 22-24.5 in. (56-63 cm) / Weight: 8-19 oz (230-530 g) / Nests: from Northern Texas all the way to Alaska / Found: AC, coastal, near coast, inland / Months found: **JF**MAMJ**JASOND**.

Blue-winged teal pair, male (left) female (right) © Bob Gress, BirdsInFocus.com

The blue-winged teal is one of the first birds to head south for the winter and one of the last to leave Florida in the spring. Because it waits so long to leave, this is one of the few birds you can find in Southwest Florida that begins to show its bright breeding plumage before its migration north. The female resembles the Florida mottled duck but is much smaller. The teal feeds primarily on aquatic vegetation and marine insects but will also graze on land, eating seeds and berries.

This bird can cover great distances in its migration, summering in northern Alberta and wintering in Colombia, a distance of more than 7,000 miles. Despite being heavily hunted on its annual migration southward, the blue-winged teal is one of the most common wintering ducks in Florida. You can often find flocks of up to 50 or 60 in larger wetlands. Because it is targeted by hunters, the teal is extremely skittish; you are unlikely to get much closer to one than gunshot range.

Its primary threat is loss of wetlands habitat, both in the United States and in Central and South America where many of the birds winter. Tens of thousands are taken every year during duck-hunting season. The nests and chicks fall victim to otters, mink, fishers, snapping turtles, snakes, and birds.

❐ ________ **Lesser Scaup** (*Aythya marila*) Other names: bluebill, bullhead, raft duck, blackhead, broadbill / Status: FL = declining, IUCN = LC / Length: 14.4-18.1 in. (39-46 cm) / Wingspan: 26.8-30.7 in. (68-78 cm) / Weight: 1-2.6 lb (454-1089 g) / Life span: to 18 years / Nests: in the northern great plains and well up into northwestern Canada / Found: AC, near coast, inland / Months found: **JFMA**MJJAS**OND.**

Lesser Scaup © Judd Patterson, BirdsInFocus.com

This bird was once Florida's most abundant duck species, with estimates of more than 500,000 scaups wintering in the Sunshine State 50 years ago. In different parts of the J.N. "Ding" Darling National Wildlife Refuge on Sanibel it was not uncommon to find flocks of 3,000 to 4,000 scaups floating close together in their favorite freshwater ponds (hence the nickname raft duck). Today, primarily because of decreasing nesting habitat along its northern breeding grounds, the lesser scaup has seen a huge decline in numbers across the state, making this once-plentiful bird a fairly uncommon sighting in Southwest Florida.

The lesser scaup, like its saltwater-loving cousin, the greater scaup, is a diving duck. It feeds not by tipping its bottom up and stretching to reach the bottom vegetation as does the mallard and Florida mottled duck, but by actually diving and swimming to depths of 60 feet where they feed on clams, snails, aquatic insects, seeds, and deep aquatic plants. Although a few lesser scaups are believed to be year-round residents of Florida, most of these ducks migrate north, all the way to the Northwest Territories and Alaska, every summer to breed and nest. The scaup frequently winters at Lake Okeechobee, where large flocks can still be found.

Lesser scaup chicks are born precocial, able to dive below the surface the same day they hatch. The chicks are taken by turtles and snakes, and adults are taken by owls, bobcats, and human hunters.

❒ ________ **Red-breasted Merganser** (*Mergus serrator*) Other names: sawbill, fish duck, hairy-head / Status: FL=stable, IUCN=LC / Life span: to 9 years / Length: 20-25 in. (51-64 cm) / Wingspan: 26-29 in. (66-74 cm) / Weight: 2.5 lb (1.2 kg) / Nests: in the far north all the way to the edge of the Arctic Ocean / Found: AC, coastal, near coast, inland / Months found: **JFMAMJJASOND**.

Red-breasted Merganser © Bob Gress, BirdsInFocus.com

A good-sized diving duck, the red-breasted merganser is quite common and prefers the saltwater estuaries to lakes and ponds when in Florida. The female merganser can often be found in midwinter feeding in the tidal flows found in estuaries all along the coast. The male tends to prefer the offshore habitat to the back bays and estuaries and as a result is much harder to find.

Its annual migration takes the merganser to the far north all the way to Hudson Bay and the coast of Greenland. In the summer, the male merganser sports a black head and crest with iridescent, greenish overtones and a clear white band around the neck. This breeding plumage is almost never apparent while the bird is wintering in Florida.

One of the fastest flying ducks, it has been clocked at more than 100 miles per hour. An extremely adept swimmer, it feeds primarily on fish but has been known to eat shrimp and crabs as well. The merganser is equipped with a serrated mandible, which greatly enhances its ability to hold on to slippery fish.

The red-breasted merganser is primarily monogamous and a solitary ground nester. Predation occurs mostly in the breeding grounds from gulls, coyotes, foxes, hawks, and owls. Because of the fishy flavor of its meat, the merganser is seldom a target of duck hunters.

❐ __________ **Northern Bobwhite** (*Colinus virginianus*) Other names: quail, partridge, bobwhite quail / Status: FL = declining, IUCN = NT / Length: 9 in. (23 cm) / Wingspan: 13 in. (33 cm) / Weight: 6.3 oz (178 g) / Life span: to 6.5 years / Nests: in mainland SW Florida / Found: SC, ChC, LC, GC, near coast, inland / Months found: **JFMAMJJASOND**.

Northern Bobwhite © Judd Patterson, BirdsInFocus.com

The call of this small, chickenlike bird gives away its presence in the flatwood pine forests it prefers. Its call is also its name, *b-bob-white*. The bobwhite has experienced a precipitous drop in population since the 1950s, with more than a 65 percent decline in the past 20 years. While some of this can be attributed to the removal of almost all of Florida's long-leaf pine forests, the exact reasons for the disappearance of this small game bird from the landscape are not well understood.

One of the best locations to find these members of the quail family is at the Babcock/Webb Wildlife Management Area in eastern Charlotte County. There, in collaboration with hunting clubs, the Florida Fish and Wildlife Conservation Commission is attempting to reestablish a permanent breeding population. While it is still a game bird in Florida with daily bag limits set at 12 per day, the bobwhite has recently been classified as a near-threatened species by the IUCN because of the dramatic population decline found throughout its range. This is one of only a few instances where the local conservation efforts lag behind the leadership of the IUCN.

Because the bobwhite is a prolific breeder, laying clutches of 10 to 15 eggs at a time, there is every reason to believe that with proper management and the kind of habitat reconstruction that is being done today at Babcock/Webb, the bobwhite will someday return to its historic populations. The adult bird is a favorite prey for owls, falcons, hawks, and bobcats, while the eggs and chicks suffer predation from feral cats, skunks, opossums, and fire ants.

❒ ______ **Osceola Wild Turkey** (*Meleagris gallopavo silvestris*)
Other names: gobbler, turkey / Status: FL = stable, IUCN = LC / Life span: to 12 years / Length: 43-45 in. (110-115 cm) / Wingspan: 49-57 in. (88-392 cm) / Weight: 5.5-24 lb (2.5-10.5 kg) / Nests: throughout SW Florida, mostly inland / Found: AC, near coast, inland / Months found: **JFMAMJJASOND**.

Male gobbler © Judd Patterson, BirdsInFocus.com

The male wild turkey is the heaviest bird living in Florida. Almost entirely terrestrial, this huge gobbler is nonetheless capable of short, powerful flights, seldom exceeding a quarter of a mile. Most of its days are spent foraging on the ground and its evenings roosting in trees, where it is safe from predators such as raccoons and bobcats. This is an important game bird throughout Florida where it is found in all 67 counties. Although the wild turkey was once common on many of the gulf coast's barrier islands, extensive development has eradicated these flocks, and the wild turkey is now found exclusively inland.

Female wild turkey with chicks Courtesy John James Audubon via Wikimedia Commons

Benjamin Franklin proposed the wild turkey as the national bird and was disappointed when Congress chose the bald eagle instead. Once abundant throughout North America, the turkey was hunted to extirpation in almost the entirety of its former range. The Florida population, however, remained healthy throughout the 1800s and 1900s, and was instrumental in repopulating the species starting in the 1950s. Today, because of the success of this reintroduction program, the wild turkey not only thrives in its former range, but can also be found in every state except Alaska and Hawaii. It has even moved into parts of southern Canada, where it was historically never a native species. The turkey also occurs in Mexico, where the domesticated stock originated. Prior to its near eradication, the turkey was an important food source for Native Americans and pilgrims.

The Osceola, or Florida, wild turkey, named for the famous Seminole chief, is a subspecies. It is slightly smaller than other wild turkeys, and its body feathers are an iridescent green-purple. The wild turkey is an omnivore, foraging on acorns, insects, worms, grubs, seeds, and even snakes and small reptiles. One of the best spots in Southwest Florida to see this large bird is Myakka State Park and Babcock Ranch, where the uplands and oak forests provide ample habitat. The wild turkey is legally hunted by man but also falls victim to a variety of natural predators including raccoons, opossums, skunks, foxes, eagles, great horned owls, bobcats, coyotes, panthers, and any number of larger snakes.

Reduced to a U.S. population of a mere 30,000 birds in 1901, the wild turkey today numbers more than 7 million birds worldwide and counting. This is a clear-cut example of how a well-monitored conservation effort coupled with a reintroduction program can make a huge difference for the future of wildlife.

❐______**Wood Stork** (*Mycteria americana*) Other names: flinthead, Spanish buzzard, wood ibis / Status: FL=Endangered species, IUCN=LC / Life span: to 18 years / Length: 33-45 in. (85-115 cm) / Wingspan: 59-69 in. (150-175 cm) / Weight: 6 lb (2.72 kg) / Nests: at Audubon Corkscrew Swamp and other remote rookeries / Found: AC, coastal, near coast, inland / Months found: **JFMAMJJASOND**.

© Judd Patterson, BirdsInFocus.com

With its distinctive black-tipped wing feathers and extended neck and legs, the wood stork is easy to recognize in flight. It can often be spotted soaring and circling high above the mainland. Because the wood stork uses thermals to travel as far as 80 miles from its roosting site to arrive at its feeding destination, you are unlikely to spot any of these birds early in the day before the land heats up sufficiently to create these rising air currents. Good places to search for the wood stork are along roadside drainage ditches, swamps, and freshwater canals, especially during times of drought.

The wood stork has a unique way of feeding, which makes it amusing to observe. It captures its prey using a specialized technique known as grope feeding or tactolocation. It prefers to feed in water 6 to 10 inches deep, with its long black bills partly open. When the fish touches the bird's bill, it snaps shut with an average response time of 25 milliseconds, one of the fastest reflexes found in all vertebrates. To put this number into perspective, humans blink at 330 milliseconds, so a stork snaps its bill shut on an unsuspecting minnow 13 times faster than the blink of a human eye.

From a high of 20,000 nesting pairs in the 1930s, the wood stork population in the southeastern United States declined to approximately 5,000 pairs by the late 1970s, mostly because of habitat and nesting-site loss. It takes up to 400 pounds of fish to feed both parents and two chicks from the time they hatch until they reach

Wood Stork

the fledgling stage. The wood stork requires almost ideal conditions to nest: summers with high rainfall (producing ample breeding ponds for small fish) followed by winters with little to no rainfall (concentrating the minnows into shallow, crowded ponds where the adult wood storks shuffle their large, pink feet to flush out crustaceans and minnows). Lacking these conditions in any given season, the wood stork does not nest.

One of the best places in Southwest Florida to observe the wood stork is the Audubon Corkscrew Swamp Sanctuary, where it roosts every evening in the ancient bald cypress trees. Although slowly rebounding from its record low numbers, the wood stork is struggling to adapt to Florida's rampant growth. Urban sprawl, coupled with the paving over of feeding ponds and wetlands, is especially hard on this large bird. It has a distinct population in Central and South America that is not endangered, but preserving the North American species may yet prove to be a challenge. Wood stork rookeries are sometimes preyed upon by snakes and owls, and the adult bird is occasionally taken by alligators. Sadly, its primary threats are humans and the demands they make on the environment.

❒ ______ **Magnificent Frigatebird** (*Fregata magnificens*) Other names: man-o'-war bird, pirate of the sea, hurricane bird / Status: FL=stable, IUCN=LC / Life span: to 19 years / Length 35-45 in. (89-116 cm) / Wingspan: 85-88 in. (217-224 cm) / Weight: 2.8-4.2 lb (1.3-1.9 kg) / Nests: in a large colony in Estero Bay in Lee County and in the Florida Keys / Found: SC, ChC, LC, CC, coastal / Months found: **JFMAMJJASOND**.

One of the most efficient flying birds in the world, the magnificent frigatebird rivals the albatross family in its ability to remain airborne for extended periods of time. Extremely light and with an enormous wingspan, it has the lowest wing-loading (weight to wingspan) of any bird in the world. Seemingly suspended in the breeze, the frigatebird resembles a kite or large black bat soaring high overhead.

Magnificent Frigate bird, male
© Judd Patterson, BirdsInFocus.com

The frigatebird is kleptoparasitic, a feeding characteristic most often found in insects but also observed in certain birds. This means that the frigatebird will often harass a gannet, anhinga, or booby into disgorging its catch, then snatch it away from the other bird in midair—hence the nickname, pirate of the sea.

On the open ocean the frigatebird survives on squid, jellyfish, fish, and even young sea turtles. A truly spectacular flyer, the frigatebird has been observed synchronizing its speed and aligning its direction perfectly to snatch flying fish

Male frigatebird in flight © Judd Patterson, BirdsInFocus.com

while the fish is airborne! In the Florida Keys, this behavior makes the frigatebird a welcome sight for anglers searching for the pelagic fishes of the Gulf Stream (dolphin, wahoo, marlin, and tuna) because the frigatebird tends to follow these fish in hopes of feeding on their by-catch or capturing the flying fish fleeing before them.

The male frigatebird has a large red pouch that it inflates during breeding season. The chicks of the frigatebird are pure white and extremely vulnerable to predation. They remain with the mother for more than a year after hatching, and because of the risk of being killed by other nesting frigatebirds, they are never left unattended. Because of this lengthy upbringing, the female frigatebird mates once every other year.

The frigatebird has been known to get swept up in major storms. In 1988 Hurricane Gilbert carried a flock deep into North America, leading to record sightings as far north as Ontario. Recent DNA testing has shown that the frigatebird is more closely related to the penguin than to the pelican family where most scientific literature still places it. Most predation to the frigatebird comes at the nesting site. It has no known predators once this large bird is at sea.

❒ __________ **Northern Gannet** (*Morus bassanus*) Other names: gannet, salon goose / Status: FL = increasing, IUCN = LC / Life span: to 27 years / Length: 32-43 in. (80-110 cm) / Wingspan: 70 in. (177 cm) / Weight: 4.85-7.9 lb (2.2-3.6 kg) / Nests: in six well-established colonies in eastern Canada / Found: AC, coastal / Months found: **JFM**AMJJASO**ND**.

This large pelagic seabird is a frequent winter visitor throughout Florida. Although sightings are more common off the Atlantic and Panhandle coasts, the gannet will come close to shore when the bait schools migrate near the beaches every fall and spring. Its size and coloration makes the gannet an easy bird to identify, especially the mature adult, which sports distinctive black-tipped wings. The gannet takes up to four years to mature. The immature bird displays a mottled brown, white, and grayish plumage. The adult gannet closely resembles the much rarer and smaller masked booby.

The gannet is related to the pelican and, like its cousin, is a plunge diver. It dives for squid and near-surface minnows in much the same fashion as the brown pelican. Unlike the pelican, however, the gannet can continue to swim downward after entering the water. This adaptation, similar to the loon, allows the bird to reach depths of up to 70 feet underwater in search of prey. Its skull is reinforced to cushion the brain from repeated impacts with the water.

Northern Gannet in flight © David Irving

The northern gannet breeds in large colonies called ganneries, which are always located along steep cliff faces to minimize predation. North America has six established ganneries, with 32 more located along coastal Europe from Brittany to Norway. The gannet breeds in large, noisy colonies (up to 60,000 couples at a single site) during the summer and wanders south during the winter in search of forage. It mates for life, but once the breeding season is over the flocks tend to disperse. Most Florida sightings are of individual birds. Because of recent protections put on harvesting the eggs from the ganneries, its worldwide population is increasing. The adult bird is still taken and eaten by people on the Isle of Lewis in the United Kingdom, though the harvest is limited to 2,000 chicks per year. At 10 weeks of age gannet chicks weigh more than the adult birds at an astounding 8.8 pounds each. The word *gannet* is derived from the Anglo-Saxon *ganot,* meaning "little goose."

The northern gannet has few predators. Eggs and nestlings are taken by herring and black-backed gulls, ravens, and ermine and red foxes. The adult bird is rarely taken by bald eagles, and sharks and seals have been known to snatch up the gannet when resting on the surface at sea. The gannet never comes ashore except to breed; any bird found on the beach is likely sick or injured. In flight it tends to skim above the surface of the sea at heights from 5 to 50 feet and is a delight to watch.

❒ _______ **Double-crested Cormorant** (*Phalacrocorax auritus*)
Other names: shag / Status: FL=stable and expanding its range, IUCN=LC / Life span: to 22 years / Length: 28-35 in. (70-90 cm) / Wingspan: 45-48 in. (114-123 cm) / Weight: 4 lb (1.81 kg) / Nests: throughout SW Florida / Found: AC, coastal, near coast, inland / Months found: **JFMAMJJASOND**.

Double-crested Cormorant in breeding plumage © Dick Fortune and Sara Lopez

Related to the pelican family, the cormorant is commonly seen across all of Southwest Florida. Often found near marinas and boat docks, it has also been known to steal small fish from anglers before they can land them. An accomplished swimmer, the cormorant can dive to 25 feet and hold its breath for well over a minute. It eats mostly fish, catching them with its hooked beak while underwater.

Nesting cormorants © Judd Patterson, BirdsInFocus.com

Although the cormorant was affected by the use of DDT and similar pesticides, it has recovered, and the population is expanding into the interior of North America where it has been known to decimate fish farms. It is sometimes killed by fishermen who blame the bird for declining fish populations in freshwater lakes. The cormorant is often mistaken for the anhinga, especially when swimming, but the cormorant has a much thicker neck and a noticeable hooked bill. It nests in colonies, most of the time exclusively with other cormorants.

❐ __________ **Anhinga** (*Anhinga anhinga*) Other names: snakebird, water turkey, darter / Status: FL=stable, IUCN=LC / Life span: Life span: to 11 years / Length: 30-37 in. (75-95 cm) / Wingspan: 45-48 in. (114-123 cm) / Weight: 2.7 lb (1.22 kg) / Nests: throughout SW Florida / Found: AC, coastal, near coast, inland / Months found: **JFMAMJJASOND**.

Anhinga in breeding plumage
© Dick Fortune and Sara Lopez

One of the most photographed birds in Florida, the anhinga can be seen at almost any time of the day along canals and drainage ditches, drying its wings. The name *anhinga,* which comes from the Tupi-speaking natives of the Amazon basin, means "evil spirit of the woods." Locally it is often referred to as the snakebird because of its ability to swim through the water with only its long, snakelike neck exposed.

When in full breeding plumage, the male anhinga sports a stunning black and white neck, back, and forewings that resemble piano keys. The female has a brown neck and breast. Because of its similar size and feeding habits, the anhinga is easily confused with the cormorant. Unlike the cormorant, however, the anhinga is an excellent flyer and can sometimes be seen soaring with wood storks and vultures high above the peninsula.

The anhinga, a distant relative of the pelican, has evolved a unique style of fishing. Unlike the cormorant and most diving ducks, the anhinga has no natural oils in its feathers. That, coupled with its dense bone structure, allows the anhinga to sink once its feathers become saturated with water. Also unlike the cormorant, the anhinga seldom grasps its prey but instead impales the pinfish or sand trout on its sharply pointed, dagger-like beak which it uses to impale the unfortunate fish. The anhinga carefully flips the minnow off of its beak, eventually working its way around to its mouth where it swallows the minnow whole.

Its unusual perching behavior, with its large wings spread wide open, occurs because the anhinga becomes completely waterlogged after fishing. Sometimes, when startled and still too wet to fly, the anhinga will tumble back into the water creating a loud, unexpected splash.

Although its principal diet is fish, the anhinga has been known to eat baby alligators, water snakes, leeches, and frogs. Monogamous and colonial, it often nests with egrets and herons. Aside from alligators and great horned owls, the anhinga has few natural predators.

Anhinga spears a freshwater bream
© Dick Fortune and Sara Lopez

❒______ American White Pelican (*Pelecanus erythrorhynchos*)

Other names: none / Status: FL=stable to increasing slightly, IUCN=LC / Life span: to 31 years / Length: 60-63 in. (152-160 cm) / Wingspan: 96-110 in. (243-279 cm) / Weight: 15.4 lb (7 kg) / Nests: in the summer in Canada and the north-central Great Plains / Found: AC, coastal, near coast, inland / Months found: **JFMAMJJASOND**.

The white pelican is one of the largest and heaviest birds found in Southwest Florida. Only the wild turkey, back from its own brush with extinction, is larger. That said, the white pelican has a much longer wingspan, measuring nine feet across for a mature bird. The white pelican is one of only seven pelican species worldwide; the only other pelican native to North America is the familiar brown pelican. There is one pelican species in South America, the Peruvian pelican, which is similar in appearance to the brown pelican but more than twice as large.

Over the past 20 years the sightings of the white pelican throughout the region have increased dramatically. In the early 1990s it was found only on remote barrier islands and along oyster bars along the coastline. Today it can be seen regularly in Myakka River State Park, Rookery Bay, and many other locations. A stunning bird to observe in flight, the white pelican has conspicuous black tips at the end of its wings and carries one of the largest bills in the world. (The Australian pelican, which is seven pounds heavier than the white pelican, has the largest bill of any bird species on earth.)

During the nesting season the white pelican develops a large, conspicuous plate on its upper bill. Its purpose is not entirely understood but is believed to be related to breeding displays. Unlike its brown cousin, the white pelican does not dive for its food. Instead it forms a communal group that herds its catch into

Five white pelicans © Dick Fortune and Sara Lopez

shallow water or surrounds a school of minnows, then feeds on them by dipping its large bill into the water and scooping them up. Although it feeds on saltwater fish during the winter months, its primary diet consists of freshwater species such as perch, sunfish, suckers, and carp. As the white pelican's numbers have rebounded, it has come increasingly in conflict with the growing aquaculture industry in the southeastern United States.

Because of its commanding size, the white pelican has few natural predators. Like many other birds, this pelican was severely impacted by the widespread use of DDT and other pesticides beginning in the 1940s until DDT was banned in the United States in 1972. The white pelican is still recovering from the effects. Despite being a protected species, it is still the target of hunters, its single largest cause of mortality. Many of the pelicans that are shot during the hunting season are cases of mistaken identity. When in flight, white pelicans often resemble snow geese and other legitimate migratory game birds.

❐ ________ **Brown Pelican** (*Pelecannus occidentalis*) Other names: none / Status: FL=species of special concern, ICUN=LC / Life span: to 27 years / Length: 40-50 in. (100-127 cm) / Wingspan: 78-84 in. (187-213 cm) / Weight: 8.2 lb (3.7 kg) / Nests: along the coastline / Found: SC, ChC, LC, CC, coastal / Months found: **JFMAMJJASOND**.

As you travel up and down the coast, it is impossible not to spot this large, easily recognized bird feeding on the threadfin herring and glass minnows that gather along the shoreline and in the shadows cast by the numerous bridges ferrying you across to the barrier islands. What is harder to grasp is that the ubiquitous brown pelican was fast approaching extinction in the 1960s and '70s.

Widespread use of DDT to control the Florida mosquito population altered the calcium metabolism in pelicans and other birds, causing them to produce eggs with shells too thin to support the embryo to maturity. In nearby Louisiana (where, ironically, the pelican is the state bird) the population completely collapsed because of the overuse of these pesticides. Louisiana had to import Florida pelicans through the 1980s to help rebuild its decimated flocks. Today, they are once again rebounding from yet another manmade disaster, the Deepwater Horizon oil spill.

Diving pelicans © Rob Pailes, Santiva Images

The brown pelican is the smallest of the seven species of pelicans in the world. The only other indigenous North American species is the American white pelican, a common winter resident of Southwest Florida. The largest pelican in the world is the Australian pelican, which can weigh more than 22 pounds (10 kilograms).

The brown pelican is unique among these species in that it is the only one that dives for its prey. The brown pelican hovers from heights of 20 to 60 feet, then collapses its wings and plunges headfirst into the water, filling its pouch with a combination of minnows and saltwater. A fully extended pouch can hold almost three gallons of water. As the bird strains out the excess water, terns and gulls flock around hoping to pick off some of the outflow.

The brown pelican is especially vulnerable to water quality. Excessive nutrient runoff and the resulting harmful algae blooms can cause severe declines in minnow populations. With each pelican chick requiring 150 pounds (67 kilograms) of fish over the eight-month nesting period, an entire breeding season can be lost to environmental degradation. The brown pelican nests in large colonies, generally on remote and smaller uninhabited mangrove islands.

Predation occurs mostly to the eggs and nestlings from raccoons, opossums, bobcats, snakes, fish crows, and exotics such as Nile monitor lizards. Adults may be taken by sharks and alligators, though rarely. Coastal development, pollution, and pesticides are the pelican's primary threats.

Brown Pelican

❐ __________ **American Bittern** (*Botarusus lentiginosus*) Other names: stake driver, thunder pump, sun-gazer, Indian hen / Status: FL = stable, IUCN = LC / Length: 23.6-33.5 in. (60-85 cm) / Wingspan: 36.2 in. (92 cm) / Weight: 13.1-17.6 oz (370-500 g) / Life span: to 8.4 years / Nests: across the northern tier of the U.S. and well up into Canada during the summer / Found: AC, coastal, near coast, inland / Months found: **JFMAMJJASOND.**

American Bittern © Bob Gress, BirdsInFocus.com

This extremely reclusive bird is often present but seldom seen during the winter months across all of mainland Florida and south to Cuba. It inhabits freshwater marshes where it feeds amidst the tall grasses and reeds. When startled the American bittern seldom flies. Instead it straightens its thick mottled neck and points its equally mottled beak skyward (hence the nickname sun-gazer), making itself all but invisible to the casual observer. It has become so adept at this camouflage technique that the bittern has learned to sway with the surrounding wind-blown vegetation.

The bittern feeds on frogs, small fish, and insects that thrive in the marshes it inhabits. Though seldom heard during the winter, the bittern is renowned for its distinctive call, often compared with a broken hydraulic machine. Because of its ability to disappear in the reeds, the adult bittern is seldom taken by predators other than alligators. The nests are sometimes raided by muskrats, water snakes, and raccoons. Its populations are in decline as a result of extensive habitat loss from the draining of marshes and swamps for agricultural and developmental uses.

❐ ____________ **Least Bittern** (*Ixobrychus exilis*) Other names: petit butor (Fr.) / Status: FL = stable, IUCN = LC / Length: 11-14.2 in. (28-36 cm) / Wingspan: 16.1-18.1 in. (41-46 cm) / Weight: 1.8-3.6 oz (51-102 g) / Life span: to 6 years / Nests: in Florida, but the population swells during the winter months when migratory birds arrive / Found: AC, coastal, near coast, inland / Months found: **JFMAMJJASOND**.

Male Least Bittern © Clair Postmus

Similar in behavior to the American bittern, the least bittern is the smallest heron found in Florida. An adult male weighs only a few grams more than a robin. This bird has a distinctive dimorphic coloration pattern rarely found in herons. The male exhibits a greenish-black head, tail, and back, whereas the female is mostly rusty brown. Both sexes forage in much the same fashion: climbing through dense stands of cattails and bulrushes in search of small fish and insects. When startled it seldom flushes, being far more inclined to freeze in place with its beak thrust skyward. Although it is

Least Bitterns © John James Audubon, via Wikimedia Commons

fairly common across the state, it is seldom seen because of its ability to vanish into the reed beds.

The least bittern enjoys an extensive range that encompasses most of the eastern United States, parts of California, most of Mexico and Central America, then south to northern Argentina. Its numbers are stable throughout the range. It is too reclusive and small to be a game bird. Chicks and eggs fall prey to snakes, rats, and other herons, but the adult is so difficult to spot amidst the reeds that it is seldom eaten. The least bittern is considered a challenging find by most birders; spotting one can be the thrill of a lifetime for a dedicated birdwatcher.

❐ ________ **Great Blue Heron** (*Ardea herodias*) Other names: blue crane, pond scoggin / Status: FL=stable, IUCN=LC / Life span: to 24 years / Length: 38-54 in. (97-137 cm) / Wingspan: 66-79 in. (167-201 cm) / Weight: 5.7 lb (2.59 kg) / Nests: throughout SW Florida / Found: AC, coastal, near coast, inland / Months found: **JFMAMJJASOND**.

Great Blue Heron in flight © Dick Fortune and Sara Lopez

The great blue heron is the largest and most widespread heron in North America. A magnificent bird to watch, this skilled hunter can be found throughout Southwest Florida. It has adapted well to human environments and can often be found leaning over open bait wells at marinas or begging for handouts at local fishing piers. Migratory herons, which frequent the region during winter, tend to be far more skittish than the resident herons.

Although there is a white morph called the white morph of the great blue heron, its range does not extend as far as Southwest Florida, though it can be readily found in the Florida Keys and may be seen rarely in southern Lee and

Coming home to roost © Hung V. Do

Collier County. There is also a mixed breed, known as Würdemann's heron, that is a meld of the blue and white morphs.

Dieting mostly on fish, which it spears with amazing precision, the great blue heron also eats mice, lizards, and snakes and has even been observed feeding on hatchling alligators. On rare occasions a great blue will choke to death when attempting to eat a fish or animal too large to swallow.

An injured or captured great blue heron must be handled with extreme caution. It has been known to drive its long, powerful beak into a person's eye. Covering its head with a towel or t-shirt is always advised if you come across a sick or injured bird.

When disturbed, the great blue heron lets loose with a very loud squawk that can be quite alarming. It is monogamous, nesting in large single-species colonies. When discovered these colonies should not be disturbed, as any intrusion could result in the agitated chicks falling from their nests where they will be preyed upon by raccoons, otters, and bobcats. The adult bird is sometimes taken by alligators. Overall, the great blue heron is thriving.

Great Egret with spotted sea trout

❒ ____________ **Great Egret** (*Ardea alba*) Other names: American egret, white crane, plume bird / Status: FL=stable, IUCN=LC / Life span: to 22 years / Length: 46-52 in. (116-132 cm) / Wingspan: 77-82 in. (195-208 cm) / Weight: 5.7 lb (2.5 kg) / Nests: throughout SW Florida / Found: AC, coastal, near coast, inland / Months found: **JFMAMJJASOND**.

Great Egret with breeding plumage
© Dick Fortune and Sara Lopez

This species, along with the smaller snowy egret, was decimated by the plume hunters in the late 1800s. During breeding season the great egret displays a long, elegant train of lacy plumes (a.k.a. aigrettes) that once made them a constant target of the hat industry. Although it has recovered statewide, the population is still impacted by this slaughter more than 100 years ago.

The great egret flies with a slow, steady beat and with its long neck tucked back. It feeds on fish, snakes, and insects and can often be seen strolling along roads and highways in search of brown anoles. The winter population is greatly increased by migratory birds, which are easily distinguishable from the resident birds by their innate fear of man.

The great egret is monogamous and nests in large colonies with other wading birds. The cover shot of this book, which was taken at the St. Augustine Alligator Farm by Sara Lopez, is a great egret with two hungry chicks. Predominant threats include water quality and habitat loss. Alligators, owls, and bobcats prey on the great egret, and various tree-climbing predators sometimes attack its rookeries.

❒ ____________ **Snowy Egret** (*Egretta thula*) Other names: snowy heron, short white, little plume bird / Status: FL=species of special concern, IUCN=LC / Life span: to 17 years / Length: 22-27 in. (56-68 cm) / Wingspan: 38-45 in. (96-114 cm) / Weight: 13 oz (360 g) / Nests: throughout SW Florida / Found: AC, coastal, near coast, inland / Months found: **JFMAMJJASOND**.

The nickname "little plume bird" best identifies this delicate bird. The snowy egret, along with its taller cousin, the great egret, was the principal target of the late 19th- and early 20th-century plume hunters. This was the most sought after of all the Florida birds because of its soft, lacy, breeding finery. It was killed in such tremendous numbers that it was driven nearly to extinction.

Snowy Egret feeding in flight © Dick Fortune and Sara Lopez

Yellow feet © Dick Fortune and Sara Lopez

The snowy and the three herons and egrets also in this section make up a quartet of similarly sized birds that are at certain times pure white, making it a challenge for the amateur birder to tell one from the other. As long as the snowy's feet are visible, however, with their bright yellow "slippers," it is simple to identify. Other identifying characteristics are the long slender black bill, yellow lores (area between eye and beak), and equally yellow eyes.

The snowy egret feeds on crustaceans, large insects, and fish. It has a peculiar feeding habit that is very entertaining to observe. It puts one of its bright yellow feet forward in the water and vibrates it rapidly in the soft bottom, scaring up fish and small crustaceans. Then it quickly runs them down and feeds on them.

The snowy egret nests in mixed colonies with other herons. This smaller egret is preyed upon by alligators, eagles, hawks, and bobcats. Its primary threat is habitat destruction, which is why the Florida Fish and Wildlife Conservation Commission currently lists it as a species of special concern.

❒ __________ **Little Blue Heron** (*Egretta caerulea*) Other names: calico crane, blue crane / Status: FL=population declining, IUCN=LC / Life span: to 13-14 years / Length: 24-29 in. (61-73 cm) / Wingspan: 40-41 in. (101-104 cm) / Weight: 12.9 oz (350 g) / Nests: across Florida / Found: AC, coastal, near coast, inland / Months found: **JFMAMJJASOND**.

Although the little blue heron was not as much a target of the millinery trade as other local species at the turn of the last century, it is suffering now from drained wetlands and habitat loss. Unlike some other herons and egrets, it is seldom seen along the barrier island beaches, preferring fresh or brackish waters where it feeds upon small vertebrates, crustaceans, and large insects.

Little Blue Heron © Hung V. Do

The little blue heron is almost the same size as the snowy egret. The immature bird, both female and male, is pure white for the first year, after which it molts into its adult purplish-maroon plumage. One theory for the white coloration in the first year is that the snowy egret tolerates the white adolescent bird over the blue-colored adult, thereby allowing it to feed in larger and, therefore, safer colonies of similarly sized egrets. When these birds transition from white to blue they are often called calico herons, a mixture of both colors.

Little Blue Heron immature calico phase © Dick Fortune and Sara Lopez

The easiest way to distinguish an immature little blue heron from a snowy egret is the absence of the bright yellow "slippers." Another method is the beak, which is grayish with a dark black tip on the little blue heron and black on the snowy egret. The little blue heron is monogamous and nests with other egrets and herons for protection. It is preyed upon by bobcats, eagles, and alligators.

❐ __________ **Tricolored Heron** (*Egretta tricolor*) Other names: Louisiana heron, blue crane / Status: FL= species of special concern, IUCN=LC / Life span: to 17 years / Length: 24-26 in. (61-69 cm) / Wingspan: 36 in. (91 cm) / Weight: 14-16 oz (450 g) / Nests: throughout SW Florida / Found: AC, coastal, near coast, inland / Months found: **JFMAMJJASOND**.

This medium-size egret is aptly named. The adult tricolored heron has a bluish head, neck, and wings, maroon coloring at the base of the neck, and a white belly. In breeding plumage it adds a beautiful white plume trailing off the crown of its head. The tricolored suffered extensive losses during the plume-hunting era. Although the species is recovering, the Florida Fish and Wildlife Conservation Commission has kept it listed as a species of special concern.

Tricolor Heron in breeding plumage
© Dick Fortune and Sara Lopez

Formerly called the Louisiana heron, the tricolored heron is known to be among the deepest waders of all the herons, sometimes going into the water all the way to its belly. Similar to the reddish egret, the tricolored is also a "canopy" feeder, making it fascinating to observe. It feeds almost exclusively on minnows.

Shying away from the beaches and only seldom seen inland, this attractive bird can be spotted near mangrove tidal flats. For the most part, the tricolored heron is monogamous and like all the egrets and herons, tends to nest in large colonies with other wading birds. Its primary threat is habitat loss and poor water quality.

❒ ______________ **Cattle Egret** (*Bubulcus ibis*) Other names: buff-backed heron, cowbird / Status: FL=population dramatically increasing, IUCN=LC / Life span: to 17 years / Length: 19-21 in. (48-53 cm) / Wingspan: 36-38 in. (91-97 cm) / Weight: 11.9 oz (330 g) / Nests: throughout SW Florida / Found: AC, coastal, near coast, inland / Months found: **JFMAMJJASOND**.

Cattle Egret with two calves © Bob Gress, BirdsInFocus.com

Although this white bird is roughly the same size as the snowy egret and little blue heron—the cattle egret is the easiest to distinguish from the others. It has yellow legs and feet and a solid yellow beak. It is also quite a bit stockier, with a larger head, thicker neck, and shorter legs than the snowy egret. During breeding season it displays patches of buff orange on its crown, nape, and lower neck.

It feeds almost exclusively inland and is far less often seen along the beaches or mangroves. True to its name, literally hundreds of these birds will sometimes follow herds of cattle in Florida's agricultural areas.

The cattle egret has one of the most fascinating stories of any bird living in Florida. Originally a native of Africa, then spreading to Europe and Asia, the cattle egret first appeared in the New World in 1877 on the northeastern tip of South America in Venezuela. There was some speculation that a flock actually rode across the Atlantic in the eye of a major hurricane and broke away from the storm near the Lesser Antilles. Seeing this bird thriving in Southwest Florida today represents one of only a few "natural" migrations of an animal. The glossy ibis, an even more recent arrival, is believed to have taken much the same path 100 years later.

After stabilizing its small immigrant population in South America, the cattle egret began expanding its range. It reached Florida in 1941, long after the devastating plume hunts, and began nesting here in 1953. Over the past 50-plus years the cattle egret has steadily increased its range throughout the United States and is now pressing into southern Canada. It nests in all the lower 48 states. It nests and roosts with other herons and egrets.

The cattle egret is an opportunistic feeder. In Africa it is often found on the backs of large ungulates such as water buffalo and rhinoceros where it forages behind them, but in the Americas it has adapted to cattle, horses, deer, and sometimes follows behind tractors or along the edges of grass fires where it feeds on fleeing insects. It also eats mice, warblers, lizards, grubs, frogs, and snakes. Because it prefers open pasture, the cattle egret is readily preyed upon by red-tailed hawks, crested caracaras, bald eagles, and red foxes. Because of its tendency to forage in urban settings, the cattle egret is vulnerable to automobile fatalities.

In the past five decades the cattle egret has become the most common heron in the Sunshine State, and unlike so many of its foreign counterparts, it is not an introduced species. It has adapted well to both agricultural and urban settings and is currently thriving.

❒ ______ Black-crowned Night-heron (*Nycticorax nycticorax*)

Other names: quock, Indian pullet / Status: FL= increasing. IUCN=LC / Life span: to 21 years / Length: 22-28 in. (56-71 cm) / Wingspan: 42-44 in. (106-112 cm) / Weight: 1.6 lb (.62 kg) / Nests: throughout SW Florida / Found: AC, coastal, near coast / Months found: **JFMAMJJASOND**.

Black-crowned Night-heron
© Mike Baird via Wikimedia Commons

With a range that spans five continents, the black-crowned night-heron is one of the most widespread herons in the world. A beautifully fashioned bird, the night-heron is a favorite of many photographers. Similar to the yellow-crowned night-heron, which is far more commonly seen, this attractive bird can be seen along the riprap in the J.N. "Ding" Darling National Wildlife Refuge, as well as in the Ten Thousand Islands region. It is seldom seen along the beaches.

Although it generally hunts at night, during the nesting season it may also be observed feeding during the day. Like the equally successful cattle egret, the night-heron feeds on a wide assortment of creatures including frogs, rodents, snakes, crabs, and young birds, as well as plant material and eggs. That being said, fish is their primary forage. The adult black-crowned night-heron does not distinguish between its own young and those from other nests and will occasionally brood chicks not its own.

❒ ______ **Yellow-crowned Night-heron** (*Nyctanassa violacea*)

Other names: crab-eater, crabier, gauldin / Status: FL=stable, IUCN=LC / Life span: to 6 years / Length: 22-28 in. (56-71 cm) / Wingspan: 42-44 in. (107-112 cm) / Weight: 1.6 lb (.72 kg) / Nests: throughout SW Florida / Found: AC, coastal, near coast, inland / Months found: **JFMAMJJASOND**.

Earning the nickname crabeater © Dick Fortune and Sara Lopez

Found only in North and South America, the yellow-crowned night-heron is virtually identical in size to its close relative, the black-crowned night-heron, but has less than one-third the life span. The easiest way to tell the two birds apart is by the large, yellowish tuft of feathers on the yellow-crowned heron, making it appear to have a punk-style haircut. Its wings are also much more variegated than the solid gray wings of the black-crowned heron.

The yellow-crowned heron tends to feed more often during daylight hours and does not have as diverse a diet as its cousin. As its nicknames imply, the yellow-crowned night-heron specializes in eating crabs. A curious habit of this bird is that it carefully removes all the legs on a captured crab before eating.

It is monogamous and tends to nest in small colonies of other yellow-crowned night-herons. Snakes and other birds prey on its eggs, and alligators and bobcats take the adult bird. Its population is stable, but it suffers from habitat loss resulting from the drainage of wetlands and coastal development.

❐ ________ **White Ibis** (*Eudocimus albus*) Other names: Chokoloskee chicken, Spanish curlew / Status: FL= species of special concern, ICUN=LC / Life span: to 16 years / Length: 21-27 in. (53-68 cm) / Wingspan: 38 in. (96 cm) / Weight: 2.3 lb (1 kg) / Nests: throughout SW Florida in large colonies / Found: AC, coastal, near coast, inland / Months found: **JFMAMJJASOND**.

White Ibis in the mudflats © Dick Fortune and Sara Lopez

Although statewide the population of the white ibis is in decline, this unmistakable bird is found abundantly throughout Southwest Florida. Its long de-curved beak and its legs turn bright red when the white ibis is in breeding plumage. The distinctive black tips at the end of each wing when in flight make it an easy bird to identify. The juvenile is a mottled brown, similar in coloration to an adult limpkin. On the mainland you can sometimes find a similar species, the glossy ibis, which is the same size and shape but a dark blue-brown color similar to an oil slick. The immature glossy looks virtually identical to the immature white ibis.

The ibis was a particular favorite with early Florida homesteaders, producing an edible breast slightly larger than that of a popular game bird, the ruffed grouse—hence the nickname Chokoloskee chicken. Ibis were hunted throughout Florida well into the 1950s. Even today it is an easy bird to approach and still is hunted illegally in certain areas.

The white ibis feeds on fish, frogs, crabs, insects, and small reptiles. It mates for life and generally nests in large colonies with other wading birds. It is preyed upon by alligators and eagles, and its nesting sites are raided by raccoons and bobcats. Its predominant threat statewide is habitat destruction.

❒ __________ **Glossy Ibis** (*Plegadis falcinellus*) Other names: black curlew, bronze curlew / Status: FL = increasing, IUCN = LC / Length: 19-26 in. (49-66 cm) / Wingspan: 34.5-41 in. (88-105 cm) / Weight: 1.1-1.75 lb (500-800 g) / Life span: to 21 years / Nests: throughout SW Florida / Found: AC, near coast, inland / Months found: **JFMAMJJASOND**.

Like the cattle egret's natural migration, the glossy ibis probably made its way to this side of the Atlantic from Western Africa via the trade winds or possibly caught up in hurricane winds. It was first seen along the northern edge of South America and has been expanding its range ever since. The glossy ibis is the most widespread ibis species in the world, with populations in Europe, Asia, Africa, Australia, South America, and North America. Similar in behavior to the cattle egret, the glossy ibis is rapidly acclimatizing to urban and suburban developments. This adaptable bird can often be found foraging along the grassy fringes of parking lots, ball fields, and agricultural areas. The North American population is still expanding, moving into coastal Georgia, South Carolina, and all the way north into Maine.

Glossy Ibis © Judd Patterson, BirdsInFocus.com

The brownish immature glossy ibis can easily be mistaken for an immature white ibis. Both birds achieve adult plumage within the first year, however, after which it is all but impossible to confuse the two. The glossy ibis is slightly smaller than the white ibis. Both birds wield distinctive de-curved bills, which they use to ferret out insects, crayfish, grasshoppers, snakes, and grubs. They use these long, slender bills to probe deeply into soft, damp soil in search of prey. Unlike the white ibis, the glossy ibis is rarely found along the coastal beaches, preferring the near-coastal and mainland regions of Florida.

The glossy ibis nests in colonies of other herons and egrets. Its nests are subject to predation by snakes, raccoons, bobcats, opossums, and rats. The adult bird is taken by alligators, great horned owls, and bald eagles, but its reproductive abilities are such that the statewide population is still increasing. Its exceptionally long life span, up to 21 years, is also a factor in its ability to flourish.

❒ __________ **Roseate Spoonbill** (*Platalea ajaja*) Other names: pink curlew, pink / Status: FL=species of special concern, IUCN=LC / Life span: to 15 years / Length: 30-40 in. (76-101 cm) / Wingspan: 50-53 in. (127-135 cm) / Weight: 2.54 lb (1.13-1.81 kg) / Nests: in remote rookeries throughout SW Florida / Found: AC, coastal, near coast / Months found: **JFMAMJJASOND**.

Skimming for food © Judd Patterson, BirdsInFocus.com

Without question, the roseate spoonbill is the poster child of Sanibel Island bird lovers. A difficult bird to add to anyone's life list, the roseate is commonly found in the J.N. "Ding" Darling National Wildlife Refuge year round and thus attracts thousands of avid birders annually to the islands. It is probably the most photographed bird on Sanibel. Because of its pink coloration, the roseate is sometimes mistakenly confused with the flamingo. Flocks of spoonbills can also be found in Everglades National Park and the Myakka River State Park.

Unmistakable for its spatulate bill, bald head, and flamboyant pink coloration, the roseate was nearly extirpated from Florida during the 1800s. Not only was it taken by the plume hunters, it was also killed for its meat, and its rookeries were repeatedly raided for eggs. Now recovering, the numbers of these lovely birds are still only a fraction of what they were when Ponce de Leon first landed in Florida.

The roseate's feeding style is unique, similar to wood storks. It swishes its spatula-shaped bill back and forth through the soft, exposed muck of a tidal flat. When it comes across a shrimp or crustacean, it claps its bill together, eating the prey, then quickly resumes feeding. It also has a unique behavior called "skypointing" where it extends its bill and neck upward toward other spoonbills flying overhead.

The roseate is monogamous and tends to nest with other wading birds. Its nests are sometimes raided by raccoons and other predators. It needs extensive tidal flats to survive, and it suffers from polluted waters, as well as long-term habitat loss.

❐ ________ **Black Vulture** (*Coragyps atratus*) Other names: black buzzard / Status: FL=stable, expanding into the Northeast, IUCN=LC / Life span: to 25 years / Length: 24-27 in. (60-68 cm) / Wingspan: 54-60 in. (137-152 cm) / Weight: 4.8 lb (2.18 kg) / Nests: on the ground in remote palmetto stands / Found: AC, near coast, inland / Months found: **JFMAMJJASOND**.

The black vulture commonly soars with the turkey vulture and is hard to distinguish from its close cousin when more than 100 feet high. As it gets closer to the ground, the black vulture's grayish-black head and whitish wing tips become easier to distinguish. Another difference between the two birds is the wing shape in flight. Whereas the turkey vulture tends to keep its wings in a distinctive V shape, the black vulture keeps its wings flatter, flapping far more often than does the soaring turkey vulture.

There are other differences. The black vulture does not have the well-developed sense of smell of the turkey vulture. As a result, it often lets a solitary turkey vulture

Black vultures feeding on a dead alligator © Dick Fortune and Sara Lopez

discover the kill, then gangs up to chase the individual bird off and take over the carcass. It also sometimes preys on live chicks in heron and pelican rookeries.

Although its wingspan and body are shorter, the black vulture weighs more than the turkey vulture and is more aggressive. It tends to be less common along the coastline than inland but can sometimes be seen along the coast, especially during red tide events. It nests on the ground, preferring open spaces amidst dense saw-palmetto thickets.

❒ __________ **Turkey Vulture** (*Cathartes aura*) Other names: turkey buzzard / Status: FL=stable, IUCN=LC / Life span: to 16 years / Length: 25-32 in. (64-81cm) / Wingspan: 67-70 in. (170-178 cm) / Weight: 3.2 lb (1.45 kg) / Nests: on the ground throughout SW Florida / Found: AC, coastal, near coast, inland / Months found: **JFMAMJJASOND**.

Three turkey vultures © David Seibel, BirdsInFocus.com

The turkey vulture is one of the easiest birds to spot in Florida. All you really have to do is look up. The only time you will not see it soaring above the mainland is in the early morning before the rising thermals form. It is one of the most ubiquitous birds in the sky, and in agricultural areas such as Glades and Hendry counties it is not uncommon to see dozens of these large birds across the horizon.

A carrion feeder, the turkey vulture thrives on roadkill, red tide incidents (feeding on washed-up fish carcasses), and other dead animals. When there is a shortage of carrion, it feeds on garbage, vegetables, and even pumpkins, so it is actually an omnivore. Even though the vulture—with its unsavory eating habits, bald head, and black body—is considered unattractive by most birders, it plays an important role in the ecosystem. It quickly removes dead chicks from rookeries and feeds on stillborn livestock and other large carcasses such as deer and bear. This niche behavior greatly reduces the risk of diseases spreading from the decaying flesh. The vulture makes up the biological cleaning crew of the wilderness.

Whereas the black vulture feeds by sight, the turkey vulture feeds by both sight and smell. It has the most sophisticated olfactory sense of any bird in the world, able to spot and smell carrion from heights of up to 200 feet.

The turkey vulture tends to be less social than its close cousin, the black vulture. Although the turkey vulture is easily and frequently spotted soaring overhead, almost no one ever sees its nests. This is in large part because it nests either on the ground in dense cover such as Brazilian pepper or white mangrove thickets, where it builds a minimal nest of raked stones, dried leaves, and wood chips, or in hollowed-out tree stumps with narrow entrances.

It has several other unique behaviors. One of the weirdest of these is its propensity to defecate on its own legs, using the evaporation of the water to cool itself down. When alarmed, the turkey vulture has been known to throw up on its attackers.

Because of its tendency to feed on roadkill, the turkey vulture is often hit by automobiles. It is also sometimes killed by predators such as panthers in an effort to keep the vulture off of fresh kills. Because it is a ground nester, its eggs and chicks are subject to predation by mammals and snakes.

❐ __________ **Osprey** (*Pandion haliaetus*) Other names: fish hawk / Status: FL=species of special concern, IUCN=LC / Life span: to 26 years / Length: 21-23 in. (54-58 cm) / Wingspan: 59-71 in. (150-180 cm) / Weight: 3.1 lb (1.41 kg) / Nests: throughout SW Florida / Found: AC, coastal, near coast, inland / Months found: **JFMAMJJASOND**.

In the classic work, *The Nature of Things on Sanibel*, Sanibel author and naturalist George Campbell noted that during the 1974-75 nesting season, 24 osprey nests produced 10 offspring on Sanibel and Captiva islands. Two years later, during the 1976-77 nesting season, 37 nests produced 12 young. In the 2007-08 nesting season, the International Osprey Foundation recorded 109 nests producing 79 healthy chicks. Most of this impressive rebound is a result of the elimination of DDT and related chlorinated hydrocarbon pesticides, which caused the osprey's eggshells to thin and fail long before hatching. Although the osprey population is slowly recovering, the Florida Fish and Wildlife Conservation Commission has kept this beautiful raptor on its list as a species of special concern.

Like most birds of prey, the osprey tends to return to the same nest year after year, and it is especially fond of nesting on power poles. Taking a cue from this behavior, Mark "Bird" Westall, founder of the International Osprey Foundation, started constructing special nesting platforms on Sanibel in the mid-1970s to see if the osprey would take to them. Today you can see many of these nesting sites all across Florida, the most common design being a single pole with a sturdy square platform on top, approximately 30-40 feet above the ground. The platforms have

Osprey with fresh fish © Dick Fortune and Sara Lopez

proved popular with ospreys, though it doesn't keep them from building nests in unlikely places such as atop the buoys marking the Intracoastal Waterway, overhead signs, or high-tension power lines.

The osprey is learning to live with humans. It is one of the most widespread raptors in the world, found on all continents except Antarctica. It is sometimes mistaken for a bald eagle, though it is considerably smaller and has a mottled white head.

It can often be observed soaring along the Sanibel causeway searching for prey. With a diet that is 99 percent fish (it has been known to eat snakes and small reptiles, though rarely), the osprey is commonly found hovering over almost any good-size body of water, from inland ponds to open tidal flats. It strikes the water with incredible speed, sometimes completely submerging its body. Once the osprey grasps a suitable prey, be it a sheepshead, seatrout, mullet, or any other local fish, it quickly turns the fish to face forward into the wind, making it more aerodynamic to carry. The osprey has been known to die after sinking its powerful talons into a fish too large for the bird to lift. Unable to extricate itself in time, it drowns with a large redfish, snook, or large-mouth bass attached.

Bald eagles sometimes prey on osprey offspring, but by and large the biggest threats to the osprey come from manmade chemical pollutants and degraded water quality, which results in loss of fisheries.

❒ __________ **Swallow-tailed Kite** (*Elanoides forficatus*) Other names: none / Status: FL=stable, but endangered in South Carolina, IUCN=LC / Length: 19-25 in. (46-64 cm) / Wingspan: 48 in. (122 cm) / Weight: 13-21 oz (.37-.60 kg) / Life span: to 12 years / Nests: throughout Florida and southern Alabama and Mississippi during the summer / Found: AC, coastal, near coast, inland / Months found: **JFMAMJJASOND**.

The swallow-tailed kite, like the magnificent frigatebird, is an impressive bird to witness in flight. In fact, you are most likely to spot and identify this bird when it is soaring high above. With its pure white body, large black-tipped wings and deeply forked black tail, this bird resembles an enormous, snowy barn swallow.

Swallow-tailed Kite in flight
© Judd Patterson, BirdsInFocus.com

Unlike most of the migratory birds that arrive in Florida, the swallow-tailed kite comes up from Central and South America during the summer. In effect, Florida is its northern breeding grounds. Once a common nesting bird as far north as Minnesota, the swallow-tailed kite has suffered from extensive habitat loss through most of its former North American range.

There is a small resident nesting population at Corkscrew Swamp on the mainland, and more than likely some of the birds found flying over Sanibel and Captiva originate from there. They predominantly eat flying insects including dragonflies, bees, and beetles but while in flight will also pick off snakes, crickets, cicadas, and small birds from the canopy top. A skilled flyer, the swallow-tailed kite can turn its tail feathers almost 90 degrees, allowing it to make sharp turns and quick dives. Its only long-term threat is habitat loss, although some efforts are under way to reintroduce the kite into its former northernmost ranges.

❒ ______________ **Snail Kite** (*Rostrhamus sociabillis*) Other names: Everglades kite, snail hawk / Status: FL = Endangered and still recovering, IUCN = LC / Length: 14.2-15.7 in. (36-40 cm) / Wingspan: 3.5-4 ft (106-121 cm) / Weight: 12.7-20.1 oz (360-570 g) / Life span: to 15 years / Nests: in mainland SW Florida / Found: LC, ChC, EC, HC, inland / Months found: **JFMAMJJASOND**.

In the early 1960s, this neotropical species had been reduced to a remnant population of a scarce 25 birds. The DDT ban and the restoration of apple snail habitat resulted in a dramatic rebound. Estimates today put the snail kite population at well over 1,000 birds and growing. During extremely dry years snail kites, like wood storks, will forgo breeding entirely, and many adults will starve. During wet winters, when the snail population explodes, the snail kite's population does the same, making it a perfect "boom or bust" species. In the worldview, which is what the much larger IUCN looks at, the snail kite is in excellent shape, with stable populations in Central and South America.

All kites are raptors, related to hawks, kestrels, and eagles. They are called kites because they feed while in flight. The snail kite swoops down and grabs unsuspecting apple snails on the wing, then perches on the ground or a nearby snag and devours the animal inside the shell. The snail kite has a specialized hooked beak allowing it to remove the operculum (the small lid that seals the living mollusk inside of its shell) and the snail meat. The arrival of the much larger invasive South American island apple snail taxes the kite's beak, which is accustomed to feeding on a much smaller snail. It will be interesting to see how or if the snail kite adapts to this change. The limpkin, which is the other Florida bird that lives almost exclusively on snails, has learned to crush the shell of this larger snail and is thriving because of it.

Snail Kite in flight © Judd Patterson, BirdsInFocus.com

For birders, finding and seeing a snail kite in Florida (the only state in the U.S. where the bird occurs) is a dream come true. Several locations identified in this book make this task easy. Look for the snail kite along the fringe marshes of Lake Okeechobee in Glades and Hendry counties and in Harn's Marsh in Lee County. It can also be seen over freshwater marshes in Collier County. It is not a coastal species since the snails it feeds on are not saltwater or brackish-water tolerant.

Aside from falcons and owls, the mature snail kite has few natural predators. The chicks and eggs fall prey to snakes, alligators, and other mammalian predators. The largest impact to its population is the abundance, or lack thereof, of apple and island apple snails.

❐ ______ **Bald Eagle** (*Haliaeetus leucocephalus*) Other names: eagle / Status: FL=species of special concern, threatened in the lower 48, IUCN=LC / Life span: to 30 years / Length: 28-38 in. (71-96 cm) / Wingspan: 72-96 in. (183-234 cm) / Weight: 9.1 lb (4.13 kg) / Nests: throughout Florida / Found: AC, coastal, near coast, inland / Months found: **JFMAMJJASOND**.

Our national symbol, the bald eagle is always a bird lover's delight to observe. With a wingspan up to eight feet across, the majestic eagle soaring above the Sunshine State is a spectacular sight. Florida has the largest nesting population of bald eagles outside of Alaska. Although the National Fish and Wildlife Service still lists the bald eagle as threatened, it has been downgraded to a species of special concern in Florida.

Until the 1940s and the widespread use of DDT as a mosquito and insect control, the bald eagle flourished in the United States. By the early 1960s the bald eagle population had collapsed and was one of the first animals listed when the Endangered Species Act was passed in 1973. Only the peregrine falcon suffered as dramatically from the use of DDT and other chemicals. After 20 years of sustained conservation efforts, the eagle was reclassified to threatened on July 12, 1995. Although far below historic numbers, the bald eagle is on the road to recovery.

American Bald Eagle © David Seibel, BirdsInFocus.com

Its predominant diet is fish, although this large bird will also take waterfowl, squirrels, rabbits, muskrats, and cattle egret. The eagle will also feed on fresh carrion when the opportunity arises. The eagle and osprey do not get along. Not only has the eagle been known to take osprey chicks, but it also habitually steals captured fish from osprey in flight. It is not uncommon to see osprey aggressively shagging off a nearby eagle.

When soaring, the juvenile bald eagle can sometimes be mistaken for a turkey vulture or black vulture. The juvenile, whose coloration is a mottled brown, does not attain adult plumage until it is 5 years old. One of the best ways to distinguish an eagle from a vulture in flight is that the eagle soars with straight wings, almost like a plank, whereas the turkey vulture's wings curve upward in the shape of a V.

The eagle uses the same nest year after year, adding more twigs and branches every nesting season. Some nests become huge, weighing more than a ton.

The only viable threat to the bald eagle is man. The fine for shooting a bald eagle can be as much as $100,000 and a year in prison. The larger threat from man, however, is chemical pollution and habitat loss.

❐________ **Northern Harrier** (*Circus cyaneus*) Other names: marsh hawk, hen harrier / Status: FL = slowly declining, IUCN = LC / Length: 18.1-19.7 in. (46-50 cm) / Wingspan: 40.2-46.5 in. (102-118 cm) / Weight: 10.6-26.5 oz (300-750 g) / Life span: to 16.5 years / Nests: in the upper Midwest north to Alaska / Found: AC, near coast, inland / Months found: **JFMAMJJASOND**.

A medium-size raptor with a worldwide distribution, the northern harrier is still commonly called the marsh hawk in many parts of the country. In North America the harrier summers and breeds in the Canadian boreal forest, ranging all the way to the tundra. There it feeds heavily on lemmings, moles, mice, and

Northern Harrier © Kenneth Haley

rats, as well as small rabbits, birds, and frogs. In September it returns to the southern tier of the U.S., including peninsular Florida, where it stays for most of the winter and spring. In Florida it tends to stay well inland and is seldom found along the coast.

The harrier's stiff facial hair and owl-shaped face allow it to use hearing as well as sight to find its prey. It prefers to hunt over open fields, marshes, and agricultural areas where it descends on unsuspecting rodents from very low altitudes. The northern harrier has two easy identifiers: 1) it flies with its wings held in a distinctive and deep V, similar to a turkey vulture; and 2) it has a white patch just behind its wings and before its tail feathers that is best seen from above or when the bird is diving. The male and female harriers have pronounced coloration differences: the male is gray and the female a mottled-brown color.

The range of the northern harrier covers all of North America, Europe, Asia, and parts of northern Egypt. There are an estimated 1.3 million harriers worldwide. Its population has suffered in England where game farms and gamekeepers shoot the bird for taking grouse and other stocked birds. The harrier has few natural predators, aside from great horned owls, but the chicks and eggs are vulnerable to snakes, rats, weasels, foxes, and lynx.

❐ ____________ **Cooper's Hawk** (*Accipiter cooperii*) Other names: big blue darter, chicken hawk / Status: FL=stable, IUCN=LC / Life span: to 20 years / Length: 14.6-15.4 in. (37-39 cm) / Wing span: 24.4-35.4 in. (62-90 cm) / Weight: 7.8-14.5 oz (220-410 g) / Nests: throughout the lower 48 and across the southern tier of Canada / Found: AC, coastal, near coast, inland / Months found: **JFMAMJJASOND**.

Considered to be one of the world's most agile and skillful fliers, the Cooper's hawk readily cuts through tangles of bush, tree limbs, and heavy cover in search of prey. It specializes in taking down smaller birds, including doves, shorebirds, warblers, and grackles. This behavior comes at a price. In a study of more than 300 adult birds, 23 percent showed old, healed-over fractures in the chest and wishbone. It may well be assumed that another 5 to 10 percent did not survive the collision.

Cooper's Hawk
© Bob Gress, BirdsInFocus.com

The Cooper's hawk is adapting to people. In the early part of the 20th century its population was in decline as forests were cut down to make way for farms and ever growing urban and suburban environments. Recently the remaining birds have shown a tolerance to these changes and are moving into cities and suburbs with surprising frequency. There the Cooper's hawk can find ample prey in rock pigeons and mourning and Eurasian collared-doves. Its flying skills come in handy amidst the telephone poles, fences, and concrete of a modern city.

The Cooper's hawk can be readily distinguished from the slightly larger red-shouldered hawk by its rounded tail and more rounded wing tips. It often tends to have a bluish or darker red tint to its back as well. The chicks are well protected but still fall victim to snakes and other raptors; the adult hawk is seldom taken by anything other than the great horned owl.

❒ ____________ **Red-shouldered Hawk** (*Buteo lineatus*) Other names: chicken hawk / Status: FL=stable, IUCN=LC / Life span: to 19 years / Length: 17-24 in. (43-61 cm) / Wingspan: 37-44 in. (94-111 cm) / Weight: 1.1 lb (0.5 kg) / Nests: throughout Florida / Found: AC, coastal, near coast, inland / Months found: **JFMAMJJASOND**.

When you spot a hawk anywhere in Florida, odds are that it is a red-shouldered hawk. Sightings of other hawks, such as the Cooper's hawk, peregrine falcon, and red-tailed hawk, are infrequent at best. The medium-size red-shouldered hawk is often seen in almost every preserve and park identified in this book. Its auburn shoulders and brightly patterned wings and tail feathers make it unmistakable. It is a truly beautiful raptor.

Mice, cotton rats, marsh rabbits, snakes, amphibians, worms, snails, and an occasional bird are all on the menu of the red-shouldered hawk. It is a perch hunter, sitting on high Australian pine branches or other lofty vantage points, then quickly pouncing on prey spotted below. It can often be heard, at a considerable distance, repeating a

Red-shouldered Hawk
© Bob Gress, BirdsInFocus.com

loud, rapid *keeyah, keeyah*. It has a disdain for the great horned owl, which has been known to raid red-shouldered hawk nests, and it will shag the owls off when discovered in its area.

The red-shouldered hawk not only reuses the same nest year after year, but also has been known to remain in the same territory, though multiple generations, for more than 45 consecutive years. It is generally monogamous and builds solitary nests.

❒ ________ **Red-tailed Hawk** (*Buteo jamaicensis*) Other names: chicken hawk, buzzard / Status: FL = stable, IUCN = LC / Length: 18-26 in. (45-65 cm) / Wingspan: 43-57 in. (110-145 cm) / Weight: 1.5-3.5 lb (.68-1.6 kg) / Life span: to 29 years / Nests: throughout SW Florida / Found: AC, near coast, inland / Months found: **JFMAMJJASOND**.

Red-tailed Hawk in flight © Judd Patterson, BirdsInFocus.com

The red-tailed hawk is the largest hawk in Florida. It weighs slightly more than its cousin, the osprey, and has a wingspan that approaches five feet. There are 14 recognized subspecies found throughout North and Central America. The largest concentration of these birds in the world occurs in El Yunque National Forest in Puerto Rico. Although it is one of the most widely distributed hawks in the Americas, it has never been abundant in Florida and is a fairly uncommon sighting here.

The red-tailed hawk, when gathered young, is readily trained in the art of falconry. The endangered status of the North American falcon population has led to the red-tailed hawk as a suitable replacement, though it is larger than and not as quick as a falcon. In the wild it is both a perching bird and a soaring diver. Its broad wings allow it to float high in the air looking for suitable prey. When it spots a rabbit, duck, or small rodent, the red-tailed hawk swoops down at a speed that can exceed 120 miles per hour and makes the kill. Its screaming, shrill cry is unmistakable.

In many ways this hawk is the diurnal equivalent of the nocturnal great horned owl. In fact, these two birds are fierce rivals, both for nesting sites and hunting ranges. If a great horned owl finds an active red-tailed hawk nest, it will invariably destroy the eggs or chicks. The great horned owl is also fond of using the red-tailed hawk nest to raise its own clutch.

The adult red-tailed hawk is almost never preyed upon, since it weighs more than the largest owls, and a mature female can weigh nearly as much as a bald eagle. The eggs and chicks are preyed upon by raccoons, crows, and great horned owls.

❐ ________ **Crested Caracara** (*Caracara cheriway*) Other names: Mexican eagle, Mexican buzzard, Audubon's caracara / Status: FL = threatened, IUCN = LC / Length: 19.3-22.8 in. (49-58 cm) / Wingspan: 47.2 in. (120 cm) / Weight: 2.3-2.9 lb (1-1.3 kg) / Life span: to 17 years / Nests: in interior mainland SW Florida, predominately around Lake Okeechobee / Found: GC, HC, CC, inland / Months found: **JFMAMJJASOND**.

Crested Caracara © Bob Gress, BirdsInFocus.com

Although it looks more like an eagle and feeds like a vulture, the crested caracara is actually a member of the falcon family. Its large size and long, bright yellow legs make it an unmistakable sighting and a great subject for photography. Its unusual name is an onomatopoeic version of its froglike grating call, *cara, cara*.

The caracara is widespread throughout Mexico, the Caribbean, and the northern edge of South America, from Ecuador through Guyana. It is an uncommon sighting in Florida where the population estimate is roughly 500 birds. The consensus is that the Florida population is in decline because of the continued expansion of large citrus farms into its woodland habitat. The only other North American populations are in Arizona and Texas, where it is also fairly uncommon.

The best places to look for these large and picturesque birds are along rural highways where it loves to perch atop fence posts and forage near open pastureland or agricultural fields. It is most common around Lake Okeechobee but can also be found near Immokalee along State Road 29 or the back roads of Hendry and Glades counties.

The caracara is a carrion eater and will often harass black and red vultures until they relinquish a roadkill to this aggressive bird. Because the caracara feeds on carrion, the front portion of its face is devoid of feathers much like vultures. The caracara also preys upon reptiles, birds, and mammals when given the opportunity.

❐ ________ **American Kestrel** (*Falco sparverius*) Other names: sparrow hawk, kitty hawk / Status: FL=the smaller Florida race is considered threatened, IUCN=LC / Life span: to 14 years / Length 8.6-12 in. (21-30 cm) / Wingspan: 20-24 in. (51-61 cm) / Weight: 2.8-5.8 oz (80-165 g) / Nests: in areas of Florida and has one of the largest raptor distributions of all New World birds, from Alaska to Tierra del Fuego / Found: AC, coastal, near coast, inland / Months found: **JFMAMJJASOND**.

Two kestrels sparring © David Seibel, BirdsInFocus.com

The kestrel is the smallest member of the falcon family. It is a colorful bird of prey, with hints of blue, auburn, and white in the males. With 17 races spread across both continents, the kestrel has evolved a number of colorful variations in its plumage.

Although the American kestrel can be spotted in Florida year round, its numbers increase dramatically during the winter month. The kestrel readily adapts to human changes in the landscape and is as comfortable on a baseball field as it is in a woodland. As a result of its easy adaptation, it is thriving across North and South America. The smaller, indigenous Florida race is the only threatened subspecies.

The kestrel feeds primarily on insects and small vertebrates, including frogs and mice. It sometimes takes small birds in flight, but these are not its primary diet.

The kestrel has one unusual characteristic: after building its nest, it squirts feces on the cavity walls, allowing them to dry and reinforce the nest. With a collection of half-eaten animals lying on the bottom and walls covered in feces, its nest can become quite odiferous.

Its primary threats are pesticides and a lack of suitable nesting sites. The kestrel readily takes to wooden bird boxes, and there is a push nationwide to increase these artificial nesting sites throughout the kestrel's range.

❒ __________ **Merlin** (*Falco columbarius*) Other names: pigeon hawk / Status: FL=stable, IUCN=LC / Life span: to 11 years / Length: 9.4-11.8 in. (24-30 cm) / Wingspan: 20.9-26.8 in. (53-68 cm) / Weight: 5.6-8.5 oz (160-240 g) / Nests: in Florida but is much more commonly seen in SW Florida when the winter migrants return from northern Canada / Found: AC, coastal, near coast, inland / Months found: **JFMAMJJASOND**.

Slightly larger than the kestrel, this swift falcon is one of many birds that is slowly but steadily adapting to human landscapes. Like many species, it at first dipped in population as woodlands and fields became parking lots and cities, but the birds that survived that change are now finding these urban settings teeming with viable prey such as mourning and Eurasian collared-doves, pigeons, and rats. The merlin is finding a new home in these ever encroaching urban and suburban areas.

Over the past decade or two, the merlin has become a more common sighting in Southwest Florida. Although there are only a handful of merlins nesting in northern Florida, there is every reason to believe that in years to come, the merlin could begin nesting in Southwest Florida. One of only a handful of birds that does not build a nest, the merlin prefers to use old nesting sites, either from other raptors or sometimes from crows or other large nesting birds.

Trained Merlin © Drew Avery, Courtesy Wikimedia Commons

The male tends to be blue-gray above, while the female is brown. It does not accelerate in steep dives as the peregrine falcon but tends to hunt closer to the ground, preying on small passerines and rodents.

As an adult, the merlin is seldom taken by anything, but its chicks and eggs can fall victim to snakes, rodents, and other birds. For reasons unknown, DDT did not harm the merlin as severely as it did the peregrine falcon and bald eagle.

❒ _______ **Peregrine Falcon** (*Falco peregrinus*) Other names: duck hawk / Status: FL=endangered, IUCN=LC / Life span: to 19 years / Length: 16-20 in. (40-50 cm) / Wingspan: 43-46 in. (109-116 cm) / Weight: 1.3 lb (.58 kg) / Nests: in the High Arctic and throughout the Rocky Mountains / Found: AC, coastal, near coast, inland / Months found: **JFMAMJJASOND**.

Peregrine Falcon ©Trisa Shears, Courtesy Wikimedia Commons

The peregrine falcon, even more so than the bald eagle, was severely impacted by the widespread use of DDT and similar organochlorine chemicals. The fastest animal in the world, clocked at speeds approaching 200 miles per hour, proved no match against pesticide contamination throughout its range. The peregrine came dangerously close to extinction in North America by the late 1960s, with some estimates putting the entire population at no more than 150 breeding pairs. The good news about the peregrine is that it is fast recovering from its brush with extinction, and up to 2,000 birds migrate through the Florida Keys each year.

This beautiful raptor has had more scientific research done on it than any other bird in the world, with its bibliography exceeding 2,000 primary scientific papers. Admired by falconers from England to Saudi Arabia, the peregrine falcon has been trained to hunt for more than 1,000 years. The name *peregrine* means "wanderer," an excellent choice since some peregrines have been known to travel more than 15,000 miles (25,000 km) in a single year. On the other hand, some nesting peregrine pairs remain sedentary their entire lives.

Because of its ability to travel long distances and fly at an average speed of 25-35 mph, the peregrine inhabits every continent except Antarctica and can be found on many oceanic islands. It is a solitary nester, sometimes settling on the window ledges of tall skyscrapers and bridges in cities.

The peregrine falcon's primary diet is other birds. In urban settings it has become adept at killing pigeons, mourning doves, starlings, and a host of other city-dwelling species. In the wild it hunts ducks, shorebirds, gulls, and even small geese. It also takes rodents, bats, and other small mammals. It dives on its prey at tremendous speeds, often killing the animal upon impact.

Aside from being killed by hunters and having its eggs fail from pesticide poisoning, the peregrine falcon has few other natural threats. There simply are no other birds fast enough to catch the peregrine.

❒ __________ **Virginia Rail** (*Rallus limicola*) Other names: marsh hen / Status: FL = stable, IUCN = LC / Length: 9 in. (23 cm) / Wingspan: 13 in. (33 cm) / Weight: 3.1 oz (88 g) / Life span: n/a / Nests: from Nova Scotia across the British Columbia and south to the Ohio River Valley / Found: SC, CHC, LC, GC, coastal, near coast, inland / Months found: **JFM**AMJJAS**OND**.

This secretive and small member of the rail family is only a winter visitor to Florida and is a very uncommon sighting south of Lee County. In fact, it is so secretive and difficult to track that it is one of the few birds for which the U.S. Geological Survey team at the Patuxent Wildlife Research Center (which provided most of the life-span information in this book) does not have sufficient data to determine its average life span.

Finding or photographing a bird such as this three-ounce rail is problematic. Although it closely resembles the much larger king rail, it is only the size of a robin and is known for its ability to hide in the wet prairies, marshes, and wetlands where it forages for invertebrates, insects, and small fruits.

Although the Virginia rail is considered a game bird, it is seldom hunted. Recent declines in its overall population have made it a difficult bird to hunt, and its small size makes it hardly worthwhile to harvest.

The Virginia rail ranges from southern Canada, where it breeds, all the way into Guatemala, where it winters. It is preyed upon by raptors, snakes, and small mammals. The eggs and chicks are vulnerable to predation by a host of creatures, including other birds.

Virginia Rail © Bob Gress, BirdsInFocus.com

❐ __________ **Purple Gallinule** (*Porphyrio martinica*) Other names: blue peter, mud hen, pond chicken, bonnet-walker, purple swamphen (European species) / Status: FL = stable, IUCN = LC / Length: 14.2-14.6 in. (36-37 cm) / Wingspan: 21.7 in. (55 cm) / Weight: 7.3-10.2 oz (208-288 g) / Life span: to 22 years / Nests: in mainland SW Florida / Found: AC, near coast, inland / Months found: **JFMAMJJASOND**.

Delicate landing by a Purple Gallinule
© Dick Fortune and Sara Lopez

Clearly related to the coot, common moorhen, and the recently imported European bird, purple swamphen, the purple gallinule is a member of the rail family of birds. Other members of that family include the sora, clapper, and king rail.

Although common throughout the state in the summer months, most of the northern birds head toward the Everglades and the southern end of the peninsula during the winter months, making it an intra-state migrant. Some of the best places to view this attractive bird are on the Anhinga Trail in the Everglades and throughout the numerous overgrown canals and marshes of Glades and Hendry counties. The purple gallinule is an inland and mainland species and is only rarely observed along the barrier islands of Florida.

The species has an extensive range throughout Central and South America, where it can be found as far south as Argentina.

The purple gallinule is one of the most colorful and beautiful of all the birds of Florida. Its rich, iridescent purple plumage contrasts with its bright, candy-corn colored beak. The purple gallinule is equipped with extremely large, bright yellow feet that allow it to forage atop lily pads and other floating vegetation. There it feeds primarily on seeds, leaves, insects, frogs, snails, spiders, and fish and has even been known to feed on the eggs of other marsh-nesting birds such as redwing blackbirds and ducks.

❒ __________ **Common Moorhen** (*Gallinula chloropus*) Other names: Florida gallinule, pond chicken / Status: FL= stable to slightly declining, IUCN=LC / Life span: to 10 years / Length: 13-14 in. (32-35 cm) / Wingspan: 21-24 in. (54-62 cm) / Weight: 12 oz (340 g) / Nests: statewide / Found: AC, coastal, near coast, inland / Months found: **JFMAMJJASOND**.

Common Moorhen © Bob Gress, BirdsInFocus.com

This widely distributed member of the rail family ranges from Argentina into southern Canada. Unlike its secretive cousins, the clapper and king rail, the moorhen is not a shy bird. It is easily approached and photographed, often without need of a telephoto lens.

Using its oversized yellow-green feet, it works its way through cattails and rushes along the edges of lakes and ponds. Lacking webbed feet, the moorhen has a curious swimming stroke, appearing to bob its head with every stroke. A close relative, the purple gallinule, is a beautiful maroon version of the moorhen that prefers the habitat of the Everglades and other expansive mainland wetlands.

One easy way to identify the moorhen is by its distinctive candy-corn bill, which has a yellow tip and red beak in the shape of a candy corn protruding from its unique red frontal shield. The moorhen is a very vocal bird, making a variety of clucks, screams, squeaks, and pips.

The moorhen is preyed upon by weasels, raccoons, and bobcats, and its nests are targeted by snakes. Its biggest problem is continued loss of wetlands habitat. It is common in Florida but a species of special concern in several states in the Midwest and Northeast.

❒ __________ **American Coot** (*Fulica americana*) Other names: mud hen, pull-doo, pond crow, splatterer / Status: FL=stable, probably increasing, IUCN=LC / Life span: to 22 years / Length: 15 in. (38 cm) / Wingspan: 23-38 in. (58-71 cm) / Weight: 1.6 lb (.72 kg) / Nests: north of the Ohio Valley all the way into the southern Northwest Territories of Canada / Found: AC, coastal, near coast, inland / Months found: **JF**MAMJJA**SOND**.

American Coot at take off © Judd Patterson, BirdsInFocus.com

The American coot is related to both the common moorhen and the purple gallinule. It is easy to distinguish from the moorhen by the all-white beak and solid black coloration, except for a spot of white along the tail feathers and wingtips.

This bird is widespread, found in all the lower 48 states, all of Mexico and Central America, and more than half of Canada. It prefers freshwater to saltwater wetlands. It is a game bird in Florida, often taken in the fall along with ducks, geese, and other waterfowl. In Southwest Florida the coot is far more common in the winter months. It appears to breed in Florida, though not consistently.

The coot is primarily an herbivore, eating mostly leaves, seeds, and roots of aquatic plants. It can be spotted paddling quietly in ponds or diving to depths of up to 25 feet. Similar to the grebe, the coot does not have webbed feet like those of ducks, but wide lobes that flare out when it swims. The chicks are taken by snakes and snapping turtles, and the adult is a favorite food of bald eagles.

❐ ________ **Limpkin** (*Aramus guarauna*) Other names: crying bird / Status: FL = species of special concern, IUCN = LC / Life span: to 12 years / Length: 25-29 in. (63-73 cm) / Wingspan: 40-42 in. (102-107 cm) / Weight: 31.7-45.9 oz (900-1300 g) / Nests: throughout SW Florida / Found: AC, near coast, inland / Months found: **JFMAMJJASOND**.

Hunted nearly into extirpation in Florida from the late 1800s through the 1950s, the limpkin population is on a slow but steady rebound across the peninsula. Its range once extended all the way to the Okefenokee Swamp in southern Georgia but now the vast majority of Florida's limpkins are found in South Florida, especially around Lake Okeechobee. The name *limpkin* is derived from its irregular gait, which can give you the impression that the bird is lame.

Limpkin © Dick Fortune and Sara Lopez

While Florida labels the limpkin a species of special concern, the IUCN considers it a species of least concern, because it is still plentiful in Central America and most of South America. Early settlers found the limpkin delicious and very easy to harvest. Because the bird was so unfamiliar with human predation early on, historic accounts of catching limpkins included the use of fishing nets. Because of its drab coloration, it was never impacted by plume hunters.

The limpkin's bill is adapted specifically for eating apple snails. A slight tweezers-like opening at the very tip allows it to extricate the snail from the shell with little effort. On some birds the bill actually curves to the right slightly, allowing even greater access to the right-handed curve of the apple snail. The arrival in recent years of the invasive and much larger island apple snail from South America has given the limpkin a new, larger source of protein. Whereas the smaller Everglades, or snail, kite is struggling with these giant snails, the limpkin is having a field day. It can pick up these fist-sized invasives from the reeds and marshes where they thrive, then carry them to shallower waters and smash the shells wide open with its powerful beak. Florida should begin to see a sharp rise in the limpkin population because of this new food source; indeed, around the shoreline of Lake Okeechobee you can now see scores of limpkins in a single day.

The limpkin is the only member of its taxonomic family. Although it resembles an ibis, it is now considered to be genetically closer to the crane and trumpeter (a small family of birds restricted to the forests of the Amazon and Orinoco basins of South America). The nickname, "crying bird," comes from the limpkin's primeval call, which is often used in the background of *Tarzan* and other jungle movies. Its unmistakable cry has an eerie, haunting quality and can be heard for miles on a calm morning. Sometimes the cry of this reclusive bird is the only way of knowing one is nearby.

Predation of this marsh- and wetlands-dwelling bird is done mostly by alligators and large turtles. Water snakes, water moccasins, raccoons, and muskrats raid its nests, for eggs and hatchlings. In addition to apple snails and island apple snails, the limpkin feeds on freshwater mussels, insects, frogs, lizards, and worms.

❐___ Sandhill Crane (*Grus canadensis, Grus canadensis pratensis*)

Other names: whooper / Status: FL = threatened, IUCN = LC / Length: 47.2 in. (1.2 m) / Wingspan: 78.7 in. (2 m) / Weight: 7.4-10.75 lb (3.3-4.8 kg) / Life span: to 31 years / Nests: resident populations nest in mainland SW Florida, migratory Sandhills nest in the northern U.S. and well into Canada / Found: AC, near coast, inland / Months found: **JFMAMJJASOND**.

Sandhill Cranes in flight © Dick Fortune and Sara Lopez

Like the endangered whooping crane today, the sandhill crane once came very near to extinction. In 1940 the entire North American population of the greater sandhill crane stood at a paltry 1,000 birds. Through careful management and severe fines for shooting one of these large cranes, the population has rebounded to approximately 100,000 greater sandhill cranes and 400,000 lesser sandhill cranes. These combined populations make this now the most numerous crane on earth. Across the globe cranes have suffered tremendous habitat losses from ever-expanding human populations. This is especially true in Asia, India, and parts of Africa where killing and eating cranes is still commonly practiced. In fact, the sandhill crane is still hunted in Texas, Kansas, and other states.

In Florida, the size of sandhill cranes follows a well-established formula known as Bergmann's rule, which states that any species that inhabits cooler or more northern latitudes tend to have a larger body mass than the species in the warmer latitudes of the tropics. The Florida subspecies of the sandhill crane, which is non-migratory and numbers around 5,000 birds, follows this general rule in that it falls on the smaller end of the weight, wingspan, and size ranges. Farther north, the migratory sandhill crane is much larger. It breeds and nests all the way north to Baffin Island, Canada.

The sandhill crane is a near-coast and inland bird. It can often be seen in pairs or small groups in dry and wet prairies, agricultural areas, or even near airports, golf courses, and other open areas. Even if not seen, this loud bird can be heard from great distances. It has a deep, rolling trumpet-like call that is followed by a rattling sound. It is a graceful flyer, and its large wings allow it to soar in much the same fashion as the vulture and wood stork.

One of the truly great migrations in North America can still be observed along the Platte River in Nebraska every spring when tens of thousands of sandhill cranes stop to rest on their long journeys from Texas to the far north. The California subspecies migrates all the way to eastern Siberia.

The sandhill crane is predominantly vegetarian. It forages on a variety of plants, seeds, and invertebrates. The adult crane is too large for most predators except bobcats, panthers, and alligators, but the chicks and eggs are vulnerable to a host of mammals including raccoons, opossums, rats, and reptiles such as snakes and the invasive Nile monitor lizard.

❒ ______ **Snowy Plover** (*Charadrius alexandrinus*) Other names: Cuban snowy plover / Status: FL=threatened, IUCN=LC / Life span: to 11 years / Length: 67 in. (15-17 cm) / Wingspan: 13 in. (34 cm) / Weight: 1.22 oz (34-58 g) / Nests on Gulf beaches / Found: SC, ChC, LC, CC, coastal / Months found: **JFMAMJJASOND**.

The snowy plover is a very small, delicate-looking shorebird that is suffering from extensive coastal overdevelopment. Disturbances such as unleashed dogs, children at play, and in some areas, automobiles being driven on the beaches have all contributed to the rapid decline of this once familiar species. Arguably Florida's most threatened bird, some estimates put its total number between 220 and 400 nesting pairs.

Snowy Plover
© Judd Patterson, BirdsInFocus.com

The snowy plover is often mistaken for the piping plover but has darker, grayish legs and an all-black beak as opposed to the yellow-orange legs and orange and black bill of the piping plover. Another tell is that the piping

Snowy Plover and chick © Dick Fortune and Sara Lopez

plover has more of a point to its bill than does the snowy. The snowy plover is quite a bit smaller than the killdeer or Wilson's plover.

It feeds on small crustaceans and soft invertebrates such as sand flies. Its nest consists of some shallow scrapes of assorted shells upon which two to three pale, dotted eggs are laid, sometimes up to two broods annually. Young plovers leave the nest within three hours of hatching.

The plover's only defense is camouflage, flattening itself against the ground when a predator or a person approaches. Predation to the nests comes from dogs, gulls, rodents, snakes, and ghost crabs. Its primary threat is continued coastal development and loss of suitable beach dune habitat. On many coastal beaches plover nesting areas are marked off by stakes and yellow police tape. Under no circumstances should dogs, children, or adults be allowed into these roped-off areas, as the tiny eggs of the snowy plover are all but impossible to spot and are easily stepped on and crushed.

❒ ____________ **Killdeer** (*Charadrius vociferus*) Other names: kildee, meadow plover / Status: FL=thriving because of its ability to adapt to urban environments, IUCN=LC / Life span: to 11 years / Length: 8-11 in. (20-28 cm) / Wingspan: 18-19 in. (46-48 cm) / Weight: 3.2 oz (90 g) / Nests: throughout SW Florida / Found: AC, coastal, near coast, inland / Months found: **JFMAMJJASOND**.

Perhaps most famous for its loud, familiar call, *killdeeahdeedee,* the killdeer's scientific name aptly describes its behavior: *vociferous*, meaning loud and vocal. Often found in pastures and open fields, the killdeer is a fairly large plover that frequents uplands, as well as beaches. Larger than the Wilson's plover, the killdeer is most easily recognized by its double-banded neck and its distinctive call.

Killdeer © Judd Patterson, BirdsInFocus.com

One of the most successful of all plovers, the killdeer is an example of an animal that not only has learned to adapt to the ways of man, but also flourishes in any number of urban or suburban environments. It nests in baseball fields, gravel rooftops, railroad yards, and scores of similarly unlikely locations. Because of this adaptation, the killdeer is prone to pesticide poisoning, and traffic and window collisions, among a host of other metropolitan dangers. Despite some losses, the killdeer population continues to expand its range, reaching all the way from the northern fringe of Chile to British Columbia.

The killdeer's diet consists almost entirely of insects, but it will also take small crustaceans and an occasional seed. It is a solitary nester and will feign a broken wing if you approach too near to its nesting locale. Its tiny chicks rely completely on camouflage to survive to adulthood.

❒ ________ **Black-necked Stilt** (*Himantopus mexicanus*) Other names: none Status: FL=stable to increasing slightly, IUCN=LC / Life span: to 12 years / Length: 13.8-15.4 in. (35-39 cm) / Wingspan: 28 in. (71 cm) / Weight: 4.8-7.8 oz (136-220 g) / Nests: throughout SW Florida in the summer / Found: AC, coastal, near coast, inland / Months found: **JFMAMJJASOND**.

Only the flamingo rivals this bird in having the longest legs in proportion to its body. When the stilt takes flight, its long pinkish-red legs trail behind the bird, giving it a most unusual and unmistakable look. The stark contrasts of the black-and-white markings also make this an easy bird to identify.

There are five species of stilts in the world, with the most endangered being the Hawaiian subspecies, called the ae'o. In Hawaii a deadly combination of over-hunting, habitat loss, and introduced predators such as rats and feral cats reduced the entire population of Hawaiian stilts to fewer than 400 birds by the mid-1940s. With careful management and habitat restoration, it has recovered to a stable population of more than 1,400 birds.

The stilt is a very noisy bird. When approached, an agitated stilt will yap incessantly until the person or predator passes. Its call, as opposed to its graceful

Stalking prey © Hung V. Do

feeding habits, lacks any pretense of refinement. The stilt arrives in Southwest Florida in early summer to nest. It can generally be found from late April through September in salt flats, coastal marshes, and wetlands, as well as some inland locations. It can sometimes be seen along the beaches and, rarely, can be found foraging in the mangrove flats.

This is one of a handful of birds whose summer migration takes it north to Florida from its wintering grounds in Cuba, Puerto Rico, and the northern fringe of South America. The stilt eats primarily small fish, crustaceans, and marine worms. It uses its thin, needle-like beak to prod deep into the soft bottom in search of prey.

Its eggs, which are laid directly on the ground or on floating vegetation, are vulnerable to snakes and rats. Because it lays its eggs directly on the ground they are also vulnerable to excessive spring rains, which can drown out the embryos before hatching. The adult is sometimes taken by hawks and falcons.

❒ ________ **Laughing Gull** (*Larus atricilla*) Other names: black-headed gull / Status: FL=stable, increasing its range, IUCN=LC / Length: 15-18 in. (39-46 cm) / Wingspan: 36-47 in. (92-120 cm) / Weight: 11.5 oz (.33 kg) / Life span: to 19 years / Nests along coastal Florida / Found: AC, coastal, near coast / Months found: **JFMAMJJASOND**.

© Judd Patterson, BirdsInFocus.com

Known for its distinctive, laugh-like call, the laughing gull is the most common gull found in Southwest Florida. It dons a black cap during breeding season, but during most of the year is far less conspicuous, with a white head, gray wings, and blackish markings. The juvenile coloration is a mottled gray before reaching adult plumage in three years.

This gull gathers along the spoil islands, as well as almost anywhere along

Laughing Gull © Judd Patterson, BirdsInFocus.com

the beaches. It feeds on fish, crustaceans, insects, carrion, eggs, young birds, and refuse. It frequently raids unattended picnic grounds when the unsuspecting tourists head out for a swim. It may also sit atop a pelican's head waiting for it to strain out the saltwater and feed on the overflowing minnows.

The laughing gull is monogamous and a strong colonial nester. In nearby Tampa Bay there are islands where up to 10,000 laughing gulls mate and nest at one time.

❒ __________ **Ring-billed Gull** (*Larus delawarensis*) Other names: none / Status: FL=stable, IUCN=LC / Life span: to 27 years / Length: 16.9-21 in. (43-51 cm) / Wingspan: 41.3-46 in (105-115 cm) / Weight: 10.6 oz -1.9 lb (300-720 g) / Nests: across the northern tier of the U.S. and well into northern Canada / Found: SC, ChC, LC, CC, coastal / Months found: **JFMAMJJASOND**.

The ring-billed gull is easy to identify. Look for the bright yellow bill with a clear black ring extending around both the upper and lower beaks. No other gull or tern has this distinctive characteristic. The ring-billed gull has adapted well to human landscapes and is frequently found in parking lots, near landfills, on golf courses, and in other urban locations.

This is a fairly large gull and has been known to interbreed and hybridize with smaller gulls such as Franklin's, black-headed, and laughing gulls. It is an attractive bird, with lovely white spots mottled over the black tips at the end of its wings. It can be readily found along the beaches or sitting on the large exposed sandbars during low tide almost anywhere along the coastline.

This gull feeds on fish, carrion, shrimp, and crabs. Because it has adapted so well to humans, it also feeds on potato chips, Doritos, and bread crumbs, and has even been known to beg. Feeding the ring-billed gull, or any bird, makes it more aggressive and can create a nuisance bird. However tempting, feeding any wildlife should always be avoided.

The ring-billed gull is sometimes preyed upon by falcons and eagles, and its nests can be raided by Arctic foxes, coyotes, and bobcats. A colony nester, the adult ring-billed gull has been observed returning to nest within three feet of where it was born.

Ring-billed Gulls © David Seibel, BirdsInFocus.com

❒ ______________ **Herring Gull** (*Larus smithsonianus*) Other names: none / Status: FL = stable, IUCN = LC / Length: 22-26 in. (56-66 cm) / Wingspan: 53.9-57.5 in. (137-146 cm) / Weight: 1.75-2.7 lb (.79-1.25 kg) / Life span: to 28 years / Nests: in the Maritime Provinces across to Alaska / Found: AC, coastal, inld. / Months found: **JFM**AMJJASO**ND**.

The herring gull is the quintessential gull in North America: a loud, raucous bird that is a frequent visitor to landfills and garbage dumps where it feeds on almost everything. In the wild it is an aggressive gull that steals food from other birds, feasts on dead fish and carrion along the shoreline, and surface-dives for fish, mollusks, and squid. In its northern nesting ranges it is also known to feed on tern eggs and chicks.

The herring gull is a migratory species in Florida with no known breeding pairs found in the state. Believe it or not, this plentiful gull was once brought to the edge of extinction through a combination of hunting it for its large, white and black wing feathers and harvesting its large eggs for human consumption. In 1900 the entire North American population was estimated at only 8,000 birds, all in Maine. By 1990, after decades of intense conservation efforts, the population in Maine stood at 27,000

Herring Gull © David Seibel, BirdsInFocus.com

but tens of thousands more had spread across its historic range from the Gulf of St. Lawrence to Alaska, and its numbers are now estimated to be in the millions. In the north this large gull is often in conflict with a similar but larger bird, the great black-backed gull.

Among ornithologists considerable controversy surrounds the extended herring gull family. Once believed to be closely related to the European herring gull, recent DNA studies indicate this is not the case, and there is considerable debate over the relationship of the American herring gull to several other subspecies. The herring gull is known to hybridize with other species of gulls including the lesser black-back and the glaucous-winged gull, making the situation even more complex.

Most herring gull mortality arises from its close interactions with humans. In dump sites it is often killed by bulldozers pushing over piles of garbage, while at sea it becomes tangled in fishing line and nets, and considerable numbers of herring gulls die from toxicity from manmade chemicals and plastics. The nests and chicks are often raided by jaegers and black-backed gulls.

❒ ___________ **Least Tern** (*Sterna antillarum*) Other names: sea swallow, pigeon de la mer, little tern / Status: FL=threatened, IUCN=LC / Life span: to 24 years / Length: 8.3-9.1 in. (21-23 cm) / Wingspan: 18.9-20.9 in. (48-53 cm) / Weight: 1.1-1.6 oz (30-45 g) / Nests: in Florida in the summer months, mostly along the coastline, and it winters in Colombia and Venezuela / Found: SC, ChC, LC, CC, coastal / Months found: **JFMAMJJASOND**.

True to its nickname sea swallow, this is the smallest tern in the Western Hemisphere. Weighing half that of a robin, this tiny tern feeds on small fish, crustaceans, and sand eels. Its cap is similar to other terns, but its diminutive size and black-tipped yellow bill are the best methods of identifying this bird.

Like several other summer species, the least tern has made Florida its northern nesting site, although several small populations nest as far north as Massachusetts. Once hunted for its plumes, the least tern is still considered threatened in much of its range, and its

Courting Least Terns © Judd Patterson, BirdsInFocus.com

population is being closely monitored. There is also a West Coast population that summers in California and winters deep into Mexico.

The least tern suffers from habitat and nesting-site loss. It prefers to nest on beaches where it is often in conflict with humans and their pets. If agitated by an unwanted intruder, the least tern has a nasty habit of hovering over the potential predator and defecating, so be forewarned. The least tern is monogamous but always nests in colonies with other terns.

Least Tern chicks in nest © Bob Gress, BirdsInFocus.com

❒ ________ **Royal Tern** (*Sterna maxima*) Other names: big striker, redbill, cayenne tern / Status: FL=stable, but declining in some areas, especially California, IUCN=LC / Life span: to 28 years / Length: 17.7-19.7 in. (45-50 cm) / Wingspan: 49-53 in. (124-134 cm) / Weight: 12.3-16 oz (350-460 g) / Nests: in a small area along the Eastern Seaboard during the summer / Found: SC, ChC, LC, CC, coastal / Months found: **JFMAMJJASOND**.

Royal terns stacking up © Bob Gress, BirdsInFocus.com

Sporting a cool hairdo, the royal tern is a fairly common sighting along the spoil islands of the Intracoastal waterway during the winter months. It crouches low against the wind and is often seen in flocks of 20 or more. One of the largest terns in North America, the royal can be found all the way to southern Argentina.

The royal tern is larger than its cousins, the Sandwich and Forster's terns. It also has a yellow-orange bill, whereas the smaller Sandwich tern has a black bill with a yellow tip. Royal terns are also fond of causeway islands and remote beaches, where it nests during the heat of summer.

The royal feeds mostly on small minnows, shrimp, and crustaceans, primarily by plunge diving, a similar technique to that used by the brown pelican. It hovers 40 to 60 feet in the air, then falls headfirst on its prey, sometimes going completely underwater. The royal is also known to raid the by-catch of pelicans and can sometimes be seen sitting on a pelican's head looking for strained-off minnows as the pelican empties its pouch of saltwater.

The royal tern is monogamous and a colony nester, most often with other species of terns. It is preyed upon by falcons, and its nests are vulnerable to mammals such as raccoons and weasels. Because it is so reliant on a stable minnow population, water-quality degradation can devastate royal tern populations.

❐ ___________ **Black Skimmer** (*Rynchops niger*) Other names: shearwater, scissorbill, sea-dog, razorbill / Status: FL=the local population of black skimmers are declining, IUCN=LC / Life span: to 20 years / Length: 15.7-19.7 in. (40-50 cm) / Wingspan: 42-50 in. (106-127 cm) / Weight: 7.5 oz-1 lb (210-450 g) / Nests: all along the barrier island beaches and spoil islands / Found: SC, ChC, LC, CC, coastal / Months found: **JFMAMJJASOND**.

Black Skimmers © David Seibel, BirdsInFocus.com

The black skimmer's nickname sea-dog comes from the barking sounds the bird makes as it glides over the water's surface in search of minnows. The skimmer feeds in a most unusual fashion. It is the only bird in the world whose lower mandible (beak) is longer than the upper. It flies, generally in pairs or small groups, directly over the surface of the water with its extended lower bill slicing through the water. When it detects a fish or crustacean, it snaps its head down and snatches the creature directly from the water. Because of the constant wear on this extended lower mandible, the black skimmer's bill continues to grow throughout its adult lifetime.

North and South America are home to three races of skimmer. The northern population, *Rynchops niger,* is the only one that frequents the Southwest Florida coastline. Although its numbers in Florida are declining as a result of a lack of suitable nesting sites, the South American population, which prefers freshwater rivers and lakes to estuaries, is healthy. Two other species of skimmers inhabit Africa and India.

The skimmer tends to feed at dawn and dusk, a timeframe scientifically defined as *crepuscular,* and has even been known to feed nocturnally, especially under a full moon. The best place to view the skimmer is along the coastline in the late afternoon or anywhere in the back bays. Another reliable viewing opportunity is just after dawn along the gulf beaches, but only when it is very calm. The skimmer prefers very still water for feeding. It is monogamous and nests in colonies of other skimmers, generally on beaches, sandy islets, or sandbars.

❒ ____________ **Rock Pigeon** (*Columa livia*) Other names: rock dove, city pigeon, pigeon / Status: FL = increasing, IUCN = LC / Length: 11.8-14.2 in. (30-36 cm) / Wingspan: 19.7-26.4 in. (50-67 cm) / Weight: 9.3-13.4 oz (265-380 g) / Life span: to 6 years / Nests: throughout SW Florida / Found: AC, coastal, near coast, inland / Months found: **JFMAMJJASOND**.

Rock Pigeon © Bob Gress, BirdsInFocus.com

Introduced in North America in 1606 at Port Royal, Nova Scotia, by well-meaning but misguided pilgrims, the rock pigeon now inhabits every major city and park in North America. Only the northernmost tier of the continent, from the Yukon Territories to Labrador, does not have these ubiquitous birds. The pigeon inhabits every continent except Antarctica, where it is too cold for it to survive. When it comes to animal populations that ride the coattails of human population growth, only the rat rivals the pigeon; hence the nickname often given the pigeon, "flying rat."

The pigeon is believed to have originated somewhere in the Middle East or Eastern North Africa and was domesticated by humans 6,500 years ago. Cuneiform tablets from Mesopotamia describe domesticated pigeons more than 5,000 years ago, and their uses over the ages have been well documented. The Chinese still eat pigeons, serving them as "squab." In both World War I and II homing pigeons were used to communicate military intelligence across enemy lines. The United Kingdom used about 250,000 pigeons during WWII, and the Dickin Medal of Honor was awarded to 32 homing pigeons for valor, not that they had any real use for the medals.

Today, the pigeon is everywhere. The North American population is so enormous that there are no reliable census counts. The Centers for Disease Control, which has expressed concern about the pigeon harboring the West Nile Virus and the deadly avian influenza (H5N1), estimates the population of these birds to be as high as 4.6 million just in the greater Atlanta area. Since the pigeon can be found in every metropolitan area in the country means the total North American population possibly exceeds 300 million, making it potentially the most populous bird in the United States.

The pigeon breeds year round and has a clutch size of one to three eggs. Originally adapted to nesting on cliffs, the pigeon has taken to nesting under bridges, overpasses, buildings, stairwells, eaves, overhangs, abandoned buildings, gutters—in essence, just about everywhere. Pigeon mortality comes from many directions. In recent years it has become a favorite target for peregrine falcons, which are also adapting to urban centers. Rats, feral cats, raccoons, mice, opossums, bobcats, and anything else that can eat eggs and chicks feast on this prolific bird. Some municipalities use net traps to keep park pigeon populations in check, and in a single day, tens of thousands of these birds may be captured and euthanized. Because of its interaction with humans, the pigeon is vulnerable to industrial and chemical poisoning. Mature birds are sometimes trapped and used for live skeet-shooting practice.

The pigeon eats practically anything, thriving in urban centers where it is often fed by humans in parks. In the wild its main diet consists of grains and seeds, along with occasional insects. Needless to say, it will be a very, very long time before the pigeon joins the endangered species list.

❒ __________ Eurasian Collared-dove (*Streptopelia decaocto*)

Other names: collared turtle dove / Status: FL=thriving, rapidly expanding its current range northward, IUCN=LC / Life span: to 5 years / Length: 11-12 in. (29-31 cm) / Wingspan: 14 in. (35 cm) / Weight: 5.6 oz (150-170 g) / Nests: year round throughout SW Florida / Found: AC, coastal, near coast, inland / Months found: **JFMAMJJASOND**.

The Eurasian collared-dove is rapidly expanding its range across North America. Originally from western India, this bird has flourished because of repeated human introductions. It was first imported to Turkey in the 1600s, then spread into the Balkans, Greece, Italy, North Africa, and finally swept across all of Europe where it is firmly entrenched. It can also be found throughout North Africa as far west as Morocco where, as elsewhere, it prefers living close to human development.

Eurasian Collared-dove © Judd Patterson, BirdsInFocus.com

It came to Florida via the Bahamas, where approximately 50 doves were released in 1974. The species reached the Florida Keys in the late 1970s and has been moving north and west ever since. It now breeds west of the Mississippi, and there are established pockets of Eurasian collared-doves in Southern California. Within the next 20 to 40 years this dove will probably inhabit every state in the lower 48, as well as Mexico, Central America, and southern Canada.

The Eurasian collared-dove is slightly larger than the native mourning dove and can be readily distinguished from that bird by the black ring extending halfway around its nape and by its tail, which is squared off with white outer feathers. Unlike the mourning dove, it does not whistle when taking flight but has been known to make a catbird-like mew when taking off and landing, as well as a similar but much quicker *cacoocuk* when roosting. This dove is monogamous and makes a solitary nest.

Its diet is almost identical to the mourning dove, consisting chiefly of seeds, grains, and occasional insects. This dove has already interbred with the native ringed turtle-dove, and there is some speculation that it may be interbreeding with the mourning dove as well. Because of its growing numbers, the Eurasian collared-dove has become an important item in the winter diet of Florida hawks, including the red-shouldered hawk.

❐ __________ **Mourning Dove** (*Zenaida macroura*) Other names: turtle dove, Carolina dove, wood dove / Status: FL=thriving, Florida's population alone is estimated at 50 million birds, IUCN=LC / Life span: to 31 years / Length: 12 in. (30 cm) / Wingspan: 17-19 in. (37-48 cm) / Weight: 4.3 oz (120 g) / Nests: year round throughout SW Florida / Found: AC, coastal, near coast, inland / Months found: **JFMAMJJASOND**.

With a total population in the United States of approximately 350 million birds—even with an annual harvest of more than 20 million doves by hunters (2 million are taken in Florida alone)—the mourning dove is in no imminent danger of extinction. Although impressive, these numbers pale in comparison with its extinct cousin, the passenger pigeon, whose numbers at the time of European contact have been estimated at 5 to 7 billion.

Mourning Dove © Judd Patterson, BirdsInFocus.com

The mourning dove has two characteristics that distinguish it from its European relative, the Eurasian collared-dove: it is the dove responsible for the familiar *ooah, woo, woo, woo* call; and it whistles when it takes flight. It is also considerably smaller but that difference can be easy to miss when either bird is in motion.

A highly adaptable bird, the mourning dove has flourished under the environmental changes brought on by mankind. It has learned to live comfortably in urban, suburban, and agricultural settings. Across Southwest Florida the mourning dove is ubiquitous, seen perched on telephone wires, sign posts, and almost any tall tree.

It feeds predominantly on grains and seeds, and it can be found filling its crop with sandy grit along almost any unpaved road. The grit assists in digesting the various seeds and fruits the dove thrives on. It is also famous for its "crop milk" or "pigeon's milk," which it regurgitates and feeds to its chicks for the first few weeks after hatching.

The mourning dove is preyed upon by falcons, bobcats, and sportsmen. It is monogamous, often pairing for life, and it nests in individual nesting sites, often in very unusual places. It is the most heavily hunted game bird in Florida.

Mourning Dove chicks in nest
© Bob Gress, BirdsInFocus.com

❒ __________ Common Ground-Dove (*Columbina passerina*)

Other names: eastern ground-dove / Status: FL=declining populations throughout the Southeast and along the gulf coast, IUCN=LC / Life span: to 7 years / Length: 67 in. (15-18 cm) / Wingspan: 11 in. (27 cm) Weight: 1.1 oz (31 g) / Nests year round throughout SW Florida / Found: AC, coastal, near coast, inland / Months found: **JFMAMJJASOND**.

The translation of its scientific name accurately describes this beautiful, small bird: sparrow-like dove. The underside of the common ground-dove has a reddish hue, and its wings have gray, brown, and purplish spots. It is an attractive bird and relatively common throughout Southwest Florida. The ground-dove is readily spotted at Harn's Marsh in Lee County and along the Indigo Trail at J.N. "Ding" Darling National Wildlife Refuge on Sanibel.

Ground Dove © Judd Patterson, BirdsInFocus.com

Most often seen in pairs or groups of four, it is usually happened upon by accident as it feeds along shell-covered hiking trails or gravel roads. Because of its diminutive size, the ground-dove is easy to distinguish from either of the region's two larger doves.

When disturbed it tends to fly a short distance and land, only to do the same thing again and again until it finally turns and flies behind you. Like its larger cousins, the ground-dove feeds on seeds, grains, and small berries. It is monogamous, and it is widely believed that pairs mate for life. Because of its small size, the ground-dove is seldom hunted.

❒ ____________ **Eastern Screech-Owl** (*Otus asio*) Other names: squinch owl, death owl, shivering owl, mottled owl / Status: FL=Declining population, IUCN=LC / Life span: to 20 years / Length: 8-10 in. (16-25 cm) / Wingspan: 18-24 in. (45-61 cm) / Weight: 5.9 oz (170 g) / Nests: year round throughout SW Florida / Found: AC, coastal, near coast, inland / Months found: **JFMAMJJASOND**.

Eastern Screech-Owl
© Judd Patterson, BirdsInFocus.com

One of the smallest owls in North America, the eastern screech owl has been known to consume one-third of its body weight every day. It has a distinct call, similar to a horse's whinny, then descending in pitch to a drawn-out trill. Because of its size and its nocturnal habits, this owl, like the great horned owl, will more likely be heard and seldom, if ever, seen.

The eastern screech owl has two distinct color morphs: red and gray. The red phase seems to be more heat tolerant and is the color most often observed in South Florida. The screech owl's broad diet consists of insects, spiders, crayfish, mammals, amphibians, reptiles, fish, and small birds, including starlings and songbirds.

This small owl nests in hollow cavities and dense foliage, as well as manmade bird boxes. Although it is fundamentally monogamous, the male owl has been known to take up with two females and remain in this avian ménage à trois throughout its lifetime. The screech owl suffers from loss of habitat and pesticide poisoning.

Eastern Screech-Owl, red phase
© David Seibel, BirdsInFocus.com

❒ __________ **Great Horned Owl** (*Bubo virginianus*) Other names: cat owl, hoot owl / Status: FL=stable, IUCN=LC / Life span: to 27 years / Length: 18-25 in. (46-63 cm) / Wingspan: 40-60 in. (101-152 cm) / Weight: 3 lb (1.36 kg) / Nests: year round throughout SW Florida / Found: AC, coastal, near coast, inland / Months found: **JFMAMJJASOND**.

Chances are you will never actually see a great horned owl anywhere in Southwest Florida. This nocturnal feeder comes out at dusk and retires just before sunrise, the exact opposite of predominantly diurnal hominoids. A far better way of knowing if there is a great horned owl in your area is by hearing it. Both the male and female make a loud, resonant *Whoo! Whoowhoowhoo! Whoo!* call that is unmistakable.

Easily recognized by the two tufts of feathers on its head resembling ears, this large owl is a formidable predator. It is the only bird known to kill full-grown skunks, falcons, and domestic cats. It also eats marsh rabbits, rats and mice, insects, coots, and other owls. Because of its ability to tackle prey weighing more than itself, the great horned owl is scorned by all other major raptors: osprey, red-shouldered hawks, and bald eagles. Crows have been known to mob the great horned owl's nest and kill its chicks.

The great horned owl ranges from the High Arctic to Argentina. Though it is not common in Southwest Florida, there are several nests scattered around. A solitary nesting bird, the great horned owl is monogamous and aggressive. It has been known to strike at humans in defense of its nest. Its powerful grip and long talons can inflict serious injury.

Great Horned Owl with chick in nest

© DIck Fortune and Sara Lopez

Great Horned Owl in Flight

© Heather Green

❐ __________ **Barred Owl** (*Stix varia*) Other names: swamp owl, hoot owl, eight hooter, rain owl, wood owl, striped owl / Status: FL = stable, IUCN - LC / Length: 16.9-19.7 in. (43-50 cm) / Wingspan: 39-43.3 in. (99-110 cm) / Weight: 1-2.3 lb (470-1050 g) / Life span: to 18 years / Nests: throughout SW Florida / Found: AC, near coast, inland / Months found: **JFMAMJJASOND**.

Perhaps best known as the hoot owl, this bird is famous for its call, which sounds similar to, *Who cooks for you? Who cooks for you-all.* Found primarily in swamps and mixed hardwood forests, the barred owl has thus far avoided urban areas. Several barred owls make their home at the Audubon Corkscrew Swamp Sanctuary in Collier County. It is increasing in population and expanding westward across the continent.

This is a large and attractive owl with dark brown eyes and multistriped feather pattern. It is one of the most active daytime owls, and although it hunts primarily at dusk and dawn, it can sometimes be found hooting and feeding during daylight hours, especially on dark, cloudy days. It hunts by roosting in tall trees, then looking and listening for the small mammals, reptiles, crayfish, muskrats, and birds it dines on. It swoops down silently and grasps its prey in its talons, then returns to its perch to feed.

Barred Owl © Judd Patterson, BirdsInFocus.com

One of the biggest predators of the barred owl is the larger and more aggressive great horned owl. Likewise, the barred owl is fond of feeding on the smaller screech owl. Because the barred owl nests in cavities high up in trees, its eggs and chicks are not subject to predation by most mammals. Snakes have been known to take both eggs and chicks. The barred owl breeds almost all year round.

❒ __________ **Burrowing Owl** (*Athene cunicularia*) Other names: ground owl, howdy owl, burrow owl / Status: FL = species of special concern, IUCN = LC / Length: 7.5-9.8 in. (19-25 cm) / Wingspan: 21.7 in. (55 cm) / Weight: 5.3 oz (150 g) / Life span: to 9 years / Nests: throughout SW Florida / Found: AC, near coast, inland / Months found: **JFMAMJJASOND**.

Burrowing Owls in Cape Coral © Dick Fortune and Sara Lopez

The burrowing owl is best described as adorable. It was the subject for the 2002 children's book *Hoot* by Carl Hiaasen and is a popular wildlife calendar subject in Florida. Its diminutive size, coupled with its long legs and large yellow eyes make it a favorite for photographers everywhere. One of the best places to find this owl is in Cape Coral, where it has adapted to living in a suburban environment. There are an estimated 1,000 breeding pairs here (see the Four-Mile Ecological Park in the Lee County section of this book for specific locales to find these owls). Every winter Cape Coral celebrates this fascinating bird with the Burrowing Owl Festival.

The conversion of much of its former range into farmland, suburban, and urban settings has had a major impact on the burrowing owl. It is believed that before these changes in the landscape, the burrowing owl inhabited every state in the union. Today its eastern range is limited to Florida, where it is a species of special concern. Its New World range runs from Tierra del Fuego at the tip of South America all the way into the Northwest Territories of Canada. In this vast and open range it is not considered endangered.

As the name implies, the burrowing owl lives in burrows. While capable of digging its own burrow, it often takes up residence in abandoned gopher tortoise nests, prairie dog holes, and an assortment of human excavations. It is both diurnal and nocturnal, feeding on insects during daylight hours and small rodents such as moles and mice during the evening. The burrowing owl has been known to bring mammal dung to its burrow to attract dung beetles, which it then consumes. It is, in essence, bird farming.

Because it is a ground-dwelling and nesting bird, the burrowing owl is preyed upon by feral cats, snakes, and coyotes. Its nests are often raided by snakes and rats.

❒ __________ **Chuck-will's-widow** (*Caprimulgus carolinensis*)
Other names: Dutch whip-poor-will, Spanish whip-poor-will / Status: FL = stable, IUCN = LC / Length: 11-12.6 in. (28-32 cm) / Wingspan: 22.8-24 in. (58-61 cm) / Weight: 2.3-6.6 oz (66-188 g) / Life span: to 15 years / Nests: in northern Florida and the Southeastern U.S. / Found: AC, coastal, near coast, inland / Months found: **JFMAMJJASOND**.

© Judd Patterson, BirdsInFocus.com

Like the chimney swift, the chuck-will's-widow makes Florida and the southeastern United States its summer nesting home. In the winter it returns to feed in Central America and the northern tip of South America, in Colombia and Venezuela. Although this reverse migratory bird is nowhere near as numerous as the species that winter in Florida and spend the summer in the far north, it is among a few equatorial migrants, including the black skimmer and least tern, for which Florida is the far north. The chuck-will's-widow is difficult to distinguish from the similar whip-poor-will except for its slightly different call and its darker plumage, which lacks the white tips of the smaller whip-poor-will.

The name of this bird is onomatopoeic, describing the sound of its nightly call, which is a variation of chuck-will's-*wid*ow, with the emphasis on *wid*. This call can sometimes be repeated through the entire night and well into morning, occasionally mixed in with the similar though distinct call of the related whip-poor-will.

The chuck-will's-widow has unusual stiff, forward-facing feathers called rictal bristles that extend outward on either side of its beak. These are believed to act as a funnel helping the bird take in bugs and moths during its nocturnal foraging. It has also been known to consume small birds such as warblers and white-eyed vireos.

The chuck-will's-widow nests in Florida but doesn't really make a nest. Instead it lays its eggs on the ground or on fallen leaves where its mottled brown coloration makes it all but invisible when roosting. The eggs are a mottled gray to white. As a ground nester, the chuck-will's-widow leaves its eggs and chicks vulnerable to snakes, rodents, and fire ants. The adult chuck-will's-widow has few natural predators since it is almost entirely nocturnal and extremely adept in flight.

❒ ___________ **Chimney Swift** (*Chaetura pelagica*) Other names: chimney swallow, chimney bat, chimney sweep, flying cigar / Status: FL = expanding range, IUCN = LC / Length: 4.7-5.9 in. (12-15 cm) / Wingspan: 10.6-11.8 in. (27-30 cm) / Weight: 0.6-1.1 oz (17-30 g) / Life span: to 14 years / Nests: in northern Florida and the entire eastern U.S. / Found: AC, coastal, near coast, inland / Months found: **JFMAMJJASOND**.

The chimney swift, which winters in South America, has only recently arrived in Southwest Florida. During the 1930s this flying acrobat was seldom if ever seen south of Orlando, but in the past 50 years it has moved as far south as Naples and Miami. It is easily identified during the spring, summer, and fall months by its constant chattering while in flight and its apparent lack of tail feathers. This unusual shape has earned it the nickname, "flying cigar."

Chimney Swift in flight

© David Seibel, BirdsInFocus.com

Related to the bird that provides the Chinese with one of the most expensive food delicacies on earth, bird's nest soup, the chimney swift uses its saliva to builds its nest on the walls of chimneys, caves, and cement structures. Unlike the black-nest swiftlet of Thailand, whose nests are made up entirely of saliva and can cost as much as $10,000 a kilo, only the inside edge of the chimney swift's nest is constructed with this salivary cement; the rest is built out of small twigs.

The swift is amazing in that it seldom stops flying. It bathes in flight, mates in flight, eats in flight, and migrates to and from the jungle regions of South America, from Colombia to southern Peru, every winter. In the summer it ventures as far north as southern Canada and across most of the Eastern United States. It consumes nothing but insects, which are always caught mid-air.

Its feet are so small that it cannot roost but instead clings, right-side-up (it does not hang upside down as bats do), to the walls of its nesting sites. The chimney swift has flourished in modern times because of the construction of so many chimneys in North America. Since it arrives after winter and nests during the summer months when most of America's chimneys are inactive, it has made itself right at home here.

Because of its aerial prowess, the swift is almost never a target for falcons, owls, or flying predators. The safety of residential chimneys also protects the swift from easy predation by snakes or raccoons. This is one creature that has taken advantage of the changes in its landscape brought about by the march of civilization. Beautiful to watch in flight and strange to hear chattering above your home, the chimney swift has flourished, in large part, because of you.

❒ ______ Ruby-throated Hummingbird (*Archilochus colubris*)

Other names: none / Status: FL=stable, IUCN=LC / Life span: to 9 years / Length: 2.8-3.5 in. (7-9 cm) / Wingspan: 3.1-4.3 in. (8-11 cm) / Weight: 0.1-0.2 oz (2-6 g) / Nests: in northern Florida to southern Canada / Found: AC, coastal, near coast, inland / Months found: **JFMAMJJASOND**.

One of North America's smallest birds, the ruby-throated hummingbird is an amazing creature. One of the few birds able to hover and the only bird able to fly backwards and upside down, the ruby-throated hummingbird beats its wings so fast it creates a humming sound. When in flight its feet virtually disappear into its tiny body, making it more aerodynamically perfect.

This bird is found in Southwest Florida only on occasion and is far more commonly seen in the summer throughout its northern range. Despite its tiny size, the ruby-throated hummingbird stores enough fat (a whopping two grams!) to enable it to fly nonstop across the 600-mile expanse of the Gulf of Mexico twice a year.

The hummingbird family is found only in the Americas, from Tierra del Fuego to Alaska. There are an amazing 325 species of hummingbirds, though the vast majority of these birds live in Central and South America.

Unlike humans, the hummingbird is able to see things in the ultraviolet color spectrum. This allows it to spot the flowering plants upon which they rely for nectar. It seems to be attracted to the color red. Sadly, this is also a cause of mortality, since it is attracted to the red tops of certain power-line capacitors and is electrocuted when attempting to feed on them.

The hummingbirds, not just the ruby-throated, are important pollinators but also consume nectar-eating insects and tiny spiders. The high-energy diet of nectar is essential to its metabolic needs, with some hummingbirds known to have heart rates as high as 1,260 beats per minute. That is roughly 1,200 beats faster than the heartbeat of a well-trained athlete. As if that weren't amazing enough, it has also been calculated that when flying forward, a hummingbird's wings can exceed 4,500 beats a minute, or 75 beats per second. One other astounding ability of many hummingbirds is there abilities to reduce their core body temperatures on command. During periods of rainy weather with little nectar to collect, the hummingbird will go torpid, lowering its core body temperature from a normal 104° F to as low as 50° F. If it were not able to do so, it would starve to death by morning.

Ruby-throated Hummingbird in flight
© Bob Gress, BirdsInFocus.com

The ruby-throated hummingbird will readily come to artificial feeders, attracted by sugar water. Only white granulated sugar has been proven safe to use: a ratio of one cup sugar to four cups water is the most common recipe. The practice of adding red dye to the sugar water in the feeders is not recommended however, since the chemicals in the dye can damage these delicate birds.

The hummingbird is seldom preyed upon as an adult, but the size of its tiny eggs—smaller than jellybeans—and chicks make them vulnerable predators as small as lizards, mice, and tiny snakes. Some of the South American species, especially the highly specialized birds, are endangered, but the ruby-throated hummingbird appears to be doing well throughout its range, possibly in part because of the innumerable feeders placed in the backyards of North America every summer.

❐ ___________ **Belted Kingfisher** (*Ceryle alcyon*) Other names: eastern belted kingfisher / Status: FL=stable to a slight decline, IUCN=LC / Life span: to 5 years / Length: 11-13.8 in. (28-35 cm) / Wingspan: 18.9-22.8 in. (48-58 cm) / Weight: 4.9-6 oz (140-170 g) / Nests: from northern Florida to the northern tier of North America from Alaska to Newfoundland / Found: AC, coastal, near coast, inland / Months found: **JFMAMJJASOND**.

The distinctive loud and rattling call of the belted kingfisher generally announces its arrival or departure from a roosting site. A plunge diver that often hovers in the air studying its potential meal before diving, the kingfisher prefers freshwater to saltwater environments. This is a bird that has taken advantage of human

Belted Kingfisher © Dick Fortune and Sara Lopez

activities and can readily be found along highways where drainage swales and ponds have been dredged. The kingfisher is often spotted sitting on a telephone pole or power line over these small bodies of water waiting for an errant minnow or tadpole to get close to the surface.

The belted kingfisher is one of only a handful of avian species in which the female is more brightly colored than the male. There are 93 different species of kingfishers worldwide, including the famous Australian kingfisher, the kookaburra. The best places to find these birds locally are around inland lakes or along the banks of the rivers and streams.

The kingfisher lives year round throughout most of the United States, but some do migrate south during the winter months. Its nests are robbed by grackles, various snakes, and tree-climbing mammals, while the adult is taken by alligators and falcons. The kingfisher is unusual in that, like the cliff swallow, it digs tunnels and makes cavities in riverbanks where it builds its nests and raises its offspring. It is adapting well to human-designed changes in the landscape, and despite some regional losses, it is fundamentally successful.

❒ ________ Red-bellied Woodpecker (*Melanerpes carolinus*)

Other names: zebra woodpecker, ladderback, orange sapsucker / Status: FL=stable to slightly expanding its range, IUCN=LC / Life span: to 12 years / Length: 9 in. (24 cm) / Wingspan: 13-17 in. (33-42 cm) / Weight: 23 oz (65-91 gm) / Nests throughout SW Florida / Found: AC, coastal, near coast, inland / Months found: **JFMAMJJASOND**.

Anyone with a home located near a nesting pair of red-bellied woodpecker may be all too familiar with the habits of this medium-size woodpecker. In the spring, during the breeding season, it loves to hammer on tin roofs, hollow trees, or anything loud that might attract a mate but will assuredly drive the homeowners half-crazy. This noisy bird also makes a trill-like sound that is fairly easy to identify, resembling a rolling *churrr, churr, churr* sound, like a gargled chirp.

This species is misnamed because it doesn't have much of a red belly. Its underside has a slightly rosy hue, but it is far easier to identify from its partially red head and beautiful back markings, which resemble a black and white ladder—hence its nickname, ladderback (not to be confused with the smaller Southwestern ladder-backed woodpecker).

One amazing characteristic of the woodpecker is the length of its tongue. Although shorter than that of some species, the male red-bellied woodpecker's tongue can be up to four inches long, protruding deep into holes and crevices where it pulls out arthropods, a primary part of the woodpecker's diet. It also eats seeds, nuts, sap, and fruit and has been known to feed on tree frogs and small lizards.

Red-bellied Woodpecker displaying tongue
© Dick Fortune and Sara Lopez

The red-bellied woodpecker loves nesting boxes and can be found using them when available anywhere in its range. It sometimes competes with starlings for the best nesting boxes, and it's not unusual to see the two species quarreling over them. This woodpecker is sometimes taken by hawks, and its nests, when in trees rather than nesting boxes, can be raided by palm rats and snakes. It is monogamous and mates for life.

❒ ____________ **Downy Woodpecker** (*Picoides pubescens*) Other names: sapsucker / Status: FL = stable, IUCN = LC / Length: 5.5-6.7 in. (14-17 cm) / Wingspan: 9.8-11.8 in. (25-30 cm) / Weight: 0.7-1 oz (21-28 g) / Life span: to 12 years / Nests: throughout SW Florida / Found: AC, near coast, inland / Months found: **JFMAMJJASOND**.

The downy is America's smallest woodpecker. It looks almost identical to the hairy woodpecker. The only real difference is in size (the hairy woodpecker is three times heavier) and in the downy's bill, which is short and stubby. It is often found flocking with chickadees.

Roughly the same size as a house sparrow, this tiny bird has adapted well to the changes in the North American landscape over the past 500 years. Today, the downy inhabits almost all of the U.S. and Canada but does not fare well in the drier regions of Texas and Arizona, nor does it cross over into Mexico.

Male Downy Woodpecker

© Bob Gress, BirdsInFocus.com

The resident breeding populations extend farther north than almost any other bird. This dainty bird lives year round well into Northern Alberta, Canada, where it has adapted to surviving the extremely cold winters of the Canadian Rockies. It has found a niche eating beetles, cockroaches, ants, and other insects, but during the winter it change its diet to seeds and sap because of a lack of insects.

The downy woodpecker has done well in urban and suburban landscapes. A cavity nester, the downy prefers dense, old-growth forests, but as these have been eradicated from the Florida landscape, this small woodpecker has moved into smaller trees and snags and is now commonly found throughout the year in Southwest Florida. It is preyed upon by kestrels, merlins, and other raptors, and its eggs are vulnerable to snakes, reptiles, and tree-climbing mammals.

❒ __________ Red-cockaded Woodpecker (*Picoides borealis*)

Other names: sapsucker / Status: FL = endangered, IUNC = E / Length: 7.9-9.1 in. (20-23 cm) / Wingspan: 14.2 in. (36 cm) / Weight: 1.5-1.8 oz (42-52 g) / Life span: to 16 years / Nests: in mainland SW Florida / Found: ChC, CC, inland / Months found: **JFMAMJJASOND**

Without intervention by the Florida Fish and Wildlife Conservation Commission and a host of other agencies across the southeastern U.S., the red-cockaded woodpecker would inevitably follow the path of the ivory-billed woodpecker toward extinction. Both birds suffer from an inability to adapt their behavior to a rapidly altered environment. Whereas some species such as the wild turkey and downy woodpecker make it through the gauntlet of civilization and come out thriving on the other side, the red-cockaded woodpecker is in serious trouble across its entire former range.

Like its ivory-billed cousin, which relied heavily on old-growth cypress trees for foraging and nesting habitat, the red-cockaded woodpecker was intimately connected to old-growth longleaf pine forests. In Florida alone, 97 percent of this pine have been harvested for profit, and the population of this once-plentiful bird crashed as a direct result. Today the single largest concentration of the red-

Red-cockaded Woodpecker
© Judd Patterson, BirdsInFocus.com

cockaded woodpecker can be found in the Apalachicola National Forest. Remnant populations can still be found in Southwest Florida as well, but spotting one of these rare woodpeckers takes considerable effort. The bird is about the same size as a northern cardinal, and only the male has the red cockade (i.e., a rosette or knot of ribbons worn on a hat), which is located behind its eye. This dash of red is so small that it is all but impossible to identify in the field.

The best way to see this bird is by finding a nest. At the time of this writing, 27 colonies of red-cockaded woodpeckers make their home in the Babcock/Webb Wildlife Management Area in eastern Charlotte County. The staff there has identified the locations of these nests by painting a white ring around the base of the nesting tree. This bird can also be found in the Fakahatchee and Picayune Strand forests, though their nests in these preserves are not marked.

One fascinating behavior of this woodpecker is that it takes up to three years to create the perfect cavity in which to raise its broods. Once the cavity is completed, the red-cockaded woodpecker continues to drill a series of "resin wells" around the bark surrounding the entrance that leak sticky pine sap (the source of turpentine) for years to follow. This sap is believed to help repel tree-climbing snakes and other predators.

Because older trees have softer hearts, sometimes rotted through by a fungus called red heart rot, the red-cockaded woodpecker prefers these to younger, stronger, and denser pines. Once the old-growth forests were cut down, so fell the communities of red-cockaded woodpeckers that thrived in them. Today there are an estimated 12,000 red-cockaded woodpeckers, including 5,000 nesting pairs, left in the U.S. To put this into perspective, this number represents less than 1 percent of its original estimated population. In an effort to rebuild the remaining population, states such as Texas, Louisiana, and Georgia are creating artificial cavities in longleaf pine trees. Hopes are that these manmade cavities will be adopted by nesting pairs, thereby saving them three years of careful excavation. The only other measure is to stop all cutting of mature pines in regions where these birds are still located, a prospect that does not go over well with loggers or developers.

Like all woodpeckers, the adult bird is taken by small raptors, owls, and bobcats, and the eggs and chicks fall victim to a host of tree-climbing predators. The only real problem with the future of this small woodpecker, however, lies with us.

❒ __________ **Northern Flicker** (*Colaptes auratus*) Other names: yellowhammer, highhole, golden-winged woodpecker / Status: FL = stable, IUNC = LC / Length: 11-12.2 in. (28-31 cm) / Wingspan: 16.5-20.1 in. (42-51 cm) / Weight: 3.9-5.6 oz (110-160 g) / Life span: to 9 years / Nests: in mainland SW Florida / Found: AC, near coast, inland / Months found: **JFMAMJJASOND**.

Northern Flicker © Judd Patterson, BirdsInFocus.com

The northern flicker is fairly common near the coast and well inland but is a less-frequent visitor to the coast and barrier islands. This bird was once categorized as two species: the yellow-shafted flicker (found mostly in the eastern U.S.) and the red-shafted flicker (found mainly in the western U.S.), but recent DNA analysis indicates that these are essentially the same bird with localized plumage variations. They interbreed along the boundary lines of both species' regions, creating a host of plumage and marking variations.

Unlike most woodpeckers, the flicker is migratory. In the summer individual birds will go as far north as the Arctic Circle, then return south for the winter. The southern migrants tend to swell Florida's numbers as they join the resident birds that remain in the state year round.

Like its red-bellied woodpecker cousin, the flicker loves to "drum" on tin, hollow logs, or anything else that makes noise. This drumming is a form of courtship similar to the songs of warblers and mockingbirds. For homeowners who have a flicker waking them up at dawn while hammering away at a fireplace cap, this offers little solace.

The flicker is unlike other woodpeckers in that it prefers to feed on the ground and not on trunks and tree branches. It forages under leaves and detritus for beetles, larvae, and mostly ants, which constitute 45 percent of its diet. In the winter, when insects are all but impossible to find, the flicker turns to seeds and fruits until spring. It has been seen breaking into old cow patties in search of dung beetles. The flicker is preyed upon by hawks, owls, feral cats, weasels, and bobcats, and their chicks and eggs are taken by snakes, rats, and raccoons.

❐ ____________ Pileated Woodpecker (*Dryocopus pileatus*)

Other names: lord-god, good-god, woodchuck, cock-o-the-woods / Status: FL=stable, IUCN=LC / Life span: to 12 years / Length: 16-19 in. (40-49 cm) / Wingspan: 26-30 in. (66-76 cm) / Weight: 9-12.5 oz (250-350 g) / Nests: throughout SW Florida / Found: AC, coastal, near coast, inland / Months found: **JFMAMJJASOND**.

Pileated Woodpecker
© Judd Patterson, BirdsInFocus.com

This is the infamous woodpecker that was the role model for the cartoon character, Woody the Woodpecker. Its unmistakable call is a loud, ringing *kukkukkuk*. A fairly large bird, about the same size as a fish crow, the pileated can be seen flying around Southwest Florida and is noted for a series of quick, rapid wing flaps followed by a pause that always results in the bird quickly losing altitude.

With its bold red crest and large black bill, the pileated woodpecker is a very attractive bird. It could be mistaken for the ivory-billed woodpecker, which is slightly larger, has a bone-white bill, and is in all likelihood extinct.

The pileated is a formidable drilling machine, known to peck so deep into smaller trees that the tree breaks in half. With its very strong beak and a special shock-absorbing head, the pileated working on a hollow log can produce a noise that can carry for blocks on a still morning. Particularly irritating to homeowners is the pileated's obsession with drilling holes into the outside of houses, wood siding, window frames, pilings, you name it.

The pileated feeds extensively on ants, beetles and beetle larvae, seeds, and fruit. It is monogamous and known to nest in wooden bird boxes (you can generally tell if a pileated is using the box if the entranceway has been chiseled open to the size of your fist), hollowed-out telephone poles, and larger trees. Its eggs and chicks are sometimes preyed upon by snakes, rats, and raccoons, but for the most part it has few natural enemies once it reaches adult size. Because it prefers taller trees, the pileated, along with its brood, is vulnerable to lightning strikes.

Loggerhead Shrike © Judd Patterson, BirdsInFocus.com

❒______**Loggerhead Shrike** (*Lanius ludovicianus*) Other names: butcher bird, French mockingbird, catbird / Status: FL=stable, IUCN=LC / Life span: to 12 years / Length: 7.9-9.1 in. (20-23 cm) / Wingspan: 11-12.6 in. (28-32 cm) / Weight: 1.2-1.8 oz (35-50 g) / Nests: throughout Florida year round; expands into southern Canada in the summer / Found: AC, coastal, near coast, inland / Months found: **JFMAMJJASOND**.

The loggerhead shrike is an amazing example of nature doing the unexpected when it finds a niche not being utilized by other creatures. It belongs in the *Passeriformes* order, which includes most of the songbirds such as the warbler, cardinal, and sparrow. These birds, commonly called passerines and known for their singing and perching abilities, are hardly considered predators in the same sense as hawks, owls, and eagles, but the loggerhead shrike is a songbird predator, and an excellent one at that.

The nickname butcher bird aptly describes this unusual bird. Lacking the strong feet and powerful talons of a raptor, the shrike has devised another method of holding and devouring its prey. It catches mice, frogs, insects, and other birds, then impales the catch on a large thorn or barbed-wire fence and rips it apart with its strong beak. If you examine the shrike closely, you will note that the beak is shaped much more like a hawk's than that of a typical songbird.

In appearance, the loggerhead shrike vaguely resembles and is roughly the same size as a mockingbird. It has a distinctive black eye band. The shrike is not a common sighting along the coastline but can be found far more readily on the mainland. There is a resident Florida population that swells every winter with the return of the migratory birds from the northern tier of the shrike's range.

Because it is an aggressive predator, the adult shrike is rarely targeted by other prey. The chicks suffer from some snake and rodent predation, and the entire Eastern Seaboard population is suffering from habitat loss and pesticide and herbicide overuse.

❒ ______________ **White-eyed Vireo** (*Vireo griseus*) Other names: none / Status: FL=stable, IUCN=LC / Life span: to 7 years / Length: 4.3-5.1 in. (11-13 cm) / Wingspan: 6.7 in. (17 cm) / Weight: 0.4-0.5 oz (10-14 g) / Nests: in the Southeast as far north as southern Iowa / Found: AC, coastal, near coast, inland / Months found: **JFMAMJJASOND**.

White-eyed Vireo © Judd Patterson, BirdsInFocus.com

Identified by its whitish-colored eye, this little bird wears a pair of yellow spectacles around that bright white iris. It is a fairly common winter resident on the barrier islands but prefers to feed in thick underbrush, making it difficult to spot. It does not sing as much during the summer breeding season, saving its lovely song, which usually begins with a sharp *chick,* for Floridians to enjoy. The white-eyed vireo's migration range extends as far south as the Yucatan and as far north as Iowa.

The vireo feeds mostly on insects, snails, and spiders, but has also been known to take small lizards, fruits, and berries. Its nests may be parasitized by cowbirds that lay eggs and let the little vireo incubate and feed their much larger offspring. The end result is that the vireo chicks seldom survive to adulthood.

Blue Jay © Judd Patterson, BirdsInFocus.com

❒ ____________ **Blue Jay** (*Cyanocitta cristata*) Other names: jaybird / Status: FL=stable to expanding north and west, IUCN=LC / Life span: to 17 years / Length: 10-12 in. (25-30 cm) / Wingspan: 13-17 in. (34-43 cm) / Weight: 2.47-3.5 oz (70-100 g) / Nests: throughout SW Florida / Found: AC, coastal, near coast, inland / Months found: **JFMAMJJASOND**.

A member of the crow family, the blue jay is a fairly common sight in all six counties covered in this book. Known for its loud call, *jay, jay, jay,* or sometimes *thief, thief, thief,* this very attractive bird is also an excellent mimic, known to imitate the cry of the red-shouldered hawk and the osprey so expertly that even an experienced birder cannot tell the difference.

A fairly large bird, the blue jay often raids the nests of smaller birds, such as the Carolina wren, prairie warbler, and common yellowthroat, taking the eggs and sometimes the chicks. This characteristic is somewhat offset by the blue jay's tendency to go after other large predators that would be far more likely to take the adult bird of these same species. That includes eagles, hawks, and owls, which the blue jay harasses to no end when they fly into its territory.

Its diet includes just about anything smaller than itself: carrion, eggs, chicks, acorns, nuts, frogs, fish, snails, small mammals, seeds, and even green and Cuban anoles. Monogamous but not always for life, the blue jay tends to switch partners every few years, allowing for a number of different couplings over its 17-year life span. It is a solitary nester. Hawks and owls prey upon the adult blue jay.

❐ ________ **Florida Scrub Jay** (*Aphelocoma coerulescens*) Other names: Florida jay, smooth-headed jay / Status: FL = threatened, IUCN = VU / Length: 9.1-11 in. (23-28 cm) / Wingspan: 13-14.2 in. (33-36 cm) / Weight: 2.3-3.2 oz (66-92 g) / Life span: to 15 years / Nests: in the northern counties of SW Florida, mostly inland / Found: SC, ChC, LC, coastal, inld / Months found: **JFMAMJJASOND**.

This small member of the *Corvidea* (crow) family is the only bird found in Florida that is found nowhere else in the world. It was once believed to be related to the similar-looking western scrub jay (*Aphelocoma californica*), but recent evidence indicates it is a separate species. These two species were descended from the same genetic stock, but climate changes during the Pleistocene separated them, and over time they diverged into two unique species. The Florida scrub jay is a cooperative breeder, and the western jay is not.

Florida Scrub Jay © Judd Patterson, BirdsInFocus.com

Cooperative breeding is rare in birds but fairly common in mammals, such as elephants and great apes. It means that fledgling Florida scrub jays remain with the extended family for several years and help raise the next generation of hatchlings. These extended families can range in size from two to eight birds. This behavior indicates an advanced degree of intelligence, in keeping with the crow family.

For birders, finding a Florida scrub jay can be a daunting task made somewhat easier by visiting Oscar Scherer State Park in Sarasota County. The Florida scrub jay is so named because its preferred habitat is xeric scrub oak, an endemic and disappearing ecosystem in Florida. Scrub oak forests are upland, well-drained stretches of land that require hardly any drainage or fill to convert into strip malls and subdivisions. The 1,400-acre Oscar Scherer State Park contains one of the largest untouched remnants of Florida scrub oak forests in the Sunshine State, and

Encroaching on their backyard, Florida Scrub Jay

it is not uncommon to see a dozen or more scrub jays in a single morning along the park's miles of hiking and biking trails.

Another unique but problematic characteristic of the Florida scrub jay is its friendliness. Most wild birds are secretive and shy: ducks rarely let people get within gunshot range; most warblers fly off long before you can get them in focus; and wading birds seldom allow birders to get close. The Florida scrub jay, on the other hand, seems to enjoy people and is often tame enough to take food right out of your hand, land on your shoulder, or beg for a handout. Feeding the scrub jay is not recommended because it not only tends to make the bird less adept at finding its own food, but also increases its chances of being harmed by humans. When you are stalking this rare bird, remember to talk loudly and behave normally, and the friendly scrub jay will find you.

The scrub jay feeds on caterpillars, spiders, grasshoppers, and crickets. It also has an interesting habit of hiding and eating acorns. One jay alone was documented to have stashed some 8,000 acorns in a single year. Those acorns that the bird fails to locate and retrieve can germinate and grow into oak trees. The scrub jay also eats tree frogs, small snakes, and lizards. Black racers, which thrive in the same scrub habitat, are common predators of the chicks and eggs, and owls, hawks, and bobcats take the adult scrub jay. In another example of its superior intelligence, the Florida scrub jay actually posts sentinels during foraging to warn the extended family about potential predators. It has one specific warning call for snakes and terrestrial predators, and another for hawks and owls.

The most recent statewide census of the Florida scrub jay indicates there are 7,000 to 10,000 in the state. This is considered good news because that number is up from the 6,500 counted a decade previous. Losing this smart, attractive bird would be a tragedy. Losing it for another strip mall or subdivision would be even worse.

❒ ______ **American Crow** (*Corvus brachyrhynchos*) Other names: southern crow, cawin' crow, corn crow / Status: FL = stable, IUCN = LC / Length: 15.7-20.9 in. (40-53 cm) / Wingspan: 33.5-39.4 in. (85-100 cm) / Weight: 11.1-21.9 oz (316-620 g) / Life span: to 14 years (note: one captive crow lived to be 59 years old!) / Nests: in mainland SW Florida / Found: AC, coastal, near coast, inland / Months found: **JFMAMJJASOND**.

The only place where the American crow is uncommon is along the coast, where it is often replaced by the fish crow, a slightly smaller but similar species. On the mainland and near-coastal regions the American crow can be found just about anywhere. It is commonly found along highways where it feeds on roadkill, from deer to dragonflies. It is a regular at garbage dumps, dumpsters, and residential garbage cans where it pick through our refuse looking for scraps of food, potato chips, and everything in between.

The crow is extremely opportunistic and intelligent. It has been observed not only using tools, but also fabricating them. For example, the crow has been seen pulling the leaves off of small twigs, then inserting these stripped twigs into holes in fence posts in search of termites and ants. It knows which day the trash is put out and shows up accordingly. Native Americans held crows in high esteem. They recognized

American Crow © Bob Gress, BirdsInFocus.com

this bird's intelligence and based many of their myths and tales on the crow.

Once considered an agricultural pest, the crow is now widely seen as mitigating some crop damage by eating the insects that destroy the wheat and corn fields.

The crow is similar to the Florida scrub jay in that it is a cooperative breeder. The fledglings remain with their extended families for several years to help raise future broods. Flocks of crows, called murders, have been known to reach 2 million birds. When these extended families chance upon a resting great horned owl or a perching hawk, they exhibit another interesting behavior called "mobbing," harassing the owl or raptor until it leaves the area. Birders can be alerted to a well-hidden roosting owl by paying attention to this avian behavior.

Recently the American crow population has been decimated by the West Nile virus. The crow appears to be the most vulnerable species to this form of encephalitis. To date, more then 45 percent of the North American crow population has died from this pathogen. That's more than 25 million birds. For the moment this pandemic appears to be subsiding, but there are regions in the U.S. where the crow has virtually vanished from the landscape.

The adult crow has quite a few predators, including owls and Cooper's and red-shouldered hawks. Its nests are often raided by raccoons and squirrels. No crow-on-crow predation has ever been observed. In past decades bounties placed on killing crows by state and local governments accounted for considerable mortality in crows, but most of these have been repealed or discontinued.

❐ ____________ **Fish Crow** (*Corvus ossifragus*) Other names: crow / Status: FL=stable, IUCN=LC / Life span: to 14 years / Length: 14-16 in. (36-40 cm) / Wingspan: 33 in. (84 cm) / Weight: 7-12 oz (190-340 g) / Nests: along the coast / Found: SC, ChC, LC, CC, coastal, near coast / Months found: **JFMAMJJASOND**.

Fish Crow © Korall, Courtesy Wikimedia Commons

The fish crow, although slightly smaller, is all but impossible to discern from the American crow. The American crow is almost never found along the coastline, however, so the chances are that any crow you see along the coast is a fish crow. One distinctive difference between the two birds is the call; the fish crow is famous for its nearly constant *cah, uh-uh.*

The fish crow is unique in that it is one of very few birds endemic to North America. It does not have the range of the American crow, extending only as far north as Rhode Island, while the American crow's range extends all the way to the Northwest Territories. The American crow far outnumbers the fish crow. Unlike its cousin, however, the fish crow does not appear to be as vulnerable to the West Nile virus, which in some regions has decimated American crow populations.

A highly adaptable bird, the fish crow feeds on garbage, eggs, insects, carrion, ticks from livestock, various berries, and some fruit. Like all crows, jays, and ravens, the fish crow appears to be capable of learned behaviors. The fish crow, for example, has learned to pick up a mollusk, fly high above a rock pile or highway and release it, breaking the shellfish open so the bird can feed on it. While not quite at the same level as the tool-using green heron, it is a fascinating example of avian intelligence.

Huge flocks of fish crows, called *murders*, roost on islands in and around St. Petersburg and Tampa where they number in the thousands. The fish crow has adapted well to the habits of *Homo sapiens* and because of that is expanding its range throughout the Southeast.

❒ ____________ **Purple Martin** (*Progne subis*) Other names: black martin, gourd martin, house martin / Status: FL = stable, IUCN = LC / Length: 7.5-7.9 in. (19-20 cm) / Wingspan: 15.4-16.1 in. (39-41 cm) / Weight: 1.6-2.1 oz (45-60 g) / Life span: to 14 years / Nests: throughout SW Florida / Found: AC, coastal, near coast, inland / Months found: **JFMAMJJASOND**.

Purple Martin © Judd Patterson, BirdsInFocus.com

Very few birds have their own websites. The purple martin, however, has several. The largest of these is *The Purple Martin Conservation Association* (www. purplemartin. org). Two other popular sites are *The Purple Martin Society* (www.purplemartins. com) and *The Nature Society* (www.naturesociety.org). All offer cornucopias of advice to purple martin fans on how to attract them into your yard, the best gourds to use or houses to construct, management tips, tending to sick or injured martins, and the 12 reasons why people lose their martin colonies. No other bird comes close to the symbiotic relationship between purple martins and the people who cherish them.

Purple Martin © Clair Postmus

This lovefest between North America's largest swallow and humans began long before Columbus landed. Native Americans were the first members of the purple martin booster club. They learned early on that this bird is capable of consuming a prodigious amount of troublesome insects, including spiders, wasps, bees, beetles, and flies. Even though the myth persists that the purple martin eats 2,000 mosquitoes a night, scientific studies indicate that it seldom if ever eats mosquitoes at all. The purple martin feeds at heights up to 500 feet, which is higher than most mosquitoes fly.

Native Americans learned that the martin will readily abandon its cavity or cliff nest in favor of a gourd or other suitable hollowed-out cavity. Today an entire industry revolves around the construction of purple martin houses. You can order pre-built houses, house kits, and house plans, spending from a few dollars to more than $1,000 on an elaborate, decorative, multi-unit bird house for these popular metallic-blue birds. In the east, the martin has nested in such birdhouses almost exclusively for the past 100 years. Out west, where the martin is far less common, it still uses nesting sites such as abandoned woodpecker cavities, natural rock caves, and cliff crevices. The western bird also tends to be more solitary than the eastern population.

Few birds have so readily adapted to the rise of humanity as has the purple martin. As a result, its population is thriving across the entire range. Although the martin winters in South America, its stay is brief, sometimes lasting only a month or two. It ranges all the way into the Yukon and Alaska, but these sparse populations represent the fringe of its northern journey since its vulnerable fledglings are subject to frosts and freezes.

The purple martin is an insectivore. It not only eats entirely on the wing, but also drinks on the wing by skimming across ponds and taking in a sip of water in flight. With all of the protections people build into the thousand-dollar martin condos, from special squirrel-prevention skirting to snake-proof posts, few natural predators can access their eggs and chicks. Blue jays, crows, and magpies sometimes alight on their birdhouses and pull adults or juvenile birds out of their nest cavities during the day, while owls may do the same at night. Hawks and, surprisingly, great blue herons, sometimes snatch adults out of the air while in flight, but overall, predation is minimal for one of America's favorite birds.

❐ ________ **Tree Swallow** (*Tachycineta bicolor*) Other names: white-bellied swallow / Status: FL=thriving, IUCN=LC / Life span: to 12 years / Length: 4.7-5.9 in. (12-15 cm) / Wingspan: 11.8-13.8 in. (30-35 cm) / Weight: .06-.09 oz (16-25 g) / Nests: in the northern tier of the U.S. all the way into the Northwest Territories / Found: AC, coastal, near coast, inland, sometimes flocking in hundreds of birds / Months found: **JFMAMJJASOND**.

Over the past decade the tree swallow population, along with a number of other swifts and swallows, has been steadily increasing across Florida. From November through May hundreds, if not thousands, of tree swallows can be spotted forming what appears to be insect-like swarms above open pastures and fields throughout Southwest Florida. This agile flyer can be found early in the morning or at sunset feeding on midges and insects midair. The tree swallow is readily distinguished from its cousin, the barn swallow, by the lack of a deeply forked tail and its coloration, which is metallic green rather than chestnut.

Tree Swallow © David Seibel, BirdsInFocus.com

The tree swallow winters as far south as Panama and Cuba but does not make it into South America, and it nests farther north than any other American swallow. It uses other birds' feathers to line its cavity nest, which is believed to help prevent various ecto-parasites such as mites and provide additional warmth to the growing chicks.

The tree swallow is doing well in part because of its unique ability among swallows to survive on seeds and fruit, as well as insects. In Florida it feeds on wax myrtle trees when insects are scarce because of strong winter cold fronts. Nests of the tree swallow are sometimes invaded by predatory birds, including shrikes, and there is some mortality caused by snakes. By and large the tree swallow has a stable to increasing population across all of North America.

❐ ________ **Tufted Titmouse** (*Baeolophus bicolor*) Other names: peter bird, peto bird, tomtit / Status: FL = stable, IUCN = LC / Length: 5/5-6/3 in. (14-16 cm) / Wingspan: 7.9-10.2 in. (20-26 cm) / Weight: 0.6-0.9 oz (18-26 g) Life span: to 13 years / Nests: in northern Florida and the Southeast / Found: AC, coastal, near coast, inland / Months found: **JFMAMJJASOND**.

The tufted titmouse, a close relative of the chickadee, is known for its call, a series of *peter, peter, peter* that has landed it the nickname, peter bird. This flitting little bird is a popular and frequent visitor at birdfeeders, where it prefers sunflower seeds.

Tufted Titmouse with seed © Al Tuttle

The titmouse does not migrate, but changes its diet in the winter from insects to seeds and acorns. As fall and winter draw near the tufted titmouse begins hoarding food, stashing sunflower seeds all around its territory. Because of the slow drift of warmer winters across the northern tier of the United States, this diminutive bird has slowly moved northward, expanding its range all the way into Minnesota and Michigan, where it was seldom seen 50 years ago.

Like most birds, the titmouse appears to be monogamous, and in the wild seldom lives longer than a decade. One curious behavior of this bird is that it lines the inner cup of its nest with animal hair from raccoons, opossums, mice, woodchucks, rabbits, livestock, and even humans. Because most of its life is spent in the dense understory, little research has been done on predation of the tufted titmouse, but most ornithologists believe this bird is taken by feral cats, owls, and snakes.

❒______ **Carolina Wren** (*Thryothorus ludovicianus*) Other names: Florida wren / Status: FL=stable to declining, IUCN=LC / Life span: to 9 years / Length: 56 in. (12-14 cm) / Wingspan: 7 in. (16 cm) / Weight: .64.-78 oz (18-22 g) / Nests: throughout Florida / Found: AC, coastal, near coast, inland / Months found: **JFMAMJJASOND**.

Anyone owning a home in Southwest Florida is probably familiar with this energetic little brown bird. The Carolina wren is not only comfortable with human enterprises, but it also takes full advantage of them. You may find this small songbird building its deep, circular nests around your home in minnow buckets, bike helmets, or under the rafters. Other unlikely nesting locations may include car

Carolina Wren © Bob Gress, BirdsInFocus.com

radiators, mailboxes, or even in clothes hanging a bit too long on the line.

The Carolina wren is famous for its *teakettle, teakettle, teakettle* song. One captive male was observed to sing his melody 3,000 times in a single day. This bird is extremely inquisitive. It will enter enclosed areas through an open door, turn over pieces of paper, and forage through just about anything in its search for insects, small invertebrates, and seeds.

Monogamous and mating for life, a pair of Carolina wrens can have up to three broods in a given year if conditions are favorable. Because it prefers to forage in the understory in and around human habitation, the Carolina wren is especially vulnerable to domestic cats and dogs, as well as snakes, rats, and larger birds.

❒ ________ **Blue-gray Gnatcatcher** (*Polioptila caerulea*) Other names: none / Status: FL=stable, IUCN=LC / Life span: to 4 years / Length: 4 in. (10-11 cm) / Wingspan: 6 in. (16 cm) / Weight: .18-.25 oz (57 g) / Nests: throughout SW Florida / Found AC, coastal, near coast, inland / Months found: **JFMAMJJASOND**.

Blue-gray Gnatcatcher © David Seibel, BirdsInFocus.com

Sometimes called a miniature mockingbird, the blue-gray gnatcatcher is similar in coloration and, like the mockingbird, loves to mimic other bird songs. Although a number of these diminutive birds are year-round Florida residents, the population greatly increases during the winter months with the southern migration of additional gnatcatchers. Thus, it is far easier to find this bird during the tourist season.

If you do see a blue-gray gnatcatcher, don't expect it to stay still for very long. Like many of the smaller birds, it is a hyperactive creature, flitting around the understory in a constant search for midges, gnats, spiders, and small insects. This is one of very few birds on Sanibel that feeds on the notorious no-see-um. It not only picks insects off of branches and vegetation but also can nab them in flight.

The gnatcatcher is monogamous and a solitary nester. It has to deal with cowbird parasitism, wherein the much larger cowbird female lays her eggs in the gnatcatcher's nest, eliminating any chance of survival for the gnatcatcher's offspring and forcing it to rear a chick nearly 10 times the size of an adult gnatcatcher. It is also vulnerable to insecticides and related chemical pollutants.

❒ ________ **Eastern Bluebird** (*Sialia sialis*) Other names: Florida bluebird / Status: FL = stable, IUCN = LC / Length: 6.3-8.3 in. (16-21 cm) / Wingspan: 9.8-12.6 in. (25-32 cm) / Weight: 1.-1.1 oz (28-32 g) / Life span: to 10.5 years / Nests: in northern Florida all the way into southern Canada / Found: SC, ChC, LC, GC, near coast, inland / Months found: **JFMAMJJASOND**.

Eastern Bluebird eggs Courtesy Wikimedia Commons

Considered rare south of Lee County, the bluebird has recently been reintroduced into the Everglades and portions of Collier and Hendry counties. Hopefully these transplants will take root and re-establish themselves throughout mainland Florida. The bluebird was severely impacted by the cutting down of most of Florida's longleaf pines, where it made its nest in abandoned woodpecker cavities. Unlike the red-cockaded woodpecker, however, this small member of the thrush family took readily to nesting in artificial boxes. Today these plain wooden boxes can be spotted along highways and in backyards across Florida and probably represent the majority of bluebird nesting sites in Florida.

Eastern Bluebird
© Bob Gress, BirdsInFocus.com

Although the Florida population does not migrate, the chances of seeing a bluebird during the winter months are greatly increased by the influx of many northern migrants. In the summer it ranges well into Saskatchewan, Manitoba, Ontario, and the Canadian Maritimes, but it cannot handle the harsh winters and retreats annually to well below the Mason-Dixon Line.

The bluebird is known for its sweet song, often described as *cheery*. It is an exceptionally pretty bird, showing a deep blue back and a brick-red breast. The male has the deeper coloration, while the female displays a more grayish head and subdued orange-brown breast.

The bluebird is frequently taken by kestrels, Cooper's hawks, owls, and other raptors. Its eggs and chicks are subject to predation by squirrels, rats, raccoons, and snakes.

❐ ________ **Gray Catbird** (*Dumetella carolinensis*) Other names: black mockingbird / Status: FL=stable, IUCN=LC / Life span: to 17 years / Length: 8.3-9.4 in. (21-24 cm) / Wingspan: 8.7-11.8 in. (22-30 cm) / Weight: .08-2 oz (23-56.5 g) / Nests: in southern Georgia all the way to New England / Found: AC, coastal, near coast, inland / Months found: **JFMAMJJASOND**.

Gray Catbird © Bob Gress, BirdsInFocus.com

Related to thrushes and mockingbirds, the catbird can also string together its own varied and personal song. It is more widely known for its *meow*-like cry, which it sings incessantly during the winter evenings to establish its feeding territory. Some songs may last up to 10 minutes and can be every bit as endearing as the mockingbird's.

Found almost exclusively in the understory, the catbird, with its dark gray body and black cap, is difficult to spot in a dense thicket. Its scientific name, *Dumetella*, means small thicket. It is best spotted in upland areas where it flits its way through Brazilian pepper and heavy brush. It can sometimes be seen flying from one side of the path or road to the other, then quickly disappearing into the underbrush. At times these fleeting glances of the catbird allow you to notice the rufous-colored under-tail coverts. The catbird is fond of drupes, the fruit produced by female gumbo limbo trees in the spring.

The catbird is taken by red-shouldered hawks, falcons, and snakes. It is thriving but has yet to transition comfortably into urban environments as its close cousin, the mockingbird, has.

❒ ________ **Northern Mockingbird** (*Mimus polyglottos*) Other names: mockingbird, eastern mockingbird / Status: FL=stable, IUCN=LC / Life span: to 14 years / Length: 8-10 in. (21-26 cm) / Wingspan: 12-14 in. (31-35 cm) / Weight: 1.59-2.05 oz (45-48 g) / Nests: throughout SW Florida / Found: AC, coastal, near coast, inland / Months found: **JFMAMJJASOND**.

"Mockingbirds don't do one thing but make music for us to enjoy...but sing their hearts out for us. That's why it's a sin to kill a mockingbird."

Northern Mockingbird © Bob Gress, BirdsInFocus.com

Made famous by Harper Lee's riveting tale of racism and intolerance in *To Kill a Mockingbird*, this small passerine (perching bird) is Florida's state bird and its most beloved singer. Scientific observation has confirmed that the scope and beauty of its songs are nothing short of amazing. A northern mockingbird, which might live to be 14 years old, will add variations to its own song throughout its entire adult life. It has been noted to sing more than 400 song types and has a unique ability to mimic other species' songs, hence the name. The male has two distinct sets of songs: one for spring and another for the fall. It is sheer joy to sit back and take in the lovely serenade of this magnificent songbird perched high atop a telephone pole in the early evening. On moonlit nights the mockingbird has been known to sing straight through the evening until dawn.

The mockingbird is easily distinguished from its close cousin, the catbird, by its gray and white plumage. It has adapted well to *Homo sapiens*, expanding its range all the way into Alaska by learning to live in proximity to human development. It feeds predominantly on insects, berries, and invertebrates. It is monogamous and breeds for life.

❐ __________ **Brown Thrasher** (*Toxostoma rufum*) Other names: brown thrush, sandy mocker, thrash, fence corner bird / Status: FL = stable, IUCN = LC / Length: 9.1-11.8 in. (23-30 cm) / Wingspan: 11.4-12.6 in. (29-32 cm) / Weight: 2.2-3.1 oz (61-89 g) / Life span: to 12 years / throughout Florida all the way up into central Canada / Found: AC, coastal, near coast, inland / Months found: **JFMAMJJASOND**.

Brown Thrasher © David Seibel, BirdsInFocus.com

Related to the catbird and mockingbird, the brown thrasher is also a songbird of extraordinary talent. Though far less renowned than the mockingbird for its singing abilities, the sandy mocker, as it is sometimes nicknamed, actually outperforms the mockingbird. There are estimates of more than 3,000 distinctive song combinations from a single performance. Unlike the mockingbird, which often repeats song phrases in patterns of three, the thrasher never repeats a phrase, making it perhaps the most accomplished songbird in all of North America.

This large songbird can be found statewide except in the Florida Keys where it is a very rare sighting. A single thrasher was once spotted in England, where its presence made quite an impression on local birders. It is the state bird of Georgia and lends its name to Atlanta's National Hockey League team, In Florida the thrasher is both migratory and a year-round resident. The migrating portion of the species summers and nests as far north as southern Canada and returns to the Southeast and Texas every winter to forage on seeds, berries, and insects. The thrasher is aptly named because it "thrashes" the leaf litter and understory in search of prey, which during the warmer months consists chiefly of ground-dwelling beetles, weevils, crickets, wasps, and bees. Because it prefers dense foliage, it is far easier to hear a thrasher than it is to see one.

Although the thrasher does well in suburban and agricultural areas, its preference for feeding on the ground has kept it from establishing significant populations in urban areas. Because of its ground-dwelling and understory habits, this bird falls prey to cats and dogs. Its chicks and eggs are taken by black and yellowbelly racers, garter snakes, and king snakes. The thrasher protects its nest fiercely and has been known to draw blood on people who approach too closely.

❒ _______ **Cedar Waxwing** (*Bombycilla cedrorum*) Other names: cedar bird, seal, cherry robin, Canadian robin / Status: FL=stable, IUCN=LC / Life span: to 8 years / Length: 5.5-6.7 in. (14-17 cm) / Wingspan: 8.7-11.8 in. (22-30 cm) / Weight: 1.1 oz (32 g) / Nests: north of the Mason-Dixon Line up into north-central Canada / Found: AC, coastal, near coast, inland / Months found: **JFMAMJJASOND**.

The cedar waxwing is a spectacular sighting when encountered, though it is not a common bird in Florida. Its gorgeous coloration—brownish above, yellow belly, and white under-tail coverts—makes it easy to identify. It is lightly smaller than a cardinal and has a similar crest. The adult waxwing secretes a waxy, reddish substance from the feather shafts of its secondary flight feathers, perhaps as a signal of age or social status, though no one has been able to determine exactly why these waxy secretions occur. The waxwing ventures all the way north to central Canada in the summer and as far south as the northern edge of South America during the winter.

Cedar Waxwing

© Judd Patterson, BirdsInFocus.com

The waxwing survives almost entirely on fruit and berries. That characteristic sometimes dooms parasitic cowbird chicks because the food that the waxwing brings to the young cowbirds does not contain enough of the insect protein they need to thrive. The cedar waxwing has been known to ingest fermented berries not only to the point of intoxication, but also to the point of death from alcohol poisoning.

It builds solitary nests but will sometimes roost in loose colonies. Its nests can be raided by any number of winged and four-legged predators, and the adult is sometimes taken by falcons.

❒ ________ **Northern Parula** (*Parula americana*) Other names: southern parula warbler, finch creeper, blue-yellow back warbler, little titmouse / Status: FL = stable, IUCN = LC / Length: 4.3-4.7 in. (11-12 cm) / Wingspan: 6.3-7.1 in. (16-18 cm) / Weight: 0.2-0.4 oz (5-11 g) / Life span: to 5 years / Nests: mostly east of the Mississippi throughout the U.S. and southern Canada / Found: AC, coastal, near coast, inland / Months found: **JFMAMJJASOND**.

Northern Parula © Bob Gress, BirdsInFocus.com

The northern parula is one of the smallest songbirds in North America. Its diminutive size makes spotting one of these dainty birds a daunting task. The parula is far easier to identify by its song, a buzzy trill followed by a sharp note. It prefers the mid-to-upper levels of the canopy where it forages for insects such as moths, ants, wasps, bees, flies, and scales. During the winter months when it migrates south, the parula feeds on seeds and nectar.

This little warbler builds its nest using beard moss in its northern summer range and Spanish moss in Florida. It lays three to four eggs in these epiphyte nests and may produce up to two broods a year, depending on the availability of local forage. Little is known about predation of the northern parula, but it is thought to be preyed upon by small owls, kestrels, and merlins. Its eggs are so small that even brown and green anoles have been known to raid the nests, and the chicks are taken by snakes, rats, and mice.

❐ ______ **Yellow-rumped Warbler** (*Dendroica coronata*) Other names: myrtle warbler, Audubon's warbler / Status: FL=stable, IUCN=LC / Life span: to 8 years / Length: 4.7-5.5 in. (12-14 cm) / Wingspan: 7.5-9.1 in. (19-23 cm) / Weight: 0.4-0.5 oz (12-13 g) / Nests: throughout Canada and in the Rocky Mountains during the summer / Found: AC, coastal, near coast, inland / Months found: **JFMAMJJASOND**.

Yellow-rumped Warbler © Bob Gress, BirdsInFocus.com

Far and away the most abundant wintering warbler in Florida, the yellow-rumped warbler is a common sighting from October through April. A clue to its abundance lies in one of its nicknames, the myrtle warbler. It is the only warbler able to digest the waxes found in bayberries and wax myrtle trees, both of which are a common shrub across Southwest Florida.

An extremely versatile feeder, the yellow-rumped warbler takes advantage of a wide array of habitats and the various foods it might encounter there. Sometimes found on beaches picking through the rack line, sometimes skimming insects from the surface of rivers and ponds, and even gleaning insects from piles of manure, this warbler is adept at taking a meal anywhere it can.

Its summer breeding plumage is much more colorful than its plainer winter coats, but it seldom molts into that plumage before arriving in its nesting area. That being said, its yellowish rump can still be found during the winter months, though it is far more subdued in color.

Like all smaller birds, most predation occurs at the nest, both to the chicks and eggs, and the adult yellow-rumped warbler is occasionally taken by kestrels, merlins and small owls. Overall this very adaptable bird is thriving and is not likely to be placed on any threatened lists anytime soon.

❒ ________ **Prairie Warbler** (*Dendroica discolor*) Other names: Northern Prairie Warbler / Status: FL = stable, IUCN = LC / Length: 4.3 in. (11 cm) / Wingspan: 7-7.5 in. (17-19 cm) / Weight: 0.2-0.3 oz. (6-9 g) / Life span: to 10 years / Found: SC, ChC, LC, CC, coastal, near coast / Months found: **JFMAMJJASOND**.

Prairie Warbler © Judd Patterson, BirdsInFocus.com

The prairie warbler is never found on the prairie. It prefers the scrubby fields and forests of the eastern and south-central deciduous forests. How this bird became misnamed remains a mystery. In Florida there is a subspecies that lives in the coastal mangrove forests and is slightly larger with white spots located on its tail feathers. This subspecies possibly evolved from interbreeding with the migratory birds that winter in Cuba and the Caribbean Islands.

Although the color combination indicates that some of these warblers nest here, most do not. For the vast majority of these warblers, Florida is primarily a migratory path that takes them all the way to Maine in the summer. Some of these migratory birds might be found in Glades and Hendry counties, but this bird seems to prefer the coastline, perhaps because of its affiliation with the thick mangrove forests in which it winters in Cuba.

This very small bird is easy to identify by observing its behavior. The prairie warbler is a tail wagger, constantly flicking its short tail about as it rifles through the understory in search of insects, spiders, and an occasional seed or berry. It is preyed upon by Cooper's hawks, merlins, and small owls. Its nests may be raided by mangrove snakes, rats, and raccoons. Its primary threat is habitat and mangrove destruction.

❐ ________ **Pine Warbler** (*Dendroica pinus*) Other names: Pine-creeping Warbler / Status: FL = stable, IUCN = LC / Length: 5.1-5.5 in. (13-14 cm) / Wingspan: 7.5-9.1 in. (19-23 cm) / Weight: 0.3-0.5 oz. (9-15 g) / Life span: to 7 years / Found: AC, coastal, near coast, inland / Months found: **JFMAMJJASOND**.

Pine Warbler © David Seibel, BirdsInFocus.com

The pine warbler is only one of a handful of warblers that remains in Florida throughout the year. It is fairly common along most of the west coast of Florida; the only county where sighting one of these tiny birds might be a challenge is Hendry County. While Southwest Florida has a sizable resident population, many of these birds leave during the summer months to venture as far north as southern Canada. When in Florida the populations will readily mix and pine warblers have been known to form flocks as large as 50 to 100 birds.

The pine warbler is true to its namesake in that it prefers pine flatlands and xeric pine scrub, especially during the breeding and nesting season in early spring. Amidst the pines this bird feeds mostly on pine seeds, occasional insects, and berries.

Its call is a high-pitched trill that sounds a bit like a musical sewing machine; it is often the best method of identifying this secretive bird. The pine warbler falls prey to hawks and owls, and its nests, mostly located in pine forests, are vulnerable to climbing snakes, squirrels, and blue jays.

❏ ______ **Hooded Warbler** (*Wilsonia citrina*) Other names: none / Status: FL = stable, IUCN = LC / Length: 5.1 in. (13 cm) / Wingspan: 7 in. (17 cm) / Weight: 0.3-0.4 oz (9-12 g) / Life span: to 8 years / Nests: in northern Florida and the Southeast U.S. / Found: AC, coastal, near coast, inland / Months found: **JFMAMJJASOND**.

Male Hooded Warbler © Judd Patterson, BirdsInFocus.com

The name of this striking songbird is derived from the black cap, or hood, that encircles the bright yellow face of the male. Its coloring is exactly opposite the common yellowthroat, which sports an olive green cap and a black mask around the eyes. Finding one of these manic little birds in your binoculars, even for a brief moment, is a real treasure.

The hooded warbler does not nest or stay very long in Florida, but uses it as a rest stop on its long journey across the Gulf of Mexico every spring and fall. The months it is found here can vary, depending on the onset of winter. The northern range of the hooded warbler is not as expansive as some warblers; it tends to stay within the boundaries of the great eastern hardwood forest from Pennsylvania to eastern Texas and north to the Ohio River Valley.

Although its population dropped after the removal of most of this hardwood forest during the first wave of European settlement (1600-1900), this bird is returning in lockstep with the gradual return of the second- and third-growth forests. In southeastern Canada the hooded warbler is considered endangered, though numbers are increasing in that range as well.

As it passes through Florida the hooded warbler feeds on weevils, fungus and bark beetles, and various flies. As is the case with all small songbirds, predation can occur from many sources. Birds such as the chuck-will's-widow have been known to catch and eat the hooded warbler on the fly, and raptors such as merlins, Cooper's hawks, and screech owls also take their toll. In its South American wintering grounds, predation comes from a most unlikely creature, the neotropical green frog. Its nests are raided by almost all of the smaller inhabitants of the hardwood forests, from opossums to crows to black rat snakes.

❒ ______ **American Redstart** (*Setophaga ruticilla*) Other names: flamebird / Status: FL = stable, IUCN = LC / Length: 4.3-5.1 in. (11-13 cm) / Wingspan: 6.3-7.5 in. (16-19 cm) / Weight: 0.2-0.3 oz (6-9 g) / Life span: to 10 years / Nests: in the southern U.S. north to Alaska, mostly east of the Mississippi / Found: CC, coastal, near coast, inland / Months found: **JFMAMJJASOND**.

Male **American Redstart** © Bob Gress, BirdsInFocus.com

Aptly nicknamed the flamebird, the American redstart is one of the most colorful and distinctive warblers. Only the male displays the black and Halloween-orange coloring on its tail and wing feathers. The female coloration is much more subdued, and is best described as a pale yellow.

The male redstart, perhaps because of his flashy wardrobe, is a bit of a rogue. While many redstarts are monogamous, this boldly patterned warbler has also been known to mate with more than one female simultaneously. He attracts the second mate shortly after the first begins incubating the eggs, and sets up a second nest, generally within 500 meters of the first.

According to some bird books, the only place the redstart winters in Florida is the very southern portion of the peninsula, from southern Collier County, Dade County, and the Florida Keys (Monroe County). That doesn't mean you won't see any of the thousands of redstarts that pass through Southwest Florida on their annual migration from as far north as the Yukon Territory to the Caribbean and Central and South America. The redstart is observed every fall and spring across all six counties covered in this book. The only county it remains in over the winter is Collier.

Predation of this small warbler comes from sharp-shinned hawks, small owls, and domesticated and feral cats. Its northern nests are often raided by red squirrels, blue jays, fishers, chipmunks, and snakes.

❒ _______ **Scarlet Tanager** (*Piranga olivacea*) Other names: none / Status: FL = stable, IUCN = LC / Length: 6.3-6.7 in. (16-17 cm) / Wingspan: 9.8-11.4 in. (25-29 cm) / Weight: 0.8-1.3 oz (23-38 g) / Life span: to 10 years / Nests: in the Eastern U.S. north of the Mason-Dixon line into southern Canada / Found: AC, coastal, near coast, inland / Months found: **JFMAMJJASOND**.

Scarlet Tanager © Bob Gress, BirdsInFocus.com

Like the two dozen warblers that pass through Florida every spring and fall, the scarlet tanager is only a seasonal visitor. It nests and summers along the Appalachian mountain range north into Minnesota and the Maritime Provinces and winters in South America from Colombia to Bolivia, in the mountainous regions and the headwaters of the Amazon River. As is the case with almost all birds, only the male is exquisitely painted with its brilliant red body and jet-black wings and tail. The female coloration is a combination of olive green and a pale greenish-yellow.

Although the tanager has a stable population overall, in certain areas of heavy forest fragmentation this bird does not appear to have sufficient foraging habitat, leading to regional declines in its numbers. In larger patches of standing forests the tanager can be quite plentiful. It feeds on bees, wasps, hornets, ants, cicadas, treehoppers, termites, and dragonflies. It is preyed upon by screech, long-eared, and short-eared owls, merlins, and kestrels. Its nests are raided by crows, blue jays, and squirrels. The parasitic cowbird lays its eggs in tanager nests and lets the tanager raise and feed its young. Since the cowbird weighs considerably more than the tanager, the tanager chicks are outcompeted for food, and generally only the cowbird chick survives. This behavior, called brood parasitism, is discussed in detail in the brown-headed cowbird article later in this section.

❒ ________ **Chipping Sparrow** (*Spizella passerina*) Other names: none / Length: 4.7-5.9 in. (12-15 cm) / Wingspan: 8.3 in. (21 cm) / Weight: 0.4-0.6 oz (11-16 g) / Life span: to 12 years / Nests: in almost all of the U.S. and Canada / Found: AC, coastal, near coast, inland / Months found: **JFMAMJJASOND**.

Adult Chipping Sparrow © Bob Gress, BirdsInFocus.com

The chipping sparrow has one of the largest geographical summer breeding territories of any bird in North America. It breeds and nests in every state of the union except Hawaii, and in all the Canadian provinces. Easily identified by its chestnut-brown cap, this small bird is only slightly smaller than that of the much more common imported house sparrow. Another prominent feature is the black band that runs through its black eyes, making it look as if it is wearing sunglasses.

The chipping sparrow is so named for its song, which is a series of up to 55 consecutive chips that it trills in less than four seconds. These evenly spaced notes sound almost mechanical. This sparrow eats mostly seeds, grasses, and weedy plants. It also eats some insects, especially when nesting, but most of its diet consists of plants. Florida is its winter destination, and it does not migrate farther south than Central America and the island of Hispaniola.

The adult chipping sparrow falls prey to kestrels, merlins, cats, snakes, prairie falcons, loggerhead shrikes, and ground squirrels. The eggs and chicks are eaten by crows, blue jays, and climbing snakes. It does not appear to be subject to cowbird parasitism, and its populations are stable throughout its range.

❐ ______ **Savannah Sparrow** (*Passerculus sandwichensis*) Other names: none / Status: FL = stable, IUCN = LC / Length: 4.3-5.9 in. (11-15 cm) / Wingspan: 7.9-8.7 in. (20-22 cm) / Weight: 0.5-1 oz (15-28 g) / Life span: to 7 years / Nests: in the northern tier of the U.S. on into Canada to the Artic Ocean / Found: AC, coastal, near coast, inland / Months found: **JFMAMJJASOND**.

This small seed eater is one of five widespread sparrow species found in North America. The second half of its scientific name, *sandwichensis,* is derived from Sandwich Bay, Alaska, where it can be found in the summer. The Savannah sparrow breeds as far north as the Bering Sea, Hudson Bay, and the very tip of Labrador. In Florida it is a winter resident, but migrants arrive early and remain late, making this sparrow absent from the Sunshine State only three months a year.

Savannah Sparrow © Bob Gress, BirdsInFocus.com

This bird tends to return every year to the region where it was born, a behavior that ornithologists call *natal philopatry*. Because of this tendency, the Savannah sparrow has become very regional, and this has resulted in 14 recognized subspecies. One such subspecies, breeding on Sable Island, Nova Scotia, is curiously 50 percent heavier than the other subspecies, though there is no clear explanation for that variation.

Because the Savannah sparrow is partial to dense understory and secretive in nature, it is easier to identify by its song than it is to find visually. Its song consists of several short, high-pitched notes followed by two or more high, thin buzzes. The buzzes result from a very fast trill that is almost a whistle.

This little bird is preyed upon by owls, northern harriers, and in its northern range herring gulls. Eggs and nests are raided by grackles, blue jays, and weasels.

❒ ______ **Song Sparrow** (*Melospiza melodia*) Other names: none / Status: FL = stable, IUCN = LC / Length: 4.7-6.7 in. (12-17 cm) / Wingspan: 7.1-9.4 in. (18-24 cm) / Weight: 0.4-1.9 oz (12-53 g) / Life span: to 11 years / Nests: in the northern U.S. into southern Canada / Found: SC, ChC, GC, LC, coastal, near coast, inland / Months Found: **JFMAMJJASOND**.

With more than 29 named subspecies, 24 of which have been diagnostically verified, this small sparrow is also one of the most widespread native sparrows in North America. Its vast range stretches from the Aleutian Islands to Newfoundland and south to Central Mexico. There is a 150 percent differential in the weight of this one species, which is rare in any animal. Its size varies from 0.4 to 1.9 ounces, with the heaviest birds found along the northern tier, in keeping with Bergmann's rule that as a species moves north, it tends to have a larger body mass.

Song Sparrow © Bob Gress, BirdsInFocus.com

The wide geographical and subspecies variations are also evident in its songs. These songs tend to last two to four seconds and start with abrupt, well-spaced notes followed by a clear, buzzing trill.

In Florida the song sparrow prefers the edges of grasslands, marshes, and woodlands where it feeds on seeds and assorted insects. The song sparrow is hunted by loggerhead shrikes, northern harriers, red fox, and Glaucous-winged gulls. The young are eaten by garter snakes and deer mice and are subject to cowbird parasitism.

❐ ______ **Indigo Bunting** (*Passerina cyanea*) Other names: indigo bird, swamp bluebird / Status: FL=stable, IUCN=LC / Life span: to 9 years / Length: 4.7-5.1 in. (12-13 cm) / Wingspan: 7.5-8.7 in. (19-22 cm) / Weight: 0.4-0.6 oz (12-18 g) / Nests: from northern Florida to the northern edge of the lower forty-eight / Found: AC, coastal, near coast, inland / Months found: **JFMAMJJASOND**.

A neotropical traveler, the indigo bunting is most commonly seen in late April and May and again in August through October as it flies to and from its northern nesting grounds. The indigo bunting winters in the Caribbean, southern Mexico, and Central America. It is a joy to see, but as is the case with so many passerines, it is best observed through a pair of binoculars.

Indigo Bunting in flight © David Seibel, BirdsInFocus.com

An interesting characteristic of the indigo bunting is that it migrates at night. Scientists believe this tiny bird has somehow learned to navigate by starlight. Another fascinating aspect is its song. Each individual bunting's song is unique to its locale. Males as close together as a few hundred yards have different songs, sometimes retaining these through two or three generations, then slowly changing them over the decades.

The indigo bunting is an omnivore, eating a variety of seeds, grains, and wild berries, as well as insects and larvae. It is semi-monogamous and a solitary nester. Because it forages around fields, it is vulnerable to pesticide and fertilizer poisoning. It also suffers from cowbird parasitism and habitat loss.

Painted Bunting © Judd Patterson, BirdsInFocus.com

❒ ______ **Painted Bunting** (*Passerina ciris*) Other names: nonpareil / Status: FL=declining, IUCN-NT / Life span: to 9 years / Length: 4.7-5.1 in. (12-13 cm) / Wingspan: 8-8.5 in. (20-21 cm) / Weight: 0.5-0.7 oz (13-19 g) / Nests: along the Eastern Seaboard to North Carolina, and a separate race nests in east Texas through Arkansas / Found: AC, near coast, inland / Months found: **JFMAMJJASOND**.

Perhaps the single most colorful bird that passes through Southwest Florida, the male painted bunting is a curious palate of blue, lime-green, red, and gray. The female is more of a greenish-yellow color and nowhere near as brilliantly colored as the male.

The painted bunting has two distinct populations: eastern and western. The eastern bird that comes through Florida generally winters in Cuba and Central America, while the western race winters in Northern Mexico. Some birds remain in South Florida for the winter; locating any during the summer is very difficult. One of the best places to find the painted bunting consistently is near the bird feeder located just off the main boardwalk at Audubon Corkscrew Swamp Sanctuary in Collier County, where it comes to feed throughout the winter.

This bird has one unexpected characteristic, especially because of its small size: the male is very territorial and aggressive toward other male buntings. Fights between rival males can become extremely animated, involving fierce pecking, beating each other with their wings, and grappling, sometimes resulting in the death of the defeated bird, a highly unusual outcome among avian rivals.

The painted bunting is approaching threatened status primarily because of habitat loss in its eastern population. It prefers dense thickets and mixed pine and hardwood forests. A handful of birds never leave Florida, nesting along the southern edge of the great Eastern deciduous forest along the border of Georgia and Alabama. It is not adapting well to human alterations to the environment, although it can be spotted on occasion in urban locations.

❐ ____________ **Bobolink** (*Dolichonyx oryzivorus*) Other names: ricebird / Status: FL = stable, IUCN = LC / Length: 5.9-8.3 in. (15-21 cm) / Wingspan: 10.6 in. (27 cm) / Weight: 1-2 oz (29-56 g) / Life span: to 9 years / Nests: in the northern tier of U.S. and the great plains of Canada / Found: AC, coastal, near coast, inland / Months found: **JFMAMJJASOND**.

Male Bobolink © David Seibel, BirdsInFocus.com

For the bobolink, Florida is little more than a pit stop on its annual migration from North to South America. Unlike most migrants that make this same journey, the bobolink doesn't stop in Colombia or Venezuela, but continues south to Paraguay and northern Argentina. Likewise, it does not nest until it makes it north of the Ohio River valley, making each trip a total of 12,500 miles. One female, believed to be nine years old, had presumably made this journey nine times, the equivalent of flying around the equator 4.5 times in less than a decade.

When passing through Florida, the bobolink sometimes flies high overhead, giving off a clear *pink* call that is hard to miss. Its song is a series of rolling, bubbling, jangling notes that sound as if someone has taken a songbird's song and shaken it up in a jar. This medium-size passerine tends to stay together in flocks. It is polygynous, with a single male mating with multiple partners, sometimes as many as four females in any given breeding season.

The bobolink eats mostly seeds but will take insects when the opportunity arises and has been known to feed on rice; hence the nickname ricebird. The bobolink is commonly taken by Cooper's hawks, owls, and ring-billed gulls. Its nests are raided by both garter and milk snakes. Along its nesting grounds, field mice often take the eggs and hatchlings.

❒ ________ **Red-winged Blackbird** (*Agelaius phoeniceus*) Other names: Florida red-wing, red-wing / Status: FL=stable, IUCN=LC / Life span: to 15 years / Length: 6.7-9.1 in. (17-23 cm) / Wingspan: 12.2-15.7 in (31-40 cm) / Weight: 1.1-2.7 oz (32-77 g) / Nests: throughout SW Florida / Found: AC, coastal, near coast, inland / Months found: **JFMAMJJASOND**.

The male of this species is readily identified by its bright red epaulets with equally bright yellow trim on the upper edges of its wings. Another indication that a red-winged blackbird is nearby is by its familiar song, an oft-repeated *konk-ler-eeee, konk-ler-eeee.*

Partial to cattails and the habitat found along the edge of marshes and ponds, the red-winged blackbird is quite common in subdivisions and golf courses with retention ponds and small manmade lakes. Unlike most birds, the red-winged blackbird is a highly polygynous avian, with a single male red-winged blackbird having as many as 15 mates at a time. Recent DNA studies have shown that these blackbird harems are far from faithful. Only 25 percent of those chicks tested were actually sired by the resident male.

Red-winged Blackbird © Bob Gress, BirdsInFocus.com

The blackbird is fiercely territorial. If you approach its nest, it will dive-bomb and attack. It has even gone so far as to shag off cattle and horses. It eats mostly aquatic insects such as beetle larvae in the summer and switches to seeds and grains in the cooler winter months. Its nests and chicks are sometimes raided by snapping turtles and otters, and the adult may be taken by hawks and owls.

❐ ______ **Eastern Meadowlark** (*Sturnella magna*) Other names: field lark, southern meadowlark / Status: FL = stable, IUCN = LC / Length: 7.5-10.2 in. (19-26 cm) / Wingspan: 13.8-15.7 in. (35-40 cm) / Weight: 3.2-5.3 oz (90-150 g) / Nests: in mainland SW Florida / Found: AC, near coast, inland / Months Found: **JFMAMJJASOND**.

The eastern meadowlark is actually not a lark at all but a member of the family *Icteridae*, whose other members include the blackbird and oriole. Farmers across the upper Midwest await the song of this accomplished singer announcing the arrival of the planting season. In Florida the meadowlark is a year-round resident commonly found across the central mainland of Florida near agricultural fields and pastureland. Look for the eastern meadowlark singing atop fence posts or telephone poles in Hendry and Glades counties.

Eastern Meadowlark © Judd Patterson, BirdsInFocus.com

This is an easy bird to identify, with its golden breast and black patch just below the neck. The western meadowlark looks almost identical to its eastern counterpart. Both species share the same diet of crickets, grasshoppers, cutworms, and grubs. The meadowlark uses its long bill to probe into cow manure and earthen clots to ferret out these morsels. During the winter months, when insects are more difficult to find, the meadowlark turns to wild fruits, waste grains such as corn and wheat, and weed seeds.

Because the meadowlark prefers open land, hawks are a common predator of this fair-sized bird, and its ground nests are vulnerable to skunks, cats, dogs, and foxes. The eastern meadowlark is not a very migratory bird, and with climate change its northern range continues to expand. It may migrate into southern Canada during the summer but is a year-round resident from southern Minnesota through northern South America.

❒ _____ **Northern Cardinal** (*Cardinalis cardinalis*) Other names: none / Status: FL=stable, IUCN=LC / Length: 89 in. (21-23 cm) / Wingspan: 10-12 in. (25-31 cm) / Weight: 1.48-1.69 oz (42-48 g) / Life span: to 15 years / Nests: throughout SW Florida / Found: AC, coastal, near coast, inland / Months found: **JFMAMJJASOND.**

Northern Cardinal

© Bob Gress, BirdsInFocus.com

The brilliantly colored northern cardinal holds the record for being named a state bird, having achieved that honor in seven states: Illinois, Indiana, Kentucky, North Carolina, Ohio, Virginia, and West Virginia. (The meadowlark comes in second with six states, and the mockingbird, Florida's state bird, is a close third with five.) In Southwest Florida, the northern cardinal is always a delight to see, especially during the spring when the male takes on its richer breeding plumage, giving its bright red color an almost fluorescent hue. The female has a duller coloration that sometimes resembles a cedar waxwing. The cardinal raises up to three broods during the breeding season, which runs from March through August.

The male northern cardinal can often be found pecking at itself in rearview mirrors, tinted windows, and even hubcaps. Extremely territorial, the male will shag off rivals that stray into its well-defended area. The cardinal feeds primarily on seeds and berries, and contributes to the dissemination of poison ivy throughout Florida by eating the seeds of the ivy then scattering them via its digestive tract.

The cardinal is monogamous and a solitary nester. It is occasionally subject to parasitic cowbird hatchlings, and its nests are sometimes raided by fish crows, grackles, snakes, and rats. The cardinal is expanding its range westward and northward across the United States.

❐ ________ **Common Grackle** (*Quiscalus quiscula*) Other names: jackdaw, Florida grackle, crow, blackbird / Status: FL=stable to expanding, IUCN=LC / Life span: to 22 years / Length: 11-13 in. (28-34 cm) / Wingspan: 14-18 in. (36-46 cm) / Weight: 2.65 oz (74-142 g) / Nests: throughout SW Florida / Found: AC, coastal, near coast, inland / Months found: **JFMAMJJASOND**.

© Judd Patterson, BirdsInFocus.com

The grackle is one of the most common birds found in Southwest Florida. Like the starling, house sparrow, and its cousin, the boat-tailed grackle, the common grackle is most often found in and around parking lots, dumpsters, and similar urban or suburban settings. Readily identified by several telltale signs, the common grackle is an easy bird to add to your wildlife life list.

One of those signs is the bird's distinct call: a short, high-pitched squeak that sounds like a metal gate in desperate need of oil. Other identifiable details are the pale yellow eyes and the oil-slick coloration, especially on the male. The grackle is easy to distinguish from the similar-size starling by the color of its bill—the grackle's bill is solid black, whereas the starling has a long, pointed yellow bill.

The common grackle engages in an odd behavior called anting. It allows ants to crawl all over its body or sometimes catches them, squishes them in its beak, then rubs them all over its feathers in a practice believed to reduce parasites. The common grackle will sometimes resort to lemons or mothballs when it cannot find the ant-based formic acid.

The grackle is an opportunistic feeder. It eats insects, mice, seeds, berries, and garbage and has been observed wading into the water to catch minnows. For the most part the grackle is monogamous, but some males are known to be polygamous. It nests in colonies with other blackbirds. Large flocks sometimes cause problems in agricultural areas.

❒ ________ **Boat-tailed Grackle** (*Quiscalus major*) Other names: jackdaw / Status: FL=stable to expanding, IUCN=LC / Life span: to 12 years / Length: 10-15 in. (26-37 cm) / Wingspan: 15-20 in. (39-50 cm) / Weight: 3.28-8.44 oz (92-239 g) / Nests: throughout SW Florida / Found: AC, coastal, near coast, inland / Months found: **JFMAMJJASOND**.

© Judd Patterson, BirdsInFocus.com

Similar to but quite a bit larger than the common grackle, the boat-tailed grackle is not quite as common as its close cousin. Easy to recognize by its unusually long, keel-shaped tail, the boat-tailed grackle is Florida's largest blackbird. The female of this species is much browner in color and slightly smaller than the male.

The boat-tailed grackle is one of the few birds that are not monogamous, and it has developed an unusual mating system similar to that of American elk and other ungulates. A single bird becomes the dominant male and defends his personal harem in a form of avian polygamy. Although the dominant male may get almost 90 percent of the copulations in his harem, we now know, thanks to modern DNA testing, that he actually sires only 25 to 30 percent of the offspring. The female grackle steps out repeatedly on the male while off foraging for food. This behavior helps to keep the gene pool far more diverse than it would first appear.

Like the other blackbirds, the boat-tailed grackle is an opportunistic feeder. It eats small fish, snails, aquatic and terrestrial insects, small birds, bird and reptile eggs, berries, grains, and seeds.

❒ ______ **Brown-headed Cowbird** (*Molothrus ater*) Other names: buffalo bird / Status: FL = stable, IUCN = LC / Length: 7.5-8.7 in. (19-22 cm) / Wingspan: 14.2 in. (36 cm) / Weight: 1.5-1.8 oz (42-50 g) / Life span: to 17 years / Nests: throughout SW Florida / Found: AC, coastal, near coast, inland / Months found: **JFMAMJJASOND**.

Brown-headed Cowbird © Bob Gress, BirdsInFocus.com

Birders and naturalists alike lament the success of this native blackbird and the toll it has taken on many of the continent's songbirds. That is because the brown-headed cowbird is North America's most notorious and successful brood parasite. The medium-size blackbird never builds its own nest, relying completely on this parasitic behavior. It is known to lay its eggs in the nests of at least 220 different species. The female may lay as many as 40 eggs in a single season, depositing only one in each nest.

Of the 220 victim species, 144 raise the young cowbird, almost always at the expense of their own offspring. Because the cowbird often lays its eggs in the nests of much smaller warblers, the larger fledgling cowbird hatches first and out-competes the warbler and vireo chicks, causing them to starve or be ejected from the nest. Some species, such as the American robin, gray catbird, and brown thrasher, have adapted to the parasitism by either ejecting or burying the unwanted eggs. The yellow warbler will often desert its nest upon discovery of a brown-headed cowbird egg, or, in some cases, build a second nest on top of the egg, effectively killing the embryo inside. Studies have indicated that after laying its unwelcome egg in a nest, should the host bird eject it, the cowbird will actually return to ransack the nest, forcing the host bird to build a second nest. Once the nest is rebuilt, the same female cowbird will then lay a second egg, hoping for better results.

The cowbird's unusual parasitic behavior has been a boon to its survival. Originally called the buffalo bird, it was first identified in the late 1700s in the short-grass western plains where it often followed the immense buffalo herds. In recent times it has abandoned that practice and greatly expanded its range to cover almost all of North America except the boreal forests and tundra of northern Canada and Alaska. This expansion has come at a tremendous cost to certain passerines that have become the favorite target species of the cowbird. These include the painted bunting, black-whiskered vireo, and Florida prairie warbler.

The adult cowbird is subject to the same predation as all smaller birds. Owls and hawks take their toll, as do weasels and feral cats. One interesting form of chick mortality comes when the cowbird accidentally lays its eggs in the nests of vegetarian species such as house finches and mourning doves. The young cowbirds, which require insect protein to thrive, eventually starve to death on the vegetarian bird's diet of seeds, fruits, and drupes. The fledglings are also taken by black rat snakes, rats, and blue jays.

The cowbird is a year-round resident of Florida, although the interior mainland population swells during the winter months from migratory northern birds.

❒ ________ **House Sparrow** (*Passer domesticus*) Other names: English sparrow, weaver finch / Status: FL=thriving, IUCN=LC / Life span: to 15 years / Length: 6 in. (14 cm) / Wingspan: 7-10 in. (19-25 cm) / Weight: .92-1.13 oz (26-32 g) / Nests: throughout SW Florida / Found: AC, coastal, near coast, inland / Months found: **JFMAMJJASOND**.

Birders can find a well-established flock of these imported sparrows at almost every supermarket and corner store in Southwest Florida. There, as in other urban settings, the sparrow flits about the grounds and spends most of the day foraging for insects, bread crumbs, and whatever else it can find in and around the parking lot. Well adapted to human beings, the house sparrow is another runaway import whose present-day population numbers in the hundreds of millions.

Originally introduced from England into New York City in 1850 and 1851, possibly by the same literary group that brought the European starling over, this small brown sparrow now ranges from the Northwest Territories of Canada to Tierra del Fuego in Chile. The house sparrow is not as controversial an import as is the starling, however, since it is not a cavity nester and prefers urban environments. It is a flying mouse in that it is hardly ever found away from human agricultural or urban settings. The house sparrow loves fast-food joints, gas stations, and grocery stores. There are well-established colonies of this bird living inside (yes, *inside!*) large chain stores

House Sparrow

© Bob Gress, BirdsInFocus.com

such as Target, Home Depot, and Lowe's.

The house sparrow feeds on seeds and grains. Its biggest threats are housecats, sparrow hawks, and encounters with vehicles. The sparrow is monogamous and nests in loosely formed colonies. Its call is a consistent *chirrup, chirrup, chirrup.* The male of this species wears a far more interesting feather pattern than the female.

❒ ____________ **American Goldfinch** (*Carduelis tristis*) Other names: wild canary, thistle bird, eastern goldfinch / Status: FL = stable, IUCN = LC / Length: 4.3-5.1 in. (11-13 cm) / Wingspan: 7.5-8.7 in. (19-22 cm) / Weight: 0.4-0.7 oz (11-20 g) / Life span: to 10.5 years / Nests: most of the U.S. and southern Canada / Found: AC, coastal, near coast, inland / Months found: **JFMAMJJASOND**.

The goldfinch is the state bird of New Jersey, Iowa, and Washington, where it is a welcome visitor at bird feeders. It prefers sunflower seeds and nyjer (a.k.a. niger thistle seed). When the male is in its breeding plumage, this finch is perhaps one of the prettiest birds in North America. The bright, road-stripe yellow contrasts sharply with the jet-black cap and black and white wingtips and tail feathers, making the bird all but impossible to miss when it is flitting around an oak tree in May. In Florida, where thousands of goldfinches winter, the bird dons a more subdued molt of pale yellow and muted black wingtips.

The goldfinch is one of the most strictly vegetarian birds in North America. A granivore, the goldfinch eats insects only rarely and generally by accident when feeding on thistle seeds, grains, buds, and unusual items such as maple sap and green algae. An interesting by-product of this exclusive diet is that when the brown-headed cowbird lays its egg in a goldfinch nest, the chick starves to death within days because it cannot sustain itself on the goldfinch's all-grain diet.

Predation for the adult goldfinch comes from small owls, hawks, and northern and loggerhead shrikes. Nests are often raided by garter snakes, domestic and feral cats, blue jays, and weasels. The range of the American goldfinch covers the continental U.S., southern Canada, and the gulf coast of Mexico. The goldfinch can be found throughout Florida during the winter, but no nesting sites have been verified here.

American Goldfinch

The Additional Birds of Southwest Florida

© BirdsInFocus.com

❒ ______ **American Wigeon** (*Anas americana*) Other names: baldpate, gray duck / Status: FL=stable, IUCN=LC / Life span: to 20 years / Length: 16.5-23.2 in (42-59 cm) / Wingspan: 33.1 in (84 cm) / Weight: 19-46.9 oz (.54-1.33 kg) / Nests: in northern U.S. and Canada / Found: AC, coastal, near coast, inland.

© BirdsInFocus.com

❒ ___ **Northern Shoveler** (*Anas clypeata*) Other names: spoonbill, spoon-billed wigeon / Status: FL=stable, IUCN=LC / Life span: to 18 years / Length: 17.3-20.1 in (44-51 cm) / Wingspan: 30 in (76 cm) / Weight: 14.1-28.9 oz (400-820 g) / Nests: in western U.S. and Canada / Found: AC, coastal, near coast, inland.

© BirdsInFocus.com

❒ ________ **Northern Pintail** (*Anas acuta*) Other names: sprig, sprigtail, spike, spiketail / Status: FL=stable, IUCN=LC / Life span: to 22 years / Length: 20.1-29.9 in (51-76 cm) / Wingspan: 34 in (88 cm) / Weight: 1-3.2 lb (.50-1.45 kg) / Nests: in northern plains and Canada / Found: AC, coastal, near coast, inland.

© BirdsInFocus.com

❒ _______ **Green-winged Teal** (*Anas crecca*) Other names: greenwing, common teal / Status: FL=stable, IUCN=LC / Life span: to 20 years / Length: 12.2-15.4 in (31-39 cm) / Wingspan: 20.5-23.2 in (52-59 cm) / Weight: 4.9-17.6 oz (140-500 g)/ Nests: mostly in Canada / Found: AC, coastal, near coast, inland.

© BirdsInFocus.com

❒ ______ **Hooded Merganser** (*Lophodytes cucullatus*) Other names: fish duck / Status: FL=stable, IUCN=LC / Life span: to 11 years / Length 16-19 in. (42-46 cm) / Wingspan: 23-26 in. (58-66 cm) / Weight: 1-1.5 lb (.45-.68 kg) / Nests: in northern Florida all the way to southern Canada / Found: AC, coastal, near coast, inland.

❒ __________ **Common Loon** (*Gavia immer*) Other names: great northern diver / Status: FL=stable, IUCN=LC / Life span: to 19 years / Length: 26-36 in. (66-93 cm) / Wingspan: 41-52 in. (105-133 cm) / Weight: 9.1 lb (4.1 kg) / Nests: along the far northern tier of North America / Found: AC, coastal, in the fall, winter, and spring on occasion in the back bays and estuaries but far more common in the Gulf of Mexico well offshore.

© BirdsInFocus.com

❒ ________ **Pied-billed Grebe** (*Podilymbus podiceps*) Other names: didapper / Status: FL=stable, IUCN=LC / Life span: to 5 years / Length: 12-15 in. (34-38 cm) / Wingspan: 17.7-24.4 in. (45-62 cm) / Weight: 9-20 oz (.25-.57 kg) / Nests: along the northern tier of North America from the Ohio Valley into far northern Canada / Found: AC, coastal, near coast, inland.

© BirdsInFocus.com

© BirdsInFocus.com

❒ ________ **Reddish Egret** (*Egretta rufescens*) Other names: none / Status: FL=species of special concern, IUCN=LC / Life span: to 12 years / Length: 27-32 in. (68-81 cm) / Wingspan: 46 in. (117 cm) / Weight: 15.9 oz. (.44 kg) / Nests: throughout SW Florida / Found: AC, coastal, near coast.

❒ ______ **Green Heron** (*Butorides virescens*) Other names: little green heron, shietpoke, skeow / Status: FL=stable, IUCN=LC / Life span: to 7 years / Length: 18-22 in. (46-56 cm) / Wingspan: 26 in. (66 cm) / Weight: 78 oz (.20 kg) / Nests: throughout Southwest Florida / Found: AC, coastal, near coast, inland.

© BirdsInFocus.com

© BirdsInFocus.com

❒ ________ **Sharp-shinned Hawk** (*Accipiter striatus*) Other names: little blue darter / Status: FL=stable, IUCN=LC / Life span: to 19 years / Length: 9.4-13.4 in (24-34 cm) / Wingspan: 16.9-22 in (43-56 cm) / Weight: 3.1-7.7 oz (87-218 g) / Nests: from the Mason/Dixon line north to Canada / Found: AC, coastal, near coast, inland – rare.

© BirdsInFocus.com

❒ _______ **Broad-winged Hawk** (*Buteo platypterus*) Other names: none / Status: FL=stable, IUCN=LC / Life span: to 16 years / Length: 13.4-17.3 in (34-44 cm) / Wingspan: 31.9-39.4 in (81-100 cm) / Weight: 9.3-19.8 oz (265-560 g) / Nests: in northern Florida to Canada / Found: AC, coastal, near coast, inland – rare.

❒ _________ **Short-tailed Hawk** (*Buteo brachyurus*) Other names: none / Status: FL=stable, IUCN=LC / Life span: n/a / Length: 16 in (40 cm) / Wingspan: 35 in (90 cm) / Weight: 14-20 oz (400-500 g) / Nests: in the mainland of Florida / Found: AC, coastal, near coast, inland – rare.

© BirdsInFocus.com

© BirdsInFocus.com

❒ ________ **Barn Owl** (*Tyto alba*) Other names: monkey-faced owl, white owl / Status: FL=stable with a slight decline, IUCN=LC / Life span: to 15 years / Length: 13-16 in. (32-40 cm) / Wingspan: 39-49 in. (100-125 cm) / Weight: 14-25 oz (.39.70 kg) / Nests: throughout SW Florida / Found: AC, coastal, near coast, inland.

❒ ________ **Mangrove Cuckoo** (*Coccyzus minor*) Other names: none / Status: FL=rare but not formally endangered, common in the Caribbean and Mexico, IUCN=LC / Life span: to 5 years / Length: 11-13 in. (28-32 cm) / Wingspan: 16 in. (40 cm) / Weight: 2.29-2.5 oz (65-72 g) / Nests: in the mangroves / Found: LC, CC, coastal, near coast – very rare.

© Clair Postmus

❒ _____________ **American Oystercatcher** (*Haematopus palliatus*) Other names: mantled oystercatcher, brown-backed oystercatcher / Status: FL=declining, species of special concern, IUCN=LC / Life span: to 14 years / Length: 16-17 in. (40-44 cm) / Wingspan: 30-36 in. (7691 cm) / Weight: .87-1.5 lbs (.39-.68 kg) / Nests: along the barrier islands / Found: AC, coastal, near coast – rare.

© BirdsInFocus.com

❒ _____ **Clapper rail** (*Rallus longirostris*) Other names: saltwater marsh hen / Status: FL=stable, IUCN=LC / Life span: to 7 years / Length: 12.6-16.1 in (32-41 cm) / Wingspan: 19 in (48 cm) / Weight: 5.6-14.1 oz (160-400 g) / Nests: in the mainland of Florida / Found: AC, near coast, inland – rare.

© BirdsInFocus.com

© BirdsInFocus.com

❒ _____ **King Rail** (*Rallus elegans*) Other names: freshwater marsh hen, mud hen / Status: FL=declining, IUCN=LC / Life span: n/a / Length: 15-18.9 in (38-48 cm) / Wingspan: 20 in (51 cm) / Weight: 10.8-13.1 oz (305-370 g) / Nests: throughout SW Florida / Found: AC, coastal, near coast, inland – rare.

❒ ______ **Sora** (*Porzana carolina*) Other names: Carolina crake, meadow chicken, ortolan / Status: FL=stable, IUCN=LC / Life span: n/a / Length: 7.9-9.8 in (20-25 cm) / Wingspan: 14 in (35 cm) / Weight: 1.7-4 oz (49-112 g) / Nests: north of the Mason-Dixon line / Found: AC, coastal, near coast, inland – rare.

© BirdsInFocus.com

© Wikimedia Commons

❒ ________ **Solitary Sandpiper** (*Tringa solitaria*) Other names: tip-up, wood sandpiper / Status: FL=stable, IUCN=LC / Life span: n/a / Length: 7.5-9.1 in (19-23 cm) / Wingspan: 22 in (56 cm) / Weight: 1.1-2.3 oz (31-65 g) / Nests: in northern Canada / Found: AC, coastal, near coast, inland.

❒ ________ **Semipalmated Sandpiper** (*Calidris pusilla*) Other names: peep / Status: FL=stable, IUCN=LC / Life span: to 19 years / Length: 5.1-5.9 in (13-15 cm) / Wingspan: 11.4-11.8 in (29-30 cm) / 0.7-1.1 oz (21-32 g) / Nests: in the high Arctic / Found: AC, coastal, near coast.

© BirdsInFocus.com

© BirdsInFocus.com

❒ ______ **Semipalmated Plover** (*Charadrius semipalmatus*) Other names: ringneck / Status: FL=stable, IUCN=LC / Life span: to 9 years / Length: 6.7-7.5 in. (17-19 cm) / Wingspan: 14-15.25 in. (35-39 cm) / Weight: 1.7 oz (47 g) / Nests: in the sub-arctic across all of Alaska to Newfoundland / Found: AC, coastal, near coast, inland.

© BirdsInFocus.com

❒ ______ **Wilson's Plover** (*Charadrius wilsonia*) / Other names: ringneck, thick-billed plover / Status: FL=stable, IUCN=LC / Life span: to 10 years / Length: 8 in. (20 cm) / Wingspan: 14-16 in. (35-40 cm) / Weight: 1.9 oz (53 g) / Nests: throughout SW Florida / Found: AC, coastal, near coast, inland.

© BirdsInFocus.com

❒ ______ **Black-bellied Plover** (*Pluvialis squatarola*) Other names: bull-head, black-breasted plover, beetlehead / Status: FL=stable, IUCN=LC / Life span: to 12 years / Length: 11 in. (28 cm) / Wingspan: 23.2-23.6 in. (59-60 cm) / Weight: 5.6-9.8 oz (160-277 g) / Nests: in the High Arctic in the summer / Found: SC, ChC, LC, CC, coastal, near coast.

❒ ________ **Spotted Sandpiper** (*Actitis macularious*) Other names: tip-up, teeter snipe, teeter tail / Status: FL= stable, IUCN=LC / Life span: to 9 years / Length: 7-7.9 in. (17-20 cm) / Wingspan: 14.6-15.7 in. (37-40 cm) / Weight: 1.2-1.8 oz (34-50 g) / Nests: just north of the Mason-Dixon Line all the way to northern Alaska / Found: AC, coastal, near coast, inland.

© BirdsInFocus.com

❒ ___________ **Greater Yellowlegs** (*Tringa melanoleuca*) Other names: telltale snipe / Status: FL=stable, IUCN=LC / Life span: unknown / Length: 11.4-13 in. (29-33 cm) / Wingspan: 23.6 in. (60 cm) / Weight: 3.9-8.3 oz (111-235 g) / Nests: across the northern tier of Canada, generally in mosquito-infested bogs and wetlands / Found: AC, coastal, near coast, inland.

© BirdsInFocus.com

© BirdsInFocus.com

❒ ______ **Lesser Yellowlegs** (*Tringa flavipes*) Other names: telltale snipe / Status: FL=stable, IUCN=LC / Life span: to 4 years / Length: 9.1-9.8 in. (23-25 cm) / Wingspan: 23.2-25.2 in. (59-64 cm) / Weight: 2.4-3.3 oz (67-94 g) / Nests: across the northern tier of Canada and Alaska all the way to the Arctic Ocean / Found: AC, coastal, near coast, inland.

© BirdsInFocus.com

❒ _______ **Piping Plover** (*Charadrius melodus*) Other names: none / Status: FL=Threatened, IUCN=NT / Life span: to 14 years / Length: 6.7-7.1 in. (17-18 cm) / Wingspan: 14-15.5 in. (35-39 cm) / Weight: 1.5-2.2 oz (43-63 g) / Nests: in the Great Plains during the summer / Found: AC, coastal, near coast.

© BirdsInFocus.com

❒ _________ **Ruddy Turnstone** (*Arenaria interpres*) Other names: calico-back, rock plover, brant bird / Status: FL=stable, IUCN=LC / Life span: to 14 years / Length: 6.3-8.3 in. (16-21 cm) / Wingspan: 19.7-22.4 in. (50-57 cm) / Weight: 3-6.7 oz (84.190 g) / Nests: in the extreme High Arctic along the shoreline of the Arctic Ocean from Baffin Island to the North Slope / Found: AC, coastal, near coast, inland.

© BirdsInFocus.com

❒ ________ **Sanderling** (*Calidris alba*) Other names: sand snipe, beach bird, whiting / Status: FL=stable, IUCN=LC / Life span: to 12 years / Length: 7.1-7.9 in. (18-20 cm) / Wingspan: 13.8 in. (35 cm) / Weight: 1.4-3.5 oz (40-100 g) / Nests: high in the Arctic on Baffin Island and farther north / Found: AC, coastal, near coast.

❒ _______ **Western Sandpiper** (*Calidris mauri*) Other names: peep / Status: FL=stable, IUCN=LC / Life span: to 9 years / Length: 5.5-6.7 in. (14-17 cm) / Wingspan: 10.2-14.6 in. (26-37 cm) / Weight: .8-1.2 oz (22-35 g) Nests: primarily along the western shore of Alaska / Found: AC, coastal, near coast.

© BirdsInFocus.com

❒ ___________ **Least Sandpiper** (*Calidris minutilla*) Other names: peep / Status: FL=stable, IUCN=LC / Life span: to 16 years / Length: 5.1-5.9 in. (13-15 cm) / Wingspan: 10.6-11 in. (27-28 cm) / Weight: .07-1.1 oz (19-30 g) / Nests: along the northern tier of North America from the Aleutian Islands to Newfoundland / Found: AC, coastal, near coast.

© BirdsInFocus.com

© BirdsInFocus.com

❒ _________ **Dunlin** (*Calidris alpina*) Other names: red-backed sandpiper, sand-snipe / Status: FL=stable to declining for unknown reasons, IUCN=LC / Life span: to 12 years / Length: 6.3-8.7 in. (16-22 cm) / Wingspan: 14.2-15 in. (36-38 cm) / Weight: 1.7-2.3 oz (48-64 g) / Nests: in the High Arctic around the northern fringe of Hudson Bay / Found: AC, coastal, near coast.

© Fortune & Lopez

❒ ________ **Marbled Godwit** (*Limosa fedoa*) Other names: none / Status: FL=declining, IUCN=LC / Life span: to 13 years / Length: 15.6-18.9 in. (42-48 cm) / Wingspan: 32 in. (81 cm) / Weight: 10.1-16 oz (285-454 g) / Nests: in the Great Plains of North Dakota, Montana, and central Canada; winters along the coast / Found: AC, coastal, near coast, inland.

❒ ________ **Whimbrel** (*Numenius phaeopus*) Other names: Hudsonian curlew / Status: FL=stable, IUCN=LC / Life span: to 13 years / Length: 17.3 in. (44 cm) / Wingspan: 31-33 in. (78-83 cm) / Weight: 10.9-17.4 oz (310-493 g) / Nests: in the High Arctic from Alaska to Hudson Bay / Found: AC, coastal, near coast, inland.

© BirdsInFocus.com

❒ ________ **Willet** (*Catoptrophorus semipalmatus*) Other names: stone curlew, bill-willie, white-wing curlew, pill-willet / Status: FL=stable, IUCN=LC / Life span: to 10 years / Length: 13-16.1 in. (33-41 cm) / Wingspan: 27.6 in. (70 cm) / Weight: 7.1-11.6 oz (200-330 g) / Nests: in the northwestern Rocky Mountains and the Great Plains of North Dakota, Montana, and central Canada / Found: AC, coastal, near coast.

© BirdsInFocus.com

❒ ________ **Red Knot** (*Calidris canutus*) Other names: robin snipe, red-breasted snipe, American knot / Status: FL=declining, IUCN=LC / Life span: to 15 years / Length: 9.1-9.8 in. (23-25 cm) / Wingspan: 20.5-22 in. (52-56 cm) / Weight: 4.8 oz (135 g) / Nests: in the extreme High Arctic along the edge of the Arctic Ocean / Found: AC, coastal, near coast.

© BirdsInFocus.com

© BirdsInFocus.com

❒ ________ **Short-billed Dowitcher** (*Limnodromus griseus*) Other names: red-breasted snipe / Status: FL=stable, IUCN=LC / Life span: to 8 years / Length: 9.8-11.4 in. (25-29 cm) / Wingspan: 18-22 in. (45-55 cm) / Weight: 3.2-4.2 oz (90-120 g) / Nests: near James Bay and across northern Quebec, as well as northern Manitoba and Alberta / Found: AC, coastal, near coast.

© BirdsInFocus.com

❒ ________ **Stilt Sandpiper** (*Calidris himantopus*) Other names: none / Status: FL=stable, IUCN=LC / Life span: n/a / Length: 7.9-9.1 in (20-23 cm) / Wingspan: 18 in (47 cm) / Weight: 1.8-2.5 oz (50-70 g) / Nests: in the Arctic / Found: AC, coastal, near coast, inland – rare.

❒ ________ **Wilson's Snipe** (*Gallinago delicata*) Other names: common snipe, Jack snipe, English snipe / Status: FL=stable, IUCN=LC / Life span: to 9 years / Length: 10.6-12.6 in (27-32 cm) / Wingspan: 16.1-17.3 in (41-44 cm) / Weight: 2.8-5.1 oz (79-146 g) / Nests: along the northern tier well into Canada / Found: AC, coastal, near coast, inland.

© BirdsInFocus.com

❒ ________ **Forster's Tern** (*Sterna forsteri*) Other names: none / Status: FL=stable but declining in some Midwest states, and in many states is now considered a species of special concern, IUCN=LC / Life span: up to 15 years / Length: 13-14.2 in. (33-36 cm) / Wingspan: 29-33 in. (73-83 cm) / Weight: 4.6-6.7 oz (130-190 g) / Nests: in the upper Midwest and lower central provinces of Canada / Found: AC, coastal, near coast.

© BirdsInFocus.com

❒ ______ **Bonaparte's Gull** (*Larus philadeplphia*) Other names: surf gull / Status: FL=stable, IUCN=LC / Life span: n/a / Length: 11-15 in (28-38 cm) / Wingspan: 29.9-31.5 in (76-80 cm) / Weight 6.3-7.9 oz (180-225 g) / Nests: in northern Canada / Found: AC, coastal, near coast.

© BirdsInFocus.com

© BirdsInFocus.com

❒ __________ **Caspian Tern** (*Sterna caspia*) Other names: none / Status: FL=staple, IUCN=LC / Life span: to 29 years / Length: 18.5-21.3 in (47-54 cm) / Wingspan: 47.2-53.1 in (120-135 cm) / Weight: 1.15-1.75 lb (530-782 g) / Nests: in Newfoundland and central Manitoba, Canada / Found: AC, coastal, near coast.

❒ ________ **Sandwich Tern** (*Sterna sandvicensis*) Other names: Cabot's tern / Status: FL=uncommon but stable, IUCN=LC / Life span: to 22 years / Length: 13.4-17.7 in. (34-45 cm) / Wingspan: 33.1-35.4 in. (84-90 cm) / Weight: 6.3-10.6 oz (180-300 g) / Nests: along the Atlantic coastline during thesummer / Found: SC, ChC, LC, CC, coastal.

© BirdsInFocus.com

❒ ___________ **Yellow-billed Cuckoo** (*Coccyzus americanus*) Other names: rain crow / Status: FL=stable, IUCN=LC / Life span: to 5 years / Length: 10.2-11.8 in (26-30 cm) / Wingspan: 15-16.9 in (38-43 cm) / Weight: 1.9-2.3 oz (55-65 g) / Nests: in the southern U.S. during the summer, winters in South America / Found: AC, coastal, near coast, inland – rare.

© BirdsInFocus.com

© BirdsInFocus.com

❒ __________ **Common Nighthawk** (*Chordeiles minor*) Other names: bull bat / Status: FL=stable, IUCN=LC / Life span: to 9 years / Length: 8.7-9.4 in. (22-24 cm) / Wingspan: 20.9-22.4 in. (53-57 cm) / Weight: 2.3-3.5 oz (65-98 g) / Nests: throughout SW Florida during the summer / Found: AC, coastal, near coast, inland.

© BirdsInFocus.com

❒ ______ **Whip-poor-will** (*Caprimulgus vociferus*) Other names: none / Status: FL=stable, IUCN=LC / Life span: to 4 years / Length: 8.7-10.2 in (22-26 cm) / Wingspan: 17.7-18.9 in (45-48 cm) / Weight: 1.5-2.3 oz (43-64 g) / Nests: east of the Mississippi across the Midwest and Northeastern U.S. / Found: AC, coastal, near coast, inland.

© BirdsInFocus.com

❒ ________ **Yellow-bellied Sapsucker** (*Sphyrapicus varius*) Other names: none / Status: FL=stable, IUCN=LC / Life span: to 6 years / Length: 7.1-8.7 in (18-22 cm) / Wingspan: 13.4-15.7 in (34-40 cm) / Weight: 1.5-1.9 oz (43-55 g) / Nests: in the upper Midwest well into Canada / Found: AC, coastal, near coast, inland.

❒ _____ **Eastern Wood-Pewee** (*Contopus virens*) Other names: none / Status: FL=stable, IUCN=LC / Life span: to 7 years / Length: 5.9 in (15 cm) / Wingspan: 9.1-10.2 in (23-26 cm) / Weight: 0.4-0.7 oz (10-19 g) / Nests: in northern Florida to the upper Midwest / Found: AC, coastal, near coast, inland.

© BirdsInFocus.com

© BirdsInFocus.com

❒ ________ **Acadian Flycatcher** (*Empidonax virescens*) Other names: green-crested flycatcher / Status: FL=stable, IUCN=LC / Life span: to 11 years / Length: 5.9 in (15 cm) / Wingspan: 9.1 in (23 cm) / Weight: 0.4-0.5 oz (11-14 g) / Nests: east of the Mississippi from northern Florida to southern Minnesota eastward / AC, coastal, near coast, inland.

❒ _________ **Great Crested Flycatcher** (*Myiachrus crinitus*) Other names: southern crested flycatcher, freight-bird / Status: FL=stable, IUCN=LC / Life span: to 13 years / Length: 6.7-8.3 in. (17-21 cm) / Wingspan: 13.4 in. (34 cm) / Weight: 1-1.4 oz (27-40 g) / Nests: from central Florida through the Upper Midwest / Found: AC, coastal, near coast and inland mostly in the winter due to the increase of migrants into Florida.

© BirdsInFocus.com

❒ ______ **Blue-headed Vireo** (*Vireo solitarius*) Other names: solitary vireo / Status: FL=stable, IUCN=LC / Life span: to 7 years / Length: 5.1-5.9 in (13-15 cm) / Wingspan: 7.9-9.4 in (20-24 cm) / Weight: 0.5-0.7 oz (13-19 g) / Nests: across southern Canada / Found: AC, coastal, near coast, inland.

© BirdsInFocus.com

© BirdsInFocus.com

❒ ________ **Red-eyed Vireo** (*Vireo olivaceus*) Other names: hanging bird, preacher bird / Status: FL=stable, IUCN=LC / Life span: to 10 years / Length: 4.7-5.1 in (12-13 cm) / Wingspan: 9.1-9.8 in (23-25 cm) / Weight: 0.4-0.9 oz (12-26 g) / Nests: throughout the lower U.S. except in the western and southwestern states / Found: AC, near coast, inland.

© Wikimedia Commons

❒ ____________ **Black-whiskered Vireo** (*Vireo altiloquus*) Other names: none / Status: FL=stable, IUCN=LC / Life span: n/a / Length: 5.9-6.3 in (15-16 cm) / Wingspan: 10 in (26 cm) / Weight: 0.6-0.8 oz (17-22 g) / Nests: throughout SW Florida / Found: AC, near coast, inland.

© BirdsInFocus.com

❒ ___________ **Northern Rough-winged Swallow** (*Stelgidopteryx serripennis*) Other names: sand martin, gully martin, gully bird / Status: FL=stable, IUCN=LC / Life span: to 6 years / Length: 4.7-5.9 in (12-15 cm) / Wingspan: 10.6-11.8 in (27-30 cm) / Weight: 0.4-0.6 oz (10-18 g) / Nests: from Central Florida north to Canada / Found: AC, coastal, near coast, inland.

© BirdsInFocus.com

❒ _______ **Bank Swallow** (*Riparia riparia*) Other names: sand martin / Status: FL=stable, IUCN=LC / Life span: to 8 years / Length: 4.7-5.5 in (12-14 cm) / Wingspan: 9.8-11.4 in (25-29 cm) / Weight: 0.4-0.7 oz (10-19 g) / Nests: across the northern U.S. deep into Canada and Alaska / Found: AC, coastal, near coast, inland.

❒ _______ **Barn Swallow** (*Hirundo rustica*) Other names: none / Status: FL=stable, IUCN=LC / Life span: to 8 years / Length: 5.9-7.5 in (15-19 cm) / Wingspan: 11.4-12.6 in (29-32 cm) / Weight: 0.6-0.7 oz (17-20 g) / Nests: from northern Florida through most of the U.S. and southern Canada / Found: AC, coastal, near coast, inland.

© BirdsInFocus.com

© BirdsInFocus.com

❒ ______ **American Robin** (*Turdis migratorius*) Other names: robin redbreast / Status: FL=stable, IUCN=LC / Life span: to 14 years / Length: 7.9-11 in. (20-28 cm) / Wingspan: 12.2-15.7 in. (31-40 cm) / Weight: 2.7-3 oz (77-85 g) / Nests: in northern Florida all the way to sections of the Arctic Ocean off the Northwest Territories / Found: AC, coastal, near coast, inland.

© BirdsInFocus.com

❒ _______ **House Wren** (*Troglodytes aedon*) Other names: eastern house wren, Jenny wren / Status: FL=stable, IUCN=LC / Life span: to 9 years / Length: 4.3-5.1 in (11-13 cm) / Wingspan: 5.9 in (15 cm) / Weight: 0.4 oz (10 g) / Nests: from the Mason Dixon line into southern Canada / Found: AC, coastal, near coast, inland.

© BirdsInFocus.com

❒ _________ **Sedge Wren** (*Cistohorus platensis*) Other names: short-billed marsh wren / Status: FL=stable, ICUN=LC / Life span: n/a / Length: 3.9-4.7 in (10-12 cm) / Wingspan: 5.5-6 in (14-15 cm) / Weight: 0.3 oz (8.5 g) / Nests: in the Midwest of the U.S. / Found: AC, coastal, near coast, inland.

© Wikimedia Commons

❒ _____ **Marsh Wren** (*Cistohorus palustris*) Other names: long-billed marsh wren, Tomtit / Status: FL=stable, IUCN=LC / Length: 3.9-5.5 in (10-14 cm) / Wingspan: 5.5-7 in (14-16 cm) / Weight: 0.3-0.5 oz (9-14 g) / Nests: in the upper U.S. into the plains of Canada / Found: AC, coastal, near coast, inland.

© BirdsInFocus.com

❒ ________ **Ruby-crowned Kinglet** (*Regulus calendula*) Other names: none / Status: FL=stable, IUCN=LC / Life span: to 5 years / Length: 3.5-4.3 in (9-11 cm) / Wingspan: 6.3-7.1 in (16-18 cm) / Weight: 0.2-0.4 oz (5-10 g) / Nests: across all of Canada and Alaska / Found: AC, near coast, inland.

❒ _______ **Veery** (*Catharus fuscescens*) Other names: Wilson's thrush / Status: FL=stable, IUCN-LC / Life span: to 10 years / Length: 6.7-7.1 in (17-18 cm) / Wingspan: 11-11.4 in (28-29 cm) / Weight: 1-1.9 oz (28-54 g) / Nests: along the U.S. / Canadian border / Found: AC, coastal, near coast, inland.

© BirdsInFocus.com

© BirdsInFocus.com

❐ ______ **Wood Thrush** (*Hylocichla mustelina*) Other names: brown thrush, swamp sparrow, branch bird / Status: FL=stable, IUCN=LC / Life span: to 9 years / Length: 7.5-8.3 in (19-21 cm) / Wingspan: 11.8-13.4 in (30-34 cm) / Weight: 1.4-1.8 oz (40-5- g) / Nests: in northern Florida all the way into the upper Midwest / Found: AC, coastal, near coast, inland.

© BirdsInFocus.com

❐ ________ **Orange-crowned Warbler** (*Vermivora celata*) Other names: none / Status: FL=stable, IUCN=LC / Life span: to 8 years / Length: 4.3-5.5 in (11-14 cm) / Wingspan: 7.5 in (19 cm) / Weight: 0.2-0.4 oz (7-11 g) / Nests: in the Rockies and high plains well into Canada and Alaska / Found: AC, coastal, near coast, inland.

❐ _________ **Nashville Warbler** (*Vermivora ruficapilla*) Other names: none / Status: FL=stable, IUCN-LC / Life span: to 10 years / Length: 3.9-4.7 in (10-12 cm) / Wingspan: 6.7-7.9 in (17-20 cm) / Weight: 0.2-0.4 oz (7-11 g) / Nests: in southern Georgia all across the U.S. and into southeastern Canada / Found: AC, coastal, near coast, inland.

© BirdsInFocus.com

❐ ______ **Common Yellowthroat** (*Geothlypis trichas*) Other names: Maryland yellowthroat / Status: FL=stable, IUCN=LC / Life span: to 11 years / Length: 45 in. (11-13 cm) / Wingspan: 67 in. (15-19 cm) / Weight: .32-.35 oz (9-10 g) / Nests: in the eastern deciduous forests / Found: AC, coastal, near coast, inland.

© BirdsInFocus.com

© BirdsInFocus.com

❐ _________ **Magnolia Warbler** (*Dendroica magnolia*) Other names: none / Status: FL=stable, IUCN-LC / Life span: to 8 years / Length: 4.3-5.1 in / Wingspan: 6.3–7.9 in (16-20 cm) / Weight: 0.2-0.5 oz (6-15 g) / Nests: across southern Canada / Found: AC, coastal, near coast, inland.

© BirdsInFocus.com

❐ _______ **Black-throated Green Warbler** (*Dendroica virens*) Other names: none / Status: FL=stable, IUCN-LC / Life span: to 6 years / Length: 4.3-4.7 in (11-12 cm) / Wingspan: 6.7-7.9 in (17-20 cm) / Weight: 0.2-0.4 oz (7-11 g) / Nests: across southern Canada / Found: AC, coastal, near coast, inland.

❐ ______ **Blackburnian Warbler** (*Dendroica fusca*) Other names: none / Status: FL=stable, IUCN-LC / Life span: to 8 years / Length: 4.3-4.7 in (11-12 cm) / Wingspan: 7.9-8.3 in (20-21 cm) / Weight: 0.3-0.5 oz (9-13 g) / Nests: from Maine through northeastern Canada / Found: AC, coastal, near coast, inland.

© BirdsInFocus.com

© BirdsInFocus.com

❐ _______ **Yellow-throated Warbler** *(Dendroica dominica)* Other names: Sycamore Warbler / Status: FL=stable, IUCN=LC / Life span: to 5 years / Length: 5.1-5.5 in (13-14 cm) / Wingspan: 8.3 in (21 cm) / Weight: 0.3-0.4 oz (9-11 g) / Nests: in northern Florida throughout the Southeast to southern Illinois / Found: AC, coastal, near coast, inland.

© BirdsInFocus.com

❐ ______ **Blackpoll Warbler** (*Dendroica striata*) Other names: none / Status: FL=stable, IUCN-LC / Life span: to 8 years / Length: 5.5 in (14 cm) / Wingspan: 8.3-9.1 in (21-23 cm) / Weight: 0.4-0.5 oz (12-13 g) / Nests: across northern Canada into Alaska / Found: AC, coastal, near coast, inland.

❐ _______ **Prothonotary Warbler** (*Protonotaria citrea*) Other names: golden swamp warbler, swamp yellowbird / Status: FL=stable, IUCN-LC / Life span: to 8 years / Length: 5.25 in (14 cm) / Wingspan: 8.5 in (22 cm) / Weight: 0.5 oz (13 g) / Nests: in northern Florida to north of the Ohio River Valley / Found: AC, coastal, near coast, inland.

© BirdsInFocus.com

❐ ______ **Yellow Warbler** (*Dendroica petechia*) Other names: Cuban golden warbler, golden warbler, wild canary, summer yellow-bird / Status: FL=stable, IUCN=LC / Life span: to 10 years / Length: 4.7-5.1 in. (12-13 cm) / Wingspan: 6.3-7.9 in. (16-20 cm) / Weight: 0.3-0.4 oz (9-11 g) / Nests: north of the Mason-Dixon Line to Alaska, as well as a remnant nesting population in the Florida Keys / Found: AC, coastal, near coast, inland.

© BirdsInFocus.com

❐ ________ **Palm Warbler** (*Dendroica palmarum*) Other names: yellow palm warbler, western palm warbler / Status: FL=stable, IUCN=LC / Life span: to 6 years / Length: 4.7-5.5 in. (12-14 cm) / Wingspan: 7.9-8.3 in. (20-21 cm) / Weight: 0.2-0.5 oz (7-13 g) / Nests: in far northern Canada and Newfoundland / Found: AC, coastal, near coast, inland.

© BirdsInFocus.com

❐ ______ **Black-and-white Warbler** (*Mniotilta varia*) Other names: none / Status: FL=stable, IUCN=LC / Life span: to 11 years / Length: 4.3-5.1 in. (11-13 cm) / Wingspan: 7.1-8.7 in. (18-22 cm) / Weight: 0.3-0.5 oz (8-15 g) / Nests: from the mid-south all the way into upper Canada to the Northwest Territories / Found: AC, coastal, near coast, inland.

© BirdsInFocus.com

© BirdsInFocus.com

❒ ______ **Worm-eating Warbler** (*Helmitheros vermivorus*) Other names: none / Status: FL=stable, IUCN-LC / Life span: to 8 years / Length: 4.3-5.1 in (11-13 cm) / Wingspan: 8.5 in (22 cm) / Weight: 0.4-0.5 oz (12-14 g) / Nests: in the southeastern U.S. / Found: AC, coastal, near coast, inland.

❒ ________ **Ovenbird** (*Seiurus aurocapillus*) Other names: golden-crown thrush, wood wagtail / Status: FL=stable to increasing, IUCN=LC / Life span: to 11 years / Length: 4.3-5.5 in. (11-14 cm) / Wingspan: 7.5-10.2 in. (19-26 cm) / Weight: 0.6-1 oz (16-28 g) / Nests: just south of the Mason-Dixon Line all the way north into Newfoundland and the Northwest Territories / Found: AC, coastal, near coast, inland.

© BirdsInFocus.com

❒ _________ **Eastern Towhee** (*Pipilo erythrophthalmus*) Other names: red-eyed towhee, ground robin, white-eyed towhee / Status: FL=stable to slightly declining for unknown reasons, IUCN=LC / Length: 6.8-8.2 in. (17.3-20.8 cm) / Wingspan: 7.9-11 in. (20-28 cm) / Weight: 1.1-1.8 oz (32-52 g) / Nests: in central and northern Florida to Minnesota / Found: AC, coastal, near coast, inland.

© BirdsInFocus.com

❒ _______ **Gray Kingbird** (*Tyannus dominicensis*) Other names: pipiry flycatcher / Status: FL=stable, IUCN=LC / Life span: to 11 years / Length: 9 in. (22 cm) / Wingspan: 14.5-16 in. (37-40 cm) / Weight: 1.5 oz (42 g) / Nests: throughout SW Florida in the summer; winters in South America / Found: AC, coastal, near coast, inland.

© BirdsInFocus.com

❒ __________ **Eastern Phoebe** (*Sayornis phoebe*) Other names: pee-wee, tick bird, bridge bird / Status: FL=expanding its range, IUCN=LC / Life span: to 10 years / Length: 5.5-6.7 in. (14-17 cm) / Wingspan: 10.2-11 in. (26-28 cm) / Weight: 0.6-0.7 oz (16-21 g) / Nests: from southern Georgia year-round all the way into the Northwest Territories in the summer / Found: during the winter only in IW, UA

© BirdsInFocus.com

❒ __________ **Northern Waterthrush** (*Seiurus noveboracensis*) Other names: none / Status: FL=stable, IUCN-LC / Life span: to 9 years / Length: 4.7-5.5 in (12-14 cm) / Wingspan: 8.3-9.4 in (21-24 cm) / Weight: 0.5-0.9 oz (13-25 g) / Nests: in northern Canada and Alaska / Found: AC, coastal, near coast, inland.

© Wikimedia Commons

© BirdsInFocus.com

❒ ________ **Louisiana Waterthrush** (*Seiurus motacilla*) Other names: large-billed waterthrush, water wagtail / Status: FL=stable, IUCN-LC / Life span: to 12 years / Length: 5.5 (14 cm) / Wingspan: 9.4 (24 cm) / Weight: 0.7-0.8 oz (19-23 g) / Nests: throughout the southeastern U.S. / Found: AC, coastal, near coast, inland.

❒ ______ **Summer Tanager** (*Piranga rubra*) Other names: summer redbird / Status: FL=stable, IUCN-LC / Life span: to 8 years / Length: 6.7 in (17 cm) / Wingspan: 11-12 in (28-30 cm) / Weight: 1.1 oz (30 g) / Nests: from central Florida through the southeast and southwest / Found: AC, coastal, near coast, inland.

© BirdsInFocus.com

© BirdsInFocus.com

❒ ______ **Swamp Sparrow** (*Melozpiza georgiana*) Other names: none / Status: FL=stable, IUCN-LC / Life span: to 6 years / Length: 4.7-5.5 in (12-14 cm) / Wingspan: 7.1-7.5 in (18-19 cm) / Weight: 0.4-0.8 oz (11-24 g) / Nests: in the upper Midwest into Canada / Found: AC, coastal, near coast, inland.

❒ __________ **Rose-breasted Grosbeak** (*Pheucticus ludovicianus*) Other names: none / Status: FL=stable, IUCN-LC / Life span: to 13 years / Length: 7.1-8.3 in (18-21 cm) / Wingspan: 11.4-13 in (29-33 cm) / Weight: 1.4-1.7 oz (39-49 g) / Nests: in the upper Midwest into Canada / Found: AC, coastal, near coast, inland.

© BirdsInFocus.com

© BirdsInFocus.com

❒ _________ **Blue Grosbeak** (*Passerina caerulea*) Other names: none / Status: FL=stable, IUCN-LC / Life span: to 10 years / Length: 5.9-6.3 in (15-16 in) / Wingspan: 11 in (28 cm) / Weight: 0.9-1.1 oz (26-31 g) / Nests: across the southern tier of the U.S. / Found: AC, coastal, near coast, inland.

❒ ______ **Baltimore Oriole** (*Icterus galbula*) Other names: northern oriole, Bullock's oriole / Status: FL=stable, IUCN-LC / Life span: to 11 years / Length: 6.7-7.5 in (17-19 cm) / Wingspan: 9.1-11.8 in (23-30 cm) / Weight: 1.1-1.4 oz (30-40 g) / Nests: throughout most of the eastern U.S. and into southern Canada / Found: AC, coastal, near coast, inland.

© BirdsInFocus.com

Masked Booby flock Courstesy NOAA Wikimedia Commons

Accidentals, Vagrants and Casuals of Southwest Florida

The following list of birds are not very common, but can sometimes be found throughout Southwest Florida. These species are generally considered to be one of the following three types:

Accidentals: Species that are represented by a single or several records but have a normal range that is distant from this region. Therefore these birds are not expected to become established in this range. Sometimes these birds are carried to into the region by a storm or weather event. Other times their appearance might be a result of an accidental release (such as in the case of various parrot or parakeet sightings) or the bird or flock of birds might have become lost or disoriented during their seasonal migration and landed here in error.

Vagrants: Species with a natural range that is close to this region, that can be expected to be observed in the region on rare occasions. Vagrants would include sightings of white-crowned pigeons or sooty terns from the Florida Keys.

Casuals: Species that have either a natural range that borders the region, or an extremely limited range within this region, and that may be expected to be recorded infrequently on an annual basis or over a period of several years in a nearby range.

To learn more about these birds, including identification of these accidental species, go to www.allaboutbirds.com, where photos, size and additional information can be found.

❒ **Horned Grebe** (*Podiceps auritus*) Other names: none.
❒ **Masked Booby** (*Sula dactylatra*) Other names: Atlantic blue-faced booby.
❒ **Greater Flamingo** (*Phoenicopteridae Flamingos*) Other names: flamingo
❒ **Snow Goose** (*Chen caerulescens*) Other names: blue goose.
❒ **Gadwall** (*Anas strepera*) Other names: gray duck, gray mallard.
❒ **Eurasian Wigeon** (*Anas penelope*) Other names: none
❒ **Cinnamon Teal** (Anas cyanoptera) Other names: none.
❒ **Surf Scoter** (*Melanitta perspicillata*) Other names: skunkhead, coot, sea coot.
❒ **Black Scoter** (*Melanitta nigra*) Other names: common scoter, American scoter, coot, black coot, sea coot, black duck.
❒ **Canvasback** (*Aythya valisineria*) Other names: can
❒ **Redhead** (*Aythya americana*) Other names: pochard.
❒ **Ring-necked Duck** (*Aythya collaris*) Other names: ringbill, ring-billed duck, blackjack, blackhead.
❒ **Bufflehead** (*Bucephala albeola*) Other names: butterball, dipper, spirit duck.
❒ **Ruddy Duck** (*Oxyura jamaicensis*) Other names: butterball, bull-necked teal.
❒ **Swainson's Hawk** (*Buteo swainson*) Other names: none.
❒ **Mississippi Kite** (*Ictinia mississippiensis*) Other names: none.
❒ **Black rail** (*Laterallus jamaicensis*) Other names: Jamaican crake, little black crake.
❒ **American Avocet** (*Recurvirostra americana*) Other names: none.
❒ **Long-billed Curlew** (*Numenius americanus*) Other names: sickle bill.
❒ **White-rumped Sandpiper** (*Calidris fuscicollis*) Other names: peep.
❒ **Upland Sandpiper** (*Bartramia longicauda*) Other names: none.
❒ **Pectoral Sandpiper** (*Calidris melanotos*) Other names: grass snipe, creaker.
❒ **Parasitic Jaeger** (*Stercorarius parasiticus*) Other names: none.
❒ **Pomarine Jaeger** (*Stercorarius pomarinus*) Other names: none.
❒ **Lesser Black-backed Gull** (*Larus fuscus*) Other names: Scandinavian lesser black-backed gull.
❒ **Great Black-backed Bull** (*Larus marinus*) Other names: none.
❒ **Gull-billed Tern** (*Sterna nilotica*) Other names: none.
❒ **Roseate Tern** (*Sterna dougallii*) Other names: none.
❒ **Common Tern** (*Sterna hirundo*) Other names: mackerel gull.
❒ **Sooty Tern** (*Sterna fuscata*) Other names: none.
❒ **Black Tern** (*Chlidonias niger*) Other names: none.
❒ **Bridled Tern** (*Sterna anaethetus*) Other names: none.
❒ **White-crowned Pigeon** (*Patagioenas leucocephala*) Other names: baldpate, white-hooded pigeon.

- ❒ **White-winged Dove** (*Zenaida asiatica*) Other names: Eastern white-winged dove.
- ❒ **Monk Parakeet** (*Myiopsitta monachus*) Other names: Quaker parakeet.
- ❒ **Budgerigar** (*Melopsittacus undulatus*) Other names: budgie, parakeet, shell parakeet.
- ❒ **Rose-ringed Parakeet** (*Psittacula krameri*) Other names: green parakeet.
- ❒ **White-winged Parakeet** (*Brotogeris vericolurus*) Other names: none.
- ❒ **Black-billed Cuckoo** (*Coccyzus erythropthalmus*) Other names: none.
- ❒ **Smooth-billed Ani** (*Crotophaga ani*) Other names: parrot blackbird, black witch, tickbird, Cuban parrot.
- ❒ **Short-eared Owl** (*Asio flammeus*) Other names: none
- ❒ **Red-headed Woodpecker** (*Melanerpes erythrocephalus*) Other names: white-wing, redhead.
- ❒ **Hairy Woodpecker** (*Picoides villosus*) Other names: sapsucker.
- ❒ **Least Flycatcher** (*Empidonax minimus*) Other names: none.
- ❒ **Vermillion Flycatcher** (*Pyrocephalus rubinus*) Other names: none.
- ❒ **Western Kingbird** (*Tyrannus verticalis*) Other names: none.
- ❒ **Scissor-tailed Flycatcher** (*Tyrannus forficatus*) Other names: none.
- ❒ **Yellow-throated Vireo** (*Vireo flavifrons*) Other names: none.
- ❒ **Bell's Vireo** (*Vireo belli*) Other names: none.
- ❒ **Philadelphia Vireo** (*Vireo philadelphicus*) Other names: none.
- ❒ **Solitary Vireo** (*Vireo solitarius*) Other names: none.
- ❒ **Cliff Swallow** (*Petrochelidon pyrrhonota*) Other names: none.
- ❒ **Cave Swallow** (*Petrochelidon fulva*) Other names: Caribbean cave swallow.
- ❒ **Swainson's Thrush** (*Catharus ustulatus*) Other names: olive-backed thrush.
- ❒ **Gray-cheeked Thrush** (*Catharus minimus*) Other names: none.
- ❒ **Hermit Thrush** (*Catharus guttatus*) Other names: Eastern hermit thrush, swamp sparrow.
- ❒ **American Pipit** (*Anthus rubescens*) Other names: water pipit, titlark, prairie sparrow.
- ❒ **Blue-winged Warbler** (*Vermivora pinus*) Other names: none.
- ❒ **Golden-winged Warbler** (*Vermivora chrysoptera*) Other names: none.
- ❒ **Tennessee Warbler** (*Vermivora peregrina*) Other names: none.
- ❒ **Cerulean Warbler** (*Dendroica cerulea*) Other names: none.
- ❒ **Chestnut-sided Warbler** (*Dendroica pensylvanica*) Other names: none.
- ❒ **Bay-breasted Warbler** (*Dendroica castanea*) Other names: none.
- ❒ **Kentucky Warbler** (*Oporornis formosus*) Other names: none.
- ❒ **Wilson's Warbler** (*Wilsonia pusilla*) Other names: none.

❒ **Connecticut Warbler** (*Oporornis agilis*) Other names: none.
❒ **Townsend's Warbler** (*Dendroica townsendi*) Other names: none.
❒ **Cape May Warbler** (*Dendroica tigrina*) Other names: none.
❒ **Mourning Warbler** (*Oporornis philadelphia*) Other names: none.
❒ **Canada Warbler** (*Wilsonia canadensis*) Other names: none.
❒ **MacGillivray's Warbler** (*Oporornis toimiei*) Other names: none.
❒ **Yellow-breasted Chat** (*Icteria virens*) Other names: none.
❒ **Western Tanager** (*Piranga ludoviciana*) Other names: none.
❒ **Roufus-sided Towhee** (*Pipilo erythrophthalmus*) Other names: none.
❒ **Lark Sparrow** (*Chondestes grammacus*) Other names: none.
❒ **Field Sparrow** (*Spizella pusilla*) Other names: none.
❒ **Le Conte's Sparrow** (*Ammodramus leconteii*) Other names: none.
❒ **Lincoln's Sparrow** (*Melospiza lincolnii*) Other names: none.
❒ **Henslow's Sparrow** (*Ammodramus henslowii*) Other names: none.
❒ **Sharp-tailed Sparrow** (*Ammodramus caudacutus*) Other names: none.
❒ **Seaside Sparrow** (*Ammodramus maritimus*) Other names: none.
❒ **Grasshopper Sparrow** (*Ammodramus savannarum*) Other names: none.
❒ **White-throated Sparrow** (*Zonotrichia albicollis*) Other names: none.
❒ **White-crowned Sparrow** (*Zonotrichia leucophrys*) Other names: none.
❒ **Dickcissel** (*Spiza americana*) Other names: none.
❒ **House Finch** (*Carpodacus mexicanus*) Other names: none.
❒ **Purple Finch** (*Carpodacus purpureus*) Other names: none.
❒ **Pine Siskin** (*Carduelis pinus*) Other names: none.
❒ **Yellow-headed Blackbird** (*Xanthocephyalus xanthocephyalus*) Other names: none.
❒ **Shiny Cowbird** (*Molothrus bonariensis*) Other names: glossy cowbird.
❒ **Orchard Oriole** (*Icterus spurius*) Other names: none.

© Judd Patterson, BirdsInFocus.com

Mother and child

The Mammals of Southwest Florida

Florida is home to 98 different species of mammals. Many of these are marine mammals, including 21 species of whales and dolphins, almost all of which live far offshore and are therefore not included in this book.

Sadly, several large mammals are extinct or are presently extirpated from the region. One of these was the Caribbean monk seal, weighing as much as 440 pounds. The last confirmed sighting of this animal was off the Serranilla Bank in the western Caribbean in 1952. The species was officially declared extinct in 2008. Other mammals that were once found in the region, such as the beaver and the red wolf, no longer roam here, having been trapped or hunted to the point of eradication. Believe it or not, beavers were once common along the Myakka River, and red wolves were historically found in all six counties of Southwest Florida. Florida does hold the only remnant population of mountain lion remaining in the eastern United States, the Florida panther.

While some mammals such as the West Indian manatee and panther struggle with man's impact on their environment, others appear to thrive. White-tailed deer and feral pigs are both expanding their populations, and bottle-nosed dolphin are faring well along the gulf coast despite the increase in boat traffic and unending coastal development. Bobcats, coyotes, fox squirrels, and raccoons are all doing well,

whereas mink, certain species of bats, and rice rats are battling to cope with this brave new world humans are creating.

What is most important, especially for larger mammals such as black bears and panthers, is the need to preserve open spaces large enough to give these animals the room they need to thrive. An adult male panther requires a range of 200 square miles to survive. Black bears do not fare well in suburban environments and require remote, heavily wooded environs where they can find enough forage to thrive. Places such as the Myakka Island and Big Cypress National Preserve are essential to keeping these large carnivores in Florida.

Most of the mammals in this section are small: either rodents or bats, the two most populous members of the mammalian family. Bats represent 24 percent of all living mammals, while rodents account for an impressive 40 percent of all known mammal species. Florida has its fair share of both of these orders; Southwest Florida has a total of 19 species of bats and rodents in its six counties.

So go ahead and learn about our closest living relatives outlined in this section of the book. Some of them are all but impossible not to love, such as the lumbering West Indian manatee, while others are hard not to keep out of your garbage cans, such as the masked bandit known as the raccoon. Each and every one is amazing in its own way and an exhilarating experience to chance upon when hiking, biking, or canoeing in the wild.

The Puma Courtesy Art G via Wikimedia Commons

Land Mammals

❐ _______ **Florida Panther** (*Felis concolor coryi*) Other names: puma, mountain lion, cougar, catamount / Status: FL=endangered, IUCN=CR (critically endangered) / Length: with tail, 8 ft (2.4 m) / Height: at shoulder, 2-2.5 ft (60-76 cm) / Weight: 75-160 lb (34-73 kg) / Life span: to 10 years / Reproduces: in Southwest Florida / Found: ChC, LC, CC, GC, HC, near coast, inland / Months found: **JFMAMJJASOND**.

The Florida panther is the largest feline carnivore in North America. The last remnant population of the Eastern subspecies has managed to survive in the southern portion of Florida, including Charlotte, Lee, Collier, Glades, Hendry, Monroe, Palm Beach, Brevard, and Miami-Dade counties. Although several cats have been authenticated as far north as Polk County, there appears to be no substantial breeding population north of the Caloosahatchee River and Lake Okeechobee. There are an estimated 120 to 160 panthers living in Florida.

As the Latin name (*coryi*) implies, the Florida panther was once considered a viable subspecies of the much more successful North American cougar. Recent genetic studies of mitochondrial DNA have disproved this status. There are now, according to *Mammal Species of the World,* only six recognized subspecies of puma, five of which are located in South America. The Florida panther, although still in desperate need of protection, is no longer considered a viable subspecies by the world's leading taxonomists. In fact, since the introduction of several Texas pumas in the past 20 years to prevent inbreeding, the genetically "pure" Florida panther no longer exists.

The North and South American cougar family is currently listed as LC (Least Concern) by the IUCN. The cougar is the only large feline in the world whose population is increasing throughout most of its range. This is especially true of the western population, which is expanding its numbers and range throughout the entire western edge of North America, from Colorado to British Columbia.

The panther in Florida survives largely on feral pigs, armadillos, raccoons, and white-tailed deer. The major cause of death to the Florida panther is the Florida panther. The extremely territorial male requires a tremendous range, of up to 200 square miles depending on available prey. Within that given range it may have two to five females with whom it breeds. When a male panther is born, his future is uncertain. When he matures, should he come across a dominant male in search of his own range, he will be killed.

The second leading cause of panther mortality is automobiles. This is also a byproduct of too many cats in too small of a range. As the male cat attempts to avoid the dominant male in any given range, it wanders farther a field, often placing itself in a suburban or urban environment where its chance of getting struck and killed by an automobile increases dramatically.

The Florida panther is Florida's state animal, a designation granted by the schoolchildren of the state in 1982. The irony is that Florida's incessant growth and its demand for more subdivisions, shopping malls, and asphalt put constant pressure on the ever-shrinking wild places the panther requires to survive. Scientists have calculated that to prevent further inbreeding, the state would need a resident population of approximately 240 panthers. Based on the panther's habitat needs, this equates to 8,000 to 12,000 square miles of range. With developers edging in from all directions, it is unlikely the panther will ever have sufficient range to maintain its population without genetic intervention from outside stock.

A male panther requires more than 5,000 calories a day to survive. A nursing female cat requires twice that. That translates to 3.8 pounds of meat a day for a male to survive and 8 pounds for a female with cubs. It is estimated that a single panther can kill up to 50 deer a year and 10 times that number of raccoons. The panther has also been known to kill and eat immature alligators, snakes, and iguanas.

With proper management and continued importation of Texas cougars to keep the gene pool sufficiently varied, there is every reason to believe this remnant population of pumas will survive in the heartland of south Florida for years to come. Your chances of seeing one of these elusive animals in the wild are almost nil. One of the best places to see panthers in a semi-wild environment is at the Babcock Ranch in eastern Charlotte County, covered in the Charlotte County destination section of this book.

Panther on the prowl

❐ ____________ **Bobcat** (*Lynx rufus*) Other names: wildcat / Status: FL=stable, IUCN=LC / / Length: 28-47 in. (70-120 cm) / Height: at shoulder, 20-24 in. (50-60 cm) / Weight: 16-30 lb (7-14 kg) / Life span: to 8 years / Reproduces: breeds in the winter with the kittens born in the spring or summer, one litter per year with three to four kittens born in each litter / Found: AC, coastal, near coast, inland / Months found: **JFMAMJJASOND**.

An estimated 700,000 to 1.5 million bobcats live in North America. In the far north the bobcat is replaced by the slightly larger Canadian lynx, which has longer legs, huge padded feet, and denser fur, all of which are helpful for surviving in the often snow-covered boreal forests of northern Canada. The male bobcat commonly grows to 30 pounds; the largest ever recorded in the wild was 48.9 pounds. The bobcat is a game animal in Florida, trapped and hunted for its fine-quality fur.

Bobcat in the bush © Heather Green

Unlike many of the world's cats, the bobcat population is not in trouble. In a few states, such as Ohio, Indiana, and New Jersey, the bobcat is considered endangered, but for the most part this feline is thriving. Because of protections now in place across North America, the bobcat is steadily returning to its entire original range.

Southwest Florida has a healthy bobcat population. Although most sightings occur at dawn and dusk, the bobcat can sometimes be spotted midday. Its fur pattern varies by region; there have even been 10 confirmed cases of melanistic (black) bobcats in Florida. Like most wild cats, the bobcat is a carnivore and operates as an adept ambush predator. It is capable of jumping yards into the air, sometimes plucking waterfowl right out of the air. While not common it has been known to take down white-tailed deer weighing eight times more than does the bobcat. It kills innumerable rats, mice, raccoons, opossums, armadillos, birds, snakes, feral and domestic cats, and just about anything else that can supply the daily calories it requires for survival.

Only a handful of predators feed upon the bobcat. While kittens may be taken by coyotes, male bobcats, raccoons, and fox, adults need only to fear wolves, panthers, and large alligators. The bobcat has been known to attack people, but in most cases it involves a mother attempting to protect her litter. There has never been a recorded fatal bobcat attack in North America.

It breeds year-round, but tends to favor April through September. On average it has one litter per year, with one to six kittens per litter. The bobcat is not capable of being domesticated. It will readily injure itself if caged and will bite and scratch its handlers without warning.

❐ ________ **Feral Cat** (*Felis catus*) Other names: housecat, domestic cat / Status: Domesticated and abundant / Length: with tail, 29.8 in. (75 cm) / Height: n/a / Weight: 5.5-16 lb (2.5-7 kg) / Reproduces: can have litters in the wild, breeds year round / Found: AC, coastal, near coast, inland / Months found: **JFMAMJJASOND**.

The origins of the housecat go back 9,500 years. Originally thought to have been domesticated in ancient Egypt, recent DNA studies indicate that all housecats are derived from as few as five self-domesticated African wildcats (*Felis silvestris lybica*). It turns out they domesticated us. Anyone who owns a cat can understand the truth of that statement.

Feral, urban cat Courtesy Wikimedia Commons

A skilled predator, with a similar hunting style to both the bobcat and the panther, a feral cat can decimate local populations of marsh rabbits, cotton rats, birds, anoles, insects, and mice. Worldwide, the wild housecat has been documented to hunt more than 1,000 different species for food. It relies on its multidirectional ears and acute sense of hearing to hunt, which it does mostly at night. Its retractable claws and well-padded feet make it silent and virtually undetectable to some unsuspecting foraging rodent.

The introduction of the housecat into certain ecosystems has been extremely damaging. The feral cat has single-handedly caused the eradication or extinction of dozens of species in certain areas. One notable example is the Stephens Island wren, indigenous only to an island located just off of New Zealand. This small flightless bird fed exclusively on insects. Its entire population was destroyed within five years of the arrival of semi-feral cats, originally brought onto the island by the lighthouse keeper in 1892 to control rodents. By the time the wren was extinct, the island swarmed with more than 100 cats.

People still dump their unwanted cats and kittens along the side of the road. This behavior is generally a death sentence for the cat—or should it survive, a death sentence for scores of shorebirds and passerines, including potentially threatened species. Some people take to feeding feral cats, which can be a mixed blessing, but even a well-fed cat will sometimes kill out of instinct. If you have a feral or semi-feral cat in your area, it is best to have it trapped and removed from the environment.

❐ ________ **Red Fox** (*Vulpes vulpes*) Other names: silver fox, cross fox / Status: FL = expanding its range, IUCN = LC / Length: not including the tail, 19-35 in. (49-90 cm) / Height at shoulder: 14-20 in. (35-50 cm) / Weight: 5-22 lb (2.2-10 kg) / Life span: to 15 years / Breeds: in the winter months, with kits born in the spring / Found: AC, near coast, inland / Months found: **JFMAMJJASOND**.

Red Fox © Bob Gress

The red fox is the most widely distributed and successful carnivore on earth. It has 45 recognized subspecies and is found on every continent except Antarctica. It even inhabits the High Arctic where it often out competes the smaller white Arctic fox. Although the red fox was historically found along the northern tier of Florida where the eastern deciduous forest ends, it has recently expanded its range southward and can now be found everywhere in the state except the Keys.

The red fox is similar in size to the gray fox, and the two animals coexist fairly well. True to the adage, "cunning as a fox," this small canid is a brilliant survivor. There is no doubt that its expansion into Southwest Florida has been on the coattails of our own expansion in the same environment. The red fox eats just about everything, including carrion and flotsam. It also preys on fawns, rabbits, squirrels, moles, mice, birds, raccoons, opossums, reptiles, earthworms, and insects. Although considered a carnivore, the red fox is actually an omnivore; during certain times of the year its diet may consist entirely of plant matter, berries, fruits, and tubers. This ability to alter its diet to whatever foodstuff is readily available is key to the fox's success.

The red fox is still trapped extensively for its fur. In the U.S., the Alaskan red fox has the best fur, with silky guard hairs that make it extremely desirable on the

Red Fox, silver phase Courtesy Wikimedia Commons

fur market. More than 2 million red fox pelts are harvested in the wild worldwide, particularly in Canada and Alaska. Despite this continued trapping, the red fox is not threatened or endangered anywhere in North America, and only two of the 45 subspecies in the world are listed as endangered.

The female, which is called a vixen, has one litter a year with up to 12 kits in a litter. Like its cousin, the coyote, the fox was once common prey for wolves and pumas. With these two top predators gone, many more kits survive, and the fox's numbers are steady to increasing in every state in the Union. In Australia and New Zealand, where the red fox was introduced for the British sport of fox hunting, it is considered an invasive species and has caused serious declines in many indigenous species such as bettongs, bilbies, numbats, kiwis, and wallabies.

The red fox is too small to seriously injure a human, and though it has been known to attack infants, no reported attack has been fatal. Like the coyote, the red fox will take outdoor house pets such as cats and small dogs and has been known to decimate entire flocks of chickens in a single night. The red fox will sometimes resort to an unusual behavior more commonly found in man—it will overkill prey beyond its immediate needs. Panthers and lions are also known to kill more than they can eat, though no one can explain the biological mechanism behind overkilling.

The red fox is prone to rabies and a number of other potentially lethal human diseases such as tularemia and encephalitis.

Although the red fox is increasing in number, your chances of seeing one of these small, secretive animals in the wild is extremely rare. It tends to hunt at dawn and dusk, and its keen sense of hearing keeps it at a safe distance from noise-making humans. The fox is a surprisingly fast animal, disappearing into the understory in a heartbeat.

❐ __________ **Gray Fox** (*Urocyon cinereoargenteus*) Other names: Florida fox / Status: FL=stable, IUCN=LC / Length: with tail, 41.5-58.8 in. (1-1.5 m) / Height: at shoulder, 12-24 in. (30-60 cm) / Weight: 7.9-15 lb (3.6-6.8 kg) / Life span: to 10 years / Reproduces: one litter per year in the spring with up to seven kits in a litter / Found: AC, coastal, near coast, inland / Months found: **JFMAMJJASOND**.

The gray fox is easily distinguished from its close relative, the red fox, by the lack of distinctive black boots, the dark markings along the lower half of all four legs. It is also considerably more aggressive than the red fox and will dominate that species in any given territory, although the red fox has come to outnumber the gray in the eastern portion of the U.S.; in the west the gray fox is far more common than its red-coated cousin. The gray fox is monogamous and mates for life.

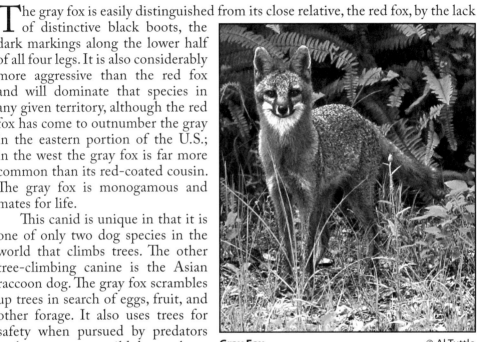

Gray Fox © Al Tuttle

This canid is unique in that it is one of only two dog species in the world that climbs trees. The other tree-climbing canine is the Asian raccoon dog. The gray fox scrambles up trees in search of eggs, fruit, and other forage. It also uses trees for safety when pursued by predators such as coyotes or wild dog packs.

The gray fox feeds on marsh rabbits, mice, rats, anoles, and birds. An omnivore, this fox also feeds on fruits and figs when available. Its hunting technique is similar to that of the bobcat. In the wild it is preyed upon by panthers and alligators, and the kits are sometimes taken by owls and coyotes.

❐ __________ **Coyote** (*Canis latrans*) Other names: Coydogs, Prairie Wolf, American Jackal, Bandit Dog, Brush Wolf, Song Dog, Wile E. Coyote, Coyotl (Aztec) / Status: FL = expanding its range, IUCN = LC / Length: 28-38 in. (71-96 cm) / Height at shoulder: 12-15 in. (30-38 cm) / Weight: 25-33 lb (11.5-15 kg) / Life span: to 15 years / Breeds: in early winter with the pups born in the spring / Found: AC, near coast, inland / Months found: **JFMAMJJASOND**.

The name *coyote* is one of very few words that have come to us from the Aztec language. The Aztec name for this adaptive and intelligent member of the *Canidae* family was coyotl, meaning God's dog. Prior to the 1930s the coyote was almost never seen east of the Mississippi River. Anyone familiar with old Western

Wild coyote © Judd Patterson, JuddPatterson.com

movies should appreciate the fact that the native habitat for this small canid was the open ranges and grasslands of the Western plains, where its familiar pose, howling at the night sky, is embedded in our collective psyche. Today the coyote has made it all the way to Cape Cod, and one was actually observed in New York's Central Park. The eastern population now tends to be larger than the western.

The coyote is a recent arrival to the South Florida landscape. There is no indication that it was ever here before now, but one thing is for certain: the coyote is in Southwest Florida and is here to stay.

While there is some debate over why the coyote so dramatically expanded its range and did it so rapidly, several factors come into play. One of these was the bounty hunting and trapping of both red and gray wolves. The wolf is a natural enemy of the coyote and will hunt and kill one when discovered within its range. Another factor appears to be the coyote's propensity to hybridize with other canines, both wolves and domesticated dogs. Indeed, DNA evidence indicates that today's coyotes are more of a genetic soup than a pure breed. The coyote may have gained additional intelligence by interbreeding with domestic dogs such as the German shepherd.

The coyote's ability to adapt and survive in agricultural, exurban, and suburban environments has also contributed to its expansion. If ever there was an animal that survived the rise of human dominance in the past 10,000 years, it is Wile E. Coyote, who in the popular cartoon not only catches the Roadrunner, but also has him for dinner with a fine bottle of wine.

Urban sprawl has provided the coyote with ample cover, along with additional food sources such as garbage, roadkill, rabbits, and rodents. Small dogs and cats are favorite prey items for the coyote.

The coyote takes advantage of its nearly invisible profile. It tends to feed at dawn, dusk, and throughout the night. Because its footprints and scat are virtually identical to those of any small dog, it is impossible to identify a coyote by its tracks. The most likely time to see one is on a rural highway late at night when it is out foraging. The coyote is primarily carnivorous but is known to feed on berries, vegetables, and insects. Out West the coyote can be a real problem for sheep ranchers where up to two-thirds of lambs may be taken in a single year. The coyote also preys in packs upon white-tailed deer and young calves.

The only animal capable of preying upon an adult coyote in Southwest Florida is the panther. Bears are simply not quick enough to catch one, and the only other native canid, the red wolf, has long since vanished from our landscape. Coyote pups might fall prey to great horned owls and rattlesnakes. Aside from human trapping or poisoning, the coyote has few natural predators to keep its population in check. In Southwest Florida, if you live along the fringes of wooded areas or in subdivisions with large lot sizes, it's probably a good idea to take your pets in at night and be on the lookout for this newcomer.

❒ __________ Domesticated Dogs (*Canis lupus familiaris*)

Other names: Rover, Fido / Status: FL=thriving, IUCN=domesticated / Length: 3.75 in.-8.2 ft (9.5-250 cm) / Weight: 4 oz-343 lb (113 g-155.6 kg) / Life span: some breeds to 20 years / Reproduces: in the wild feral dogs can breed year round / Found: AC, coastal, near coast, inland / Months found: **JFMAMJJASOND**.

Recent DNA evidence shows that all dogs, from the tiniest Yorkshire terrier at 113 grams to the massive English mastiff at 343 pounds, came from the gray wolf some 15,000 years ago. The dog is ubiquitous throughout Southwest Florida. Having been around humans for centuries, it has been bred to handle any number of chores—from bloodhounds tracking criminals to huskies pulling sleds and all points in between.

Feral dog © Dave Irving

The dog has reasonably good eyesight, very good hearing, and an astonishing sense of smell. It is this sense of smell that is the primary reason why the dog should be kept on a leash whenever it is taken outside, especially on the beaches. The dog is still a wolf, and despite our best intentions, we should always consider it a threat to wildlife.

Its olfactory ability can sometimes lead an unleashed dog directly to a fresh sea turtle nest, and within seconds an entire clutch can be destroyed. Even if the dog doesn't uncover the eggs, the strong canine scent left behind will likely lead raccoons to the nest later that evening. The dog also tends to chase shorebirds, which, after flying across the Gulf of Mexico, are sometimes far too exhausted for such behavior. If a dog should catch an adult plover or sandpiper, one shake of the dog's head will kill the bird.

Pet owners are also tempted to unleash their dogs while walking them in wildlife preserves. An injured marsh rabbit is quickly killed by an unchecked dog. Leashes are for the dog's safety as well—alligators love eating dogs, even large ones. Feral dogs are a major problem. They sometimes form wild dog packs, which have been known to take down deer, bear, and even humans. A dog's wild instincts tend to be heightened under these conditions, and anyone coming across a dog pack should use extreme caution and report the sighting to the local authorities.

❑ ________ Florida Black Bear (*Ursus americanus floridanus*)

Other names: Bear / Status: FL = endangered, IUCN = LC / Length: 4-6 ft (1.2-1.8 m) / Height at shoulder: 2.5-3 ft (.76-.91 m) / Weight: 150-300 lb (68-136 kg) / Life span: to 27 years / Breeds: in the early summer with the female giving birth to twins or triplets mid-winter / Found: AC, near coast, inland / Months Found: **JFMAMJJASOND**.

Black bear grazing

© Judd Patterson, JuddPatterson.com

Unlike the coyote, wild turkey, and white-tailed deer, the black bear has not done so well adapting to manmade changes in the environment. Secretive and with a low reproductive rate, the black bear struggles throughout its broad range to hang onto its remnant populations from the Midwest to Florida. According to the Florida Fish and Wildlife Conservation Commission, 2,500 to 3,000 black bears are left in the state; some estimates indicate less than half of that. Because of the black bear's reclusive nature and tendency to keep to dense forests with heavy understories, getting an accurate census of the largest land carnivore in Florida is a daunting task.

In Southwest Florida one of the best remaining intact habitats is the Big Cypress National Preserve in southern Collier County. The chance of actually seeing a black bear in Florida are only slightly better than seeing a panther. You might come across bear signs, however, such as scat, clawed trees, or tracks (its hind paws resemble a squat, oddly shaped human foot with claws). In the Sunshine State the bear does not hibernate, although it will sometimes remain dormant during periods of cold weather.

Bear hunting was legal in Florida until 1993 when the state imposed a moratorium that remains in place today. The bear is still hunted across the United States, where more than 18,000 bears are killed annually. Canada, which has an estimated black bear population approaching 400,000, also allows controlled hunts of this impressive predator. The largest black bear ever taken was in North Carolina in 1998. It weighed 880 pounds. The meat of black bear is said to taste similar to pork.

Black Bear © Bob Gress

Human/bear encounters are rare and seldom fatal. A mother with cubs presents one of the most obvious dangers, but a young, healthy male is also of serious concern. Most attacks occur in places where bears have been fed, such as dump sites or campgrounds, and happen because the animal loses its fear of people. There have been only 52 documented cases of fatal black bear attacks in North America in the past 100 years, none of which was ever recorded in Florida.

The bear is an omnivore. More than 85 percent of its diet consists of herbs, grasses, fruit, acorns, nuts, and tubers. It is very fond of honey and bee larvae, a trait that often brings it into direct conflict with Florida's beekeepers. It also eats termites, carpenter ants, and other colony-building insects. Less commonly, the black bear will take white-tailed deer and smaller mammals such as opossums and raccoons. It will readily feed on carrion and has been known to chase panthers off of a fresh kill.

In Florida the bear is at the top of the food chain. Only the cubs, which are born extremely small at 7.8 to 10.4 ounces, are vulnerable to predation. The majority of bear cub deaths do not come from other predators but from male black bears wanting to induce the female back into estrus. The female becomes reproductive between three and five years of age and rears two to three cubs every two years.

One of the leading causes of bear mortality in Florida are automobile collisions on remote highways. With its slow reproductive rate and need for large, unbroken tracts of forested lands, it is highly unlikely that the Florida black bear will be returning to its historical populations anytime soon.

❐ ______ **Wild Boar** (*Sus scrofa*) Other names: Wild Pig, Razorback, European Boar, Boar, Feral Pig, Feral Swine, Piney Woods Rooter / Status: FL = thriving, IUCN = LC / Length: 2.9-6 ft (.09-1.8 m) / Height at shoulder: 30-42 in. (76-109 cm) / Weight: 110-420 lb (50-190 kg) / Life span: to 20 years / Breeds: throughout SW Florida / Found: AC, coastal, near coast, inland / Months Found: **JFMAMJJASOND**.

Wild hog cutting through a marsh © Heather Green

The European wild boar is one of the most destructive invasive species ever introduced into North America. Originally transported by Hernando de Soto to the gulf coast of Florida in 1539 as domestic livestock, these escaped pigs have now expanded their range northward to the upper peninsula of Michigan, westward to California, and eastward to Virginia. Texas and Florida have the largest populations of wild hogs. In Texas the wild boar is outcompeting the native collared peccary, or javelina, which seldom weighs more than 50 pounds.

In Florida the wild boar population is estimated in excess of 500,000. More than 100,000 wild boars are taken by hunters in the Sunshine State annually, though this impressive harvest is still inadequate for keeping the soaring population in

A sounder of feral pigs © Blake Sobczak

check. It breeds year round; the sow is capable of producing two litters a year, with as many as 12 piglets per litter. Left unchecked, the wild hog population in Florida could easily overwhelm the balance of nature and do immeasurable harm to other species by consuming too much of the available food sources. A single 400-pound boar can devour bushels of acorns in a week, leaving little for the other acorn-eating species such as deer, wild turkeys, opossums, raccoons, armadillos, and any number of birds. The wild boar also eats snakes, carrion, refuse, insects, and reptiles.

Another problem with the wild boar is its habit of using its six-inch tusks to root out grubs, roots, and tubers, causing irreparable damage to the understory of forests and pastureland. As a result, many of the region's parks and preserves such as Myakka River State Park have ongoing trapping operations to reduce, or optimistically eliminate, the wild boar from the ecosystem. The hogs taken from these traps are sold by the trappers as game meat.

The wild boar story has a silver lining. In the 1920s and 1930s Florida's white-tailed deer population was intentionally eradicated by the state because it was believed to be transmitting diseases to Florida's domestic cattle. With the deer population down to 20,000 animals statewide, the only substantial food source left for the Florida panther became the wild boar. This allowed the panther to survive into the 21st century. Today the deer population has rebounded, but feral pigs, especially piglets, still play an important part in the panther's survival.

The trouble with the panther's diet of wild pig is that swine are known vectors of diseases. One of these is pseudorabies, a disease similar to rabies that is fatal to panthers. Another common disease is swine brucellosis, which can be fatal to humans as well. Care should always be taken when handling wild boar meat as both the mucous and blood can transmit disease, including trichinosis.

With a half-million wild hogs out there, it is unlikely Florida will ever be free of this intelligent and adaptive omnivore. Its primary cause of mortality is hunting by humans, followed by predation of smaller hogs by panthers; predation of piglets by owls, eagles, coyotes, bobcats, and black bears; and, finally, cannibalization by solitary male boars. Although not inherently dangerous to humans, a cornered or wounded boar wielding six-inch tusks is a formidable threat, and care should always be exercised when encountering one of these animals in the wild.

❐_____ **White-tailed Deer** (*Odocoileus virginianus clavium*)
Other names: Bucks, Jumper, Deer / Status: FL = thriving, IUCN = LC / Length: 60-90 in. (1.5-2.28 m) / Height to shoulder: 32-40 in. (.82-1 m) / Weight: 90-125 lb (41-56 kg) / Life span: to 20 years / Breeds: in the fall rut with the fawns born in the spring / Found: AC, near coast, inland / Months found: **JFMAMJJASOND**.

Three white-tailed deer © David Irving

A true survivor, the white-tailed deer has not only outlived the gauntlet of human encroachment into its realm, but also flourished because of it. There are no exact numbers for the deer population in North America at the time of first contact in the early 1500s. By the late 1800s, however, hunting and a lack of game management had reduced the population across the continent to an all-time low of 500,000 animals. In 1900, the Lacey Act, the first Federal wildlife law, prohibited the interstate trafficking of venison and other wild game, thereby restricting the market hunters' ability to sell their product. By 1908, 41 states had established departments of conservation and hunting seasons, and bag limits along with scientifically based management plans put this even-toed ungulate well on its way to recovery.

A healthy Florida buck © Heather Green

Today the population of white-tailed deer in the lower 48 states alone has been estimated at an astounding 30 million animals. This rebound is the result of a combination of factors. The absence of predators, including wolves, cougars, and black bear (in large part because of bounty hunting), has allowed the deer population to flourish in areas where such predators once held it in check. Enforcement of hunting regulations and the deer's ability to adapt to manmade changes in the landscape are also major reasons for the population explosion. The white-tailed deer has learned to survive in suburban and exurban environments where it feeds on a wide array of landscape plants, much to the consternation of homeowners.

The high population numbers also lead to the deer's inevitable involvement in automobile collisions as drivers encounter them more and more on the roads. In the lower 48 the white-tailed deer is responsible for killing more than 200 people annually, injuring more than 29,000 people, and causing $1.1 billion in property damages.

Yet another problem caused by the burgeoning deer population is the proliferation of deer ticks, which transmit Lyme disease. Although uncommon in Florida, where only a handful of cases have been reported (all in the northern tier of the state), in New England and the Midwest the spread of this debilitating and potentially lethal disease has reached epidemic proportions. More than 20,000 new cases of Lyme disease are reported every year, making it the most common vector-borne disease in America.

Because of these problems stemming from the deer's population growth, some areas have not only issued doe permits but also increased the allowable harvest to as many as 12 deer per hunting season. In essence, the white-tailed deer is so successful that it is fast approaching its maximum sustainable population.

In Florida the white-tailed deer is nowhere near as common as it is in other Southeastern states. The deer population in Southwest Florida is estimated at around 20,000. It can readily be seen in places such as Myakka River State Park, Babcock Ranch, Big Cypress Preserve, and the Audubon Corkscrew Swamp Sanctuary. The white-tailed deer is strictly an herbivore and is capable of browsing as well as grazing. It thrives on mast, which consists of the fallen acorns, leaves, and fruit found in oak and other forests. Capable of leaping over most range fencing, deer can often be found along the wooded edges of cow pastures and agricultural lands.

Worldwide there are 36 recognized species of deer (Family: *Cervidae*) and hundreds of subspecies. The largest member of this family is the North American moose (up to 1,750 lb), while the smallest member is the Southern pudu (17.5 lb) found in the lower regions of South America. In Florida the Key deer, a diminutive subspecies of white-tailed deer found solely in the lower Florida Keys (Big Pine Key and No Name Key), is listed as endangered, with an estimated 300 left in the wild. A mature Key buck weighs less than a German shepherd.

The primary cause of deer mortality is legal hunting, with roughly100,000 animals taken every year in Florida and more than 6 million harvested annually across the U.S. Illegal hunting and automobile collisions also take a heavy toll. Deer is the primary food source for Florida panthers, and the fawns are killed by coyotes, bobcats, and black bears. Although deer can live to be 20 years old in captivity, wild deer seldom survive longer than a decade.

❒ __________ **Man** (*Home sapiens*) Other names: Mankind, Human Beings, Humans, etc. / Status: FL = thriving, IUCN = LC / Length: n/a / Height: 5-6 ft (1.5-1.8 m) / Weight: 120-160 lb (54-72.5 kg) / Life span: to 100 years; the average Florida life span is 77.5 years / Reproduces: year-round throughout their extensive range / Found: AC, coastal, near coast, inland / Months found: **JFMAMJJASOND.**

Modern mitochondrial DNA evidence indicates that all modern humanoids originated in southeastern Africa, possibly near what is now Tanzania, approximately 160,000-200,000 years ago. Scientific studies of our DNA have demonstrated that a single woman, commonly referred to as Mitochondrial Eve, is believed to have given birth to the family of man thousands of generations ago. It is also held that the mutation that set humanoids apart at this time had to do with an improvement in the ability to process language, a gift that has proven indispensable to our hunting skills and the ability to survive in many of the harshest environments on earth.

The first wave of humanoids to arrive in Florida were the Paleo-Indians who came approximately 12,000 years ago. Aside from a few burial mounds, middens, and stone tools found scattered across the state, little is actually known about these ancient peoples. We know they used Clovis projectile points and atlatls, giving them the ability to kill prey much larger than themselves. They were hunter-gatherers who followed the big game they relied on for feeding their tribes, which seldom numbered more than 100 individuals. It is widely believed that these Paleo-Indians were responsible for the first wave of early extinctions across North and South America. This extinction, commonly called the Pleistocene overkill, resulted in the eradication of many of the megafauna that once inhabited peninsular Florida. These included the giant beaver, armadillo, mammoth, mastodon, cave bear, ground sloth, and saber-toothed tiger. By 6500 B.C., with most of the large, easy game eradicated, the Paleo-Indians began to settle down into distinct regions that would later give rise to the historic tribes that were living in Florida at the time of first European contact in the early 1500s. These tribes included the Calusa, Ais, Apalachee, Cherokee, Miami, Tequesta, Timucuan, and Tocobago.

With the discovery of the New World by the Spanish in 1492 the die was cast for dramatic changes for the indigenous peoples of Florida. By the 1700s almost all

We can do it! Courtesy Wikimedia Commons

of the original Native Americans were gone and the state's population was far less than it was 200 years earlier. The eradication of these native peoples did not come from warfare or enslavement, though both were factors, but predominantly from their lack of resistance to European diseases such as influenza, small pox, mumps, and measles. The state started repopulating after the Civil War ended in 1865 and has continued expanding its human population ever since.

A series of historical events, from the crash of 1929, through the Great Depression and World War II, kept Florida's human population in check. Following the end of WWII, the 1950 census put the Sunshine State's population at 2,771,305 people. By 1960 that number had increased to 4,951,560, and by 1990 the number of people calling themselves Floridians had climbed to 12,937,926. The 2010 census shows Florida with a population of 18,801,310, or an overall density of 359 people per square mile. Although this is far less than the density of nearby Haiti, which is the western world's most populated nation with a density of 900 per square mile, Florida still has the highest human density in the entire Southeast United States.

This continued growth in Florida puts unsustainable pressures on wild spaces and will, without question, eventually cause the extinction or extirpation of many of the birds, mammals, reptiles, and amphibians described in this book. Every year more than 160,000 acres of wilderness lands are destroyed to make way for agricultural, industrial, urban, and suburban uses. Given this relentless growth, in 100 years Florida, the land of flowers, could well resemble the deforested and barren western end of the island of Hispaniola, which today includes the nation of Haiti.

The 2050 population of Florida is projected to be 32,000,000 people, making the loss of hundreds of thousands of acres of open spaces, parks, and preserves inevitable. Although the impact of human development is not to be underestimated, it must be noted that we are also the primary cause of the importation of invasive species such as black and brown rats, Brazilian pepper, melaleuca trees, Australian pines, Nile monitor lizards, Burmese pythons, peacock bass, and a host of insects and pathogens, such as fire ants and West Nile virus. In short, we arrive with tremendous baggage that further impacts the native flora and fauna.

Not everything we do is bad for wildlife. Certain species thrive in the face of changes wrought on the landscape by humanoids. These species include the white-tailed deer, coyote, wild turkey, mourning dove, house sparrow, black rat, raccoon, and feral pig, among others. Species that were once seriously endangered such as the American alligator and southern bald eagle are on their way to recovery. The most serious threat to the future of all Florida wildlife will be the continued pressure to change large tracts of preserved land to accommodate humans. As the population increases over the coming decades, virulent political movements will deride the need for open spaces in favor of alternative uses. This could translate to a death sentence for animals such as the Florida panther, Florida scrub jay, and crested caracara, as well as many other species that are struggling to cope with human neediness.

To put these population numbers into perspective, consider that there are approximately 100 wild panthers left in Florida. There are three to four times that many people shopping in any given Wal-Mart or Publix right now. There are fewer than 200 breeding pairs of snowy plovers in the state and fewer than 5,000 manatees. Humans are the most populous mammal in Florida, and all indications are that this trend will continue for centuries to come. How we come to terms with our population growth and the impacts of that intractable growth will determine the future of all wild things in Florida. The future is, in the end, up to us.

❐ ________ **River Otter** (*Lutra canadensis*) Other names: common otter / Status: FL=stable but extirpated in 11 states and endangered in 13 more, IUCN=LC / Length: with tail, 26-42 in. (66-106 cm) / Height: n/a / Weight: 11-30 lb (5-14 kg) / Life span: to 20 years / Reproduces: near water in suitable dens; will often use another animal's burrow or find natural holes in riprap and tree roots / Found: AC, coastal, near coast, inland / Months found: **JFMAMJJASOND**.

There are 12 species of otters worldwide. This mammal appears on every continent except Australia and Antarctica. The largest of the freshwater species is the giant otter of the Amazonian basin, weighing up to 66 pounds; the shorter but heavier sea otter of the north Pacific coastline can weigh up to 90 pounds. Throughout its range, otter populations are declining as a result of habitat loss and the harvesting—often overharvesting—of its meat and fur.

The only aquatic member of the weasel family, the otter is renowned for its playfulness. Curious and entertaining to observe, it is a favorite at zoos and aquariums. Children seem to gravitate to the otter naturally, as they do with the dolphin. In the wild, the otter is far less playful but is still known to slide down a muddy embankment repeatedly or engage in other behavior that can only be described as play. Aside from primates, the sea otter is the only mammal known to use tools when harvesting food.

The diet of the river otter that inhabits all of Southwest Florida is largely made up of fish, both fresh and saltwater species. It prefers slower-moving fish such as gar, panfish, and catfish, but will catch just about any fish it can. It also eats crawfish, horseshoe crabs, frogs, coots, ducks, beetles, and on rare occasions, muskrats and marsh rabbits.

An otter is capable of holding its breath for up to four minutes, diving as deep as 60 feet and swimming as fast as six miles per hour. Its fur is so dense

Otter family

© Heather Green

Two River Otters © Dick Fortune and Sara Lopez

that its skin never gets wet. Young otters, even though they are born with webbed feet and will eventually spend most of their lives in the water, must be taught how to swim by their parents. The otter is very vulnerable to water quality issues and will quickly abandon any polluted lakes or streams. Poor water quality has been a major factor in the otter's decline worldwide.

The river otter is slowly being reintroduced into states where it once was plentiful, including Iowa, Kansas, Kentucky, Nebraska, New Mexico, North and South Dakota, Ohio, Oklahoma, Tennessee, and West Virginia. Over the past few centuries it has been trapped for its high-quality fur, causing localized extinctions. Most states now prohibit trapping and hunting the otter.

The otter is preyed upon by alligators, bobcats, coyotes, and wolves. Because of its unusual method of running, arching its back high into the air as it runs, it is very vulnerable to automobile collisions. Oil spills are especially troublesome for the otter. The Exxon *Valdez* spill in Prince William Sound killed more than 1,000 sea otters and dozens of river otters within days.

An offshore spill in Florida would not impact the river otter as severely because it tends to favor freshwater over saltwater or brackish environments. The same cannot be said for the manatee, a species that could literally be wiped out along the gulf should a spill like the Deepwater Horizon occur close to the coastline.

❒ ________ Everglades Mink (*Mustela vison evergladensis*)

Other names: Mink, American Mink / Status: FL = threatened, IUCN = LC / Length: 17-24 in. (43-61 cm) / Height: n/a / Weight: 1.32-2.2 lb (.59-1 kg) / Life span: to 10 years / Breeds: in midwinter, with the kits born in the spring / Found: CC, near coast, inland / Months found: **JFMAMJJASOND**.

The mink is a member of a larger family of weasels and polecats (*Mustela*), which contains 16 different species worldwide. Only two of these species are mink: the American mink and the European mink. The Everglades mink is a subspecies and is the only mink found in southern Florida; two different subspecies inhabit the northern tier of the state.

Everglades MInk Courtesy Wikimedia Commons

The mink population in Southwest Florida today is limited to Everglades National Park, Big Cypress National Preserve, and the Fakahatchee Strand in Collier County. Historically, this relative of the ferret could be found as far north as Lake Okeechobee, but agricultural development has reduced its range to the very southern tip of the state. Seeing an Everglades mink in the wild is nearly impossible. Quick, solitary, and secretive, this small carnivore is rare to witness even in areas where it is more common, such as Canada and the northern Midwest.

The mink was once trapped and hunted to the point of eradication throughout much of its range, in pursuit of its prized fur, but today almost all mink stoles and coats are fashioned out of farm-raised animals. Although this practice is controversial, as is the wearing of any fur products, mink farming has helped reduce the pressure on wild harvesting and allowed the mink to regain some of its former range. It can now be found throughout the eastern U.S., across all of Canada all the way to Newfoundland, and in Alaska.

The mink is a strict carnivore. Its razor-sharp teeth and incredible speed make it a formidable predator. Semi-aquatic, it feeds primarily in freshwater streams, lakes, and ponds where it catches crayfish, small fish, and frogs. On land it is capable of killing animals much larger than itself and has been known to prey on rabbits, ducks, rice rats, birds, mice, and voles. It in turn is taken by coyotes, great horned owls, and foxes.

❒ ______ **Raccoon** (*Procyon lotor*) Other names: common raccoon, coon, masked bandit / Status: FL=stable, IUCN=LC / Length: 16-28 in. (41-71 cm w/o tail) / Height: 9-12 in. (23-40 cm) / Weight: 8-20 lb (3.6-9 kg) / Life span: up to 20 years in captivity / Reproduces: in hollow logs, shallow burrows, under buildings / Found: AC, coastal, near coast, inland / Months found: **JFMAMJJASOND**.

Mother and juvenile raccoon © Dick Fortune and Sara Lopez

If there is one wild mammal you can expect to see in Southwest Florida, it is the raccoon. Intelligent, curious, and persistent, the raccoon has adapted well to the behavior of humans. Because of this, and in large part owing to the raccoon's ability to access both residential and commercial refuse containers, its population in urban and suburban settings is artificially higher than could be sustained with natural foraging alone. Studies have indicated that this population of urbanized raccoons can be 20 times denser than in a natural wooded environment of the same size.

In the wild the raccoon eats insects, lizards, acorns, plants, worms, nuts, and fruit. It will take young marsh rabbits, raid bird nests for eggs and chicks, and dig up sea turtle nests to reach the eggs. The raccoon also eats the small black dates found in the fall on cabbage palms, as well as the figs of the strangler fig. In urban and suburban settings it subsists predominantly on residential and commercial garbage, ferreting out everything from old milk cartons to greasy chicken wings. The word *raccoon* is derived from *arakun*, an Algonquin word meaning "he scratches with his hands."

The raccoon found in the southern part of Florida is much smaller than its northern counterpart. It also tends to have longer legs to help dissipate heat. In Colorado one raccoon was verified to weigh 62 pounds, while most Florida

Taking a dip © Dick Fortune and Sara Lopez

raccoons seldom exceed 10 pounds. The raccoon is a very distant relative of the giant panda and the bear, but it is much more closely related to the similar-looking coati and ringtail, found in Central and South America.

The raccoon is one of the primary carriers of rabies in the United States. It is also prone to picking up canine distemper. If you see a raccoon behaving strangely, especially if it appears to be disoriented or unusually aggressive, call the local authorities and report the animal. Never approach or attempt to capture a wild raccoon as it has very sharp teeth, strong jaws, and can inflict a vicious bite. If you are bitten by a raccoon, you will have to undergo rabies treatments.

The life span of a wild raccoon is much shorter than that of a captive raccoon. The young are preyed upon by owls and eagles, while the adult is taken by alligators and bobcats. Many of the young, who are weaned by 16 weeks, simply starve to death. Raccoon litters range from two to five kits; 90 percent fail to survive past the age of two. Much of the adult and juvenile mortality comes from of automobile collisions. The age-old adage "Speed kills!" should be amended to "Speed kills wildlife!" Please obey the posted speed limits and be on the lookout for wildlife, especially at night, dusk, and dawn when the majority of wild animals become active.

Look for raccoons just about anywhere, but especially the same night you put your garbage cans out for pickup. Considered as intelligent as dogs, local raccoons seem to know the garbage pickup days better than do most husbands.

❐ __________ **Striped Skunk** (*Mephitis mephitis*) Other names: Skunk, Stinker, Pepe / Status: Florida = stable, IUCN = LC / Length with tail: 20-30 in. (50-75 cm) / Height: n/a / Weight: 6-8 lb (2.73-3.6 kg) / Life span: to 6 years / Found: AC, coastal, near coast, inland / Months found: **JFMAMJJASOND.**

Two striped skunks near den Courtesy Wikimedia Commons

Known for its stinking spray, the striped skunk is a relatively uncommon sighting in Florida, even as roadkill. The active ingredient in its spray is a chemical called butyl mercaptan, and can be easily detected by humans and other animals from as far away as a mile. If you happen to get skunk spray on your clothing, the best method for removing the odor is by burying the clothing for a week, then washing it in tomato juice or ammonia, then, as a final step, taking it out to the garbage can and throwing it away. Removing the spray from your person is equally as disconcerting. (Hydrogen peroxide and baking soda can be used to help eliminate the smell.)

The skunk is a known vector of rabies, and any skunk seen during daytime hours should be avoided because it is likely sick. The striped skunk is predominantly crepuscular or nocturnal in foraging habits, coming out at dusk and returning to its den as dawn approaches. It eats just about anything it can find, from carrion to garbage, insects to mice. Because of its odiferous spray, its only consistent predation is by two common owls in Florida, the great horned and the barred owl, neither of which appears to be affected by the skunk's odor.

In Florida the striped skunk does not go dormant, as it does in the more northern reaches of its range, all the way into Canada. It feeds heavily in the summer and fall to build up enough stored fat to survive the long northern winter. It has one litter a year, producing between four and six young with each litter.

With its scent glands removed, a skunk can actually be kept as a pet, though because of its susceptibility to the rabies virus, it is not generally regarded as a preferred wild pet. It can also deliver a nasty bite, though if reared properly, it is not prone to biting its owner. Skunk pelts were once highly desired, marketed creatively as "Alaskan sable." Today, however, wild skunk trapping is mostly a thing of the past.

❒ ________ **Spotted Skunk** (*Spilogale putorius*) Other names: Weasel Skunk, Civet Cat, Hydrophobia Cat, Civvy Cat / Status: FL = stable, IUCN = LC / Length with tail: 21-25 in. (53-63.5 cm) / Height: n/a / Weight: 1-3 lb (.50-1.4 kg) / Life span: to 6 years / Reproduces: in the spring and fall / Found: AC, near coast, inland / Months found: **JFMAMJJASOND.**

Spotted Skunk © Bob Gress

The spotted skunk is roughly half the size of the striped skunk, and like its cousin, it is equipped with a strong, foul-smelling secretion that is sprayed at potential predators accurately at a distance of up to 15 feet. The spotted skunk stores about one tablespoon of the malodorous oil in its glands, making it capable of up to five discharges in a row.

The chemistry of the spotted skunk's secretion differs from the striped skunk in that it contains several different components, and many people feel that the spray of this smaller animal is even worse than that of the striped skunk. Hydrogen peroxide and baking soda can be used to help eliminate the smell should you be unfortunate enough to get sprayed by either skunk species.

The spotted skunk is an agile climber, known to frequent oak trees in search of acorns and other forage. Its primary diet consists of insects, including beetles, cockroaches, and grubs, but like its larger cousin, it will eat just about anything—berries, acorns, nuts, birds, rodents, larvae, lizards, snakes, and domestic chickens. This skunk gets its nickname, weasel skunk, from its ability to climb and move quickly when attacking small mammals and birds. It is an agile and formidable predator.

The spotted skunk, even more than the striped skunk, was once trapped heavily for its fur. In another example of clever marketing, spotted skunk skins were sold as "marten fur." Today most "marten fur" is farm raised, as the spotted skunk is readily domesticated and is a fairly common house pet.

Because of its defensive spray, the spotted skunk is seldom taken by bobcats or coyotes, but it is killed by owls, snakes, and alligators since the smell does not affect any of these predators. The only other mortality comes at the hands of humans, both from vehicle encounters and nuisance trapping.

❒ ___________ **Opossum** (*Didelphis virginiana*) Other names: Virginia opossum, common opossum, 'possum / Status: FL=stable, IUCN=LC / Length w/o tail: 15-20 in. (38-51 cm) / Height: n/a / Weight: 9-13 lb (4-6 kg) / Life span: to 7 years / Breeds: does not establish a nest but tends to wander, carrying the young along, raising two litters yearly, with up to 10 tiny opossums in each litter / Found: AC, coastal, near coast, inland / Months found: **JFMAMJJASOND**.

Opossum in the grass © Judd Patterson, JuddPatterson.com

North America's only marsupial, the opossum, along with the armadillo, is a fairly recent immigrant to Florida. The opossum is a native of South America, migrating into North America more than 2 million years ago over the Isthmus of Panama. Around the early 1600s, when the first European settlers were arriving in the northeastern United States, the opossum's range extended only as far north as Virginia, but it has since dramatically expanded. This is in large part a result of the animal's ability to adapt to the changes humans make to the environment and to increasingly moderate winters (i.e., climate change—which is also attributed to human activity). The opossum, like many of the well-established mammals, birds, and reptiles covered in this book, has done well by riding on the coattails of the recent success of us clever monkeys out of Africa.

In 1608, Captain John Smith, upon discovering this unusual animal, described it as such: *"An Opassom hath an head like a Swine, and a taile like a Rat, and is the bignes of a Cat. Under her belly she hath a bagge, wherein she lodgeth, carrieth, and sucketh her young."*

Unknown in Europe, the opossum was such a curiosity that in the early 1500s the explorer Pinzón brought one back to present to the Spanish court of King Ferdinand and Queen Isabella. The royals were amazed to find a creature that raised its young in a pouch and had 13 teats and a prehensile tail. Because the opossum also came with a foul odor—secreted involuntarily from its scent glands whenever it "plays 'possum," or pretends to be dead—it quickly fell out of favor with the royal court.

There are more than 75 species of opossum in the New World, but only one of these, the common opossum, has made it to North America. The rest range from southern Chile to Central America and vary in size from the tiny Formosan mouse opossum, weighing less than an ounce, to the largest member of the family, the Virginia opossum, which now thrives throughout Southwest Florida. There are aquatic opossums, tree-dwelling opossums, and shrew opossums. Although of the same order (*Marsupialia*) as the kangaroo and koala bear, the opossum is not directly related to the Australian orders of marsupials. Various opossum species have been introduced into New Zealand, where the invasive bushy-tailed opossum now numbers more than 60 million and presents an environmental nightmare to the native flightless birds and plant life of that remote island.

The opossum is not considered a very intelligent creature, having a brain size roughly six times smaller than a similar-size raccoon. It has a good sense of hearing and an acute sense of smell but relatively poor eyesight. Oddly enough, the opossum has more teeth (50) than any other mammal in North America (humans have 34).

An omnivore, the opossum will eat just about anything, including garbage, carrion, frogs, snakes, venomous snakes (the opossum is immune to rattlesnake and cottonmouth bites), small mammals, worms, fruit, insects, and grubs. It should never be fed or handled, as it is capable of inflicting a painful bite.

The wild opossum seldom lives beyond two years. It is heavily preyed upon by owls, bobcats, hawks, panthers, raccoons, dogs, coyotes, and foxes. Because it is slow moving and nocturnal, its single largest source of mortality today is deadly encounters with vehicles. It tends to freeze when approached by an automobile and will sometimes play dead as the car gets closer, never a good choice to make.

❐ ________ Nine-banded Armadillo (*Dasypus novemcinctus*)

Other names: long-nosed armadillo, armadillo, Hoover hogs, road pizza, possum on the half shell / Status: FL=stable, IUCN=LC / Length: 15-23 in. (27-57 cm body only) / Height: n/a / Weight: 12-22 lb (5-9.5 kg) / Life span: to 15 years / Reproduces: in long deep burrows along river banks and in sandy soils / Found: AC, coastal, near coast, inland / Months found: **JFMAMJJASOND**.

Another recent Florida import, the nine-banded armadillo is now fairly common throughout Southwest Florida. The name *armadillo* means "little armored one" in Spanish. Like the opossum, the armadillo is an immigrant from South America, probably coming into Central America and Mexico during the same time period as the opossum, roughly 2 million years ago (this is referred to as

Why did the armadillo cross the road? © Dick Fortune and Sara Lopez

the Great American Interchange in scientific works). Its northern migration into the United States is a far more recent event, having been first noted north of the Rio Grande River in 1880. Once into Texas, the species continued drifting north and east, reaching the Florida Panhandle in the 1920s.

A second East Coast population was established after a pair escaped from a small zoo in Cocoa, Florida. The two populations met in the early 1970s, and now the species is firmly entrenched from the Florida Keys to the Georgia border. It continued to expand its range to the north and east, eventually inhabiting most of the lower United States to just north of the Ohio River Valley. Found only in the New World, the 20 species of armadillo range in size from the 130-pound South American giant armadillo to the tiny and endangered fairy armadillo. The three-banded armadillo, native only to South America, has the unique ability to roll itself up completely when threatened, looking like an oversized, plated softball.

The armadillo can become a lawn and garden problem. Primarily an insectivore, it uses its long, powerful snout and sharp claws to ferret out grubs and worms from the soil. Its erratic digging patterns can make quick work of a well-manicured lawn. The best way to handle this behavior is with some patience and the knowledge that it eats more than 200 pounds of insects a year, meaning it will leave you with fewer cockroaches, termites, ants, and other troublesome insects to contend with. It also eats amphibians, reptiles, fungi, tubers, and carrion.

Although it can coil itself into a ball, this behavior offers little protection from bobcats, panthers, and alligators that are able to reach the armadillo's unprotected belly or crunch through its shell. Because of its high reproductive rate and the protection its shell offers, however, the armadillo is thriving. One fascinating aspect of its reproduction is that the nine-banded armadillo always gives birth to four identical offspring. Another interesting aspect of its reproduction is that even though the armadillo breeds in July, its gestation period is delayed, resulting in a February birth, an unusual 10-month cycle.

The biggest cause of mortality is from automobile collisions. When startled, the armadillo has an even worse response to oncoming cars than the opossum: it

Portrait of an armadillo

© Dave Irving

usually either stands upright to sniff the oncoming vehicle or jumps straight into the air, making a collision with the car inevitable.

Commonly eaten in South America and said to taste like pork, very few armadillos are hunted or consumed in North America. Although mostly nocturnal, it will venture out of its burrow at dusk and dawn and can be spotted on rare occasions. Sadly, its nickname, road pizza, indicates the most likely sighting you will have of a nine-banded armadillo in Southwest Florida.

❐ ________ **Eastern Cottontail** (*Sylvilagus floridanus*) Other names: Bunny Rabbit, Rabbit, Cottontail, Peter Rabbit / Status: FL = stable, IUCN = LC / Length: 14-18 in. (35-45 cm) / Height: n/a / Weight: 2-4 lb (1.1-1.8 kg) / Life span: to 3 years / Breeds: up to seven litters a year / Found: AC, near coast, inland / Months found: **JFMAMJJASOND**.

Worldwide there are 44 species of rabbits and hares. The rabbit thrives on every continent except Antarctica and can even be found in Greenland. Florida claims only two of this diverse and widespread family (*Leporidae*): the eastern cottontail and the smaller marsh rabbit. A population of black-tailed jackrabbits, originally brought in to train racing greyhounds, has taken up residence at the Miami International Airport, but it is not native to Florida.

Eastern Cottontail © Blake Sobczak

The rabbit is a prolific breeder. It can have up to seven litters a year, with as many as 12 kits per litter. With an average litter of five, a single cottontail can have 35 kits a year. The female reaches breeding age at three months, meaning that over its lifetime, a rabbit can have 105 to 252 offspring. There is a reason for this incessant flood of newborns, and that lies in the next staggering statistic: 85 percent of all eastern cottontails do not survive the first year of life. Literally every carnivore in the Sunshine State has rabbit on its regular menu. It is preyed upon by red-tailed hawks, eagles, owls, foxes, coyotes, bobcats, dogs, panthers, mink, weasels, bear, rattlesnakes, and hunters. The rabbit's high reproduction rate, therefore, is directly tied to its long-term survival as a species. This is a fairly common adaptation in nature that is seen in other mammals such as field mice, rats, and many fish and insect species. If most of your offspring get eaten, you had better learn to have lots of them if your species plans to survive.

One rather odd behavior of the rabbit is that it eats its own excrement directly from its anus, a practice known as *coprophagia.* It is widely believed that by reprocessing the digestive material through its intestines twice, it extracts certain vitamins and proteins that survive the first digestion, similar to what a cow does by chewing its cud.

When hunting and shooting the Florida cottontail, you should take care when cleaning your catch, because it often carries tularemia, or rabbit fever, which can cause high fever, lethargy, anorexia, septicemia, and even death in humans. The microbe causing the disease is killed upon cooking, but gloves should be used to avoid contracting the disease when dressing the rabbit and handling the raw meat.

❐ ______________ **Marsh Rabbit** (*Sylvilagus palustris*) Other names: marsh hare / Status: FL=stable statewide but endangered in the Lower Keys, IUCN=LC / Length: 17 in (43 cm) / Height: n/a / Weight: 2.2-2.6 lb (1-1.2 kg) / Life span: to 7 years / Reproduces: in abandoned burrows of gopher tortoises and armadillos or in dense thickets / Found: AC, coastal, near coast, inland / Reproduces: year round / Months found: **JFMAMJJASOND**.

One of the most peculiar habits of the marsh rabbit is its tendency to let go with a strange, lizard-like squeal when startled. It is a bizarre sound coming from such an adorable little rabbit and when first encountered can startle the unsuspecting naturalist.

Commonly seen eating grass and other vegetation along trails and roadways, the marsh rabbit is the bread and butter of many of Florida's predators, especially bobcats, hawks, and owls. Although a member of the cottontail family, the marsh rabbit does not have a fluffy white tail. It has smaller ears than

Marsh Rabbit © Charles Sobczak

the cottontail and prefers wetter environments. The marsh rabbit will actually swim across tidal passes to inhabit other barrier islands. It ranges all the way north to Virginia and west to Alabama.

The marsh rabbit is a strict herbivore and eats a wide variety of vegetation. It is a game animal in Florida, as it is in most of its range. Because a subspecies, *Sylvilagus palustris hefneri* (named after Hugh Hefner of *Playboy* fame), located in the lower Florida Keys, is endangered, the marsh rabbit is not hunted south of the Everglades.

It would be easy to think that the marsh rabbit is also prone to roadkill, but in fact it is rare to see one hit by an automobile. Like the white-tailed deer, the marsh rabbit appears to be adapting to the automobile. Its primary cause of mortality is predation, including being taken by alligators when swimming.

❒ ______________ **Nutria** (*Myocastor coypus*) Other names: Coypu, Nutra-rat / Status: FL = expanding range, IUCN = LC / Length: 16-24 in. (40-60 cm) / Height: n/a / Weight: 11-20 lb (5-9 kg) / Life span: to 12 years / Breeds: year round / Found: AC, near coast, inland / Months found: **JFMAMJJASOND**.

Nutria feeding © Cottbus courtesy Wikimedia Commons

An invasive species introduced into the Tampa area in the 1950s from the released stock of the fur trade industry, this large rodent in now established in every area of Florida except the Keys. This species originated in South America, where it thrives in the swamps and wetlands of the Amazon all the way to the southern tip of the continent at Tierra del Fuego.

The nutria resembles a cross between a beaver and the capybara, the largest living rodent. A large nutria can weigh more than 20 pounds. In Maryland, where there is a large feral population, the nutria has caused extensive damage to wetlands in the Chesapeake Bay region. Today both Louisiana and Maryland have state-sponsored eradication programs and offer bounties on the nutria.

Although fairly common in Florida, the nutria has yet to pose a serious risk to the environment here. In the Everglades it is a common prey for another invasive, the Burmese python. It is also taken by bobcats, coyotes, alligators, and panthers. It is still raised for its fur in some regions, but the demand worldwide has fallen dramatically. The meat of the nutria is reputed to be quite delicious and low in cholesterol, but attempts to market it have, for the most part, failed. In Kyrgyzstan and Uzbekistan nutria meat is sold as "poor-man's meat."

The nutria is strictly a herbivore, with large front teeth similar to those of beavers. Its tail resembles the muskrat's. Because it is so widespread, this import from South America is more than likely here to stay.

❒ ____________ **Eastern Gray Squirrel** (*Sciurus carolinensis*)

Other names: squirrel / Status: FL=stable, IUCN=LC / Length: with tail, 16.5-22 in. (42-55 cm) / Height: n/a / Weight: 14-18 oz (400-510 g) / Reproduces: in the forks of trees or abandoned tree cavities, mostly live oaks, and has two litters a year / Found: AC, coastal, near coast, inland / Months found: **JFMAMJJASOND**.

Gray squirrel on railing © Gareth Pinckard

This adaptive arboreal animal is common in Southwest Florida. The gray squirrel is a member of the *Rodentia* order of mammals, which consists of

Gray squirrel with a peanut © Gareth Pinckard

30 families, 389 genera, and some 1,702 species—more than 40 percent of all mammals. Other members of the order include the beaver, gopher, mouse, rat, porcupine, paca, capybara, and chinchilla.

Predominantly vegetarian, the gray squirrel survives on acorns, buds, seeds, fungi, and fruit. It eats insects and larvae and an occasional bird egg but does not have a major impact on nesting birds or their chicks. The squirrel is preyed upon by bobcats, feral cats, and snakes. The single largest cause of mortality among adult squirrels is hunting; an estimated 500,000 gray squirrels are harvested annually in Florida alone.

In Florida the gray squirrel is found predominately in deciduous forests of oak and other hardwoods. It has two litters a year and is very prolific. Although it prefers nesting in the forks of trees, in nests called dreys, it will on occasion build its nest in attics and under eaves, much to the consternation of the people living in those houses.

❒ ______________ **Fox Squirrel** (*Sciurus niger*) Other names: Monkey-faced Squirrel, Raccoon Squirrel, Stump-eared Squirrel / Status: FL = threatened, IUCN = LC / Length: 17.7-27.6 in. (45-70 cm) / Height: n/a / Weight: 1.1-2.2 lb (.50-1 kg) / Life span: to 12 years / Breeds: up to two litters annually / Found: AC, near coast, inland / Months found: **JFMAMJJASOND.**

Fox squirrel with acorn Courtesy Wikimedia Commons

Three subspecies of this large North American squirrel live in Florida: Sherman's fox squirrel, Carolina fox squirrel, and mangrove or Big Cypress fox squirrel. Once a legal small game animal in Florida, recent population declines have prompted the Florida Fish and Wildlife Conservation Commission to change the fox squirrel's status and ban the hunting of any fox squirrel in the Sunshine State. Because a fox squirrel can reach a sizable three pounds, this ruling has not gone over well with hunters, and poaching of fox squirrels is fairly common throughout the state.

While the Sherman's fox squirrel is listed as species of special concern and the Big Cypress squirrel is listed as threatened, the Carolina fox squirrel, whose range runs from the northern tier of Florida well up into the Appalachian forests, is not in any imminent danger. The trouble is that in regions where these subspecies overlap, it would prove all but impossible for most hunters to distinguish one kind of squirrel from the other.

The rarest by far is the Big Cypress squirrel (*Sciurus niger avicennia*). It can be found only in southern Lee and all of Collier County. The best places to see a Big Cypress fox squirrel are the Big Cypress National Preserve and the Audubon Corkscrew Swamp Sanctuary in Collier County. This elusive creature also has a preference for the numerous golf courses found throughout Collier County, where it is known to beg for food.

The Big Cypress fox squirrel is best identified by its coloration, which tends to be a chestnut red underside and a dark, almost black coat with grizzled tips. All fox squirrels have 20 teeth (grey squirrels have 22) and strong incisors, allowing them to pry open the hard seeds they prefer to feed upon. These include the seeds located inside the longleaf pine cone, as well as other nuts and plant forage such as acorns, cypress seeds, cabbage palm fruit, fungi, and the inner bark of certain trees. The fox squirrel has also been known to eat bone, bird eggs, nestlings, moths, beetles, birds, frogs, and even dead fish.

Although it is an agile climber, the fox squirrel spends more time on the ground than in the trees. It buries nut and seed caches in numerous locations throughout its 40-acre range, a behavior called *scatter hoarding*. It often forgets many of its buried nuts, which ultimately sprout into new trees, making the fox squirrel the Johnny Appleseed of the forest.

Although no longer hunted, the fox squirrel is attractive to plenty of other predators, including bobcats, owls, and coyotes. With good management, hopefully this beautiful squirrel will roam the backcountry of Florida for generations to come.

❐ ______________ **Eastern Mole** (*Scalopus aquaticus*) Other names: Common Mole / Status: FL = stable, IUCN = LC / Length: 5-6.5 in. (12.7-16.5 cm) / Height: n/a / Weight: 2.6 oz (75 g) / Life span: to 3 years / Reproduces: one liter a year / Found: AC, near coast, inland / Months found: **JFMAMJJASOND.**

In Florida the eastern mole rarely builds the characteristic molehill. Instead it prefers to make long continuous tunnels just beneath the surface of the earth. A single tunnel was once measured to be more than 3,300 feet long! The eastern mole is extremely good at digging in Florida's dry, sandy soil, which is the habitat

Eastern Mole Courtesy Wikimedia Commons

it prefers. A healthy mole can dig a hole and bury itself in five seconds. The chances of actually seeing an eastern mole in Florida are extremely slim since it spends its entire life underground.

Its underground life also makes it difficult to study. We do know it is virtually blind, able only to distinguish dark from light with what remains of its eyes. It is a prodigious insectivore and can eat from 25 percent to 100 percent of its own body weight in a day. Its diet consists of earthworms, slugs, snails, centipedes, larvae, scarab beetle grubs, and ants. When an insect accidentally breaks through into an open tunnel, the mole senses the intrusion and scurries over to devour the intruder.

The mole we find in South Florida tends to be smaller and darker than those found in the East and Midwest. It ranges all the way into the very southern sections of Ontario. When the mole comes into contact with any of Florida's many golf courses, it is, for obvious reasons, not very welcome. Most of these nuisance moles are trapped or poisoned.

The mole has a single litter of two to seven pups per year, which suffer from a high mortality rate. As many as two-thirds of its offspring are unable to find suitable habitat in time to avoid predation. The mole pups must leave their mother's tunnel territory and travel above ground in search of their own two- to five-acre range. The young, defenseless moles are taken by coyotes, foxes, snakes, and shrews. Take a good look at the photo in this article because, in all likelihood, it's the only mole you will ever actually see.

Marine Mammals

❐ ____________ **West Indian Manatee** (*Trichechus manatus*)
Other names: sea cow, sea siren / Status: FL=endangered, IUCN=V / Length: 10-15.2 ft (3.1-4.6 m) / Weight: 880-3,300 lb (400-1,500 kg) / Life span: to 60 years / Reproduces: a slow reproductive rate of one calf every two to five years, generally born in the spring / Found: SC, ChC, LC, CC, coastal / Months found: **JFMAMJJASOND**.

Until 1768 there were five species of *Sirenia* (manatees) in the world. First discovered and scientifically identified by German naturalist Georg Steller in 1741 off of three subarctic islands in the Steller Sea, the Steller's Sea cow was the largest of the five species. Feeding exclusively on giant kelp, this 10-ton manatee did not have teeth but crushed the algae using two huge bony plates. It was too large to submerge itself and thus became an easy target for seal and whale hunters in the north Pacific. Growing to a length of 27 feet, the slow-moving, docile Steller's Sea cow was hunted to complete extinction within 27 years of its discovery.

The West Indian manatee is the second-largest member of this order. The female once obtained a length in excess of 15 feet and a weight approaching two tons. Today the average length is 10-12 feet. The other three remaining species are the West African manatee, similar in habits and size to the West Indian; the Amazonian manatee, which inhabits the freshwater system of the Greater Amazonian basin; and the dugong, which has a whale-shaped tail and is more closely related to the extinct Steller's Sea cow.

The closest land-based relatives to the manatee are two very different mammals: the elephant and the hyrax, a rabbit-size herbivore from Africa. The manatee adapted to its salt- and freshwater environment beginning in the Miocene period, some 26 million years ago.

The manatee is an herbivore, eating a variety of aquatic vegetation from turtle grass to freshwater reeds. An adult can consume up to 65 pounds of vegetation a day. Because it roots out these grasses, it also consumes vast amounts of sand. This gritty diet wears down its front teeth, which are replaced from back to front throughout its life; the manatee is one of only a few mammal species on earth that has this adaptation. The shark has a similar tooth replacement system, although for different reasons.

Because of its docile nature and the ease with which *Homo sapiens* have been able to harvest the manatee, all five species have been dramatically impacted by man. Ample archaeological evidence proves that the West Indian manatee has been hunted unabatedly since the arrival of the first Paleo-Indians into Southwest Florida approximately 12-14,000 years ago. This continuous harvesting, until the passage of the Endangered Species Act (1973) and the Marine Mammal Protection Act (1972), has greatly reduced the manatee's former range and placed the animal on the endangered species red list (vulnerable) of the IUCN.

The meat of the manatee is said to be delicious, similar in texture and taste to the finest cuts of beef (think filet mignon). The Calusa Indians, Cuban fishermen, and early settlers all ate manatee. Native Americans used manatee hide for war shields,

West Indian Manatee © Judd Patterson, JuddPatterson.com

canoes, and shoes, the fat for oil, and the bones for "special potions." Hunting the manatee in the United States was officially banned in 1893, but poaching this gentle giant continues today.

Because of its enormous size, the manatee is almost never taken by sharks, saltwater crocodiles, or alligators. The number-one cause of manatee death is cold water, which results in hypothermia. Florida is the very northern extent of the manatee's range, and the recent wave of long, cold winters has resulted in the death of hundreds of these gentle giants.

The second leading cause of death is boat collisions. Because of its slow speed and large size, almost every adult manatee in the state has been scarred by boat propellers on its head, back, or tail. Biologists use these ubiquitous scars to identify individual manatees in any given range. Since a manatee swims at less than five miles per hour, it is no match for boats with 300-horsepower engines speeding across an

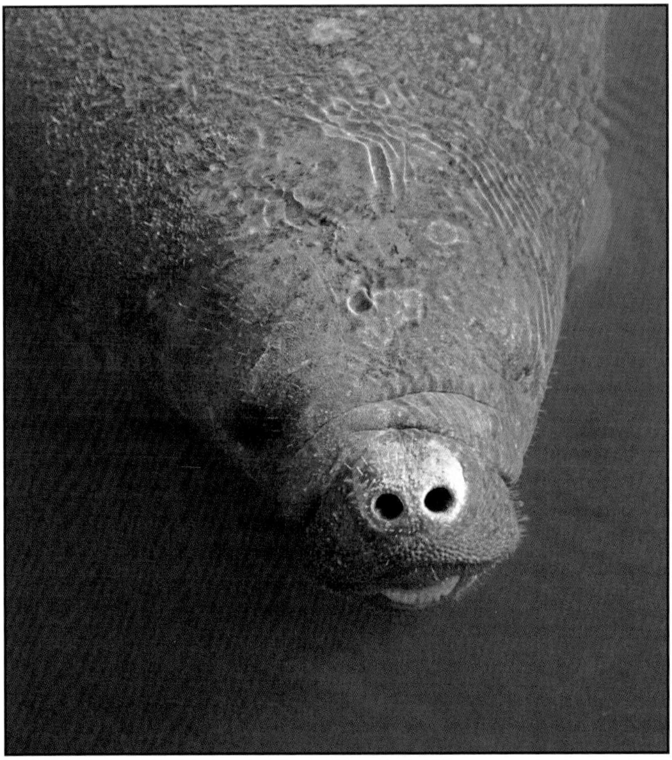

This is how we usually see them

© Dick Fortune and Sara Lopez

estuary at 60 miles an hour. Laws requiring boaters to slow down in manatee zones are instrumental in saving this species, though they are often ignored by hurried boaters. Another major cause of manatee deaths is red tide.

One reason the manatee population cannot recover easily is the animal's incredibly slow reproductive rate. It has one calf every two to four years and, depending on availability of mates, may go years without having a calf at all. Although rare, the sea cow will, on occasion, have twins. A highly intelligent mammal, the manatee requires extended nursing periods to teach the calf where to find food, when to migrate to warm waters, and what dangers to avoid.

The combination of a docile nature, slow speed, delicious meat, and low reproductive rate has not been a prescription for success when competing with a smart, fast, and hungry hominoid. Estimates are that between 1,500 and 2,500 manatees are living in the coastal areas of Florida. In 2007 the United States Fish and Wildlife Service attempted to upgrade the status of the manatee from endangered to a lesser, threatened status. There was an immediate outcry from organizations such as Save the Manatee Club, which argued that changing the status would result in far less regulation and would certainly contribute to increased manatee mortality throughout its range.

In winter one of the best places to see manatees is near the warm outflow of the Florida Power and Light plant off of Palm Beach Blvd. (State Road 80) in North Ft. Myers. Attracted by the warm water, manatees gather by the hundreds in the power-plant discharge canal that flows into the Orange River, a tributary of the Caloosahatchee. Although the water is stained from tannic acid, the chances of seeing one of these rare animals is almost 100 percent as they seek shelter from winter cold fronts from mid-October through the end of March. Go to www.leeparks.org for a complete printout of hours, directions, and additional information. Manatee Park is also covered in the eco-destination section of this book.

The manatee may well prove to be a litmus test for us. It is what biologists refer to as a "keystone species." That means that in protecting this docile marine mammal we must also protect the expansive grass flats upon which it feeds. These grass flats in turn support hundreds of additional species, such as sea horses, spotted sea trout, pinfish, tunicates, and shrimp. Like an umbrella, everything beneath the manatee is sheltered from the adverse impacts that seem to follow our every step. Hopefully, 100, or 1,000, years from now and because of our dedication to conservation, someone reading this text will still be able to share their moment in time with West Indian manatees. That cannot be said today about the Steller's Sea cow.

❐ ____________ Bottle-nosed Dolphin (*Tursiops truncatus*)

Other names: flipper, porpoise, dolphin, common bottlenose dolphin / Status: FL=stable, IUCN=LC / Length: 7.5-9.5 ft (2.28-2.9 m) / Weight: 330-1,400 lb (150-650 kg) / Life span: to 25 years / Reproduces: in the back bays and estuaries year round / Found: SC, ChC, LC, CC, coastal / Months found: **JFMAMJJASOND**.

Dolphin feeding on striped mullet © Dick Fortune and Sara Lopez

Any visitor to the coastal regions of Southwest Florida would be hard pressed not to spot a bottle-nosed dolphin over the course of a week's stay. The dolphin is often observed swimming in the gulf just off the beaches or can be spotted inshore while kayaking or canoeing through the Intracoastal Waterway, back bays, and estuaries that grace the coastline. The dolphin can also be readily observed from many causeways and bridges where it gathers to feed in the huge tidal flows. It is always a delight to watch and shows little fear of man.

Worldwide there are 32 different species of toothed whales, the family (*Delphinidae*) to which the bottle-nosed dolphin belongs. The largest member of this extensive family is the orca, or killer whale, which can reach a length of 30 feet and weigh as much as 9,000 pounds. The orca will attack and eat bottle-nose dolphins given the opportunity.

Mother and juvenile Courtesy Wikimedia Commons

The dolphin is an extremely social animal, living in groups of 15 to 100 animals called pods. Several larger pods have been identified with as many as 1,000 members. The dolphin has a unique and special relationship with man. Tales of bottle-nosed dolphins saving drowning sailors date back to Greek times, although recent studies indicate that this may be part of an instinctive behavior.

With a brain size larger than our own, the bottle-nosed dolphin has been studied extensively for decades. Highly intelligent, it has been trained to perform in places such as Sea World in Orlando, as well as to carry out tactical exercises including the detection of sea mines and enemy divers for the U.S. Navy. In some parts of the world the dolphin has actually learned to cooperate with local fishermen, driving schools of fish into their nets, then taking any escaping fish as a form of payment for services rendered. In 1997, at an observation station in Shark Bay, Australia, female dolphins were discovered to be using marine sponges on their rostrums (the pointed beak of dolphins) to protect them from damage while searching for prey along the sandy sea floor. This primitive use of tools, along with teaching the skill to their daughters (culture), is found only in giant sea otters, whales, and great apes.

The dolphin makes a wide array of sounds and noises, including many in ranges far above the audio capacity of the human ear. An interesting study is being conducted by neurologists at Caltech University in California where scientists have verified that the dolphin has distinctly shaped brain cells (called von Economo neurons), which are found only in the great apes, elephants, and whales. This may be biological evidence for behaviors that were once considered to be strictly human.

These elongated neuron cells appear to be responsible for language, as well as empathy, trust, guilt, embarrassment, love, and humor.

Another amazing though seldom discussed fact about the bottle-nosed dolphin is its highly unusual sexual activity. Like humans, the dolphin is one of only a handful of species that has no set breeding or calving season, but mates and procreates any time of the year. Numerous studies of both wild and captive bottle-nosed dolphins have verified that this marine mammal engages in group sex, bisexuality, cross-species sex with the spotted dolphin, and homosexual activity. Some male pairs appear to partner for life, while the female dolphin, who may raise up to 10 calves in her breeding lifetime, will have a different father for every calf she births. Recent evidence indicates that as many as 1,500 species of wild animals engage in some form of homosexual or bisexual activity, including giraffes and chimpanzees. Some of this behavior may be related to social bonding and establishing dominance.

The dolphin eats mostly fish but also takes squid and octopus. Along the west coast of Florida its predominant prey is mullet, which it stuns with its powerful tail, flipping the fish high in the air, then swimming back to dine on it while it is still stunned and disoriented. Several dolphins will sometimes be seen working together as a team to corral schools of striped mullet in a behavior similar to that of lion prides or wolf packs. High-frequency vocalizations help the dolphins coordinate these mullet hunts.

Although the temptation exists to feed this marine mammal, it is never advisable. It can make the dolphin dependent on humans for food and can lead to it becoming entangled in cast nets and fishing line, resulting in injury or death. Another concern is that the dolphin can and will bite. Feeding any wild animal, from shark to alligator, is not advisable.

In the wild, the dolphin has several natural predators. In Australia and New Zealand, scores of bottle-nosed dolphins display scarring from past shark attacks. In Florida the bottlenose has been known to be killed by bull, tiger, and hammerhead sharks, as well as killer whales. It is also infrequently killed when it gets entangled in crab-pot lines and gill and trawl nets. Water pollution, especially raw sewage that can bring on diseases, nutrient-rich dead zones from the overuse of fertilizers, and red tides also take their toll. The dolphin is also known for stranding itself en masse on beaches, though no one has been able to explain this bizarre and often fatal behavior. It is still killed and eaten in Japan (see the documentary film, *The Cove*) and parts of China but is protected throughout most of its range.

One of the most difficult things for a self-centered species such as *Homo sapiens* to come to grips with is the concept that we may not be the most advanced or sophisticated species on the planet. While it is obvious that we, as toolmakers and tool users, can out compete and hence eradicate the entire world population of bottle-nosed dolphins, it is another thing entirely to admit that the dolphin has a better world to live in. It doesn't make tools because in its environment it doesn't need them. It has far more habitat than humans because the oceans cover more than 70 percent of the globe. It has no gravity to contend with, ample food, few natural predators, a complex and rich social environment, and in all probability some kind of language, though we have yet to decode or understand it. It is a hard pill to swallow, the concept that we are just a vain species in second place, but it may well prove true in the end.

Additional Mammals of Southwest Florida

❒ __________ **Southern Short-tailed Shrew** (*Blainna carolinensis*) Other names: Shrew, Sherman's Shrew / Status: FL = species of special concern in some counties, IUCN = LC / Length w/o tail: 4 in. (10 cm) / Height: n/a / Weight: 0.5-0.75 oz (14-21 g) / Life span: 2 to 3 years / Found: AC, coastal, near coast, inland / Months found: **JFMAMJJASOND.**

© Wikimedia Commons

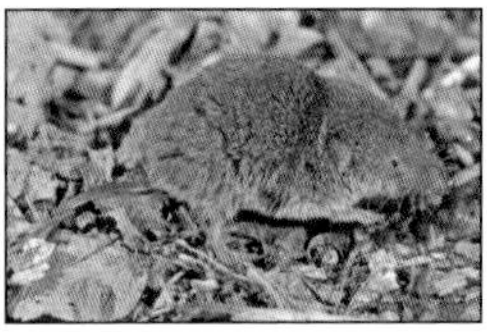
© Bob Gress

❒ ______ **Least Shrew** (*Cryptotis parva*) Other names: Shrew, Bee Shrew / Status: FL = stable, IUCN = LC / Length w/o tail: 3 in. (7.6 cm) / Height: n/a / Weight: 0.1-0.2 oz (4-6.5 g) / Life span: to 2 years / Found: AC, coastal, near coast, inland / Months found: **JFMAMJJASOND.**

❒ ____ **Hispid Cotton Rat** (*Sigmodon hispidus*) Other names: cotton rat / Status: FL=stable, IUCN=LC / Length with tail: 11-20.5 in. (27-52 cm) / Height: n/a / Weight: 2.75-4.25 oz (80-120 g) / Life span: to six months / Reproduces: in marshes, wetlands, and mangrove regions having up to 15 offspring per litter and breeding up to nine litters per year / Found: AC, coastal, near coast, inland / Months found: **JFMAMJJASOND**.

© Bob Gress

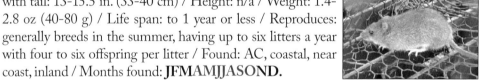

❒ ____ **Marsh Rice Rat** (*Oryzomys palustris*) Other names: Rice Rat, Rice Field Mouse, Swimming Rice Rat, Florida Marsh Mouse / Status: FL = stable, IUCN = LC / Length with tail: 13-15.5 in. (33-40 cm) / Height: n/a / Weight: 1.4-2.8 oz (40-80 g) / Life span: to 1 year or less / Reproduces: generally breeds in the summer, having up to six litters a year with four to six offspring per litter / Found: AC, coastal, near coast, inland / Months found: **JFMAMJJASOND.**

© Wikimedia Commons

❒ ____ **Black Rat** (*Rattus rattus*) Other names: ship rat, roof rat, palm rat, house rat, Alexandrine rat, Old English rat / Status: FL=thriving, IUCN=LC / Length: with tail, 13.6-18 in. (34-45 cm) / Height: n/a / Weight: 2.5-10.5 oz (70-300 g) / Reproduces: breeds year round and can have up to six litters a year with 10 offspring per litter / Found: AC, coastal, near coast, inland / Months found: **JFMAMJJASOND**.

© Wikimedia Commons

© Wikimedia Commons

❒ __________ **Norwegian Rat** (*Rattus norvegicus*) Other names: brown rat, Norway rat, wharf rat, common rat / Status: FL=thriving, IUCN=LC / Length: with tail, 20 in. (50 cm) / Height: n/a / Weight: 9-12 oz (250-350 g) / Life span: to 18 months / Reproduces: year round and is a prolific breeder / Found: AC, coastal, near coast, inland / Months found: **JFMAMJJASOND**.

❒ _______ **House Mouse** (*Mus musculus*) Other names: mouse / Status: FL=thriving, IUCN=LC / Length with tail: 5-7.8 in. (12-19 cm) / Height: n/a / Weight: 0.35-0.88 oz (10-25 g) / Reproduces: breeds year round having up to 10 litters per year with as many as 14 offspring per litter / Found: AC, coastal, near coast, inland / Months found: **JFMAMJJASOND**.

© Wikimedia Commons

❒ _______ **Cotton Mouse** (*Peromyscus gossypinus*) Other names: Key Largo Cotton Mouse / Status: FL = stable, IUCN = LC / Length with tail: 7-8 in. (17.8-20 cm) / Height: n/a / Weight: 1-2 oz (28-56 g) / Life span: to 6 months / Reproduces: in Florida the cotton mouse breeds year round / Found: AC, coastal, near coast, inland / Months found: **JFMAMJJASOND.**

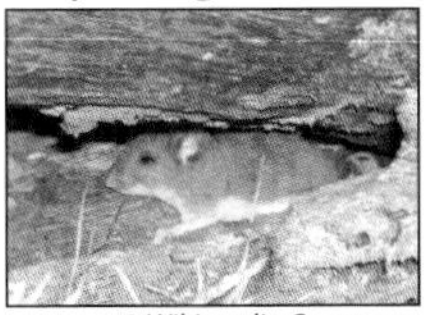

© Wikimedia Commons

❒ _______ **Mexican Free-tailed Bat** (*Tadarida brasiliensis*) Other names: Brazilian free-tailed bat / Status: FL=stable but a species of special concern in several states, IUCN=LC / Length: 3.5 in. (9 cm) / Wingspan: 12.5 in. (32 cm) / Weight: 0.43 oz (12.3 g) / Life span: to 18 years / Reproduces: in caves, under overpasses, in crevices, and in bat houses / Found: AC, coastal, near coast, inland, nocturnal / Months found: **JFMAMJJASOND**.

© Jennifer Beltran

©Jennifer Beltran

❒ _____ **Northern Yellow Bat** (*Lasiurus intermedius*) Other names: yellow bat / Status: FL=stable, IUCN=LC/ Length: 2.8 in. (7 cm) / Wingspan: 14-16 in. (35-40 cm) / Weight: 0.5-1.1 oz (14-31 g) / Life span: to 20 years / Reproduces: in hanging Spanish moss and cabbage palms / Found: AC, coastal, near coast, inland / Months found: **JFMAMJJASOND**.

❒ _______ **Big Brown Bat** (*Eptesicus fuscus*) Other names: brown bat / Status: FL=stable, IUCN=LC / Life span: to 19 years / Length: 4.33-5.12 in. (11-13 cm) / Wing span: 12.99 in. (33 cm) / Weight: 0.81 oz (23 g) / Life span: to 19 years / Reproduces: one litter a year that is born in the spring / Found: AC, coastal, near coast, inland / Months found: **JFMAMJJASOND**.

© Jennifer Beltran

❒ _____ **Evening Bat** (*Nycticeius humeralis*) Other names: Cypress Bat, Bat / Status: FL = stable, IUCN = LC / Length: 3-4 in. (7.5-10 cm) / Wingspan: 10-11 in. (25-27.5 cm) / Weight: 0.17-0.50 oz (5-14 g) / Life span: to 5 years / Reproduces: one litter of one to three pups a year, usually twins that are born in June / Found: AC, coastal, near coast, inland / Months found: **JFMAMJJASOND.**

© Jennifer Beltran

❒ _______ **Eastern Pipistrelle** (*Pipistrellus subflavus*) Other names: Bat / Status: FL = stable, IUCN = LC / Length: 3-3.5 in. (7.5-9 cm) / Wingspan: 8-10 in. (21-26 cm) / Weight: 0.2-0.3 oz (5-8 g) / Life span: to 15 years / Reproduces: mating occurs in late summer, the sperm is stored in the female, and the pups, generally twins, are born in the late spring or early summer / Found: AC, coastal, near coast, inland / Months found: **JFMAMJJASOND.**

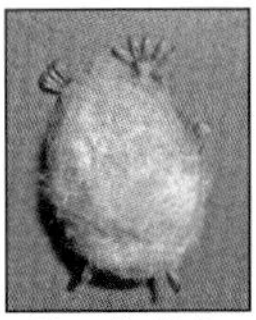

©Jennifer Beltran

Alligator Hatchling

The Reptiles and Amphibians of Southwest Florida

Florida leads the nation in the number of native and invasive reptiles and amphibians. There are an estimated 184 species of frogs, toads, lizards, caecilians, snakes, turtles, terrapins, tortoises, newts, salamanders, and crocodilians found within its borders. Regrettably this number is increasing annually with the introduction of more invasive species such as the Burmese python in the Everglades and the Nile monitor lizard in northern Lee County. For the most part, Florida's native species are holding their own, with only a handful, such as the indigo snake and gopher tortoise, showing signs of vulnerability.

Southwest Florida has somewhere around 95 different species of reptiles and amphibians, a number far too large to cover thoroughly in this work. Many of these creatures spend much of their life under leaf litter or in the soil itself and will rarely, if ever, be seen by anyone other than the scientists who study them. For those of you reading this who love the study of herpetology, a complete list of all the additional species, with thumbnail photos when available, is included at the end of this section.

For most of us, Florida's reptiles consist of alligators, a handful of commonly seen snakes, and the fascinating, if environmentally challenging, infamous invasives.

© Dick Fortune and Sara Lopez

These include the green and spiny-tailed iguanas, the huge pythons roaming our swamps, and the numerous outbreaks of local invasions by released pets such as the Tokay gecko, curly-tailed lizard, cane toad, and the massive and problematic Nile monitor lizard. The challenge here is trying to keep up with what's new this year that can be added to a list of invasive species that is already far too long.

Southwest Florida's climate is close enough to the tropics that many of these foreigners can survive the mild winters and wet, steamy summers without much trouble. Whether from tropical Africa, such as the African rock python, or from Southeast Asia, such as the reticulated and Burmese pythons, these snakes feel right at home in the vast wetlands and swamps of Lee, Collier, Hendry, Monroe and Glades counties. Hopefully, recent changes in the law regarding the importation of these exotics and microchip identification of the original owners will help curtail this escalating problem.

Included in this section are a number of our most fascinating cold-blooded creatures. Some are absolutely huge, weighing more than half a ton (American crocodile), while others are simply amazing, such as the greater siren (*Siren lacertina*), which is capable of surviving, encased in a mud cocoon, without any food or water for up to two years during times of drought. Each has its story to tell, and all of them are compelling.

What lies beneath? © Dick Fortune and Sara Lopez

Crocodilians

❒ ______ **American Alligator** (*Alligator mississippiensis*) Other names: gator, el lagarto (Spanish), alli / Status: FL=species of special concern, IUCN=LC / Length: 8.2-14.5 ft (2.5-4.4 m) / Weight: 160 (female)-1,200 lb (male) (72-544 kg) / Life span: to 66 years / Reproduces: throughout SW Florida / Found: AC, coastal, near coast, inland / Months found: **JFMAMJJASOND.**

The alligator, along with birds, survived the fifth extinction some 65.5 million years ago at the end of the Jurassic period. Its lineage goes back 230 million years. Despite the obvious difference in appearance, the alligator is more closely related to birds than to other cold-blooded animals such as turtles, snakes, and lizards. The alligator builds nests, lays eggs, and remains with its offspring for as long as a year after they are hatched—all characteristics commonly found in birds. Another similarity is that, like birds, the alligator, especially the American alligator, is very vocal.

Because the alligator was over-harvested for its hide and flesh, the species was placed on the endangered species list in 1967. At that time experts estimated that fewer than 400,000 alligators were left in the state of Florida. Restrictions on hunting, strong conservation efforts, and the alligator's ability to reproduce rapidly all helped to bring this primeval predator back, and 20 years later its status was changed to a species of special concern. Today an estimated 1-1.5 million alligators are living in Florida. Only Louisiana has more, with an estimated 1.5-2 million living in its swamps and bayous.

The American alligator has the strongest bite of any living animal, measured in laboratory conditions at 2,125 pounds per square inch. The only known animal to have ever exceeded that level of bone-crushing jaw power was Tyrannosaurus rex.

The alligator can hold its breath and remain underwater for as long as six hours. It does this by shunting off the blood supply to its extremities and circulating all of its blood between its brain and heart. It can survive temperatures as low as 26° F but only for brief periods. Its optimum functioning temperature is 89° F.

The alligator has a high reproductive rate. After breeding in the spring, the male and female separate. The female generally lays one clutch of 20 to 50 eggs, covering them with decaying vegetation that generates heat and serves as an incubator. The warmer eggs (90-93° F) become males, and the cooler eggs (82-86° F) become females. Hatchling mortality is very high, with 93 percent succumbing to predation before reaching sexual maturity around seven years of age. Almost every animal living in the wetlands habitat eats alligator eggs or hatchlings, including herons, egrets, raccoons, otters, snakes, bobcats, panthers, bears, fire ants, fish, crocodiles, and other alligators.

The alligator has a unique relationship with birds, and nowhere does that play out more dramatically than in rookeries. Most rookeries are located on islands or along wetlands where alligators are readily found. In an unusual symbiotic relationship, birds use the alligator as a reptilian sentinel guarding their nests. When a hungry raccoon, bobcat, or rat attempts to swim to an island of nesting egrets and herons, the resident alligator stands ready to kill the predator long before it can reach its intended target. The alligator has little trouble drowning a predator as large as a Florida panther. The bobcat poses little danger to a creature with a hide as thick and almost as effective as a bulletproof vest. There is a price to be paid for this service, however. The alligator is not above snatching fledglings from low-hanging branches, and if a nestling should end up on the ground or in the water below, the alligator quickly disposes of the wayward chick.

American Alligator eating a Burmese python US Fish & Wildlife Service

The alligator eats just about anything. It has the strongest digestive acids found in any living creature, capable of converting hair, bone, and teeth into usable proteins. Its diet consists of fish, birds, turtles, snakes, mammals, and amphibians. Hatchlings also eat insects, snails, mollusks, frogs, mice, and rats. A mature bull alligator will eat deer, wild boar, and cattle and will even take down prey as large as black bears and horses.

People are often tempted to feed alligators, but this is not a good idea. Once this pattern is established, the animal equates humans with food, and anyone approaching the reptile is in grave danger.

You should never swim in any Southwest Florida freshwater lakes, ponds, or rivers, unless they are clearly marked as safe for swimming. In the water, which is the alligator's domain, it takes only a small alligator to bite and drown a person. The alligator is capable of very quick attacks and can actually propel itself almost completely out of the water with a few swishes of its massive tail. Since 1948 there have been more than 346 unprovoked alligator attacks on humans in Florida and 22 fatalities. (For more information about alligators and these attacks, read *Alligators, Sharks & Panthers: Deadly Encounters with Florida's Top Predator—Man,* published by Indigo Press in 2007.)

Alligators are common throughout Southwest Florida. During the rainy season they travel over land and find their way into many residential ponds, golf courses, and manmade canals. They are easy to spot while kayaking along Fisheating Creek, the Peace and Myakka rivers, as well as the marshes and swamps of interior Florida. You should always take care when in the immediate area of any alligator. Female alligators are very protective of their offspring, and males can be aggressive. The alligator is primal and beautiful and with proper management should be a part of Florida for all time.

❐ ______ **American Crocodile** (*Crocodylus acutus*) Other names: American croc, saltwater croc, salty, croc / Status: FL=threatened, IUCN=VU / Length: 9.8-13 ft (3-4 m) / Weight: 380-840 lb (173-382 kg) / Life span: to 70 years / Reproduces: Along the southern edge of Florida, mostly in Monroe County / Found: LC, CC, coastal / Months found: **JFMAMJJASOND.**

The crocodile is a rare sighting in Southwest Florida. Extremely vulnerable to cold temperatures, it seldom ranges as far north as Lee County, with the vast majority of the region's sparse population living along the southern coastal edge of Collier County, predominantly in the Ten Thousand Islands and Everglades National Park. Because this region represents the northern edge of its range, the Florida croc seldom grows as large as those found farther south. In South America there have been official reports of 20-foot crocs. The longest croc skull ever measured was 28.6 inches (72.6 cm) and came from a mature male estimated to be at least 22 feet long. That animal would have weighed more than 3,000 pounds. A crocodile this size could eat a horse. Whole.

Waiting for a snack. © Dick Fortune and Sara Lopez

Sadly, because of over-harvesting and hunting, the American crocodile is in trouble throughout its range. Venezuela banned the taking of crocodiles in 1972. Other nations such as Costa Rica and Cuba have followed suit, and in these locales the croc is making a slow but steady recovery from the brink of extinction.

American Crocodile close-up © Dick Fortune and Sara Lopez

Ironically, a major reason for the recovery of the American crocodile in Florida, where its numbers are now estimated at more than 1,500, is the nuclear power plant at Turkey Point, built in 1972 south of Miami near Homestead. The power plant encompasses some 3,300 acres of wetlands through which a series of canals were dug to assist in cooling the water used to keep the reactor core from overheating. Shortly thereafter, a handful of American crocodiles discovered these canals, which teemed with fish that thrived in the artificially warmed waters.

Like the endangered manatee that frequents the Florida Power and Light plant in North Fort Myers at Manatee Park, the Florida croc has found a safe haven at Turkey Point. The power plant has become the primary recovery engine for the entire Florida population, helping to upgrade the status of this impressive animal from endangered to threatened in 2007.

Despite its size, the crocodile is far less aggressive than the alligator toward humans. Aside from an injured croc named Zulu that killed the man who shot him in 1925 on the outskirts of Miami, there has never been a confirmed attack by any crocodile in the U.S., though there have been several fatal attacks reported in Mexico and Central America. You should never approach a crocodile in the wild. If its nest is anywhere near, the female crocodile will kill in defense of its eggs. The croc, like the alligator, is capable of explosive charges that occur almost faster than the human eye can follow. In the water the croc can obtain speeds of 20 miles per hour and is capable of launching its 2,000-pound body completely out of the water with its powerful tail.

Turtles and Tortoises

❐ ______ **Loggerhead Sea Turtle** *(Caretta caretta)* Other names: loggerhead / Status: FL=threatened, IUCN=EN / Length: 36-42 in. (.92-1.1 m) / Weight: 250-350 lb (113-158 kg) / Life span: to more than 100 years (maximum life span is still unknown) / Reproduces: lays multiple clutches along the coastal beaches during the summer / Found: AC, coastal / Months found: **JFMAMJJASOND.**

Juvenile Loggerhead Sea Turtle Courtesy Wikimedia Commons

By far the most common nesting sea turtle found in Southwest Florida, the loggerhead has been visiting the gulf beaches since they were formed thousands of years ago. The loggerhead used to be much larger than is commonly found today. When Ponce de Leon arrived in Florida there were turtles weighing 1,000 pounds or more. A loggerhead of 600 to 800 pounds was quite common until the turn of the 20th century. Today, a loggerhead approaching 500 pounds is considered remarkable.

The range of the loggerhead is worldwide, though only in tropical or subtropical waters. There are still a couple of sites where up to 10,000 females nest every year: one is in South Florida and another in Oman at the tip of the Saudi Arabian peninsula. Approximately 68,000-90,000 loggerhead turtle nests are recorded in the United States every year. The world population of the species is unknown.

The loggerhead is an omnivore, eating jellyfish, Portuguese man o' war (a toxic jellyfish the loggerhead is immune to), sponges, small fish, crustaceans, mollusks,

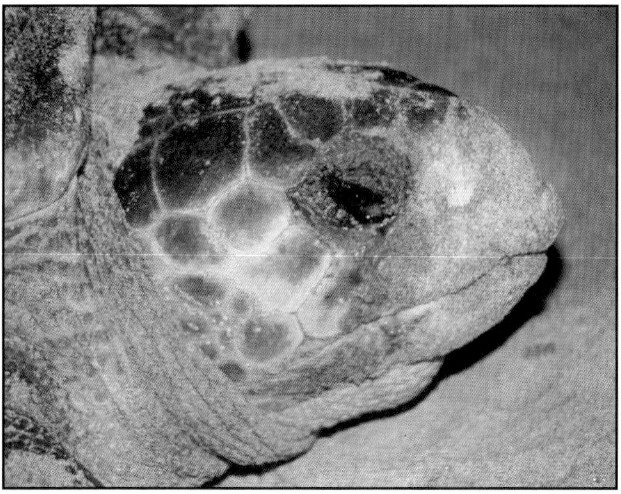

Loggerhead Courtesy SCCF

crabs, and shrimp. Juveniles eat sea grasses and marine worms at first, moving to larger prey as their powerful jaws develop. The adult sea turtle has few natural predators. Sharks have been known to bite off turtle limbs but only an extremely large shark is capable of piercing the thick carapace.

The hatchlings are another story. Literally everything preys upon them for the first year of life, including raccoons, dogs, herons, seagulls, crows, birds of prey, ghost crabs, shorebirds, snook, catfish, tarpon, shark, and even fire ants. To counter this constant predation, the female loggerhead can lay as many as four or five clutches of eggs in a breeding season, which may occur only every two or three years. Every clutch holds between 50 and 150 eggs, which helps the species since the mortality rate of sea turtle hatchlings is precariously close to 100 percent. Studies have shown that only one out of every 1,000 sea turtles makes it to adulthood. Therefore, any additional pressure on its fecundity puts its long-term survival in jeopardy.

Once heavily preyed upon by humans, all the world's sea turtles are now endangered. Illegal taking of mature turtles still occurs throughout much of its range. An even larger threat to the population comes from people raiding turtle nests for eggs. Finding a sea turtle nest is not difficult since the female hauls herself up beyond the surf line and leaves a clearly evident crawl track. Eggs are still taken illegally throughout much of the Third World. Roughly the size of a large Ping-Pong ball, the egg is a free source of protein in a hungry world.

Other leading causes of mortality for the loggerhead are long-line fishing and shrimp trawlers, which the turtle gets caught in and drowns. In 1989 the National Marine Fisheries Service required all U.S. shrimp boats to install turtle extruder devices (TEDs). These large metal contraptions allow turtles and larger fish to escape entanglement in the trawling net. TEDs have helped tremendously, but many shrimp fleets throughout the world refuse to install them, or in some instances they fail to work correctly because of improper installation.

Thousands of sea turtles also die annually from choking on plastic trash. To a sea turtle that feeds on jellyfish, a plastic bag or a six-pack ring floating offshore looks like food. Once ingested, this plastic can become lodged in the intestines, causing a slow and painful death. As if these gauntlets aren't enough, still another cause of loggerhead mortality is boat and propeller collisions. This is especially true in the early spring when the loggerhead comes to the surface to mate. Because of these and other impacts, the loggerhead turtle has suffered a 40 percent decline in population in the past decade.

Green Turtle swimming Courtesy Wikimedia Commons

❒ ____________ **Green Turtle** (*Chelonia mydas*) Other names: soup turtle / Status: FL=endangered, IUCN=EN / Length: 3.2-5 ft (1-1.5 m) / Weight: 400-600 lb (181-272 kg) / Life span: to 80 years / Reproduces: lays multiple clutches along the coastal beaches during the summer / Found: AC, coastal / Months found: **JFMAMJJASOND.**

The green turtle has, and always has had, a serious problem—it tastes too good. When a vulnerable animal has to nest on land every two to three years, crawls slightly faster than a snail, weighs as much as 800 pounds, and tastes delicious, its chances of thriving on a planet filled with a subspecies of clever apes with an appetite and an ax are not good.

From Sarasota to Matanzas Pass the early settlers were particularly fond of the green turtle. Its nests were often raided for the eggs, and the adult was a common item on the settlers' menus. There is every reason to believe that this region once had as many green turtle nests as loggerhead nests, and that predation around the turn of the 20th century severely diminished the green turtle population. Today green turtle nests in Southwest Florida are rare events, averaging fewer than a dozen per year.

The green turtle is not named for the color of its carapace, which is actually black. Green is the color of the fat and flesh found beneath the carapace.

Its range was once even greater than that of the loggerhead, extending well down into Australia, the Red Sea, Madagascar, and everywhere in between. Like all sea turtles, the green turtle is an expert open ocean navigator, though the mechanism used for its long transoceanic voyages is unknown. The current speculation is that it has trace elements of magnetic rock in certain parts of its brain, helping it to use the earth's magnetic field to locate nesting sites. It has been known to swim more than 1,400 nautical miles to return to the exact beach where it was born.

Today the green turtle is in serious trouble throughout its range, largely because of human predation. Other than humans, only the 20-foot-plus tiger shark is known to feed on the adult green turtle.

One reason humans prefer the taste of the green turtle is its diet. Unlike the loggerhead, hawksbill, and leatherback, the green turtle is an herbivore feeding on sea grasses, algae, kelp, and seaweed. Its meat is considered a delicacy and today is a product of aquaculture in the Cayman Islands. Green turtle soup can still be found on menus in the Florida Keys and elsewhere in the world.

Oceanic pollution, habitat destruction, shrimp and fish trawlers, egg raids, and illegal hunting of adults all conspire to make the future of the green turtle anything but certain. That's the trouble with tasting so good—it's not a healthy attribute on a planet filled with close to 7 billion hungry mouths.

❐ ______________ **Kemp's Ridley Turtle** (*Lepidochelys kempi*)

Other names: bastard turtle / Status: FL=Endangered, IUCN=CR / Length: 24 in. (60 cm) / Weight: 100 lb (45 kg) / Life span: to 50 years / Reproduces: lays multiple clutches along the coastal beaches during the summer / Found: SC, LC, coastal / Months found: **JFMAMJJASOND.**

The Kemp's ridley sea turtle may well be one of the rarest animals in the world. The last time one is known to have nested in Southwest Florida (on Sanibel) was in 1996. This is one of the smallest of the world's sea turtles, and its numbers have been drastically reduced since Richard Kemp, a fisherman from Key West, first submitted the species for identification in 1906. It is similar to the olive ridley, another seriously endangered sea turtle.

Kemp's Ridley baby turtle Courtesy NOAA

Predominantly a carnivore, the Kemp's ridley survives on mollusks, crustaceans, jellyfish, algae, seaweed, and sea urchins. Because it is smaller than most sea turtles, a fair number of adult ridleys are taken by sharks, goliath grouper, and other large fish.

One of the most unique aspects of the Kemp's ridley turtle is a behavior called *arribada*, Spanish for arrival. At a certain time and date, determined by natural phenomena still not understood, hundreds of these turtles gather near a particular nesting beach near Rancho Nuevo, Mexico; then they all come ashore to nest at exactly the same time.

In Mexico, the skins of these turtles became a popular material for cowboy boots, resulting in tens of thousands of Kemp's ridley turtles being taken during the past

Kemp's Ridley sea turtle release Courtesy Georgia Fish & Wildlife Service

70 years. In 1947 the number of nesting females at Rancho Nuevo was estimated at 89,000; by the mid-1980s that population had been reduced to fewer than 1,000. Fortunately, due to a shortage of raw materials, the turtle-skin boot business has disappeared.

Perhaps as a survival response to the slaughter of these turtles in Mexico, a few have begun to show up in new nesting locations. In 2007, Texas wildlife officials found 128 Kemp's ridley sea turtles nesting near Corpus Christi, and in 2009 some 10,594 hatchlings were safely released along the Texas gulf coast. Perhaps the few individuals that have crawled up to lay their clutches on Sanibel Island have done so in an effort to find a new safe haven, but the future of this small reclusive turtle remains in question.

❒ ______________ Leatherback Turtle (*Dermochelys coriacea*)

Other names: glass eater / Status: FL=Endangered, IUCN: CR / Length: 6-8.4 ft (1.8-2.5 m) / Weight: 1,100-2,000 lb (500-916 kg) / Life span: to 45 years / Reproduces: lays multiple clutches along the coastal beaches during the summer / Found: SC, LC, coastal / Months found: **JFMAMJJASOND.**

On June 3, 2009, Linda Gornick, a volunteer with the Sea Turtle Research and Monitoring Program of the Sanibel-Captiva Conservation Foundation (SCCF) discovered an unusual turtle crawl on the east end of Sanibel. She notified permittee Tom Krekel, who, upon further inspection, determined it was not a loggerhead crawl, but possibly a green turtle or, however implausible, a leatherback crawl. After seeing photos of the crawl, the Florida Fish and Wildlife Conservation

Commission confirmed it was probably a green turtle that had made the unusual tracks up the beach.

The nest was appropriately marked and staked off, and the only thing left to do was to wait for hatching to begin. Two months later SCCF's sea turtle coordinator Amanda Bryant and staff herpetologist Chris Lechowicz were amazed to discover that it was a leatherback nest. They discovered 90 empty eggshells and rescued four live baby leatherback turtles, releasing all of them the following night.

Hatchling leatherback turtle Courtesy SCCF

What is so surprising about this event is that from the earliest records of the Calusa Indians and the early settlers, all the way through the sea turtle research conducted by Charles LeBuff and his Caretta Research team, there had never been a documented leatherback sea turtle nest in all of Lee, Collier, or Charlotte counties. The closest and most recent leatherback nesting occurred in Sarasota County in 2001. The leatherback does nest in the Panhandle and along the East Coast of Florida. It also nests in South America, Africa, India, China, Australia, and Albania. There are only an estimated 34,000 nesting females left in the world.

The leatherback turtle is a spectacular creature, the fourth-largest reptile in the world behind three crocodilians: the Nile and Indo-Pacific crocodiles and the rare freshwater gharial of the Indian subcontinent. The leatherback is not entirely cold blooded. In a mechanism similar to that of the great white shark, it has a counter-current heat exchanger that allows the turtle to maintain a body temperature as much as 32 degrees warmer than the surrounding water. This ability greatly extends the leatherback's range as far north as Newfoundland and as far south as New Zealand.

It is also the deepest-diving and fastest-swimming reptile on earth. It has been documented to dive to a depth of 3,937 feet and obtain a speed of 22 miles per hour. Its front flippers can grow as large as 8.8 feet across, giving it the ability to fly through the water at more than four times the speed of the fastest Olympic swimmer.

The leatherback turtle cruises the open ocean in search of prey. One turtle was tracked covering 13,000 miles in 647 days. It feeds primarily on jellyfish. Its digestive system appears to be immune to the toxins found in jellyfish, some

Leatherback Turtle in open ocean Courtesy Las Boulas National Park

of which are fatal to humans. It has also been known to feed on tunicates and cephalopods such as squid and octopus.

As is true of all sea turtles, the hatchlings suffer high predation, and only one or two leatherbacks in a thousand make it to breeding age. The leatherback turtle does not have a hard-shell carapace for protection as do other sea turtles. Instead, its carapace is covered by a thick, leathery skin embedded with minuscule bony plates. Because of its immense size, only the largest of sharks (great white, tiger, and bull) feed on the leatherback. It may also be attacked by killer whales, but this is not known for sure.

Its largest threat comes from the harvesting of its eggs by humans, which in China and the Caribbean are erroneously considered to be aphrodisiacs. In Southeast Asia, egg harvesting has resulted in the complete eradication of nesting sites along most of the beaches the leatherback once frequented. It is also an accidental by-catch in commercial fishing vessels, long-lining fishing fleets, and shrimp trawlers. Turtle extruder devices are generally too small to free leatherbacks from nets.

Another cause of mortality is intestinal blockage following the ingestion of Mylar balloons and plastic bags, which resemble jellyfish in the open ocean. Chemical and bacterial water pollution also takes its toll on these marine giants. Efforts to save the critically endangered leatherback are taking place worldwide, but sadly, the future of this oceanic voyager remains uncertain.

❐ ________________ **Gopher Tortoise** (*Gopherus polyphemus*)
Other names: Hoover chicken (from the days of the Great Depression), gopher, landlord of the sand / Status: FL=threatened, IUCN=VU / Length: 9.25-14.5 in. (23-37 cm) / Weight: 9-30 lb (4-13.6 kg) / Life span: to 80 years / Reproduces: digs deep, long nesting burrows on dry ground throughout SW Florida / Found: AC, coastal, near coast, inland / Months found: **JFMAMJJASOND.**

Gopher Tortoise at Koreshan State Historical Site Courtesy Florida State Parks

Considered a keystone species, the gopher tortoise plays an important role in the lives of many other creatures. Some 300 to 400 species use active or abandoned gopher tortoise burrows, including the threatened indigo snake, gopher frog, burrowing owl, cotton mouse, rattlesnake, coachwhip snake, and 32 types of spiders. An excellent excavator, the gopher tortoise digs burrows that have been documented to be as long as 47 feet and more than 18 feet deep.

The gopher tortoise is strictly a land animal. It is related to the Galapagos tortoise, which can grow to 880 pounds and is also strictly terrestrial. The easiest way to distinguish the gopher tortoise from another turtle is by its high, dark, rounded shell and its front feet, which are spade-like with heavy protective scales.

The gopher tortoise is known to stop traffic on occasion as it forages. If you discover a turtle or tortoise crossing a road and are unsure what kind it is, take it to the edge of the road and let it continue on but do not release it into any body of water. There is an empty shell at the Clinic for the Rehabilitation of Wildlife (CROW) on Sanibel from a gopher tortoise that was placed into the Gulf of Mexico by a well-meaning but seriously misguided tourist who found it browsing on beach-dune

Gopher Tortoise © Kenneth L. Krysko, UF

vegetation and thought it was a lost sea turtle. The combination of saltwater and wave action quickly drowned the poor gopher tortoise.

No matter the species of turtle you help across any road or bike path, always ferry it along in the direction it was heading. It may be following the scent of a mate, changing habitat, nesting, or looking for food. Returning the animal to where it just came from will likely result in it crossing the same street or intersection a few minutes later, putting itself at risk again. It is now believed that some water turtles can see polarized light and use this ability to navigate over land to find other habitable bodies of water.

The gopher tortoise's natural range runs from extreme southwestern South Carolina across Georgia and into southeastern Louisiana. Its population has been severely impacted by development. Until July 30, 2007, when Florida rescinded the incidental take permits, the gopher tortoise was commonly plowed under by commercial and subdivision developers. It has moved from a species of special concern to its current status as threatened in Florida, and its population statewide is in decline. It has also been impacted by upper respiratory tract disease, which can result in death.

Although predominantly an herbivore, feeding on berries, grass, fruit, and cactus flowers, the gopher tortoise will sometimes scavenge carrion as well. It is preyed upon by a host of creatures, the smallest being the fire ant, which has been known to attack hatchlings. Other predators include gray fox, armadillos, snakes, and raptors. The slow-moving gopher tortoise was once a favorite with early settlers who would, upon finding one, simply turn it over on its back and return later to bring it home for the kettle; hence, the comical but accurate nickname, Hoover chicken.

The best way to find a gopher tortoise is to find an active burrow. It has a home range of two to five miles but generally does not stray more than several hundred yards from its burrow to forage. If you do come upon one, please let it feed and do not pick it up or disturb it. The gopher tortoise is one of only four species of land tortoise remaining in North America. The others are the desert tortoise of California, Nevada, and New Mexico; the Berlandier's tortoise of southern Texas; and the Bolson tortoise of Mexico, which was reintroduced into New Mexico in 2007.

❐ __________ **Ornate Diamondback Terrapin** (*Malaclemys terrapin macrospilota*) Other names: none / Status: FL=species of special concern, IUCN-NT / Length: 5-9 in. (12-23 cm) / Weight: 0.90-1.7 lb (300-1,400 g); the male is much smaller than the female / Life span: unknown / Reproduces: lays up to 3 clutches a year with 6-7 eggs in each clutch / Found: SC, ChC, LC, CC, coastal / **JFMAMJJASOND.**

Ornate Diamondback Terrapin Courtesy Wikimedia Commons

In all four coastal counties of Southwest Florida the ornate diamondback terrapin spends most of its life in and around the mangroves where it forages on carrion, snails, crabs, and salt-marsh plants. Along the Eastern Seaboard and west to Texas it lives in salt marshes. The terrapin is equipped with a special gland next to its eyes that allows it to secrete excess salt. It has one of the most heavily embossed shell patterns of any turtle and a unique spotted lavender skin. It is also becoming extremely rare.

The reason for its demise is simple: it is delicious. Until recently the terrapin was hunted in much of its range for terrapin soup. It has also suffered from coastal development. Its biggest threat today is crab traps, which it enters to feed on the bait, then drowns. There are five subspecies in Florida and two more in its greater range from southern New England to Corpus Christi, Texas.

Ornate Diamondback Terrapin hatchling

❐ ________ **Florida Box Turtle** (*Terrapene carolina bauri*) Other names: box turtle / Status: FL=species of special concern, IUCN=LC / Length: 6.5 in. (16.5 cm) / Weight: 5 lb (2.3 kg) / Life span: to more than 100 years / Reproduces: lays up to 3 clutches of 4-6 eggs each on land / Found: AC, coastal, near coast, inland / Months found: **JFMAMJJASOND.**

Florida Box Turtle © Kenneth L. Krysko, UF

The Florida box turtle is semi-aquatic, at home in both terrestrial and aquatic habitats. In freshwater it prefers to remain in the shallows and does not appear to be a good swimmer. It has a life expectancy of more than 100 years, making it the longest-living organism in this book.

Easily identified by its high, arching domed carapace with bright orange-yellow markings, the box turtle is commonly kept as a pet. Collecting this turtle for the pet industry was recently outlawed, however, and the species is now protected in Florida. Because of the box turtle's popularity, Florida has imposed a two-turtle possession limit.

The box turtle's diet consists of insects, carrion, dung, and toxic fungi. The box turtle cannot be eaten by humans or other mammals because of the build-up of toxicity in its flesh from eating poisonous mushrooms and other fungi. Because of that, the box turtle is seldom preyed upon as an adult. That may be why it is so brightly patterned, much like other toxic and poisonous species. Some juveniles and hatchlings are taken by fire ants, herons, and skunks.

❒ __________ **Florida Softshell Turtle** (*Apalone ferox*) Other names: flatback, pancake turtle, river flyer / Status: FL= stable, IUCN=LC / Length: 6-25 in. (15-63 cm) / Weight: 20-50 lb (9-22.5 kg) / Life span: to 30 years / Reproduces: lays 2-3 clutches of 12-20 eggs in burrows on land / Found: AC, coastal, near coast, inland / Months found: **JFMAMJJASOND.**

Florida Soft Shell Turtle © Sarah Pinckard

A favorite food of the American alligator, the Florida softshell turtle can be found in almost every pond and lake in Southwest Florida. It is easily recognized by its unusually long snorkel-like snout and flat, olive-black carapace, which resembles stretched leather. The largest Florida softshell on record topped the scales at 93 pounds (42 kg). The average size found in this region is 25-35 pounds.

The softshell turtle is capable of pharyngeal breathing. This means it can bypass its lungs by taking in oxygen and releasing carbon dioxide through a special membrane that lines the throat, creating a direct gas exchange with the water. Think of it as a turtle gill device, giving the softshell the unique ability to remain underwater for extended periods of time. It is, in effect, part fish.

The Florida softshell turtle is primarily a carnivore, dieting on insects, crustaceans, mollusks, fish, waterfowl, and amphibians. It has also been known to eat other turtles. Softshell eggs and hatchlings are heavily preyed upon by otters, raccoons, skunks, and snapping turtles. Adults are taken by alligators and humans, who turn it into turtle soup.

On land the softshell turtle can be very aggressive and should never be handled. It is capable of delivering a nasty bite, and because of the habitat it thrives in, infection is a strong possibility.

❒ ______________ **Florida Snapping Turtle** (*Chelydra serpentina osceola*) Other names: common snapping turtle, snapper / Status: FL=stable, IUCN=LC / Length: 10-20 in. (25-50 cm) / Weight: 10-35 lb (4.5-16 kg) / Life span: to 40 years / Reproduces: lays 25-80 eggs in burrows on land / Found: AC, coastal, near coast, inland / Months found: **JFMAMJJASOND.**

Large Florida Snapping Turtle Courtesy Wikimedia Commons

Aside from the sea turtles that nest along our beaches, the Florida snapping turtle and Florida softshell turtle are the two largest turtles in Southwest Florida. In captivity the snapping turtle has been known to grow to 75 pounds; a close relative, the endangered alligator snapping turtle of northern Florida, can reach an astonishing 200-plus pounds.

This turtle, especially when discovered on land, has a powerful bite and an ornery disposition. Picking one up by the carapace is ill advised, as its long neck is capable of reaching halfway back across its body. Picking it up by its tail can injure or kill it. Take extreme care if you come across one of these turtles while it is laying its eggs or crossing over land from one watershed to another.

The snapping turtle is an omnivore, consuming a wide variety of aquatic vegetation, as well as frogs, fish, snakes, other turtles, small birds, and mammals.

Alligators prey on the adult snapping turtle, and the young are preyed upon by herons, otters, and even tarpon. Although nowhere near as common as the cooter, the snapping turtle can sometimes be seen basking on a log but is more likely to be seen when it comes up on land to lay its clutch of eggs in the late spring or summer. The snapping turtle, just like the cooter, is only recently protected from harvesting (July 20, 2009).

❐ ______ **Peninsula Cooter** (*Pseudemys floridana peninsularis*)
Other names: cooter, Florida river cooter / Status: FL=stable, IUCN=LC / Length: 12-15 in. (30-38 cm) / Weight: 6-8 lb (2.7-3.6 kg) / Life span: to 12 years / Reproduces: lays 12-20 eggs near freshwater rivers, lakes, and ponds / Found: AC, coastal, near coast, inland / Months found: **JFMAMJJASOND.**

Peninsula Cooter © Kenneth L. Krysko, UF

Southwest Florida's most commonly seen turtle, the cooter is often observed basking on logs and banks or rising to the surface to breathe in almost any pond, river, or lake in the region. It is readily identified by bright, road-stripe yellow facial markings, although this can sometimes lead to confusion with the Florida redbelly turtle, which has a similar facial pattern. The name *cooter* may be derived from the African *kuta,* which means turtle in several dialects.

Until very recently the cooter was commonly harvested for the dinner table in Florida. On July 20, 2009, U.S. Fish and Wildlife extended full protection to this species, so it is no longer legal to harvest wild cooters.

The mature cooter feeds on aquatic vegetation, while juveniles feed on aquatic insects and tadpoles. This turtle is a favorite food of adult alligators, which can easily crush its shell with powerful jaws. Hatchlings and juvenile cooters are eaten by snakes, great blue herons, raccoons, and otters.

❐ ________ **Red-eared Slider** (*Trachemys scripta elegans*) Other names: red-eared terrapin, pond slider / Status: FL=stable (introduced species), IUCN=LC / Length: 8-12 in. (20-30 cm) / Weight: 3-5.5 lb (1.5-2.5 kg) / Life span: to 40 years / Reproduces: digs nesting burrows on land / Found: LC, coastal, near coast, inland / Months found: **JFMAMJJASOND.**

Originally found only west of the state of Mississippi, this small, colorful turtle early on became the most popular species for the turtle pet trade. In 1958, after several were released into the freshwater canals of Miami, the red-eared slider established a breeding population in Dade County. Over time, with the help of more and more releases from pet owners who grew tired of caring for them, this species has successfully moved into nearby counties, including Collier and Lee.

Red-eared Slider © Kenneth L. Krysko, UF

The red-eared slider is easily identified by the distinctive red marking located directly behind its eye. This slider is an omnivore, feeding on crayfish, carrion, tadpoles, snails, crickets, and wax worms, as well as aquatic vegetation.

Although the red-eared slider does not yet appear to have a major impact on the environment, it is displacing native turtles in other regions. Though not considered invasive, this is an introduced species we should keep an eye on.

❐ ________ **Yellow-bellied Slider** (*Trachemys scripta scripta*) Other names: slider / Status: FL=stable, IUCN=LC / Length: 5-13 in. (13-33 cm) / Weight: 3-5.5 lb (1.5-2.5 kg) / Life span: to 35 years / Reproduces: digs nesting burrows on dry land / Found: AC, coastal, near coast, inland / Months found: **JFMAMJJASOND.**

Originally found only in northern Florida from Levy County across the Panhandle, the yellow-bellied slider has been extending its range southward over the past 50 years. It can now be found in all six Southwest Florida counties.

Since the ban on sales of the red-eared slider went into effect in fall 2008, people have begun farming the yellow-bellied slider in huge numbers, and the spread of this turtle through the pet trade will likely follow the same pattern as the red-eared slider.

Yellow-bellied Slider © Sara Kim

The indigenous yellow-bellied slider is believed to be interbreeding with the introduced red-eared slider, which has led to concern for the future of the yellow-bellied slider and motivated Florida to ban sales of the red-eared slider.

The yellow-bellied slider is a small turtle, rarely exceeding a foot in length in the wild. It is easy to distinguish from the cooter in that it has much more yellow on its face and carapace. Although it starts its life as an omnivore, by the time it reaches maturity almost 95 percent of its diet is derived from aquatic vegetation.

The yellow-bellied, like all turtles, is a common prey for the alligator. Eggs and hatchlings are preyed upon by a variety of species, including herons, otters, other turtles, snakes, fire ants, and raccoons.

❐ ______ **Striped Mud Turtle** *(Kinosternon baurii)* Other names: three-striped mud turtle / Status: FL=stable, IUCN=LC / Length: 5 in. (12 cm) / Weight: 0.35-0.50 lb (160-230 g) / Life span: to 50 years / Reproduces: burrows nest into dry land / Found: AC, coastal, near coast, inland / Months found: **JFMAMJJASOND.**

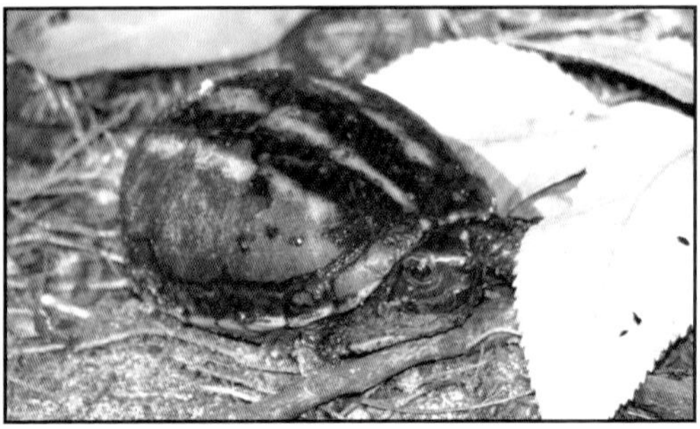

Striped Mud Turtle © Daniel Parker/SCCF

One of the smallest turtles in the world, the striped mud turtle is rarely longer than five inches. Only the narrow-bridged musk turtle from Central America is as tiny. The striped mud turtle can readily be identified by the three distinctive stripes running across the top of the carapace. Its docile disposition and small size make it a favorite of the turtle pet trade. The striped mud turtle is now protected in the Keys but is still captured in the wild throughout most of the state. Because of its small size, the mud turtle is seldom used as food.

An omnivore, the mud turtle feeds on aquatic vegetation but will also eat insects, aquatic animals, and carrion. It is easily caught with small baited hooks. In the wild it can be taken by herons, skunks, raccoons, and alligators.

Snakes

❒ _____ **Eastern Diamondback Rattlesnake** (*Crotalus adamanteus*)
VENOMOUS! Other names: rattler, rattlesnake, diamondback, water rattler / Status: FL = declining, IUCN = LC / Length: 3.5-7 ft (1-2.1 m) / Weight: 10-24 lb (4.5-10.8 kg) / Life span: to 20 years / Reproduces: oviviviparous, giving live birth to 7-21 baby snakes in the summer or early fall / Found: AC, near coast, mainland / Months found: **JFMAMJJASOND.**

The largest rattlesnake in the world, this venomous pit viper is still common throughout Southwest Florida. Once found in Louisiana, Mississippi, Alabama, Florida, Georgia, and South and North Carolina, this snake has been relentlessly persecuted and hunted to extirpation throughout much of its historical range. Today it is reduced to remnant populations in southern Georgia, most of Florida, and parts of southern Alabama.

One reason for the decline of the diamondback throughout the Southeast is development. The rattlesnake prefers upland habitats such as longleaf and slash pine forests. These same habitats are coveted by developers since their dry, sandy soils can readily be turned into strip malls and subdivisions. As a result, the eastern diamondback rattlesnake is fast approaching threatened status because of the continued encroachment on its range.

Rattlesnake © Kenneth L. Krysko, UF

Another cause of the snake's declining numbers is the popularity of commercial rattlesnake roundups in which patches of saw palmetto are burned to drive the rattlers out from their cover so they can be killed. Another method used in these roundups is to illegally pour gasoline into gopher tortoise burrows (a popular den for diamondbacks and indigo snakes) killing the tortoises and dozens of other species that frequent these excavations. After such a roundup, the rattlesnakes are eaten and the hides sold for the production of snakeskin purses and boots. In a paper published in 2008 by the American Society of Ichthyologists and Herpetologists, thousands of scientists united in strongly opposing these cruel and environmentally harmful roundups.

Another disturbing by-product of these roundups affects natural selection. The eastern diamondback has large, loud rattles located at the end of its tail that it uses to warn potential predators when they get within close proximity of the animal. Rattlesnake hunters use this behavior to locate the snakes they kill. Over time only the snakes that *do not rattle* or *have little to no rattle* survive. This results in a form of unintentional selective breeding, allowing the silent snakes to survive and pass on that genetic tendency, leading to a population with no means of warning its predators (or humans) of an impending attack.

Do not try this at home.
Courtesy Wikimedia Commons

The eastern diamondback rattlesnake is a lethal adversary, and any encounter with one of these large snakes in the wild should be taken seriously, but the best thing to do is walk away without trying to harm it. A mature snake has up to one-inch fangs that can readily penetrate clothing, shoes, and leather boots. A lethal dose of the venom has been estimated at between 100-150 mg; an adult snake averages three to five times that amount (400-850 mg). The bite is extremely painful and highly necrotizing. Untreated, death can occur within hours.

On average, 7 to 12 people a year die in the United States from snakebites, as opposed to 100 deaths recorded annually from lightning strikes. The last recorded fatal rattlesnake bite in Florida occurred in Putnam County, Florida, in 2005 when Joe Guidry, 54, reached under his neighbor's shed for a snake he thought he had shot and killed only to have it bite him in the hand, hitting a vein and killing him within seconds. Fortunately, unlike the grim situation with eastern coral snake antivenom, there is ample pit-viper antivenom available throughout the country.

The rattlesnake plays a vital role in the balance of any given ecosystem. It keeps rodent populations in check, feeding primarily on marsh rabbits, cottontails, squirrels, and rice rats. It also eats bobwhites and large insects. Aside from opossums, which are immune to their venom, the diamondback has few natural predators, for obvious reasons.

❒ ______ Cottonmouth (*Agkistrodon piscivorus*) VENOMOUS!

Other names: water moccasin, swamp moccasin, black moccasin, viper / Status: FL = stable, IUCN = LC / Length: 34-52 in. (.86-1.3 m) / Weight: 2-4 lb (.90-1.8 kg) / Life span: to 10 years / Reproduces: ovoviviparous, giving live birth to 7-21 baby snakes in the summer or early fall / Found: AC, near coast, mainland / Months found: **JFMAMJJASOND.**

The longest known cottonmouth specimen was taken from the Dismal Swamp of Virginia and measured 74 inches. The Florida average is half of that, at approximately 36 inches. Highly aquatic and an exceptional swimmer, the cottonmouth prefers the numerous swamps, marshes, and wetlands found throughout the Southwest Florida landscape. It is fairly commonly seen at the Audubon Corkscrew Swamp Sanctuary and Big Cypress National Wildlife Preserve in Collier County and Myakka River State Park in Sarasota County.

Cottonmouth close-up © Kenny L. Krysko, UF

In these black waters, the cottonmouth is a skilled predator, feeding on an array of animals. It has been known to feed on banded water snakes, mud snakes, fish, frogs, salamanders, sirens, lizards, turtles, baby alligators, birds, small mammals, insects, crayfish, snails, and even bats. Because its diet is so varied, it is sometimes referred to as being omni-carnivorous.

When approached, it is not overtly aggressive, and sadly, many similar-looking banded water snakes are killed every year in a lamentable example of mistaken identity. Fatal cottonmouth bites are far rarer than those of rattlesnakes, both because of the smaller size of the snake and the fact that the cottonmouth is generally found in wet environments avoided by humans.

The venom of a cottonmouth is similar in composition to that of a rattlesnake. It is rich with tissue-destructive enzymes and causes extensive bleeding. Immediate emergency medical attention is mandatory. It is preyed upon by kingsnakes, which are virtually immune to the cottonmouth's venom, great horned owls, opossums, alligators, snapping turtles, and great blue herons.

❐ __________ **Dusky Pigmy Rattlesnake** (*Sistrurus miliarius barbouri*) **VENOMOUS!** Other names: ground rattlesnake, pigmy rattler, hog-nosed rattler / Status: FL = stable, IUCN = LC / Length: 18-30 in. (45-76 cm) / Weight: 5-6.5 oz (141-185 g) / Life span: to 20 years / Reproduces: live birth of 5-7 baby snakes, generally born in the spring / Found: AC, coastal, near coast, inland / Months found: **JFMAMJJASOND.**

The smallest venomous snake found in Florida, the pigmy rattlesnake's bite is seldom fatal. The record length for this diminutive rattler is a mere 30 inches, more than a foot shorter than the average length of a mature coral snake. Because of its size, this pit viper delivers roughly 18 mg of venom, which, while

Pigmy rattlesnake © Kenneth L. Krysko, UF

extremely painful to the victim, is only a tenth of the amount delivered by an eastern diamondback rattlesnake. A handful of people have lost digits to these bites, but deaths are extremely rare. The same readily available antivenom serum used for the eastern diamondback is used to treat pigmy rattler bites.

The pigmy rattlesnake is carnivorous, foraging primarily on green and brown anoles, cotton mice, and insects. It tends to strike its prey quickly, then withdraw and wait out the effects of its toxin. While most small rodents succumb quickly, some reptiles can escape, only to die 10 to 15 minutes later. This small pit viper is a fairly common sighting at Myakka River State Park, especially along the road in the fall when the first cold snaps leave the snake seeking the warmth of the pavement.

Because it is so small, the pigmy is taken by a host of predators, including kingsnakes, opossums, great blue herons, and owls.

❐ ____________ **Eastern Coral Snake** (*Micrurus fulvius*)

VENOMOUS! Other names: American cobra, coral adder, thunder-and-lightning snake, candy-stick snake / Status: FL=stable, IUCN=NE / Length: 30-48 in. (0.76-1.2 m) / Weight: 8-15 oz (226-425 g) / Life span: to 6 years / Reproduces: lays up to 7 eggs, probably in underground burrows / Found: AC, coastal, near coast, inland / Months found: **JFMAMJJASOND.**

The coral snake is a distant relative of the cobra and has one of the most toxic and lethal venoms of any reptile. Fortunately, it is a small, secretive snake that is seldom encountered in the wild. According to the National Institutes of Heath,

Yellow against black = Coral Snake © Kenneth L. Krysko, UF

only 15 to 25 coral-snake bites are recorded each year in the United States. Because it is a fossorial snake (i.e., it spends most of its life under leaf litter or underground), it is rarely encountered while hiking. Most of the bites occur to individuals while doing yard work or gardening when the leaf litter and soil are disturbed. Because it takes only 3-5 mg of venom to kill a person, immediate medical attention is mandatory. The venom of the eastern coral snake is a powerful neurotoxin that starts to affect the victim's ability to breathe within 30 minutes. Death occurs within two to three hours.

Unfortunately, coral-snake bites are about to become more deadly. Because of the infrequent number of bites annually, none of the big pharmaceutical companies is interested in producing its antivenom. The U.S. supply expired in 2010 and there is very little of it available. The best advice at this point is to avoid getting bitten.

The coral snake eats ring-necked snakes, anoles, small insects, and mice. Its small size makes it incapable of taking large prey. It is seldom fed upon by other snakes and animals with the exception of opossums, which are immune to most snake venom and have little trouble subduing a small coral snake.

The brightly patterned coloration of the coral snake is a common characteristic of toxic species throughout the world. The black, red, and yellow of a coral snake, just like the brilliant colors of Central America's poisonous frogs, ward off potential predators by boldly announcing their presence and danger. It is as if to say, eat me if you dare!

❒ __________ **Burmese Python** (*Python bivittatus*) **INVASIVE!**
Other names: python / Status: FL = invasive and thriving, IUCN = NT / Length: 12-16.5 ft (3.7-5 m) / Weight: 110-200 lb (49-91 kg) / Life span: to 25 years / Reproduces: egg laying, breeds in the early spring and lays clutches up to 79 eggs in March and April / Found: CC, HC, EC, near coast, inland / Months found: **JFMAMJJASOND.**

Burmese Python © Tim Vickers via Wikimedia Commons

Although this species is commonly singled out, it is not the only known large constrictor found in the Everglades. Other species include African rock pythons, boa constrictors, anacondas, and reticulated pythons, making the task of removing these massive snakes all the more troublesome. The Burmese python is native to Southeast Asia, where it feeds as a constrictor on wild chickens, peacocks, and an assortment of mammals as large as domestic goats and pigs.

In Florida it is known to take nutria, alligators (including some large ones), deer, raccoons, an assortment of wading birds. In 2010 personnel from Everglades National Park removed 322 pythons, though most biologists believe this is only a fraction of the current population. In 2000, when the snakes were first discovered in the park, only two were removed. To date, more than 1,334 have been taken out, and the numbers captured every year are increasing exponentially. In short, the Burmese python is a snake Florida will be dealing with for decades to come.

Some biologists project that the Burmese python might eventually make it all the way into southern Georgia and become established in places such as the Okefenokee Swamp.

Capturing a 15-foot-long, 200-pound snake isn't easy. Thus far, firearms and traps are not permitted, and the only way to catch this huge reptile is by hand, with nets, or by using snake snares. There is currently a program in place allowing concerned trappers and citizens to capture the python, though there is no bounty paid. In Asia, the Burmese python is readily consumed by humans, but in the Everglades it contains unacceptably high levels of mercury and eating one is ill advised. Its skin is also harvested in Asia, but to date, no market has been found for python hides in the United States.

Alligators, black bears, and panthers are known to feed on the Burmese python, but nothing smaller than these top predators is capable of tackling a snake this large. Young pythons are probably eaten by herons, raccoons, and other predators, though no sightings or records are available to confirm this.

The influx of Burmese pythons and other large constrictors in Florida is directly related to the pet trade. This python can be deadly. A two-year old girl was strangled to death by a nine-foot Burmese python in Sumter County, Florida, in 2009 after the snake escaped from its cage.

❒ ____________ **Eastern Indigo Snake** (*Drymarchon couperi*)

Other names: indigo snake, gopher snake / Status: FL=threatened, IUCN=LC-population declining / Length: 6-8.6 ft (1.8-2.6 m) / Weight: 8-10 lb (3.6-4.5 kg) / Life span: to 25 years in captivity / Reproduces: little is known about this egg-laying (8-11) snake but it is believed it uses gopher tortoise burrows for dens / Found: AC, rare, coastal, near coast, inland / Months found: **JFMAMJJASOND.**

Eastern Indigo Snake close-up © Kenneth L. Krysko, UF

The eastern indigo snake is the largest non-venomous snake in North America. A long, thick-bodied snake, it can grow to nearly nine feet and weigh more than 10 pounds. Its coloration resembles that of a black racer, except that it sometimes has a rusty to blood-red hue under its chin as opposed to the brown hues of the black racer. It catches its prey with powerful jaws and uses its body weight to pin down its prey, which, like all snakes, it swallows whole.

Indigo Snake Courtesy FL Fish & Wildlife Service

This beautiful species has been in steady decline in Florida for the past 30 years. A century ago the indigo snake was quite common, but today it is listed as threatened in Florida. Although attempts are being made to stabilize the population, it continues to vanish. A number of factors all seem to be coming into play. The indigo snake relies heavily on the burrows made by gopher tortoises, which because of habitat loss and upper respiratory tract disease have suffered dramatic losses across the state. Another factor is the high demand for this species as a pet and hence the pressure put on the wild population by snake collectors. In the past decade the state of Florida placed a ban on taking wild indigos without a special permit. Fortunately, it is fairly easy to breed in captivity, and the captive snakes are meeting the demand in the pet trade.

The indigo snake eats a variety of animals including reptiles and other snakes (especially other snakes), birds, and small mammals such as marsh rabbits. Because of its size, the adult indigo snake is taken only by alligators, bobcats, and crocodiles. Birds of prey are unable to lift a 10-pound snake, and even the aggressive great horned owl shies away from tackling such a formidable predator.

❒ __________ **Corn Snake** (*Pantherophis guttatus*) Other names: red rat snake / Status: FL=stable, IUCN=LC / Length: 3.9-5.9 ft (1.2-1.8 m) / Weight: 1.5-3 lb (0.68-1.3 kg) / Life span: to 23 years / Reproduces: deposits its eggs (10-30) in old logs, stumps, sawdust, and detritus / Found: AC, coastal, near coast, inland / Months found: **JFMAMJJASOND.**

Corn Snake © Maggie May Rogers/ SCCF

The corn snake's name is derived from the beautiful maize-like pattern on its belly and its preference for cornfields. The name appeared as far back as 1676

Corn snake eating a brown anole © Kenneth L. Krysko, UF

when these colorful snakes were first discovered in America. Its docile nature, attractive skin pattern, and reluctance to bite make it a popular pet.

The range of the corn snake is much smaller than that of the black racer or yellow rat snake and does not extend much above the Mason-Dixon Line. It does survive at elevations up to 6,000 feet. In colder climates it hibernates during the winter. The best time for viewing one of these gorgeous snakes is early morning or near sunset. It tends to feed nocturnally and is seldom spotted midday.

When threatened, the corn snake coils up in much the same fashion as a rattlesnake. Its bite is swift and painful, and because of its heavily patterned coloration, it may easily be confused with the deadly rattlesnake. In yet another form of rattlesnake mimicry, the corn snake often rattles its tail, even though it lacks the rattle.

In the wild this small constrictor dines predominantly on rodents—mostly rats and mice—but will also take lizards, anoles, and frogs. The corn snake is preyed upon by all the major raptors, and juvenile snakes are taken by black racers.

❐______ **Eastern Rat Snake** (*Pantherophis alleghaniensis*) Other names: yellow rat snake, Everglades rat snake / Status: FL=stable, IUCN=LC / Length: 4.5-7 ft (1.4-2.1 m) / Weight: 2-4 lb (0.9-1.80 kg) / Life span: to 20 years / Reproduces: deposits its eggs (4-28) in old logs, stumps, and detritus / Found: AC, coastal, near coast, inland / Months found: **JFMAMJJASOND.**

Eastern Rat Snake © Kenneth L. Krysko, UF

After the black racer, the yellow rat snake is the second most commonly seen snake in Southwest Florida. Various subspecies and color variations extend the range of the yellow rat snake across most of the eastern U.S., and as far west as western Texas. Growing to lengths of seven feet, with a circumference about the size of a man's wrist, this snake can be quite startling when you happen upon one. It is nonvenomous, however, and aside from a nasty bite, will not cause any real harm to a person. Nonetheless, it should never be picked up or handled.

The yellow rat snake is an impressive predator. It is a true constrictor, seizing its prey, then coiling its muscular body around the animal and slowly constricting the life out of it through suffocation. The yellow rat snake is one of the leading predators of invasive black and brown rats and is therefore beneficial to wildlife. It also preys upon birds, frogs, lizards, eggs, insects, and small mammals.

Extremely arboreal, the yellow rat snake can often be spotted climbing into trees and up onto porches, rooftops, and rafters. It has nowhere near the speed of the black racer on the ground and often falls prey to hawks, ospreys, eagles, owls, raccoons, bobcats, and otters. Unlike the black racer, the yellow rat snake takes readily to humans, and after it becomes socialized, seldom bites.

❐ ________ **Southern Black Racer** (*Coluber constrictor*) Other names: black racer, racer / Status: FL=stable, IUCN=LC / Length: 2-4.5 ft (0.61-1.4 m) / Weight: 0.75-1 lb (340-453 g) / Life span: to 10 years / Reproduces: deposits its eggs (7-22) in old logs, stumps, and sawdust / Found: AC, coastal, near coast, inland / Months found: **JFMAMJJASOND.**

Black Racer © Blake Sobczak

The most commonly seen snake in this region, the southern black racer is also one of the most common in Florida. One reason for the frequent sightings is that the black racer is a diurnal hunter, so it is out at the same time when most people are working in their yards, biking, or doing other activities that might bring them into contact with this snake. The black racer has one of the most extensive ranges of any North American snake, extending to the Canadian border, west to Washington, and east to Maine.

The black racer is nonvenomous but will inflict a bite if grabbed. It will shake its tail in the grass or dry leaves when cornered or threatened, imitating a rattlesnake. It cannot be domesticated and should not be kept as a pet. It will continue to bite its captors throughout its life span and repeatedly bash its head against a glass enclosure until it seriously injures itself.

Despite its species epithet (constrictor), the black racer is not a true constrictor. It tends to chase down, bite, then suffocate or crush its victims on the ground rather than coiling around them in true constrictor fashion. Its diet includes brown and green anoles, insects, moles, birds, frogs, eggs, smaller snakes, and rodents. It is preyed on by red-shouldered hawks, owls, and larger snakes.

The black racer is extremely quick and agile, making it difficult to catch. When spotted crossing a trail or road, it vanishes into the understory with amazing swiftness.

❐ __________ **Ring-necked Snake** (*Diadophis punctatus*) Other names: none / Status: FL=stable, IUCN=LC / Length: 8-18.5 in. (20-47 cm) / Weight: 0.6-2 oz (17-56 g) / Life span: to 6 years / Reproduces: deposits its eggs (4-7) in old logs, stumps, and detritus / Found: AC, coastal, near coast, inland / Months found: **JFMAMJJASOND.**

Ring-necked Snake © Kenneth L. Krysko, UF

The smallest snake found above ground in Southwest Florida, the diminutive ring-necked snake is usually less than a foot long. It is easily recognized by the distinctive red ring located just behind the head. Its range extends through all of Florida and across much of North America except in the higher elevations of the Rocky Mountains and the central plateau.

Although it has recently been discovered that the saliva of this species may have some toxicity, it is not considered poisonous and has no ability to inject its saliva into a human. It seldom if ever attempts to bite. Its mouth is so small that even biting a baby finger is unlikely. When picked up, the ring-necked snake releases a strong, unpleasant musk smell. It does not make a good pet because as soon as it is placed into captivity, it refuses to eat and dies within weeks.

The ring-necked snake feeds upon insects, grubs, frogs, and newborn rodents. In the wild this tiny snake has an average life span of little more than a year. Because of its small size and defenseless nature, it is taken by a wide variety of predators, from hawks to rats, and is one of the favored preys of the coral snake and other larger snakes.

❐ ________ **Eastern Coachwhip Snake** (*Masticophis flagellum*)

Other names: coachwhip / Status: FL=stable, IUCN=LC / Length: 6-8.5 ft (1.8-2.6 m) / Weight: 2-3 lb (.90-1.4 kg) / Life span: to 17 years / Reproduces: deposits its eggs (12-16) in old logs, stumps, and detritus / Found: AC, coastal, near coast, inland / Months found: **JFMAMJJASOND.**

Coiled Coachwhip © Mark Kenderdine

Aptly named because its long, slender body resembles a whip, the eastern coachwhip snake is capable of short bursts of speed up to 12 miles per hour. It is perhaps even more difficult to capture than the black racer. Its coloration is similar to that of a black racer across the first third of its head and body, but fades into a dark brown near the tail. Across its range, which is most of the southeastern U.S., the coachwhip exhibits a variety of color phases, from dark brown to pink.

The coachwhip prefers dry, upland environments and is best spotted along high ridges. Its most common habitat is the vegetated dune area along the coast. It is a daytime predator, focusing on lizards, small birds, and rodents. It tends to raise its head in cobra-like fashion when hunting, scanning the horizon in search of prey. Although it is nonvenomous, under no circumstances should you attempt to catch a coachwhip. It is renowned for its aggressive nature and will inflict repeated bites. In captivity it will strike at anyone approaching its glass terrarium to the point of harming itself. Because of that behavior, the coachwhip cannot be kept as a pet or displayed in zoos.

Young coachwhip snakes succumb to any number of predators, including raccoons, raptors, and bobcats. Once it reaches adult size, the coachwhip is seldom taken by birds of prey, but can be killed by rattlesnakes.

❒ _____ Peninsula Ribbon Snake (*Thamnophis sauritus*) Other names: garter snake / Status: FL=stable, ICUN=NE / Length: 2.6-3.4 ft (0.79-1 m) / Weight: 1-1.5 lb (453-680 g) / Life span: to 10 years / Reproduces: live bearing (3-20) during spring through summer / Found: AC, coastal, near coast, inland / Months found: **JFMAMJJASOND.**

Peninsula Ribbon Snake © Hung V. Do

Related to the common garter snake, the peninsula ribbon snake ranges throughout the eastern United States from the Mississippi River to New England. The primary difference between the two snakes is that the garter snake is considerably stockier, and its striping is more pronounced.

The ribbon snake is not easy to find. It is an extremely shy snake that prefers dense underbrush and wetlands, and is seldom seen during the daytime. When captured it does not bite as readily as other snakes but does release an unpleasant musk odor. The ribbon snake does not do well in captivity and is seldom kept as a pet.

It feeds on crickets, small fish, and frogs. Alligators, snapping turtles, gar, birds of prey, and otters all prey upon the peninsula ribbon snake.

❒ _______ Florida Water Snake (*Nerodia fasciata pictiventris*) Other names: water snake, Florida banded water snake / Status: FL=stable, IUCN=NE/ Length: 4-5.2 ft (1.2-1.6 m) / Weight: 2-4.5 lb (.90-2 kg) / Life span: to 9 years / Reproduces: gives live birth to between 20 to 30 offspring / Found: AC, coastal, near coast, inland / Months found: **JFMAMJJASOND.**

Because of its aquatic nature, size, and coloration, the Florida water snake is commonly confused with the venomous cottonmouth. Far too many of these harmless water snakes are killed as a result of this mistaken identity. When cornered, the Florida water snake does behave like a cottonmouth, coiling itself back as if to strike, and because it can grow quite large, its bite can be vicious. Sadly, many people kill all snakes out of fear. This is a tragedy because snakes play a vital role in keeping rodent populations down; no wild creature should be killed simply because we fear it.

The Florida water snake ranges across most of the Southeast. It is a fairly heavy-bodied snake, with faint brown banding. It has two color phases: blackish-green and reddish-orange. It feeds on a variety of aquatic prey, including tadpoles,

Florida Banded Water Snake © Kenneth L. Krysko, UF

frogs, fish, juvenile turtles, and toads. Although it will survive in captivity, it can never really be handled as it tends to bite throughout its lifetime. In the wild it is preyed upon by crocodiles, alligators, gar, snapping turtles, and otters.

❒_____ **Florida Brown Snake** (*Storeria victa*) Other names: brown snake / Status: FL=stable, IUCN=NE / Length: 12-19 in. (30-46 cm) / Weight: unknown / Life span: to 7 years / Reproduces: gives live birth to 3-18 offspring / Found: AC, coastal, near coast, inland / Months found: **JFMAMJJASOND.**

Florida Brown Snake © Kenneth L. Krysko, UF

The second-smallest terrestrial snake in Southwest Florida, the Florida brown snake is only slightly larger than the ring-necked snake. It has a distinctive pattern, and some adult brown snakes have a light tan marking that rings the back portion of the head. It prefers a moist or aquatic habitat and can be found around ponds, drainage ditches, or homes where there is a source of water such as air conditioning units and garden hoses, but it is not a common sighting.

When captured this tiny snake will flatten its body and strike repeatedly, but its head and teeth are too small to inflict a serious bite. In time it does well in captivity and is commonly kept as a pet.

The brown snake feeds on earthworms, slugs, and small invertebrates such as crickets and roaches. It is fed upon by other snakes, birds of prey, and small mammals such as rats.

❒ ____ **Mangrove Water Snake** (*Nerodia clarkii compressicauada*)
Other names: mangrove snake, salt marsh snake / Status: FL=stable, IUCN=LC / Length: 30-37 in. (76-93 cm) / Weight: 1.2-2.2 lb (0.54-1 kg) / Life span: to 20 years / Reproduces: gives live birth to up to 22 young snakes throughout the summer / Months found: **JFMAMJJASOND.**

Because of its size and coloration, the elusive mangrove water snake is virtually impossible to spot during the day. As evening approaches, especially in the fall, this small snake will come out of the mangroves to bask on paths and roadways while they are still warmed from the sun. Like all reptiles and amphibians, the mangrove snake is cold blooded and has to regulate body temperature by basking in the sun or absorbing the warmth of rocks or roadways when it is cold, and hiding in the shadowy understory or entering the water when it is too warm.

Grey phase of Mangrove Snake © Mark Kenderdine

Red phase of Mangrove Water Snake
© Mark Kenderdine

The mangrove snake is closely related to the Florida water snake. It has a variety of color variations throughout its range: some varieties have a reddish hue, whereas others can be yellow and/or brown.

This snake is unusual in that it tolerates brackish water and prefers the habitat of red and black mangroves. It feeds on mangrove crabs, snails and slugs, small fish, and marine insects and worms. In the wild it is preyed upon by raccoons, otters, ospreys, and larger fish such as snook and tarpon. The mangrove snake is not commonly kept as a pet.

❐ _______ **Brahminy Blind Snake** (*Ramphotyphlops braminus*)
Other names: flowerpot snake, worm snake / Status: FL=invasive, introduced and thriving, IUCN=LC / Length: 2.5-6.5 in. (6.35-16.5 cm) / Weight: 1-4 oz (28-113 g) / Life span: to 2 years / Reproduces: unknown, it lays eggs or may be live bearing — all individuals are females and reproduce unisexually without sperm from a male. Up to eight genetically identical females are born / Found: AC, coastal, near coast, inland / Months found: **JFMAMJJASOND.**

Originally introduced into the Miami area from Asia, this very small, completely blind snake is easily mistaken for a black earthworm. One of the primary reasons for its success at establishing itself on every continent except Antarctica is that it is parthenogenetic, meaning it reproduces asexually. A rare characteristic in vertebrates, shared by Komodo dragons, Nile monitor lizards, some sharks, and a handful of other reptiles and amphibians, parthenogenesis allows a single individual to establish a beachhead in any given environment by essentially cloning itself, though the process is far more complex than that.

Brahminy Blind Snake © Kenneth L. Krysko, UF

The Brahminy blind snake lives most of its life underground. It feeds on larvae, eggs, and the pupae of ants and termites. It is eaten by moles, armadillos, and opossums. Because of its subterranean habitat, it is very unlikely that you will find a Brahminy blind snake, but it has become fairly well established here and is thriving somewhere beneath us.

Black Spiny-tailed Iguana Courtesy Wikimedia Commons

Lizards

❒ ________ **Black Spiny-tailed Iguana** (*Ctenosaura similis*)
INVASIVE! Other names: black iguana, iguana / Status: FL = invasive and expanding its range, IUCN = LC / Length: 3.3-5 ft (1-1.6 m) / Weight: 2.6-8.8 lb (1.2-4 kg) / Life span: to 25 years / Reproduces: egg laying with as many as 70 eggs laid per clutch / Found: LC, ChC, coastal / Months found: **JFMAMJJASOND.**

On Gasparilla Island, located in southern Charlotte and northwestern Lee County, the invasive and environmentally damaging black spiny-tailed iguana has become a major concern to both environmentalists and residents. Unlike the invasive green iguana found on Sanibel and Captiva, which is an herbivore, the spiny-tailed iguana is an omnivore. It eats not only native vegetation, but also local birds, marsh rabbits, green anoles, young gopher tortoises, and snakes. Since 2006 Lee County has spent an average of $100,000 a year in an attempt to eradicate this invasive from Gasparilla Island. To date, nearly 10,000 spiny-tailed iguanas have been caught and euthanized, mostly from the northern end of the island. The sheer numbers of these lizards, coupled with their high fecundity, make their removal a daunting and expensive task.

The eradication program is having results. In 2010 the number of mature, breeding adults was down considerably from the previous estimates of more than 12,000 lizards. The rise of this invasive on one small island is an ominous tale of a well-meaning but misguided individual who released a few breeding pairs from his backyard cage some 30 years ago. One man, George Cera, has personally captured and killed more than 16,000 black iguanas. He wrote a book about his experiences called *The Iguana Cookbook—Save Florida, Eat an Iguana.*

To date, this incredibly fecund lizard has made it to many areas on the Florida mainland. As an omnivore, great climber, and prolific breeder, this large iguana could quickly overrun entire ecosystems. In fact, the black spiny-tailed iguana is noted in the Guinness Book of World Records as the fastest lizard alive, having been clocked at speeds of more than 21 miles per hour, just shy of the fastest recorded human running speed of 23.4 miles per hour.

The black iguana has few natural predators in Florida. Bobcats have learned to hunt and eat adults, and owls and great blue herons take the juveniles. Alligators would readily eat them but there are no alligators found on Gasparilla Island. The recent cold winters have also helped to keep the burgeoning population in check.

❐______ **Green Iguana** (*Iguana iguana*) **INVASIVE!** Other names: common iguana, bamboo chicken, chicken of the tree / Status: FL=invasive, increasing, IUCN=VU / Length: 3.5–6.5 ft (1-2 m) / Weight: 10-20 lb (4.5-9.1 kg) / Life span: to 20 years / Reproduces: lays between 20 and 71 eggs in the spring / Found: CC, LC ChC, HC, coastal, near coast, inland / Months found: **JFMAMJJASOND.**

The current green iguana population in Southwest Florida is a direct result of the release of this large Central and South American reptile by pet owners who no longer want the animal. After time, due in part to its long life span, the released reptiles find each other, mate and propagate. Because of its size and ability to adapt to the climate and vegetation of the region, a species like the green iguana can quickly get out of control. The first verified sighting of a feral green iguana occurred in the Miami area in 1966. Since then it has spread northward into seven counties. In an effort to control this invasive species, the city of Sanibel has undertaken a green

Green Iguana © Arthur Pedziwilk via Wikimedia Commons

Large male green iguana © Gareth Pinckard

iguana eradication program. To date it has captured and euthanized more than 750 iguanas at a cost in excess of $50,000. Although nowhere near as devastating to wildlife as the spiny-tailed iguana, this huge lizard destroys ornamental vegetation, eating shrubs, orchids, fruits, mangoes, berries, and tomatoes. It also digs nesting burrows that can undermine sidewalks, seawalls, and foundations. It often leaves droppings in private swimming pools and is known to harbor salmonella bacteria.

The green iguana's high reproductive rate makes its eradication difficult. A single clutch can contain as many as 71 eggs. Unlike its native habitat in Central and South America, where these large lizards are fed upon by ocelots, pumas, jaguars, caimans, anacondas and boa constrictors, the green iguana has only alligators, bobcats and owls to fear in Florida.

Although South Florida represents the northernmost part of its range, the green iguana appears to be undergoing a slow process of natural selection. The more cold-tolerant members of the species are surviving, while the others die off during the winter. Eventually, the cold-resistant iguanas will continue to move northward, possibly as far as central Florida. Thus far, most individuals have not been able to survive a hard freeze and the recent rash of unusually cold winters has helped to keep further population growth in check, at least in the short term.

In Central and South America many people eat the green iguana. The level of harvest in some areas has become so severe that the ICUN is considering listing it as an endangered species. It is said to taste like chicken, especially when fried; hence, the nickname "chicken of the tree."

Do not attempt to capture or kill a feral green iguana. Their sharp claws and powerful jaws can inflict serious injuries and they should only be dealt with by an experienced trapper.

❐ ________ **Nile Monitor Lizard** (*Varanus niloticus*) **INVASIVE!**
Other names: leguaan (African) / Status: FL=invasive, expanding its range, IUCN=LC / Length: 4.5-7.5 ft (1.5-2.3 m) / Weight: 20-40 lb (9-18 kg) / Life span: to 15 years / Reproduces: parthenogenetic, lays up to 60 eggs in a single clutch / Found: LC, CC, near coast / Months found: **JFMAMJJASOND.**

Currently known to exist in seven south Florida counties, the Nile monitor lizard represents a serious potential environmental threat. This powerful lizard is a carnivore. It is a distant relative of the Komodo dragon of Indonesia, the largest lizard in the world, known to obtain lengths of 10 feet and weigh more than 300 pounds. The Komodo has been known to kill children, goats, and dogs.

With a keen sense of smell, excellent speed, and sharp eyesight, the monitor lizard, once established in a region, could quickly decimate a wide range of native animals. In Africa, where it originates, it is one of the leading predators of crocodile nests. On barrier islands, if it becomes established there, it could turn its attention to alligator and sea turtle eggs. Equipped with sharp claws, it would have no trouble digging up loggerhead nesting sites and devouring all the eggs in a single night. A strong climber, this predator could do significant damage to bird rookeries and small mammal populations.

The Nile monitor has established a beachhead in northern Cape Coral where it can sometimes be spotted foraging for food during the day. These massive lizards were probably released as pets, though importing and keeping the Nile monitor in Florida is now allowed by special permit only. Every imported animal must also be identified with a microchip, ensuring that the owner will remain responsible for each lizard's continued captivity. A young Nile monitor lizard can be easily handled as a pet, but by the time it reaches two or three years of age, it is a ferocious lizard capable of killing a housecat with a single bite and swallowing it whole. Not surprisingly, the pet owner may want to remove this danger from the household.

NIle Monitor Lizard
Courtesy Wikimedia Commons

The first reported sighting of a Nile monitor in Southwest Florida was in 1990, and the population is now estimated at more than 1,000. It may lay up to 60 eggs in a clutch and is capable of parthenogenesis, which means that a single individual can reproduce without mating. In Africa this lizard is kept in check by other lizards and birds of prey that feed on the eggs and young. Larger lizards are sometimes killed and eaten by leopards and other wild cats. In Florida, alligators, panthers, and bobcats are its only natural predators.

If you see or suspect you see one of these lizards, which resemble giant brown anoles only much darker and without the dewlap, please call Florida Fish and Wildlife at 850-488-4676 to report the sighting.

❐ ______ **Green Anole** (*Anolis carolinensis*) Other names: Carolina anole, American chameleon / Status: FL=in decline, IUCN=LC / Length: 6-8 in. (15-20 cm) / Weight: 0.05-1.5 oz (1.5-4 g) / Life span: to 4 years / Reproduces: breeds throughout SW Florida, prefers heavily wooded environments to lay its two small eggs / Found: AC, coastal, near coast, inland / Months found: **JFMAMJJASOND.**

Before the arrival of the brown anole from the Caribbean, the green anole was the only anole living in Southwest Florida. The more aggressive and invasive brown, or Cuban, anole has all but eliminated this emerald green lizard from many of its former locales. Finding one today is a difficult undertaking. Its range extends throughout the Southeast from Mississippi to North Carolina.

Green Anole © Kenneth L. Krysko, UF

It is easiest to spot when in its green coloration. Although not a true chameleon, the green anole is capable of swiftly changing its color to brown, tan, or gray depending on the background material where the lizard is located. A brown-phase green anole is almost impossible to distinguish from the much more common brown anole. Look for the green anole's long, pointed snout, which differs from the blunt snout of the brown anole.

Because of its coloring, the green anole prefers foraging in the green foliage of bushes and trees, unlike the ground-dwelling brown anole. The green anole eats moths, ant larvae, flies, and crickets to mention a few of the many insects it preys upon. It in turn is part of the diet of herons, egrets, snakes, rats, and a number of different bird species, including grackles, merlins, and kestrels. The green anole makes an excellent pet and can live in captivity for more than seven years if cared for properly.

❐ ________ **Brown Anole** (*Anolis sagrei*) INVASIVE! Other names: Cuban anole, Key West anole / Status: FL-Invasive, still expanding its range, IUCN=LC / Length: Length: 6-8 in. (15-20 cm) / Weight: 0.05-1.5 oz (1.5-4 g) / Life span: to 5 years / Reproduces: lays its two eggs in early summer, generally on the ground / Found: invasive species, AC, coastal, near coast, inland / Months found: **JFMAMJJASOND.**

Brown Anole close-up © Jennifer Beltran

This small, athletic lizard probably hitchhiked over to Southwest Florida in the root balls and canopies of the many ornamental palms imported from the Miami area when the region was experiencing the rapid growth of the early 1970s. Once here, it quickly became the most prolific lizard in the area. An invasive species, its sheer numbers now prohibit any viable attempts to contain its spread or effectively remove the species. Its range continues to expand across the Southeastern U.S.

The brown anole has a number of subtle color and pattern variations, but its dewlap, the throat fan you can often see the male extending when announcing its territory to other males, is always yellow or reddish-orange. It is one of the easiest reptiles to find in SW Florida, occurring around condominiums, homes, pools, screen enclosures, and the bike path—virtually every habitat harbors at least a few, if not scores of brown anoles.

It feeds mostly in the daytime and prefers foraging on the ground where it eats beetles, grasshoppers, spiders, and roaches. The brown anole is a favorite food for white and cattle egrets, as well as great blue herons. An injured lizard often succumbs to overwhelming attacks of fire ants, and it is also favored by many of the islands' indigenous snakes. When grabbed by a predator from the tail, it is able to release just its long, slender tail and survive the attack. The tails re-grow in a month or two.

❒ ______ **Six-lined Racerunner** (*Aspidoscelis sexlineata*) Other names: racerunner / Status: FL=stable, IUCN=NE (Not Evaluated) / Length: 8-9.5 in. (20-24 cm) / Weight: n/a / Life span: to 6 years / Reproduces: four to six eggs are laid in rotting logs or other vegetation in the spring / Found: SC, LC, CC, HC, coastal, near coast, inland / Months found: **JFMAMJJASOND.**

The racerunner is well named as it is the fastest lizard in SW Florida, capable of short bursts of speed approaching 20 miles per hour. That, coupled with its breakaway tail, makes this reptile virtually impossible to catch.

The tail of the six-lined racerunner makes up 70 percent of its total body length. Some studies have shown that this tail helps the lizard obtain its remarkable speed. A member of the teiid family of lizards, common only in the New World, the racerunner has approximately 200 members in its family, including the largest teiid, the three-foot tegu lizard of South America.

Six-lined Racerunner © Mark Kenderdine

Preferring drier upland habitats, the six-lined racerunner is most commonly seen in the upper reaches of the beaches and the beach dunes. It is a common sighting at Oscar Scherer State Park, which is in the destination section of this work. In these more upland habitats the racerunner feeds on beetles, mosquitoes, flies, cockroaches, grasshoppers, and crickets. Because of its speed, the racerunner is seldom caught by anything other than birds of prey, which have no trouble swooping down on an unsuspecting lizard.

❒ __________ **Ground Skink** (*Scincella lateralis*) Other names: little brown skink / Status: FL=stable, IUCN=LC/ Length: 3.5-5 in. (9-13 cm) / Weight: n/a / Life span: to 3 years / Reproduces: throughout SW Florida / Found: AC, coastal, near coast, inland / Months found: **JFMAMJJASOND.**

The smallest lizard found in Southwest Florida and rather uncommon, the ground skink is most likely to be found beneath moist leaves, under logs, or hiding in woodpiles and debris. It feeds during the daytime, but its size and feeding habits make it a rare sighting. The ground skink ranges throughout the Southeast and north to the Ohio River valley.

Ground Skink Courtesy Wikimedia Commons

This somewhat comical lizard has been known to take a bite out of its own tail, mistaking it for a small centipede or insect. Like all skinks, its tail is quick to break off, allowing the animal to escape and leaving the predator with more of a snack than the meal it was originally in pursuit of. The ground skink is a favorite prey for smaller snakes such as the coral and ring-necked.

The home range of this diminutive skink may be as small as 20 square meters, wherein it consumes insects, spiders, and isopods such as woodlice and pill bugs.

❒ ___ **Southeastern Five-lined Skink** (*Plestiodon inexpectatus*) Other names: blue-tailed skink, red-headed skink / Status: FL=stable, IUCN=LC / Life span: to 6 years / Length: 4.9-8.5 in. (12.5-21.5 cm) / Weight: n/a / Life span: to 6 years / Reproduces: six to eight eggs are laid in early spring / Found: AC, coastal, near coast, inland / Months found: **JFMAMJJASOND.**

Blue tail juvenile
© Maggie May Rogers/ SCCF

This relatively common skink is easily identified in its juvenile stage by its bright blue tail. It is the most colorful lizard native to Southwest Florida and a true delight to observe when spotted. It is a fairly large lizard, growing close to nine inches long, and closely resembles the broad-headed skink. It likes to sun itself during the heat of the day and can sometimes be observed on pool decks and around other concrete or asphalt surfaces.

It is incredibly agile and quick and nearly impossible to catch without a trap. It is commonly kept as a pet and can live up to 10 years in captivity.

Five-lined Male Skink © Mark Kenderdine

Although it will bite when captured, its mouth is too small to inflict serious damage.

The southeastern five-lined skink eats mostly insects but will also take young green and brown anoles. It is eaten by snakes, birds of prey, and small mammals.

❒ ________ **Indo-Pacific Gecko** (*Hemidactylus garnotii*) Other names: fox gecko / Status: FL=invasive, increasing in population, IUCN=LC / Length: 5 in. (13 cm) / Weight: n/a / Life span: to 13 years / Reproduces: parthenogenetic, capable of asexual reproduction laying two genetically identical eggs in the spring / Found: AC, coastal, near coast, inland mostly in urban settings / Months found: **JFMAMJJASOND.**

Indo-Pacific Gecko © Kenneth L. Krysko, UF

An invasive species, probably arriving into Southwest Florida around 1963, the Indo-Pacific gecko is the most commonly seen of all three introduced gecko species found in the region. Originally from India, this gecko has spread across several continents with the help of *Homo sapiens.* It is also one of a very small group of animals that breen by a process known as parthenogenesis, or asexual reproduction. Rarely exceeding five inches in length, this small lizard can be easily identified by its motion and its ability to cling to walls and ceilings, remaining upside down for hours. Sticky toe-pads allow the gecko to climb on surfaces as smooth as glass without difficulty.

The gecko moves very differently from the anole and racerunner. Its body tends to bend and twist, and it is nowhere near as fast. It is mostly nocturnal, coming out near house or condominium lights during the evening to feed on the insects these lights attract. The Indo-Pacific gecko dines on moths, flies, and termites among a host of other insects. It is fed upon by larger lizards, as well as rats and snakes. Although considered invasive, this small gecko's impact on native species appears to be minimal.

Frogs and Toads

❐ ____________ **Oak Toad** (*Anaxyrus quercicus*) Other names: hoppy toads / Status: FL=stable, IUCN=LC / Length: 0.75-1.25 in. (2-3 cm) / Weight: n/a / Life span: to 3 years / Reproduces: Lays between 700-1,900 eggs in shallow pond annually / Found: AC, coastal, near coast, inland / Months found: **JFMAMJJASOND.**

The oak toad is the smallest toad found in North America and looks more like a small, hopping insect than a toad. Most cockroaches are larger than this toad. Its size and inconspicuous coloration make it very difficult to spot. It is capable of incredible population explosions; one study found an amazing 70 oak toads per acre near Orlando. Each female toad can lay as many as 2,000 eggs per summer breeding season.

Oak Toad Courtesy USGS

The oak toad prefers pine forests, shrub lands, and marshes, and proximity to a water supply is important. In Florida this species is suffering from habitat loss as a result of urban sprawl. Its range extends throughout the Southeast. The oak toad is a carnivore and dines mainly on smaller insects. It is heavily preyed upon by snakes, lizards, birds, and fire ants.

❒ __________ **Southern Toad** (*Anaxyrus terrestris*) Other names: none / Status: FL=stable, IUCN=LC / Length: 3-4.5 in. (7.5-11.4 cm) / Weight: n/a / Life span: to 5 years / Reproduces: lays 2,500-4,000 eggs in shallow ponds and ditches in the early spring / Found: AC, coastal, near coast, inland / Months found: **JFMAMJJASOND.**

Southern Toad © Blake Sobczak

A fairly common toad throughout the region, the southern toad can sometimes be seen hopping around brightly lit convenience stores late at night looking for a meal under the insect-attracting lights. On rainy nights you will see it out on roadways foraging or mating, and, especially in the spring and early summer, you can hear its continuous high-pitched trill throughout the night.

It is generally grayish to dark brown in color and looks like a typical toad. Its diet consists of beetles, larvae, cockroaches, and moths. It is preyed upon by snakes, raccoons, small mammals such as rats, and owls. A close relative, the giant marine toad from Texas, can kill a dog or cat that is foolish enough to bite it.

❒ ________ **Green Treefrog** (*Hyla cinerea*) Other names: American green treefrog, cowbell frog, bell frog, fried bacon frog / Status: FL=stable, IUCN=LC / Length: 2-2.5 in. (5-6 cm) / Weight: n/a / Life span: to 5 years / Reproduces: lays 1,000-4,000 eggs annually in ditches, ponds, and marshes / Found: AC, coastal, near coast, inland / Months found: **JFMAMJJASOND.**

Once far more populous than it is now, the small green treefrog has suffered tremendous losses in competition with the larger and more aggressive Cuban treefrog, an invasive introduced to Florida in the 1920s. The green treefrog has a coastal range that extends all the way from Maryland to Corpus Christi, Texas. It also inhabits the Ohio River valley all the way to southern Illinois. Its pretty, lime-green color makes it very popular as a pet. It is also the state amphibian of both

Georgia and Louisiana (oddly, Florida, which has an abundance of amphibians, doesn't designate a state amphibian).

The green treefrog is primarily nocturnal in nature. As a tadpole its diet consists of plants, algae, and aquatic insects, but once it undergoes its metamorphosis, it becomes a carnivore feeding on crickets, moths, and flies. The green treefrog is eaten by snakes and lizards, and the smaller ones are sometimes eaten by the much larger Cuban treefrogs.

Green Treefrog © Kenneth L. Krysko, UF

❒ ______ **Squirrel Treefrog** (*Hyla squirella*) Other names: rain frog, Morse-code frog / Status: FL=stable, IUCN=LC / Length: 0.9-1.75 in. (2.25-4.5 cm) / Weight: n/a / Life span: to 6 years / Reproduces: lays approximately 900 eggs in seasonal ponds and wetlands in the early spring / Found: AC, coastal, near coast, inland / Months found: **JFMAMJJASOND.**

The squirrel treefrog derives its name from its loud, persistent chatter in early spring, resembling a squirrel's. During the mating season it also produces a unique call that sounds a bit like sending Morse code but with an alphabet that makes no sense. When the squirrel treefrog joins in with the oak toad on a rainy night in early spring, the noise can be deafening.

The squirrel treefrog's range covers the southeastern U.S. from Virginia to the Texas gulf coast. It does not extend as far north as the green treefrog. It is easily mistaken for the green treefrog but is quite a bit smaller and has more of a brownish hue. It has some chameleon-like characteristics, capable of changing its coloration in mere seconds from green to brown, or spotted to plain, depending upon the surface it is resting upon.

Highly arboreal and nocturnal, this frog spends most of its adult life in trees, shrubs, and vines. It eats insects, including ants, beetles, moths, and termites. It is heavily preyed upon by Cuban treefrogs, snakes, small rodents, and birds.

Squirrel Treefrog © Kenneth L. Krysko, UF

❒_____ **Cuban Treefrog** (*Osteopilus septentrionalis*) Other names: none / Status: FL=invasive, rapidly expanding its range, IUCN=LC / Length: 3-5.5 in. (7.5-14 cm) / Weight: n/a / Life span: to 10 years / Reproduces: lays 100-130 eggs in any standing water, including highly saline water, in early spring / Found: AC, coastal, near coast, inland / Months found: **JFMAMJJASOND.**

The invasion of the Cuban treefrog is a case study in what happens when an interloper that is a prolific breeder enters a new environment through human commercial activity. First identified in the Florida Keys in the 1920s, this frog is now found throughout Florida and is rapidly moving into Georgia and the Carolinas, as well as westward toward the Texas coast. The Cuban treefrog spreads not only via ornamental plants, but also by motorized vehicles, trailered boats, and many other unusual methods.

This spread is devastating to the indigenous frogs because the Cuban treefrog grows to twice the size of both the green and squirrel treefrogs and is capable of eating them. Furthermore, the Cuban treefrog

Two Cubans © Rob Pailes

Cuban Treefrog

tadpole is a superior competitor to native tadpoles, causing even more pressure on the indigenous species. It also appears to be negatively impacting certain smaller fish in the locales it has moved into.

The situation has become so dire that Dr. Steve Johnson, assistant professor of urban wildlife ecology at the University of Florida, wrote an article in which he instructs homeowners on how to euthanize and dispose of all the Cuban treefrogs they might encounter around their homes. This document is available on the Web site of the UF Institute of Food and Agricultural Sciences (http://edis.ifas.ufl.edu/UW259). The recommended method is to catch the frogs using a plastic bag and freeze them.

The Cuban treefrog readily gets into homes and condominiums, swims in toilets, can be found under sinks, has been known to short out electrical boxes, and generally wreaks havoc on the environment. Studies are now under way to explore the use of biological or chemical deterrents to halt or at least slow the continued spread of this invasive species.

The Cuban treefrog eats a wide variety of insects, but has also been known to consume Indo-Pacific geckos, green and brown anoles, and bird eggs, as well as some smaller hatchlings. It has become the prey of choice for yellow rat, coral, and corn snakes and is heavily preyed upon by rodents.

You should always take care in handling the Cuban treefrog as its skin secretes a sticky substance that is extremely irritating to the mucous membranes of humans, such as the eyes, ears, and nose. People with allergies are especially vulnerable, and recovery from contact with a Cuban treefrog may take several hours. Although it has not been documented to be responsible in any dog or cat deaths, pets should be kept away from this potentially harmful frog. Given its ability to adapt and thrive in urban environments, the Cuban treefrog battle will probably end with the frog winning.

❐ ________ Greenhouse Frog (*Eleutherodactylus planirostris*)

Other names: none / Status: FL=invasive, IUCN=NE / Length 1-1.25 in. (2.5-3 cm) / Weight: n/a / Life span: to 5 years / Reproduces: lays 3-26 eggs in any damp environment in the spring / Found: AC, coastal, near coast, inland / Months found: **JFMAMJJASOND.**

Greenhouse Frog © Kenneth L. Krysko, UF

The greenhouse frog is the first known documented exotic amphibian (1863), originally from the Caribbean and Cuba. Because it is even smaller than the native green and squirrel treefrogs, it does not appear to have anywhere near the negative impact of the Cuban treefrog. In fact, the greenhouse frog has also suffered from heavy predation by the Cuban treefrog.

This very small frog is unusual in that it skips the tadpole stage of development common with most amphibians. The female lays her eggs in rotting vegetation or under moist debris rather than in water. From those eggs come miniature, fully developed baby frogs. This is known as "direct development" and is extremely rare.

The greenhouse frog is not a treefrog and therefore is not equipped to climb on glass, plastic siding, or other slick surfaces. It stays in lawns, shrubs, and trees and feeds on a wide variety of small insects. It in turn is eaten by snakes, Cuban treefrogs, larger lizards, and rats.

❒ ___ **Eastern Narrow-mouth Frog** (*Gastrophryne carolinensis*)
Other names: narrow-mouth frog / Status: FL=stable, IUCN=LC / Length: 1-1.5 in. (2-4 cm) / Weight: n/a / Life span: to 4 years / Reproduces: lays 850-1,600 eggs in any standing water in the early spring / Found: AC, coastal, near coast, inland / Months found: **JFMAMJJASOND.**

Fairly common throughout the region, this small frog is easily recognized by its brown, blotchy skin color and distinctive pointed nose. In the past it has been considered a toad, but is actually a *microhylid* frog, which is a separate family. Its range extends across most of the Southeast from Texas to southern Maryland and north to the Ohio River valley.

Narrow-mouth Frog Courtesy Wikimedia Commons

It prefers living very close to moisture and is often found near ponds, under rotting logs, or hidden in debris piles. Strictly nocturnal, it is never seen in harsh sunlight. The narrow-mouth feeds on small insects and invertebrates, especially ants and termites. It is eaten by snakes, rodents, and larger lizards.

❒ __________ **Pig Frog** (*Lithobates grylio*) Other names: southern bullfrog, lagoon frog / Status: FL=stable, IUCN=LC / Length: 3.25-6.5 in. (9-16 cm) / Weight: 2 oz (57 g) / Life span: to 6 years / Reproduces: lays 8,000-15,000 eggs in ponds or any wetlands in the early summer / Found: AC, coastal, near coast, inland / Months found: **JFMAMJJASOND.**

This is the largest and loudest frog found in Southwest Florida. A mature pig frog, with its legs outstretched, can be more than 10 inches long. It is very similar in size and coloration to the slightly larger bullfrog, and both species are harvested for their prized frog legs.

Pig Frog Courtesy USGS

The pig frog is considered a game animal, although there are no harvest limits and no license is required to take one. In May 2008 the Florida Fish and Wildlife Conservation Commission issued an advisory on how many frog legs a person should eat per week because of mercury contamination. High levels of mercury have recently led to a ban on taking the pig frog in Everglades National Park and the Loxahatchee National Wildlife Refuge. Most of the frog legs served in restaurants are grown commercially, but thus far aquaculture attempts at raising the bullfrog and pig frog in Florida have not met with much success. An exported exotic, the pig frog has been introduced into China, the Bahamas, and Puerto Rico where it is doing quite well.

The pig frog is completely aquatic, seldom if ever leaving its pond, marsh, or lake. It is mostly nocturnal and tends to remain silent and hidden during the day, then starts croaking at dusk. Its loud, single calls can sound like a large pig grunting and are sometimes mistaken for alligator calls.

Its primary diet is crayfish, but it has also been known to dine on insects, tadpoles, fish, and other frogs. The pig frog is eaten by young alligators, herons, egrets, snakes, and freshwater fish such as bass and gar. The chances of seeing one are slim, but hearing them bellowing on a calm summer evening is quite easy, especially near the edges of larger wetlands and marshes.

❐ ________ **Southern Leopard Frog** (*Lithobates sphenocephalus*)
Other names: meadow frog, shad frog, and herring hopper / Status: FL=stable, IUCN=LC / Length: 3.5-5 in. (9-14 cm) / Weight: n/a / Life span: to 9 years / Reproduces: lays 1,200-1,500 eggs in freshwater marshes and ponds year round / Found: AC, coastal, near coast, inland / Months found: **JFMAMJJASOND.**

Florida Leopard Frog © Kenneth L. Krysko, UF

The southern leopard frog is similar in size and appearance to the northern leopard frog, which is the famous jumping frog described in detail by Mark Twain in *The Celebrated Jumping Frog of Calaveras County*. When people think of what a frog looks like, they generally visualize the leopard frog. Its body is green, bronze, and blotchy brown, and it has a distinctive upper iris that is a beautiful gold color.

Southern Leopard Frog Courtesy USGS

Both nocturnal and carnivorous, the leopard frog feeds on a variety of insects, earthworms, spiders, and centipedes. It breeds year round. The tadpole is a strict vegetarian, feeding on rotting vegetation and algae for the first 90 days of its life.

It is quick to dive into deeper water when threatened by predators, which include herons, snakes, raccoons, rats, and birds. It tends to do better in the cooler months than do most frogs and toads and can sometimes be heard croaking in the winter when most other amphibians are silent.

Salamanders and Sirens

❐ __________ **Greater Siren** (*Siren lacertina*) Other names: ditch eel, mud eel / Status: FL = stable, IUCN = LC / Length: 1-3 ft (.3-1 m) / Weight: n/a / Life span: to 25 years / Reproduces: lays as many as 500 eggs in rivers, swamps, ponds, and lakes / Found: AC, near coast, inland / Months found: **JFMAMJJASOND.**

While it is doubtful that anyone reading this book will ever see this giant salamander, it merits inclusion here, if for no other reason than because it is such an unusual creature. The greater siren ranges from Maryland to Florida. Strictly nocturnal and living its entire life in water, it possesses both gills and lungs and is capable of slithering out of the water, which it does on rare occasions to move from one pond or stream to another.

Totally harmless, it is so slimy and strange looking that fishermen who sometimes catch one usually cut the line to avoid touching it. Although the greater siren is quite sizable, it pales in comparison with the Chinese giant salamander, which can grow to a length of six feet and weigh an incredible 60 pounds.

Greater Siren Courtesy Wikimedia Commons

When drought strikes, as it sometimes does in Florida, the siren can aestivate (a form of hibernation) in mud burrows for months at a time, secreting a moisture-sealing cocoon over its entire body. What is amazing is that it is able to remain in this state for up to two years, living off its body fat to survive.

It is carnivorous, feeding on annelids, insects, snails, and small fish. It locates its prey using a very sophisticated and sensitive lateral line running the length of its body. The siren is preyed upon by catfish, gar, largemouth bass, and alligators.

Additional Reptiles & Amphibians of Southwest Florida

Turtles

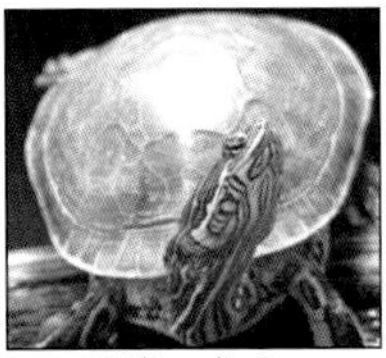

© Wikimedia Commons

❒ ________ **Chicken Turtle** (*Deirochelys reticularia chrysea*) Other names: none / Status: FL = stable, IUCN = LC / Length: 4-10 in. (10-25 cm) / Weight: n/a / Life span: to 25 years / Reproduces: lays from 2 to 19 clutches of eggs during both winter and early spring / Found: AC, coastal, near coast, inland

❒ ___________ **Florida Mud Turtle** (*Kinosternon subrubrum steindachneri*) Other names: mud turtle / Status: FL = stable, IUCN = LC / Length: 2.75-4 in. (7-10 cm) / Weight: n/a / Life span: to 38 years / Reproduces: lays its eggs in upland areas after the first spring rains / Found: AC, coastal, near coast, inland.

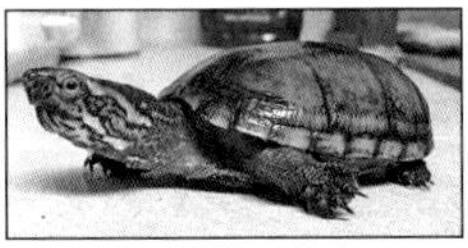

© Wikimedia Commons

❒ _______ **Stinkpot Turtle** (*Sternotherus odoratus*) Other names: common musk turtle, stinkpot / Status: FL = stable, IUCN = LC / Length: 3-5 in. (8-14 cm) / Weight: n/a / Life span: to more than 50 years / Reproduces: lays 2-9 elliptical, hard-shelled eggs in shallow burrows in the spring / Found: ChC, CC, HC, near coast, inland.

© Wikimedia Commons

Snakes

❒ ___________ **Florida Scarlet Snake** (*Cemophora coccinea coccinea*) Other names: n/a / Status: FL = stable, IUCN = LC / Length: 14-20 in. (35-50 cm) / Weight: n/a / Life span: to 15 years / Reproduces: lays 2-9 eggs in the spring / Found: AC, coastal, near coast, inland.

© Kenneth L. Krysko, UF

❒ _________ **Southern Florida Rainbow Snake** (*Farancia erytrogramma seminola*) Other names: rainbow snake, eel moccasin / Status: FL = extremely rare and may be extinct, IUCN = NE / Length: 45-56 in. (114-142 in.) / Weight: n/a / Life span: n/a / Reproduces: probably lays between 22-52 eggs as does the far more common rainbow snake found in the northern part of the state / Found: EC, near Fisheating Creek.

photo is of *F. e. erytogramma*

❒ ________ **Southern Hognose Snake** (*Heterodon simus*) Other names: puff adder, hissing adder, blow viper, hissing sand snake / Status: FL = rare, declining, IUCN = VU / Length: 14-21 in. (35.5-53.3 cm) / Weight: n/a / Life span: to 18 years / Reproduces: lays 6-14 eggs in the spring / Found: AC, near coast, inland.

❒ _________ **Southern Florida Mole Kingsnake** (*Lampropeltis calligaster occipitolineata*) Other names: n/a / Status: FL = very rare, IUCN = NE / Length: 30-40 in. (76-101 cm) / Weight: n/a / Life span: to 12 years / Reproduces: lays eggs but due to its rarity no wild nests have ever been documented / Found: EC, HC, inland.

© Kenneth L. Krysko, UF

© Wikimedia Commons

❒ _________ **Florida Kingsnake** (*Lampropeltis getula floridana*) Other names: n/a / Status: FL = stable, IUCN = LC / Length: 36-48 in. (91-121 cm) / Weight: n/a / Life span: to 15 years / Reproduces: lays 3-30 eggs in the early summer / Found: EC, ChC, near beach, inland.

❒ _______ **Scarlet Kingsnake** (*Lampropeltis elapsoides*) Other names: false coral snake / Status: FL = stable, IUCN = LC / Length: 14-20 in. (35-50 cm) / Weight: n/a / Life span: to 15 years / Reproduces: lays 2-9 eggs in the spring / Found: AC, coastal, near coast, inland.

© Wikimedia Commons

❒ ________ **Florida Green Watersnake** (*Nerodia floridana*) Other names: n/a / Status: FL = stable, IUCN = LC / Length: 30-55 in. (76-140 cm) / Weight: n/a / Life span: to 5 years / Nests: ovoviviparous, gives birth to as many as 100 live young in the late spring or early summer / Found: AC, coastal, near coast, inland.

© Wikimedia Commons

❒ _ **Florida Rough Greensnake** (*Opheodrys aestivus*) Other names: grass snake, green grass snake / Status: FL = stable, IUCN = LC / Length: 22-46 in. (55-116 cm) / Weight: n/a / Life span: to 15 years / Reproduces: lays between 3-12 eggs in the mid to late summer / Found: SC, ChC, LC, CC, GC, near coast, inland.

© Kenneth L. Krysko, UF

❒ _________ **Florida Pinesnake** (*Pituophis melanoleucus*) Other names: bull snake, black and white snake, carpet snake, pilot snake, white gopher snake / Status: FL = species of special concern, IUCN = LC / Length: 48-66 in. (122-168 cm) / Weight: n/a / Life span: to 15 years / Reproduces: lays between 4-8 large eggs in the spring / Found: ChC, near coast, inland.

❒ __________ **Pine Woods Snake** (*Rhadinaea flavilata*) Other names: littersnake / Status: FL = stable, IUCN = NE / Length: 10-13 in. (25-33 cm) / Weight: n/a / Life span: to 15 years / Reproduces: lays 2-4 eggs anytime from May through August / Found: SC, near coast, inland.

© Kenneth L. Krysko, UF

© Kenneth L. Krysko, UF

❒ _______ **Southern Florida Swamp Snake** (*Seminatrix pygaea cyclas*) Other names: n/a / Status: FL = stable, IUCN = LC / Length: 10-15 in. (25-38 cm) / Weight: n/a / Life span: to 12 years / Reproduces: ovoviviparous, gives live birth to 4-6 neonates in the late summer or fall / Found: AC, coastal, near coast, inland.

❒ __________ **Eastern Mud Snake** (*Farancia abacura abacura*) Other names: mud snake / Status: FL = stable, IUCN = LC / Length: 40-80 in. (101-202 cm) / Weight: n/a / Life span: to 12 years / Reproduces: lays between 11-104 eggs in the early summer / Found: AC, near coast, inland.

© Kenneth L. Krysko, UF

© Kenneth L. Krysko, UF

❒ ___________ **Peninsula Crowned Snake** (*Tantilla relicta relicta*) Other names: crown snake / Status: FL = stable, IUCN = LC / Length: 7-8.5 in. (17.7-21.5 cm) / Weight: n/a / Life span: to 10 years / Reproduces: lays between 1-3 eggs in late spring or early summer / Found: SC, ChC, near coast, inland.

❒ ________ **Eastern Gartersnake** (*Thamnophis sirtalis*) Other names: garter snake / Status: FL = stable, IUCN = LC / Length: 20-28 in. (50-71 cm) / Weight: n/a / Life span: to 15 years / Reproduces: live-bearing with anywhere from 6 to 60 offspring born in the late spring / Found: AC, coastal, near coast, inland.

© Kenneth L. Krysko, UF

Frogs and Toads

❒ _________ **Cane toad** (*Rhinella marina*) Other names: giant toad, marine toad, Bufo toad / Status: FL = invasive, expanding its range, IUCN = LC / Length: 3.9-5.9 in. (10-15 cm) / Weight: the largest cane toad recorded weighed 5.8 lb. (2.65 kg) / Life span: to 15 years / Reproduces: lays between 8,000-25,000 eggs in any standing water, tadpoles are poisonous / Found: CC, near coast, inland.

© Kenneth L. Krysko, UF

❒ __________ **Eastern Spadefoot Toad** (*Scaphiopus holbrookii*) Other names: none / Status: FL = stable, IUCN = LC / Length: 1.75-2.25 in. (4-6 cm) / Weight: n/a / Life span: to 5 years / Reproduces: lays its eggs in temporary ponds or puddles in early spring / Found: AC, near coast, inland.

❒ __________ **Pinewoods Treefrog** (*Hyla femoralis*) Other names: n/a / Status: FL = stable, IUCN = LC / Length: 1-1.5 in. (25-32 mm) / Weight: n/a / Life span: to one year or less / Reproduces: lays 100-125 eggs in water during the summer / Found: AC, near coast, inland.

© Kenneth L. Krysko, UF

© Kenneth L. Krysko, UF

❒ __________ **Barking Treefrog** (*Hyla gratiosa*) Other names: n/a / Status: FL = stable, IUCN = LC / Length: 2-2.6 in. (5-7 cm) / Weight: n/a / Life span: to 10 years / Reproduces: lays 1,500-2,000 eggs in marshes and ponds in the early summer / Found: AC, near coast, inland.

❒ __________ **Gopher Frog** (*Lithobates capito*) Other names: Florida gopher frog / Status: FL = declining, species of special concern, IUCN = LC / Length: 2-4.5 in. (5.1-11.4 cm) / Weight: n/a / Life span: to 3 years / Reproduces: lays eggs in any available body of water in the early spring / Found: SC, ChC, EC, near coast, inland.

❒ __________ **Little Grass Frog** (*Pseudacris ocularis*) Other names: none / Status: FL = stable, IUCN = LC / Length: .45-.90 in. (11-16 cm) / Weight: n/a / Life span: to 10 years / Note: this is the smallest frog found in North America / Reproduces: lays its eggs in any body of water in the early spring / Found: AC, coastal, near coast, inland.

❒ __________ **Florida Cricket Frog** (*Acris gryllus dorsalis*) Other names: cricket frog / Status: FL = stable, IUCN = LC / Length: .75-1.25 in. (19-31 cm) / Weight: n/a / Life span: one year or less / Reproduces: lays its eggs in any available standing water from the spring through the fall / Found: AC, coastal, near coast, inland.

© Kenneth L. Krysko, UF

Amphisbaenid

❒ __________ **Florida Worm Lizard** (*Rhineura floridana*) Other names: thunderworms / Status: FL = stable, IUCN = LC / Length: 7-12 in. (18-30 cm) / Weight: n/a / Life span: n/a / Reproduces: lays its eggs underground where the adults live almost all of their lives / Found: SC, ChC, GC, near coast, inland.

© Kenneth L. Krysko, UF

© Wikimedia Commons

Lizards

❒ __________ **Broad-headed skink** (*Plestiodon laticeps*) Other names: skink, red-headed scorpions / Status: FL = stable, IUCN = LC / Length: 5.9-17 in. (15-43 cm) / Weight: n/a / Life span: to 16 years / Reproduces: lays 8-11 ovoid eggs in the summer in rotting logs or sawdust piles / Found: LC, near coast, inland.

❒ __________ **Eastern Slender Glass Lizard** (*Ophisaurus attenuatus*) Other names: glass lizard / Status: FL = stable, IUCN = LC / Length: 30-42 in. (76-106 cm) / Weight: n/a / Life span: to 30 years / Reproduces: lays 6-17 eggs in grass clumps or heavy vegetation / Found: CC, near coast, inland.

❒ __________ **Island Glass Lizard** (*Ophisaurus compressus*) Other names: glass lizard / Status: FL = stable, IUCN = LC / Length: 20-25 in. (50-63 cm) / Weight: n/a / Life span: n/a / Reproduces: little is known about the nesting behavior of this species, believed to lay 7-10 roundish eggs in an underground nest / Found: SC, ChC, LC, CC, near coast, inland.

© Wikimedia Commons

❒ __________ **Eastern Glass Lizard** (*Ophisaurus ventralis*) Other names: glass lizard / Status: FL = stable, IUCN = LC / Length: 36-43 in. (91-109 cm) / Weight: n/a / Life span: to 30 years / Reproduces: lays 7-10 round, white eggs in clumps of grass or under forest litter / Found: SC, ChC, LC, CC, near coast, inland.

© Wikimedia Commons

© Wikimedia Commons

❒ __________ **Florida Scrub Lizard** (*Sceloporus woodi*) Other names: none / Status: FL = stable, IUCN = LC / Length: 4-5 in. (10-12.5 cm) / Weight: n/a / Life span: n/a / Reproduces: lays 2-4 round, chalky eggs in the soil or down in gopher tortoise burrows / Found: CC, near coast, inland.

❒ __________ **Peninsula Mole Skink** (*Plestiodon egregius onocrepis*) Other names: mole skink / Status: Fl = stable, IUCN = LC / Length: 5-6 in. (12.5-15 cm) / Weight: n/a / Life span: to 5 years / Reproduces: lays 2-4 elliptical white eggs in cavities up to six feet beneath the surface / Found: SC, near coast, inland.

© Kenneth L. Krysko, UF

❒ __________ **Bark Anole** (*Anolis distichus*) **INVASIVE!** Other names: none / Status: FL = non-native, invasive, IUCN = LC / Length: 6-8 in. (15-20 cm) / Weight: n/a / Life span: to 5 years / Note: can be distinguished from the brown anole by a yellow dewlap / Reproduces: lays its eggs in early summer / Found: AC, coastal, near coast, inland.

Courtesy USGS

❒ ________ **Tokay Gecko** (*Gekko gecko*) **INVASIVE!** Other names: bulldog gecko / Status: FL=invasive, populations increasing, IUCN=LC / Life span: to 10 years / Length: 11-15 in. (30-40 cm) / Weight: n/a / Reproduces: has multiple pairings and lays multiple clutches for 4-5 months every year, mostly in the summer / Found: AC, coastal, near coast, inland.

© Kenneth L. Krysko, UF

❒ ________ **Northern Curly-tailed Lizard** (*Leiocephalus carinatus*) **INVASIVE!** Other names: lion lizard / Status: FL=invasive, slowly expanding its range, IUCN=NE / Life span: to 8 years / Length: 8-10.5 in. (20-27 cm) / Weight: n/a / Reproduces: n/a / Found: LC, coastal though there may be other isolated pockets elsewhere.

❒ ______________ **Red-headed Agama** (*Agama agama*) **INVASIVE!** Other names: red-headed agama, rainbow agama / Status: FL=invasive and expanding, IUCN=NE / Life span: to 25 years / Length: 12-14 in. (30-35 cm) / Weight: n/a / Reproduces: n/a / Found: CC, LC, coastal, near coast, inland.

© Kenneth L. Krysko, UF

❒ _________ **Knight Anole** (*Anolis equestris*) **INVASIVE!** Other names: Cuban knight anole / Status: FL = invasive and expanding its range, IUCN = LC / Life span: to 16 years / Length: 13-20 in. (33-51 cm) / Weight: n/a / Reproduces: n/a / Found: AC, scattered populations, coastal, near coast, inland.

© Kenneth L. Krysko, UF

Salamanders and Sirens

❒ _________ **Two-toed Amphiuma** (*Amphiuma means*) Other names: congo snake, conger eel / Status: FL = stable, IUCN = LC / Length: 30-36 in. (76-91 cm) / Weight: n/a / Life span: to 27 years / Reproduces: lays up to 200 eggs in a damp cavity near the waters edge and remains with the eggs for up to 5 months during incubation / Found: AC, near coast, inland.

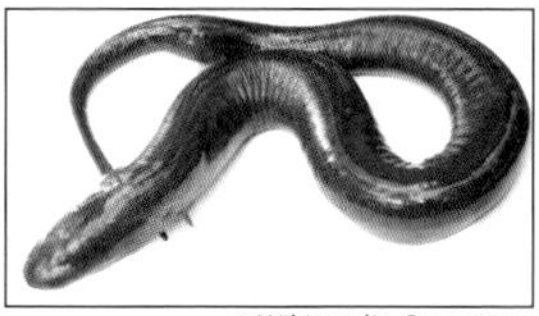
© Wikimedia Commons

© Wikimedia Commons

❒ ___________ **Peninsula Newt** (*Notophthalmus viridescens piaropicola*) Other names: eastern newt / Status: FL = stable, IUCN = LC / Length: 4-5 in. (10-12.5 cm) / Weight: n/a / Life span: to 15 years / Reproduces: lays its eggs in water, similar to frogs and develops as a tadpole into adulthood / Found: AC, coastal, near coast, inland.

Boca Grande Lighthouse

The Parks, Preserves & Eco-destinations of Southwest Florida

There are 162 destinations identified in this section of *The Living Gulf Coast*: 61 of them are described in detail, while the remaining 101 receive a paragraph or two. Choosing which destination merited the additional coverage and which received only a brief synopsis was not easy.

Of course, the flagships had to be included. Places such as Mote Marine Laboratory and Aquarium, Myakka River State Park, Babcock Ranch, J.N. "Ding" Darling National Wildlife Refuge, and the Big Cypress National Preserve were mandatory. It was the smaller, less-renowned parks and preserves that presented the real challenge. To select these I relied on personal recommendations from local naturalists and birders, as well as county and park officials. I wanted unique, genuine places that were not "roadside attractions" and offered the visitor something truly special in experiencing nature. Many of these destinations are on the Great Florida Birding Trail, a region-by-region birding guide published by the Florida Fish and Wildlife Conservation Commission. Go to www.floridabirdingtrail.com to learn more about the trail. To be certain we had made the right choices, my wife, Molly, and I, toured, hiked, biked, canoed, or kayaked all 61 major destinations.

According to the Conservancy of Southwest Florida, the six counties included in this book have a combined total of 3,853,440 acres (6,021 square miles). Of that acreage, 1,407,165 (2,198 square miles) are managed lands, which translates into parks, preserves, wetlands, and wildlife sanctuaries. That represents an astonishing 37 percent of Southwest Florida. It is a number we should be proud of. Because of this, we still have panthers roaming the wilds of Florida and some of the best birding found in North America. As time passes it will be a struggle to protect these open spaces from the encroaching hand of our own self-centered industries, whether phosphate mining, drilling, subdivisions, malls, or airports. Protecting these wild places in the future is our single greatest challenge.

The destinations chosen here flow from north to south. Mote Marine is the most northerly destination, and Everglades National Park is the farthest south. Every destination has a checkbox in front of it and a space to note the date you visited it. The park symbols are self–explanatory, but if you need help a symbol key is provided on the last two pages of this book. There is also a solitary "snowmobiling allowed" symbol hiding somewhere in this section just for fun. Good luck finding it!

While I have done everything possible to make certain the information contained herein accurately reflects what you might expect to discover at each destination, there may well be mistakes. Parks that are free might begin charging an admission fee, just as the amenities found at some destinations will change over time. To get the latest information, I recommend you visit the individual websites of each location before heading out. Many of these sites have downloadable PDF trail maps, campsite layouts, and other information you may want to have before visiting.

My hope is that this work inspires every reader to turn off the television, break out the camping gear, dust off the paddles, dig out the binoculars, toss in some water, bug spray, and sunscreen and go discover these natural treasures. Once there, amidst the birds singing and the sunlight shining on you, you'll be glad you did. Enjoy!

The sun sets over Sarasota County

© Dick Fortune & Sara Lopez

Sarasota County

Carved out of Manatee County in 1921, Sarasota County is approximately 725 square miles in size. Of that total, 572 square miles are land, and the balance is water, mostly the Myakka River, along with Sarasota Bay, Little Sarasota Bay, and Lemon Bay. A variation of the name first appeared on a 1763 land-grant map as *Zarazote*. The name is believed to have been derived from a Calusa word meaning either point of rocks or, possibly, place of the dance.

According to the Conservancy of Southwest Florida, 28 percent of Sarasota County (102,674 acres) is managed land. Most of that land is in a series of preserves, parks, and state forests that straddle the Myakka River, including one of the largest parks in Florida: the 57-square-mile Myakka River State Park. Adjacent preserves such as Deer Prairie, Mabry Carlton, and Jelks converge to create a huge section of conservation land called the Myakka Island. The spectacular Myakka River is considered by many to be one of the best "Wild and Scenic" waterways in the state. From the numerous launches found at Myakka River State Park to the put-in at Snook Haven just above the Myakka State Forest, it is well worth the time to explore at least part of this historic Florida stream.

Sarasota County also has an unusually high number of county, regional, and city-owned parks and preserves scattered throughout the district. Because of this, no one living in or visiting Sarasota County is ever more than a few minutes from quality natural open space.

Like all of Southwest Florida, however, Sarasota County continues to struggle with the onslaught of rapid growth. In 1930, nine years after incorporation, there were 12,000 people living in the county. Most of these residents were farmers, cattlemen, and commercial fishermen. By 1950 the population had doubled to 28,827. By 1990 that number had increased more than tenfold to 301,900. In 2010 the population of Sarasota County was estimated at 388,296 and is expected to increase to 414,565 by 2015. This rapid growth has put an immense strain on the natural resources of the county, which, because of its small size and high population has the second-highest

Kayaking in the Gulf of Mexico Courtesy Sarasota VC Bureau

density per square mile of any county in Southwest Florida: 678 people per square mile (Lee is first at 765 people per square mile; Collier has 164).

This growth has also affected water quality in the area. While Lemon Bay and Myakka River have largely avoided the troubles created by overtaxed municipal sewer and septic systems and the excess runoff of residential and commercial fertilizers, both Sarasota Bay and Little Sarasota Bay have not been as fortunate. For several years during the past decade a consistent red tide haunted Sarasota Bay for months on end, and parts of the bay collapsed as a result of hypoxic (oxygen-depleted) zones created by these relentless algae blooms. In an effort to help prevent future harmful algae blooms, the city of Sarasota was one of the first municipalities to adopt a residential fertilizer ordinance, forbidding the use of quick-release fertilizers during the rainy season.

In addition, Sarasota County tightened the rules and regulations governing community sewer and individual septic systems, hoping to reduce unwanted nutrients in the watershed. Mote Marine Lab has worked hand in hand with the county in monitoring the nitrogen and phosphate loads throughout the area and well out into the Gulf of Mexico in an effort to restore water quality throughout the region.

It is impossible to write about Sarasota County without mentioning its beaches. Siesta Key Beach, comprised of 99 percent pure quartz sand, has been consistently voted one of the best beaches in America since 1991. Other fabulous beaches that are included in this book include Venice, Brohard, and Caspersen, where the fabled fossilized shark's teeth can still be sifted out of the sand.

Sarasota County's well-designed website (www.scgov.net) makes it easy to find the area's parks, preserves, and paddling trails, along with printable maps for each of them. From devoted Audubon Society birders searching for the elusive scrub jay, to trekking backpackers hiking the Myakka Island Wilderness Trail through the T. Mabry Carlton Jr. Memorial Preserve, there is truly something for everyone in Sarasota County. So put down this book, grab your binoculars, bug spray, and sunscreen, and get out there and see it for yourself.

Sarasota County Eco-Destinations

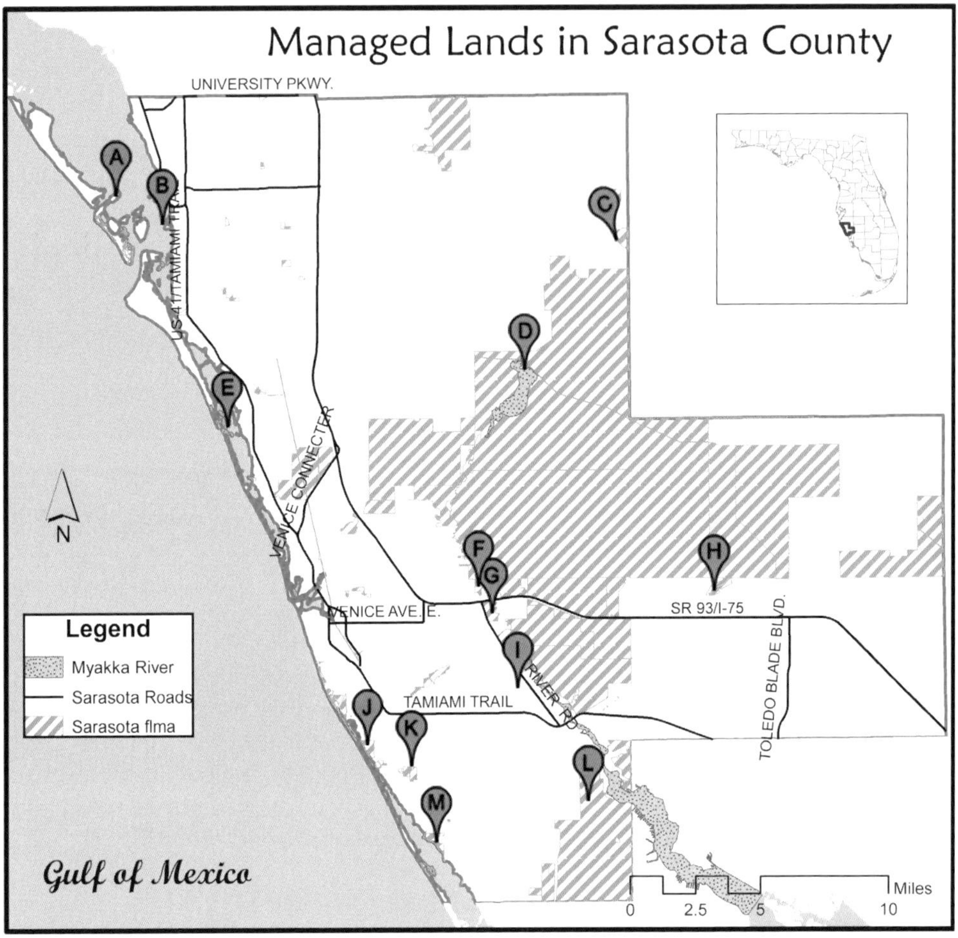

A. Mote Marine Laboratory
B. Marie Selby Botanical Gardens
C. Crowley Museum & Nature Center
D. Myakka River State Park
E. Oscar Scherer State Park
F. T. Mabry Carlton, Jr. Memorial Preserve
G. Sleeping Turtle Preserve
H. Myakkahatchee Creek Environmental Park
I. Jelks and Deer Prairie Creek Preserves
J. Caspersen & Brohard Beaches
K. Venice Audubon Rookery
L. Myakka State Forest
M. Lemon Bay Park

CONSERVANCY
Of Southwest Florida
www.conservancy.org

Managed Lands in Southwest Florida

Sarasota County
366,080 Acres
102,674 Acres Managed
28%

❒ _____ A. Mote Marine Laboratory and Aquarium

Location: 1600 Ken Thompson Parkway, Sarasota, FL 34236 / Phone: 941-388-4441 / Fax: 941-388-1872 / Website: www.mote.org / E-mail: info@mote.org / 10.5-acre campus / Admission fee charged.

Shark tank at Mote Marine Courtesy Mote Marine Lab

What began as a one-room lab in 1955 today has become one of North America's most important marine labs and public aquariums. Mote Marine Laboratory and Aquarium has nearly 200 staff members, 1,400 dedicated volunteers, and 350,000 visitors a year. The original lab was located in Cape Haze, 40 miles south of its present location on Sarasota Bay, and was funded by the Vanderbilt family. The founding director of the lab, Dr. Eugenie Clark, is the author of *Lady with a Spear*, and it was reading that book that inspired Anne Vanderbilt to provide the site and money to get the Cape Haze Marine Laboratory started.

Much of Dr. Clark's original research focused on the biology and behavior of sharks. Today Clark continues her research at Mote and is known for her studies of many species of sharks and fishes. She has served as chief scientist on 72 submersible dives to study deep-sea sharks.

Only five years after opening, the Cape Haze Lab needed more space, and the city of Sarasota mounted a campaign to have Dr. Clark move her facility to the southern tip of Siesta Key. By 1965 the Vanderbilt family for various reasons had lost interest in the lab. The following year, with the finances of the Cape

A trophy tarpon at Mote Marine Aquarium
© Charles Sobczak

Haze Marine Lab in trouble, Dr. Clark was approached by William R. Mote, a wealthy transportation executive and avid fisherman, who helped the lab back to a sound financial footing. The lab and aquarium are named in honor of Mote and his family.

Today Mote's scientists and staff work in such diverse fields as sustainable aquaculture, coastal ecology, coral reef research, the effects of oil spills on ecosystems, fisheries enhancement, and ecotoxicology, as well as the study of sea turtles, dolphins, whales, and manatees. Its sea turtle rehabilitation hospital has cared for hundreds of sick and injured loggerhead, green, and other sea turtles over the years, and its dolphin and whale hospital has provided similar aid to marine mammals in need. The hospitals are not open to the public.

In 1978 Mote Marine Lab seriously considered relocating again to a 15-acre site in Placida, Florida, but a groundswell of local support, spearheaded by community leader Jim Neville, persuaded the lab to stay in Sarasota. Neville worked with the Arvida Corporation and the city of Sarasota to lease a 6.7-acre site on City Island to the lab for $1 per year. A countywide fund-raising effort ensued, and Mote officially opened its new Marine Science Center, later renamed Mote Aquarium, on Oct. 18, 1980. The center was designed to educate the public about Mote research and local marine life.

Mote Aquarium has more than 100 marine species on display, interactive exhibits for all ages, and glimpses into Mote's working labs. Although other eco-attractions throughout Southwest Florida have touch tanks and aquariums, none compares with the enormous tanks and multitude of exhibits found at Mote. Its 135,000-gallon shark habitat tank not only exhibits several regional species of sharks such as nurse, blacknose, and sandbar sharks, but also teems with Florida's top game fish, including tarpon, snook, redfish, and jack crevalle.

Finding Nemo at Mote Marine Aquarium
© Charles Sobczak

When you enter the darkened, air-conditioned main building, you are met by a number of smaller but compelling displays of everything from Pacific clownfish to local Spanish hogfish. One display showcases convict fish studied by Dr. Clark, who discovered how they are unique among all other fish: the young feed the adults, which never leave their burrows. Mote's exhibit allows the visitor to see these elusive, eel-like adult fish

Children watching the manatees at Mote
Courtesy Mote Marine Lab

using a carefully placed reflecting mirror set below the tank. A live-feed camera also helps you to catch a glimpse of these secretive fish, native to the west-central Pacific.

Other displays include an enormous touch tank called Contact Cove that allows you to handle sea stars, horseshoe crabs, sea urchins, and other harmless marine life. Guests can even touch the sleek backs of stingrays in the Ray Touch Pool, in which the barbs have been carefully removed from the rays.

A short walk across the parking lot to the Ann and Alfred Goldstein Marine Mammal Research and Rehabilitation Center will take you to another set of large exhibits. Several contain orphaned loggerhead turtles that cannot be released back into the wild. One exhibit holds a beautiful but blind green sea turtle named Hang Tough. Another green sea turtle named Harriet and three large loggerheads named Shelley, Montego, and Edgar round out the crew. The pens they are kept in allow visitors to get within a few feet of these nearly 300-pound animals.

The largest tank at Mote is the 200,000-gallon lagoon where Moonshine, a pan-tropical spotted dolphin, and Harley, a long-snouted spinner dolphin, greet you with that enigmatic dolphin smile. Visitors can also see Hugh and Buffett, the world's only manatees trained to participate in behavioral research. Mote scientists work with these animals to learn how manatees use their five senses to navigate their environment.

In addition to its amazing displays, Mote has a gift shop, the Deep Sea Diner, and runs eco-tours of Sarasota Bay by boat. It also offers summer camps, classes, lectures, and other events throughout the year.

In addition to the Mote Marine facility on City Island, it has a campus on Summerland Key in the Florida Keys that focuses on coral reef research and aquaculture, a sustainable fish farm called Mote Aquaculture Research Park in eastern Sarasota County, and a field station in Charlotte Harbor that studies the population health, movement patterns, and habitat needs of some of Florida's most prized sport fish.

As Mote Marine Laboratory grew over the years, the board of directors and staff chose to integrate the lab's scientific work with its educational outreach programs. Because of that not only can you see large aquariums filled with fish, but you can also peer through windows into a marine lab where countless seahorses are raised for use in aquariums throughout the world. It is the dedication and work of the researchers that make up the heart and soul of Mote.

❒ ________ B. Marie Selby Botanical Gardens

Location: 811 South Palm Avenue, Sarasota, FL 34236 / Phone: 941-366-5731 / Fax: 941-366-9807 / Website: www.selby.org / E-mail: contactus@selby.org / 9.5-acre campus / Admission fee charged.

The Koi pond at the gardens © Charles Sobczak

Not surprisingly, Florida ranks third in the United States in its number of botanical gardens. Only California and Pennsylvania have more. Florida has 36, and Southwest Florida claims four of these. Two are located in Sarasota: Marie Selby Botanical Gardens and Sarasota Jungle Gardens.

Marie Selby Botanical Gardens manage to pack an unbelievable amount of greenery into a relatively small area. Its bayfront campus is just less than 13 acres. This has its advantages in that the entire property can be covered in a half-day, with a lot less walking and a lot more viewing.

The gardens are named in honor of Marie Selby, who was born in 1885 in West Virginia. Being of an adventurous nature, she was the first woman to cross the United States by car. In 1908 she married William Selby, an avid fisherman who brought her to see Sarasota a few years later. Marie fell in love with the town, and the couple purchased a seven-acre parcel bordering Sarasota Bay and Hudson Bayou. That acreage forms the cornerstone of the botanical gardens.

Vast oil and mineral holdings made the couple multimillionaires by the time they built their Spanish-style home on the grounds, but they lived modestly and kept a low profile. They were outdoors-loving people who liked raising cattle, fishing in Sarasota Bay, and, of course, gardening. William passed away in 1956, and Marie continued to plant flowers, shrubs, and trees on the grounds until her

A cactus blooms in the gardens

Courtesy Sarastoa VC Bureau

passing in 1971. She bequeathed the property to the community as a botanical garden for all to enjoy.

On July 7, 1975, Marie Selby Botanical Gardens officially opened to the public. Prior to the grand opening, the foundation purchased the adjoining Christy Payne House, which presently serves as the gardens' gallery, with constantly changing shows displaying botanical artwork and photography. In 1998 the Payne House was added to the U.S. National Register of Historic Places. In November 2001 both William and Marie Selby were reinterred in front of their beloved home on the grounds of Selby Gardens. A triangular-shaped fountain now pays lasting tribute to their generosity.

Marie Selby Botanical Gardens today are best known for their focus on epiphytes, especially orchids and bromeliads, as well as their canopy ecosystems. They currently have the largest living bromeliad collection in the world, with more than 20,000 plants from some 6,000 species in 1,200 genera and 214 distinct plant families. The orchid collection alone exceeds 6,000 plants. These plants are rotated constantly through the Tropical Display House as they come into bloom. In the gardens alone, there are approximately 2,300 plants to observe.

In addition to displaying its amazing collections, Marie Selby Botanical Gardens have nearly 26,000 vials of flowers in preservative fluids, second only to the world-renowned Royal Botanical Gardens at Kew, England. The facility has sponsored more than 150 scientific expeditions to tropical rain forests from Ecuador to Mexico. The research library contains approximately 7,000 volumes, some extremely rare, dealing with tropical plants, especially epiphytes.

The grounds at Marie Selby include more than 20 habitats. You can find immense banyans, bamboo, boa trees, live oaks, palms, mangroves, succulents, wildflowers, cycads, and a koi pond. A walkway takes you along Sarasota Bay where the breezes coming off the Gulf of Mexico make even a summer visit enjoyable. The historic Selby house offers coffee, tea, and light snacks daily, and the gift shop offers the visitor one of the largest collections of orchid and other gardening books in Florida. Beside the gift shop is a plant lover's paradise, the Garden Shop, which sells an assortment of orchids, bromeliads, trees, ferns, and seasonal offerings.

Because of its gorgeous grounds and various facilities, the Marie Selby Botanical Gardens have become a favorite for weddings, parties, and corporate retreats. There is something magical about the grounds—perhaps the spirit of William and Marie—that make this the ideal place for these special events.

❒ ________ C. Crowley Museum and Nature Center

Location: 16405 Myakka Road, Sarasota, FL 34240 / Phone: 941-400-2780 / Fax: 941-322-1000 / Website: www.cmncfl.org / E-mail: info@cmncfl.org / 190 acres / Admission fee charged.

Located roughly a mile north of Myakka River State Park off of Myakka Road, the Crowley Museum and Nature Center is an interesting side trip on your way to visit the much larger park. Crowley, consisting of a museum, pioneer cabin, working sugar cane mill, and fully restored "cracker" house, offers a first-hand view of how Florida settlers managed to get by in the late 1800s. The 190-acre site also offers some excellent nature trails.

The way it used to be © Charles Sobczak

The museum contains scores of artifacts from the pioneer era, including hand tools, household furnishings, and items from the Old Miakka General Store and Post Office. The small pioneer cabin on the property is representative of a typical one-room building found throughout Southwest Florida around the end of the 1800s and early 1900s.

The real treasure here is the completely restored two-story Tatum House. Originally built in 1889 and enlarged in 1892, this stunning example of cracker architecture was moved to its present site in 1996 and, through donations and grant money, was totally restored over the next five years by volunteers. Additional donations of pioneer artifacts, from handmade brooms to dishes, furnishings, and cookware, have made the Tatum House an excellent example of what a large family household looked like more than 100 years ago—reminiscent of the original MacIvey homestead in Patrick Smith's classic Florida novel, *A Land Remembered.*

After taking in the museum and the other attractions on site, take a stroll down the half-mile boardwalk into the surrounding countryside. A self-guided trail takes you through pine flatwoods, shady oak hammocks, over the Maple Branch swamp, and out to the edge of the expansive Tatum Sawgrass Marsh along the edge of the Myakka River. The towering slash pines at the start of the trail offer a rare encounter with a fully mature, dry pine flatwood forest. These trees are more than 100 years old and represent a prime example of what Florida's extensive pine

The boardwalk through the swamp © Charles Sobczak

forests must have looked like before loggers took out almost all of the virgin timber. Sightings of birds might include barred owls, wild turkeys, crested caracara, sandhill cranes, and seasonal buntings, warblers, and eastern bluebirds. From the two-story observation tower, birders can look out across the Tatum Sawgrass Marsh and find white pelicans, roseate spoonbills, and wood storks feeding along the edges of the Myakka River, while eagles, osprey, and hawks soar overhead.

Where the trail crosses over a small stream, look for river otters, white-tailed deer, eastern spotted skunks, marsh rabbits, and fox squirrels. Open-range cattle still graze on the property. Reptiles include a variety of snakes, gopher tortoises, lizards, and the occasional alligator. Because of the varied habitats, plant and insect life abounds. As you walk down the boardwalk look for butterflies, colorful and varied dragonflies, as well as a wide variety of wetlands-loving plants such as pickerelweed and alligator flag.

Every January the Crowley Nature Center puts on the Florida Heritage Festival, during which volunteers practice the lost art of blacksmithing, sugar-cane grinding, quilting, carving, and more. Old-time recipes of barbequed pork, roasted corn, and sweet potatoes are available while everyone enjoys hayrides, gourd painting, and country music. Another popular annual event is Starry Nite, a fundraiser for the Nature Center celebrated outdoors in early March.

Anyone with more than a passing interest in "olde Florida" should include a visit to this gem of site. With its meticulously restored buildings, interesting artifacts, and lovely trails, the Crowley Museum and Nature Center is a great way to spend an afternoon in the backwoods of Florida.

❐ ________ D. Myakka River State Park

Location: 13208 State Road 72, Sarasota, FL 34241 / Phone: 941-361-6511 / Reservations: 800-326-3521 / Fax: n/a / Website: www.floridastateparks.org / E-mail: n/a / 37,000 acres / Admission fee charged.

Encompassing more than 57 square miles (37,000 acres), Myakka River State Park is one of the largest and oldest state parks in Florida. Numerous adjacent parcels such as the Pinelands Reserve, T. Mabry Carlton Jr. Memorial Reserve, and Myakka Prairie bring the total protected lands to approximately 142 square miles (91,066 acres). Sometimes referred to as the Myakka Island, these abutting parcels in aggregate represent one of the largest tracts of undeveloped wilderness in Florida outside of the Everglades.

Myakka River Courtesy Florida State Parks

The history of Myakka River State Park dates back to 1910 and the arrival of Bertha Palmer, a wealthy Chicago socialite who began purchasing vast tracts of land in what was then Manatee County. After her death, her two sons, Honeré Palmer and Potter Palmer II, donated a strategic tract of 1,920 acres along the Myakka River to form the cornerstone of the park. That same year, President Franklin Deleno Roosevelt's Civilian Conservation Corps (CCC), operating out of primitive barracks and working amidst swarms of mosquitoes, alligators, and wild animals, began building the visitors center, cabins, and picnic pavilions, as well as laying out the park road, planting trees, and digging drainage ditches. The park opened to the public on June 1, 1942.

Myakka River State Park encompasses a variety of habitats. Along the park road lie hammocks of live oaks and cabbage palms, with very little understory able to thrive beneath the dense canopy. To the south are some of the last untouched tracts of dry prairie left in Florida. Adding to the mix are the freshwater marshes

Biking Myakka State Park
© Charles Sobczak

Canopy Walkway at Myakka
Courtesy Florida State Parks

Kayaking down the Myakka
Courtesy Sarasota VC Bureau

surrounding Upper Myakka Lake, as well as numerous smaller wetlands found throughout the region. This variety of habitats, along with the sheer size of the park, makes for some of the best wildlife viewing in the state.

On a typical bike ride or hike through Myakka, you might expect to see alligators, limpkins, roseate spoonbills, armadillos, wild turkeys, deer, wild boar, gray squirrels, pygmy rattlesnakes, and box turtles. The park has 35.9 miles of hiking trails divided into four distinct loops. Along with the two campsites (Big Flats Campground and Old Prairie) just off the road, there are six primitive campsites located deep within the interior of the park and accessible only on foot or bicycle. Several palm log cabins built by the CCC are available for rent, though the high demand for these cabins makes it necessary to book them a year in advance.

One of the most unique attractions at the park is the Myakka Canopy Walkway. Inspired by Dr. Margaret Lowman, former director of Marie Selby Botanical Gardens, this unique walkway was completed in 2000 at a cost in excess of $100,000 and with the help of countless volunteers. The 85-foot walkway is suspended 25 feet above the forest floor and takes you through a mixture of live oak and cabbage palm canopies that abound with native epiphytes such as the cardinal airplant, ball moss, and resurrection fern. A good way to conclude your canopy walk is climbing the 74-foot tower overlooking the park. The views are astounding.

A park concession rents bicycles, kayaks, and canoes, and operates what have been called the world's largest airboats. It also runs a truck-pulled tram ride with interpretive guides who help visitors better understand the history and flora and fauna of the park. A small but nicely appointed wildlife diorama at the park entrance includes mounts of Florida panthers, bald eagles, snakes, and other commonly seen critters. An interactive display allows you to push various buttons and listen to the sound of pig frogs, toads, and bullfrogs.

Myakka River State Park represents one of the finest examples of preserving key habitats such as the vanishing Florida dry prairie while simultaneously creating a beautiful playground for residents and visitors alike who want to see Florida much as it was when Ponce de Leon arrived here 500 years ago. It is, arguably, one of the finest state parks in all of Florida.

❒_______ E. Oscar Scherer State Park

Location: 1843 S. Tamiami Trail, Osprey, FL 34229 / Phone: 941-483-5956 / Reservations: 800-326-3521 / Fax: n/a / Website: www.floridastateparks.org / E-mail: n/a / 1,400 acres / Admission fee charged.

In 1955 Elsa Scherer Burrows bequeathed the 462-acre South Creek Ranch to the state of Florida with the intention of turning this pristine stretch of creek into a park in honor of her father. The following year, in 1956, Oscar Scherer State Park opened its doors to the public. Thirty years later, in an effort to protect the remnant Florida scrub jay habitat in Sarasota County, Realtor and environmentalist Jon Thaxton worked diligently to acquire the adjacent 992-acre Palmer Ranch. With the help of the Nature Conservancy, Preservation 2000, and widespread public support, Palmer Ranch ultimately became a part of Oscar Scherer State Park. In September 2008, Lee Wetherington, a local developer and park supporter, donated an additional 16.6 acres, bringing the park to its present 1,400 acres.

The dock at Oscar Scherer Courtesy Florida State Parks

The predominant habitats found in Oscar Scherer State Park consist of pine flatwoods, scrubby flatwoods, and, running along South Creek, hardwood hammocks. Several well-marked trails traverse these habitats, and two of them are ADA accessible: Lake Osprey Trail, which is approximately a third of a mile long and encircles the lake; and the half-mile Lester Finley Trail, located near the entrance to the park .

Four other trails accommodate both hikers and bicyclists. The most consistent trail for off-road biking is the three-mile Green Trail. The five-mile Yellow Trail, the 1.5-mile Blue Trail, and the two-mile Red Trail all have long stretches of soft sand that can be difficult for biking.

You can also rent a canoe or kayak and paddle up and down South Creek (approximately two miles). Upstream the creek teems with freshwater fish such as bream, bass, and the exotic tilapia, while near the mouth, which is influenced by the tides, you can find saltwater species such as snook, snapper, and seatrout, especially during the winter months. There is a designated swimming area in Lake Osprey. The Nature Center has a number of interesting displays in the main building and

A Florida scrub jay © Judd Patterson, JuddPatterson.com

a screen enclosure with Wi-Fi access (for those who cannot leave their laptops at home!).

Oscar Scherer State Park is best known for its endangered Florida scrub jays. The Yellow and Green trails are the best areas for spotting this elusive cousin to the blue jay. Scrub jays are curious birds, so with any luck at all, it's fairly easy for any dedicated birder to catch a glimpse of this attractive jay. Remember to NOT be silent when stalking the elusive scrub jay. Being naturally curious, they like noisy people. While walking along these trails, also be on the lookout for alligators, six-lined racerunners, indigo snakes, rabbits, river otters, and gopher tortoises.

A trail through scrub jay habitat © Charles Sobczak

The campground at Oscar Scherer runs right along the river. With more than 100 sites, it is one of the most popular camping destinations in Southwest Florida. The riverfront sites are gorgeous, many with captivating views of South Creek, and the outer-circle sites all back up to the preserve areas. Showers, restrooms, and recycling bins are located throughout the campground. A primitive camping area above Lake Osprey is available for youth groups. During the winter months park rangers offer guided walks, campfire discussions, and nature programs. The biggest event of the year at Oscar Scherer is the Scrub Jay Run, attracting more than 600 runners who participate in the fund-raising event for the park.

A part of the Great Florida Birding Trail, Oscar Scherer State Park attracts more than 130,000 visitors every year. It is perhaps the best location in the world to catch a glimpse of the endangered Florida scrub jay.

❐ ______ F. T. Mabry Carlton Jr. Memorial Preserve

Location: 1800 Mabry Carlton Way, Venice, FL 34292 / 941-861-5000 / Fax: 941-861-9932 / Website: www. scgov.net/NaturalLands / E-mail: parksonline@ scgov.net / 24,565 acres / Admission is free.

The visitors center © Charles Sobczak

At 38 square miles, the T. Mabry Carlton Jr. Memorial Preserve is a significant part of what has become known as "Myakka Island," a matrix of conservation lands including the Myakka River State Park, Myakka Prairie, Pinelands Reserve, Schewe Tract, and Deer Prairie Creek Preserve. All together, Myakka Island consists of more than 101,000 acres of protected contiguous parcels of environmentally sensitive land—the largest piece of undeveloped, continuous wilderness properties in Florida north of the Everglades.

Wildflowers flourish along the trails © Charles Sobczak

The park's namesake, T. Mabry Carlton Jr., was a Sarasota County commissioner who was instrumental in the negotiations to buy the first tract from the Ringling-MacArthur Trust in 1982. The preserve was renamed in his honor shortly after his death in a plane crash in 1989. Another 8,238 acres were purchased and added to the preserve that same year. In 1994, the T. Mabry Carlton Jr. water treatment plant opened, supplying Sarasota County with nearly 6 million gallons of freshwater a day.

Today, the shared use plan for the preserve includes more than 80 miles of hiking trails, including the 12-mile Myakka Island Wilderness Trail, which accommodates horses and bicycles as well. The preserve has several primitive campsites, and more are in the planning stages, including several right on the Myakka River.

While most of the preserve is designed for serious hikers, off-road bicyclists, and equestrians, a much smaller and readily accessible section of the park is located just off of Mabry Carlton Parkway north of Border Road. This area has a public parking lot, restrooms, picnic tables, and a small historic log cabin that also serves as an information center. Two trails, both three-quarters of a mile long, are connected by another short trail. One trail encircles a wet prairie; the other a forested swamp. The entire walk takes about an hour to complete and offers the day hiker a brief look at what lies deeper within the vast preserve.

❒ ________ G. Sleeping Turtles Preserve

Location: 3462 Border Road, Venice, FL 34292 / 941-861-5000 / Fax: 941-861-9932 / Website: www.scgov.net/NaturalLands / E-mail: parksonline@scgov.net / 174 acres / Admission is free.

River otters on the upper Myakka Courtesy Sarasota VC Bureau

The Sleeping Turtles Preserve, whose name comes from a landmark along the Myakka River noted on naval maps from the 1800s, consists of two tracts, both abutting sections of the Myakka River. They are divided by Border Road on the way to both the T. Mabry Carlton Jr. Memorial Preserve and Deer Prairie Creek Preserve.

The 174-acre northern tract is also known as the North Ligon Property, a former homestead purchased in 2003 and 2004 through the Environmentally Sensitive Lands Protection Project. This section has more than five miles of well-marked hiking/biking trails, part of which follow the Myakka River. From here you might spot a real sleeping turtle resting on one of the many fallen oaks or cabbage palms near the bank. There is a canoe landing near the northern edge

Welcome to Sleeping Turtles Preserve © Charles Sobczak

of the trails. The northern tract also has a picnic area, large parking area, and restroom. Pets are allowed on leashes.

The larger southern tract, also known as the South Rohlwing Property, is less developed. Its five miles of trails are unmarked. Its two entrances offer only roadside parking and no restrooms. Pets are not allowed in this section. Unlike the northern tract, the 214-acre south parcel has only one small viewing spot where a hiker can catch a glimpse of the Myakka River.

The vegetation on both tracts consists mostly of oak hammocks, pine flatwoods, and seasonal wetlands. Neither parcel is used heavily, so the wildlife viewing can be impressive. Along the river you can find alligators, river otters, and an assortment of freshwater turtles. As you walk the trails you might spot bobcats, white-tailed deer, squirrels, and armadillos. Typical bird sightings include pileated and red-bellied woodpeckers, seasonal warblers, and blue jays.

Although fairly primitive in nature, both sides of Sleeping Turtles Preserve are inviting to anyone looking to take a quiet hike in the woods. For the more adventurous, a mountain bike ride through both sections will give you quite a workout.

❒____ H. Myakkahatchee Creek Environmental Park

Location: 6968 Reisterstown Road, North Port, FL, 34291 / Phone: 941-861-5000 / Fax: n/a / Website: www.scgov.net / E-mail: gtatge@scgov.net / 206 acres / Admission is free.

Although this park is not large, it offers the casual naturalist a terrific opportunity to step back in time. A true "blackwater creek," the Myakkahatchee is stained a dark color by the leaves, roots, and detritus falling into the stream from the overhanging oaks and other vegetation. They release tannins, giving the water its coffee-like hue. The tannins, which are a mild form of tannic acid, are produced in the leaves as natural deterrents against browsing by deer and other herbivores.

Welcome to the environment © Charles Sobczak

Archaeologists have discovered nearby Indian mounds that indicate the Calusa and other tribes hunted in the river valley of the Myakkahatchee for at least 10,000 years. The name itself is Seminole in origin, from *miarca*, meaning big water, and *hatchee*, meaning river.

Prior to becoming a park in 1989, this stretch of land was used for grazing cattle, and its rich grasses and vegetation still attract deer and wild pigs. Beneath many of the sprawling live oaks you can spot the rooting of the wild boars as they search for fungi and grubs in the understory.

Much of the Myakkahatchee Creek Environmental Park consists of oak and cabbage palm hammock. Squirrels, opossum, and armadillos are plentiful, feeding on the acorns that litter the floor of the forest. You will also find seasonal marshes and pine flatwoods here. Wildflowers abound throughout the park, as do golden orb weavers and other spiders.

The bridge across Myakkahatchee Creek

© Charles Sobczak

Several well-marked trails loop through the park and are color coded, making them easy to navigate. The yellow trail is approximately a mile long and meanders along both sides of the creek, crossing over via two wooden bridges.

Although there is a launch area for canoes and kayaks, the first three miles of downstream navigation is difficult. During the drier winter season water levels drop to a point requiring numerous portages that involve considerable effort on the part of the voyager. During the summer months the kayaking is easier, but the trails can become very wet and parts of them will take you through knee-deep water. The best time to take advantage of both activities would be in the early fall when the water may still be high but the rains are diminishing.

A little farther south, the Myakkahatchee Creek runs deeper, and the three- to four-mile paddle to the larger Myakka River is much easier. For the truly adventurous there is primitive camping in the Myakka State Forest near the mouth of the Myakka River where it widens into Charlotte Harbor.

Other amenities at the Myakkahatchee Creek Environmental Park include sheltered picnic areas, a restroom, and a small fishing pier. Although not a large park, these 200 acres revolves around the steady-flowing creek and offers the visitor a window into Florida's past—peaceful, lush, and another side of paradise.

❐ ________ I. Jelks and Deer Prairie Creek Preserves

Locations: **Jelks Preserve**: 2300 North River Road, Venice, FL 34292 / 941-861-5000 / Fax: 941-861-9932 / Website: www.scgov.net/NaturalLands/Jelks / E-mail: parksonline@scgov.net / 614 acres / Admission is free.

Deer Prairie Creek Preserve: 7001 Forbes Trail, Venice, FL 34223 / 941-861-5000 / Fax: 941-861-9932 / Website: www.scgov.net / E-mail: parksonline@scgov.net / 6,439 acres / Admission is free.

The Myakka River corridor forms the backbone of a series of state parks and preserves that grace Sarasota County. Florida designated the Myakka a state Wild and Scenic River in 1985. With more than 34 miles of undeveloped wilderness shoreline, the Myakka offers one of the best freshwater paddling experiences in Southwest Florida. Only Fisheating Creek and the Peace River rival the natural beauty and serenity found on the upper Myakka.

Welcome to Deer Prairie © Charles Sobczak

The 614-acre Jelks Preserve is located on the western side of the Myakka River, roughly halfway down, near the region where the freshwater mixes with the salty tidal waters flowing up from Charlotte Harbor. As a result, you will find freshwater bass and alligators, as well as saltwater species such as snook and seatrout along this stretch of the Myakka.

The Jelks Preserve is best known for its migratory passerines. During the annual fall and summer migrations of these beautiful but elusive birds, visitors to the preserve might look for the ruby-crowned kinglet, both white-eyed and red-eyed vireos, as well as a host of warblers such as the worm-eating warbler, American redstart, and yellow-throated and pine warblers. A complete list of the birds found at the preserve is available at the Sarasota County website (www.scgov.net).

The preserve, which was purchased in 1999 through a 1-percent sales tax and a generous contribution from the Jelks Family Foundation, has more than eight miles of well-marked trails that lead you through diverse habitats: scrubby flatwoods, oak hammocks, and pine flatwoods. A self-guided tour handbook is available online, as well as in the convenient brochure holders located at the main entrance on the east side of West River Road approximately one mile south of I-75.

Just south and across the Myakka River from the Jelks Preserve lies the far larger Deer Prairie Creek Preserve, which runs along the eastern bank of the river for more than six miles. This preserve encompasses 6,439 acres and offers more

View down the Myakka at Jelks Preserve © Charles Sobczak

than 70 miles of hiking trails. Unlike the Jelks Preserve, which is restricted to foot traffic, the trails of the Deer Prairie Creek Preserve are often shared with off-road bicyclists and horses. Some of the trails can flood during the summer rainy season and may prove difficult for inexperienced hikers. Be sure to bring along ample freshwater, rain gear, and mosquito spray before heading into the trails of this preserve.

The main entrance of the Deer Prairie Creek Preserve can be difficult to find. The best way is to head north off of exit 193 (Jacaranda Blvd.) and turn right on Border Road less than a half mile north of I-75. From there you drive a little more than two miles to the Mabry Carlton Parkway and take a right onto Forbes Trail, which takes you back under I-75 to the entrance to Deer Prairie Creek. A left takes you into the immense Mabry Carlton Preserve, which is also covered in this section of *The Living Gulf Coast*.

❒ ______ J. Caspersen and Brohard Beaches

Locations: **Caspersen Beach:** 4100 Harbor Drive, Venice, FL 34285 / Phone: 941-861-5000 / Fax: 941-861-9932 / Website: www.scgov.net / E-mail: parksonline@scgov.net / 177 acres / Admission is free.

Brohard Beach: 1600 Harbor Drive, Venice, FL 34285 / Phone: 941-861-5000 / Fax: 941-861-9932 / Website: www. scgov.net / E-mail: parksonline@scgov.net / 84 acres / Admission is free.

Caspersen and Brohard beaches, both of which lie south of the Venice City Beach in southern Sarasota County, are famous for a unique form of beachcombing—hunting for fossilized shark's teeth.

The exact reason why these two beaches contain so many shark's teeth is unclear. The shark is known to shed and replace its teeth throughout its lifetime.

In the course of 10 years a mature tiger shark can produce as many as 24,000 teeth. The upper and lower jaws each contain up to 40 teeth with as many as six or seven replacement rows slowly moving forward into place as the older teeth naturally shed or break off.

While most of the teeth found along this stretch of sand are small, often no larger than your fingernail, some are much larger. The most sought-after teeth are those that were once shed by the extinct *Carcharodon megalodon.* This gigantic

The annual Shark festival Courtesy Sarasota VC Bureau

forerunner of the great white shark reached lengths of up to 67 feet and roamed the waters off of Venice between 1.6-25 million years ago. Fossilized megalodon teeth can be more than seven inches long and weigh several pounds. Other common finds include prehistoric mako, bull, tiger, and sand shark's teeth.

The most common method for locating these buried treasures is to use a small shovel and a strainer, most often a meshed bucket, and while one person scoops up a load of sand, another jiggles the basket along the surf line looking for the small black or dark brown teeth that appear as the sand washes away. Professional shark's teeth hunters prefer scuba diving along a stretch of limestone reef and sandy bottom 10 to 20 feet offshore. This is where the larger teeth are usually found, most of which are sold to wholesalers who make them into jewelry or sell them as novelties.

Digging for fossils anywhere on the Florida mainland requires a special permit, but not so the famous shark's teeth of Caspersen and Brohard beaches. There seems

Sunset at Caspersen Beach Courtesy Sarasota VC Bureau

to be an almost endless supply of smaller teeth. These teeth can be purchased at the local tourist shops or on the Internet for a few dollars, so it's not as if you're panning for gold, but the fun lies in the search. Hunting for shark's teeth has become so popular that the city of Venice holds a Shark's Tooth Festival every April.

Of course, there is much more to these two beaches than shark's teeth. They are both popular nesting sites for loggerhead and green turtles, and the birding along the shoreline is fantastic. Depending on the time of year, you might see least terns, black skimmers, ruddy turnstones, and the elusive snowy plover. Brohard Beach also offers a 740-foot-long fishing pier, a family restaurant, and a popular dog park. At the very end of Caspersen Beach hikers, bikers, and rollerbladers can connect to the Venetian Waterway Park trails that run along the manmade canal into town. These two unusual beaches on the Gulf of Mexico are worth the trip, whether or not you're in search of fossilized shark's teeth.

The shells of Caspersen Beach

Courtesy Sarasota VC Bureau

❒ ______ K. Venice Area Audubon Society Rookery

Location: 4002 Annex Road, Venice, FL 34239 / Phone: 941-412-1610 / Fax: n/a / Website: www.veniceaudubon.org / E-mail: info@veniceaudubon.org / Admission is free.

Life at the rookery © Dick Fortune and Sara Lopez

Considered one of Venice's best-kept secrets (at least before this book was written!), the Venice Area Audubon Society's Rookery, or VAAS Rookery, is a very small island in the middle of an equally small lake. It is a classic example of the symbiotic relationship between alligators and birds. Alligators in the lake protect the nesting area from snakes, raccoons, bobcats, and rats that might otherwise take eggs and chicks from the nests. A handful of fledglings are lost every year because they fall from the nest or are snatched from lower branches by the alligators, but these losses pale in comparison with the damage a single raccoon can do in one night to a rookery as dense as this one can be.

The rookery tends to be the most crowded from January through March, though different birds continue to nest on the island throughout the rest of the year. Since the various species that use the rookery tend to nest and hatch at different times of the year, there is something going on here every month of the year. The list of birds observed on the island include great blue herons, snowy and great egrets, anhingas, ibis, green herons, and cattle egrets. There is a large covered pavilion adjacent to the pond.

Because the distance between the shoreline and the island is less than 100 feet, the VAAS Rookery has become an extremely popular place to photograph immature chicks, feeding parents, and mating couples. A good telephoto lens will bring the nest so close that you can actually see the colors of the eggs being laid or catch a parent feeding hungry chicks in the afternoon light. The best viewing is down the path and to the left of the pavilion. Be sure to look up into the surrounding slash pines and live oaks for fledglings, nervous parents, or avian predators waiting for an opportunity to turn an unattended chick into dinner.

The beauty of the VAAS Rookery is that you do not need to wade though wetlands or hike miles to find this urban rookery. In fact, the road leading up to the rookery is fairly commercial in nature and seems a rather unlikely place to find an island filled to overflowing with birds. All you have to do is put the above address in your phone or GPS and drive there. You'll be glad you did.

❐ _______ L. Myakka State Forest

Location: 2000 South River Road, Englewood, FL 34223 / Phone: 941-460-1333 / Fax: n/a / Website: www. fl-dof.com/state_forest/myakka / E-mail: shumicd @ doacs.state.fl.us / 8,593 acres / Admission fee charged.

Tucked into the very southwestern corner of Sarasota County between Englewood and West Port Charlotte, the Myakka State Forest is a sprawling preserve that borders the Myakka River. Its habitats consist of pine flatwoods, hardwood hammocks along the river, and seasonal wetlands and swamps. A shell road enters the forest off of County Road 777 and bears east- southeast across the property to the county line.

The mesic flatwoods are made up of both longleaf and slash pine, while the understory is predominantly palmetto. Look for eastern towhees, red-cockaded woodpeckers, scrub jays, wild turkeys, and seasonal warblers in these regions. The numerous marshes and wetlands provide

Trails traverse the Myakka State Forest

© Charles Sobczak

Bull alligator along the Myakka River Courtesy Florida State Parks

ample habitat for wading birds such as egrets, herons, and limpkins. Along the 2.5 miles of river frontage you might find river otters, alligators, and white-tailed deer.

For the hiker, horseback rider, and off-road biker, Myakka State Forest is a real treat. Its more than 13 miles of marked trails are part of the Division of Forestry's Florida Trailwalker program. Most of these trails have fairly solid surfaces and are therefore more biker friendly than the soft sand found at many parks and preserves. A great ride runs from the shell road around a portion of the 5.4-mile North Loop, then takes a spur to the primitive campsite located directly on the Myakka River. Another popular trek is the 7.4-mile South Loop trail, which leads to two primitive campsites, known as the Watering Hole and the Pine Straw. Permits are required for use of any of the forest's five designated campsites and can be obtained by contacting the Division of Forestry at its website. For the equestrian enthusiast, the Myakka State Forest has more than 13 miles of marked trails that are part of the Division of Forestry's Trailtrotter program.

The Myakka River is designated as an Outstanding Florida Waterway. Several creeks, including Myakkahatchee Creek and Rock Creek, are located within the forest and offer additional wildlife- and bird-viewing opportunities. Like most state forests, the facilities are modest, but the pristine condition of the forest and its many inhabitants are well worth the trip, especially for the nature enthusiast who likes to keep it simple and well off the beaten path.

❒ ________ M. Lemon Bay Park

Location: 570 Bay Park Blvd. Englewood, FL 34223 / Phone: 941-861-5000 / Fax: 941-861-9932 / Website: www.scgov.net / E-mail: parksonline@scgov.net / 204 acres / Admission is free.

The boardwalk along Lemon Bay © Charles Sobczak

The people of Sarasota County exhibited some real foresight in 1986 when they purchased the first 48 acres of Lemon Bay Park as part of a $20 million county bond referendum. The county later added to the acreage when it acquired the assets of the Anita and Jacob France Foundation, whose environmental research area can still be found on the north end of the park. Several parcels have been added since then, bringing the park to its current size of 208 acres.

Welcome to Lemon Bay Park! © Charles Sobczak

With more than a mile of bay frontage on the Lemon Bay Aquatic Preserve, Lemon Bay Park is sitting on some valuable real estate. Vacant residential lots sell for more than $1 million per 100 feet of bay frontage, making the park worth more than $55 million in waterfront property alone. Add the value of the remaining acreage to the equation and Lemon Bay Park in today's real estate market is easily worth $100 million.

Because the park stretches along Lemon Bay, it offers a rare window into what much of the bayou and bayfront Florida once looked like. The half-mile bayside trail, which has a number of small boardwalk sections and bayfront overlooks, wraps around red and black mangrove forests. While hiking the trail, look for mangrove, fiddler, and horseshoe crabs. Polarized sunglasses will help you

Eagles nest spotting scope
© Charles Sobczak

see finger mullet, immature thread herring, and glass minnows in the water. Don't be surprised if you scare a redfish or snook out from under the mangroves at high tide, as they often come in to feed on the mangrove crabs and minnows that thrive in the tangled red mangrove root system.

While the park's south trail focuses on mangroves, the two-mile north trail system is decidedly more upland in nature. It wanders through pine and scrubby flatwoods and abuts a freshwater swamp near the very northern tip. Look for an entirely different kind of wildlife here, including bald eagles. A viewing scope along the Eagle Trail allows you to spot an active eagles' nest in the towering slash pines near the edge of Lemon Bay.

The Environmental Center provides a handy checklist of 123 species of birds that frequent the park, including some difficult finds such as the American oystercatcher, Caspian tern, black-crowned night heron, and elusive Florida scrub jay, a welcome addition to any birder's life list.

Mammals found at the park include bobcats, river otters, marsh rabbits, and gray fox. Reptiles include gopher tortoises, brown and green anoles, and a dozen different snake species. A butterfly garden directly north of the Environmental Center features more than two dozen varieties of butterflies, skippers, and moths. If you look closely, you might even discover a chrysalis hidden in the foliage.

The Environmental Center has an ample supply of trail maps and bird, mammal, and insect guides, as well as several informative displays. It offers a number of nature-based educational programs throughout the year. There is a lovely rose garden, amphitheater, canoe/kayak launch, picnic pavilion, and a large veranda behind the center for taking in a sunset over Lemon Bay. A meeting room is available for organizations to rent. Portions of the trail and the center itself are ADA accessible.

Lemon Bay Park is a welcome respite from what would likely have been yet another subdivision in Southwest Florida. Although relatively small, it serves as a sanctuary for any number of birds, mammals, and other living things that struggle to find a place to call their own. So, take advantage with a morning stroll though the pines or an evening walk along the shoreline of Lemon Bay Aquatic Preserve, and revel in the knowledge that sometimes we can get it right.

Additional Parks, Preserves, and Eco-destinations of Sarasota County

Wildflowers in bloom © Charles Sobczak

❐ ________ Sarasota Jungle Gardens

Location: 3701 Bay Shore Road, Sarasota, FL 34234 / Phone: 941-355-1112 Ext. 306 / Toll-free: 877-861-6547 / Fax: n/a / Website: www.sarasotajunglegardens.com / E-mail: on website / 10-acre campus / Admission fee charged.

Originally established in 1940, Jungle Gardens has been a staple in Sarasota ever since. Its programs, such as Birds of Prey and Critters & Things, Reptile Encounter and Birds of the Rainforest, are oriented toward children, but Jungle Gardens has something for every age group. The gardens include an extensive collection of palms, bromeliads, and native flora and offer visitors a chance to learn about the various species that thrive in Sarasota's semitropical environment.

❐ ________ Gulf Coast Wonder & Imagination Zone

(aka G.WIZ - The Science Museum)

Location: 1001 Boulevard of the Arts, Sarasota, FL 34236 / Phone: 941-309-4949 / Fax: 941-906-7292 / Website: www.gwiz.org / E-mail: amyf@gwiz.org / Admission fee charged.

This science center originally opened as the Gulf Coast World of Science in December 1990 with a mere 1,000 square feet of space. Today the G.WIZ home base is in a 33,000-square-foot facility in downtown Sarasota where it thrives as a world-class hands-on science and technology center. Permanent exhibits include Mindball, ExploraZone, Tech Zone, and Body Zone. These are augmented by traveling exhibits such as Renewable Energy, The Illusion Room, and Avatar to Art, 3D Works by Jeff Hazelton. The traveling exhibits change frequently so be sure to check the website for updated information. This is the perfect destination to learn the science behind our environment.

❐ ________ Sarasota History Center Museum

Location: 701 North Tamiami Trail, Sarasota, FL 34236 / Phone: 941-861-5000 / Fax: 941-861-6893 / Website: www.scgov.net/historycenter / E-mail: on website / Admission is free.

Offering an extensive collection of archives, digital images, archaeological finds, and additional resources, the Sarasota History Center promotes an understanding of Sarasota County's heritage and strives to protect its historic resources. It has an extensive collection of photos, manuscripts, news articles, and information about the life and times of Bertha Palmer, whose legacy helped shape today's Sarasota. Also affiliated with the museum are a research center and library located at 6062 Porter Way, Sarasota, FL 34232. The research center is open to the public and has tens of thousands of documents and images.

❐ ________ Historic Spanish Point

Location: 337 North Tamiami Trail, Sarasota, FL 34229 / Phone: 941-966-5214 / Fax: 941-966-1355 / Website: www.historicspanishpoint.org / E-mail: info@historicspanishpoint.org / 30 acres / Admission fee charged.

This attractive 30-acre estate near Osprey, Florida, was formerly owned by Bertha Potter Palmer, who was responsible for much of the early growth of the city of Sarasota. The property contains several gardens, including a butterfly garden and the sunken garden and pergola originally planted by Mrs. Palmer. A popular setting for weddings and family reunions, Historic Spanish Point also features the Guptill House, dating back to the turn of the 20th century.

❒ ________ Phillippi Estates Park/Edson Keith Mansion

Location: 5500 S. Tamiami Trail, Sarasota, FL 34231 / Phone: 941-861-5000 / Fax: 941-861-6893 / Website: www.scgov.net / E-mail: on website / 60 acres / Admission is free.

This expansive park includes the magnificent Edson Keith Mansion and several outbuildings, including a garden shed, servants' quarters, old farmhouse, and garage. Three gazebos on the property are often used for weddings and other special occasions. The park also offers a nature trail, canoe/kayak launch, and playground. The nature trail takes you through a rare coastal hammock, and for the anglers, there are three separate fishing piers on the property. A schedule of public events at the park is posted on its website.

❒ ________ Legacy Trail

Location: From Potter Park in Sarasota to the Venice Train Depot, with numerous trailheads in between / Phone: 941-861-5000 / Fax: 941-861-6893 / Website: www.scgov.net/legacytrail / E-mail: on website / Total length: 10 miles / Admission is free.

Similar in concept to Lee County's Calusa Blueway, but for bikes instead of kayaks, the Legacy Trail is a north/south path that follows the old CSX railroad corridor. The trail was started in 2004 and completed in March 2008. It starts just south of the city of Sarasota at Potter Park, then continues south all the way though Venice, Florida. It crosses through Bay Street Park and Oscar Scherer State Park in Osprey, Laurel Park in Laurel, Nokomis Park in Nokomis, and Patriots Park and the train depot in Venice. For serious cyclists, this is one of the best urban/suburban bike paths found on the West Coast of Florida.

❒ ________ Venice Archives and Area Historical Collection

Location: Triangle Inn, 351 S. Nassau Street, Venice, FL 34285 / Phone: 941-486-2487 / Fax: n/a / Website: www.venicegov.com/archives / E-mail: jhagler@ci.venice.fl.us / Admission is free.

This museum and its collection are located in a fascinating triangle-shaped building that dates back to 1927 when it was built as a rooming house. The museum's primary focus is on the local history of Venice and the life of Dr. Fred Albee, who was very involved with the formation of the city of Venice. The fossil collection of Roy and Helen Burgess is also on permanent display, and special exhibits are changed periodically throughout the year.

❒ ________ Sarasota Garden Club Center

Location: 1131 Boulevard of the Arts, Sarasota, FL 34236 / Phone: 941-955-0875 / Fax: 941-955-0875 / Website: www.sarasotagardenclub.org / E-mail: marveram@yahoo.com / 1-acre campus / Admission is free.

This small but compact public garden is located about a mile from the Marie Selby Botanical Gardens in downtown Sarasota. A nonprofit group of 200 people maintain this publicly owned park. A number of pathways lead through flowers, bromeliads, and a butterfly garden. The facility hosts plant sales and flower shows throughout the year and has a spacious great room that is rented out for weddings, conferences, civic affairs, and fundraisers.

❒ ________ Celery Fields

Location: Entrance is 600 feet west of Raymond Road, east of I-75 on Palmer Blvd., Sarasota, FL 34232 / Phone: Sarasota Audubon, 941-364-9212 / Fax: n/a / Website: www.sarasotaaudubon.org / E-mail: dave@sarasotaaudubon.org / 400 acres / Admission is free.

Although its primary use is as a flood mitigation zone, this half-mile-square property is a mixture of marshlands, deep ponds, shallow pools, and canals. The Sarasota Audubon Society has been conducting bird surveys on the site since 2001, with more than 200 species recorded to date, including limpkins, black-necked stilts, and any number of migratory duck species. Paths and walkways around the stormwater retention areas allow visitors access into most of the acreage.

A Florida mottled duck and her ducklings
© Charles Sobczak

❒ ________ Blind Pass Beach/The Hermitage

Location: 6725 Manasota Key Road, Manasota, FL 34223 / Phone: 941-861-5000 / Fax: 941-861-6893 / Website: www.scgov.net / E-mail: on website / 66 acres / Admission is free.

Home of the Hermitage Artist's Retreat (note: closed to the general public), this beach attracts artists, writers, composers, and playwrights from around the world. Blind Pass Beach itself is more than a half-mile long, with picnic shelters, playgrounds, and a canoe/kayak launch. There are always plenty of shorebirds to observe here.

❒ ______ South Lido County Park

Location: 190 Taft Drive and 2201 Ben Franklin Drive, Lido Key, FL 34236 / Phone: 941-861-5000 / Fax: 941-861-6893 / Website: www.scgov.net / E-mail: on website / 100 acres / Admission is free.

This attractive park is located at the very southern tip of Lido Key, just minutes from the famed shopping area known as St. Armands Circle. Most of the park lies along the shoreline of Sarasota Bay and Big Pass, with a small portion located along the Gulf of Mexico. Care should be taken when swimming near Big Pass, as the tidal currents can be strong.

Aerial of South Lido Beach Courtesy Sarasota County Parks and Recreation

❒ ______ Quick Point Nature Preserve

Location: 100 Gulf of Mexico Drive, Longboat Key, FL 34228 / Phone: 941-316-1999 / Fax: 941-316-1656 / Website: www.longboatkey.org/Parks/quick_point. / E-mail: on website / Admission is free.

This small nature park abuts New Pass on Longboat Key. It includes a manmade lagoon, nature trail, overlook, and osprey nesting pole. Interpretive signs throughout the park help visitors identify the various species of mangroves and upland vegetation.

❒ ________ Turtle Beach Park and Campground

Location: 8862 Midnight Pass Road, Sarasota, FL 34242 / Phone: 941-861-5000 / Campground reservations: 941-349-3839 / Fax: 941-861-6893 / Website: www.scgov.net / E-mail: turtlebeachcampground@scgov.net / 19 acres / Admission is free, but fees are charged for camping.

Turtle Beach Park is a work in progress. Sarasota County purchased Gulf Beach Travel Trailer Park in 2006, adding 40 campsites to Turtle Beach Park. Advance reservations are recommended. Long-term plans for the park include 219 parking spaces, 38 RV and trailer parking spaces, revamped restrooms, playgrounds, and more. Access to nearby Palmer Point Beach, which has no on-site parking, is by hiking down to it from Turtle Beach Park.

❒ ________ Jim Neville Marine Preserve

Location: Little Sarasota Bay, Sarasota, FL 34242 / Phone: 941-861-5000 / Fax: 941-861-6893 / Website: www.scgov.net / E-mail: on website / 35 acres / Admission is free.

A part of the Paddle Sarasota program, this watery park surrounds some mangrove islands in Little Sarasota Bay. It can be accessed from the canoe/kayak launch at Turtle Beach Park or from several other access points that are listed on Sarasota County's Paddle Sarasota website. There are a dozen recommended paddling trails spread out across the county.

❒ ________ Shamrock Park and Nature Center

Location: 3900 Shamrock Drive, Venice, FL 34293 / Phone: 941-861-5000 / Fax: 941-861-6893 / Website: www.scgov.net / E-mail: on website / 80 acres / Admission is free.

This park is connected via the Venetian Waterway trail to Caspersen and Brohard beaches. A 10.2-mile trail along the waterway allows visitors to hike, bike, or rollerblade into downtown Venice from the park. It also has a nature center, indoor rental space, and basketball and tennis courts. The Florida scrub jay and gopher tortoise are both known to frequent this park, which has a sizable stand of coastal scrub habitat. Guided nature hikes and environmental programs are offered during the winter months.

Boardwalk over Myakka Lake

Courtesy Florida State Parks

❐ ________ Ken Thompson Park and Fishing Pier

Location: 1700 Ken Thompson Parkway, Sarasota, FL 34236 / Phone: 941-365-2200 / Fax: n/a / Website: www.discovernaturalsarasota.org/listing/ken-thompson-park / E-mail: info @sarasotafl.org / 84 acres / Admission is free.

This predominantly urban park offers a fishing pier, boat ramp, and half-mile nature trail. It is a popular destination for jogging, wetting a line, or picnicking. Its proximity to Mote Marine Laboratory and Aquarium, located just down the street on City Island, makes it a great place to take a breather after visiting the aquarium.

❐ ________ Red Bug Slough Preserve

Location: 5200 Beneva Road, Sarasota, FL 34233 / Phone: 941-861-5000 / Fax: 941-861-6893 / Website: www.scgov.net / E-mail: on website / 72 acres / Admission is free.

Set in the suburban community of South Gate Ridge, this fair-sized parcel was purchased in 2000 and 2001 through the Environmentally Sensitive Lands Protection Program. The preserve offers hiking trails, a small playground, picnic shelters, and a fishing pier.

❐ ________ Circus Hammock

Location: 4572 17th Street, Sarasota, FL 34232 / Phone: 941-861-5000 / Fax: 941-861-6893 / Website: www.scgov.net / E-mail: on website / 22 acres / Admission is free.

Purchased in 2006 through the Environmentally Sensitive Lands Protection Program, this parcel derives its name from the nearby historic winter quarters of the Ringling Brothers and Barnum & Bailey Circus. A number of well-marked trails take you through red maples, oaks, and hackberry. Look for box turtles, woodpeckers, and an assortment of songbirds.

❐ ________ Curry Creek Preserve

Location: 1075 Albee Farm Road, Venice, FL 34285 / Phone: 941-861-5000 / Fax: 941-861-6893 / Website: www.scgov.net / E-mail: on website / 80 acres / Admission is free.

The preserve abuts Curry Creek, which can be accessed via a canoe/kayak launch just north of the park entrance. From there paddlers can work their way downstream to Roberts Bay and farther north into Dona Bay and Lyons Bay, both of which are about a mile away. The preserve also offers hiking trails and fishing opportunities.

❐ ________ Manasota Scrub Preserve

Location: 2695 Bridge Street, Englewood, FL 34223 / Phone: 941-861-5000 / Fax: 941-861-6893 / Website: www.scgov.net / E-mail: on website / 145 acres / Admission is free.

A mile-long hiking trail takes you through this mixture of Florida scrub forest, home to the Florida scrub jay, northern quail, and great-horned owls. A 330-foot boardwalk takes you from the parking lot to the trailhead over a large wetlands area.

❐ ________ Myakka Islands Point

Location: 1289 Campbell Street, Port Charlotte, FL 33953 / Phone: 941-861-5000 / Fax: 941-861-6893 / Website: www.scgov.net / E-mail: on website / 100 acres / Admission is free.

Flanked to the north by the much larger Myakka State Forest and to the east by Charlotte County, this 100-acre property abuts the Myakka River, though there is no canoe or kayak access available in the park because mangrove forests border the river. Primitive hiking trails wind through the vegetation where you can observe tidal marshes, pine flatwoods, and tropical hammocks. Sightings include swallowtail kites, kestrels, and red-shouldered hawks.

❐ ________ Old Miakka Preserve

Location: 251 Myakka Road, Sarasota, FL 34240 / Phone: 941-861-5000 / Fax: 941-861-6893 / Website: www.scgov.net / E-mail: on website / 132 acres / Admission is free.

This preserve is located in a historic, rural community once called Old Miakka, which is another spelling of the Seminole word for the Myakka River. The preserve has more than four miles of unpaved hiking trails that take you through scrub forests, pine flatlands, and seasonal wetlands.

An inviting trail © Charles Sobczak

Natural Rhythm

© Alan Maltz

Red Knots © Judd Patterson, JuddPatterson.com

Charlotte County

Dominated by Charlotte Harbor, the immense body of water named after Queen Charlotte Sophia by the English in 1775, Charlotte County remains the least developed of the four coastal counties of Southwest Florida. According to the U.S. Census, the county has a total area of 859 square miles, of which 694 are land and 166 are water. The vast majority of that water consists of Charlotte Harbor, the Peace and the Myakka rivers. Charlotte Harbor is one of Florida's largest and healthiest aquatic preserves and is the 17th largest estuary in the continental United States. The Charlotte Harbor National Estuary Program, or CHNEP, covers 2,815,988 acres (4,400 square miles). In 2005, the Conservancy of Southwest Florida gave Charlotte Harbor/Gasparilla Sound a grade of C, with 59 percent of its original wetlands unchanged and in good overall condition.

A remarkable feature of Charlotte Harbor is that most of its surrounding wetlands have been preserved as state buffer preserves. These include the Charlotte Harbor Aquatic Preserve, Charlotte Harbor State Buffer Preserve, Charlotte Flatwoods Environmental Park, Gasparilla State Park in Lee County, and the fragile 20-acre Island Bay National Wildlife Refuge. Because of this consistent buffer, the waters of Charlotte Harbor do not suffer from the same level of nutrient loading as do the waters in places such as Sarasota and Naples Bay.

Another factor in preserving the health of Charlotte Harbor is population density. The projected population of Charlotte County in 2010 is 159,488. This equates to a density of 229 people per square mile. In Sarasota County, directly north of Charlotte County, the density is almost three times higher at 678 people per square mile, whereas Lee County, abutting Charlotte County to the south, is almost 3.5 times as dense, with 765 people per square mile. In the natural world there is a consistent equation that does not seem to change: more people equal more impact on the environment.

Of the six counties included in this book, Charlotte County ranks second in the number of acres of managed land: 175,534 acres (274 square miles) are dedicated to conservation uses. Much of this consists of the Babcock/Webb Wildlife Management Area (80,335 acres) and the adjoining Babcock Ranch (90,000 acres). While a substantial portion of Babcock Ranch is slated to become the world's first solar-powered, self-sufficient city (17,000 acres), much of that development will occur in northern Lee County, leaving most of the acreage in Charlotte County unchanged.

Whereas Lee and Sarasota counties have encouraged and experienced unprecedented growth in the past few decades, the growth of Charlotte County has been far less explosive. In 1950 only 4,286 people lived in the county. By 1990 that number had grown to 110,975. The projected population of Charlotte County by 2015 is estimated to be 176,400. Growth has slowed recently, allowing time for the infrastructure to catch up with the influx of new arrivals. Adoption of stricter regulations for septic systems and municipal wastewater systems have helped to alleviate the pressure put on the fresh and saltwater estuaries found in this watery county.

That is not to say that Charlotte Harbor has escaped the ravages of development. One of the largest threats to the estuary and the Peace River lies near the headwaters of that stream in Polk and Hardee counties. This is where several different phosphate-mining companies continue to gather this important agricultural product, presenting a host of problems for the Peace River. These problems result from elevated levels of cadmium, lead, nickel, copper, chromium, and even uranium. As if this weren't enough, the phosphorus itself can leach into the stream, wreaking havoc on the ecosystem by overloading the freshwater with nutrients.

Wisely, Charlotte County has followed in the footsteps of Lee and Sarasota counties in adopting a strict fertilizer ordinance. Enacted in March 2008, this ordinance has already helped decrease the amount of dissolved nitrogen in the harbor and reduce harmful algae blooms.

Although Charlotte County does not have any high-profile conservation lands such as Sarasota's Myakka River State Park or Collier's Big Cypress National Preserve, it does have an abundance of smaller parks and preserves that present equal opportunities to commune with nature. The end of this section contains many of these smaller eco-destinations. There isn't room here to include the details of each and every one of these green spaces, but the Charlotte County website (www.charlottecountyfl.com) presents plenty of information about each, including downloadable trail and park guides.

With 40 percent of its land mass preserved as state and county parks, wildlife management areas, ranches, and preserves, Charlotte County has many great places to explore. Start your journey by paddling the splendid and tranquil Peace River and venture out from there. It's time to discover Charlotte County.

Charlotte County Eco-Destinations

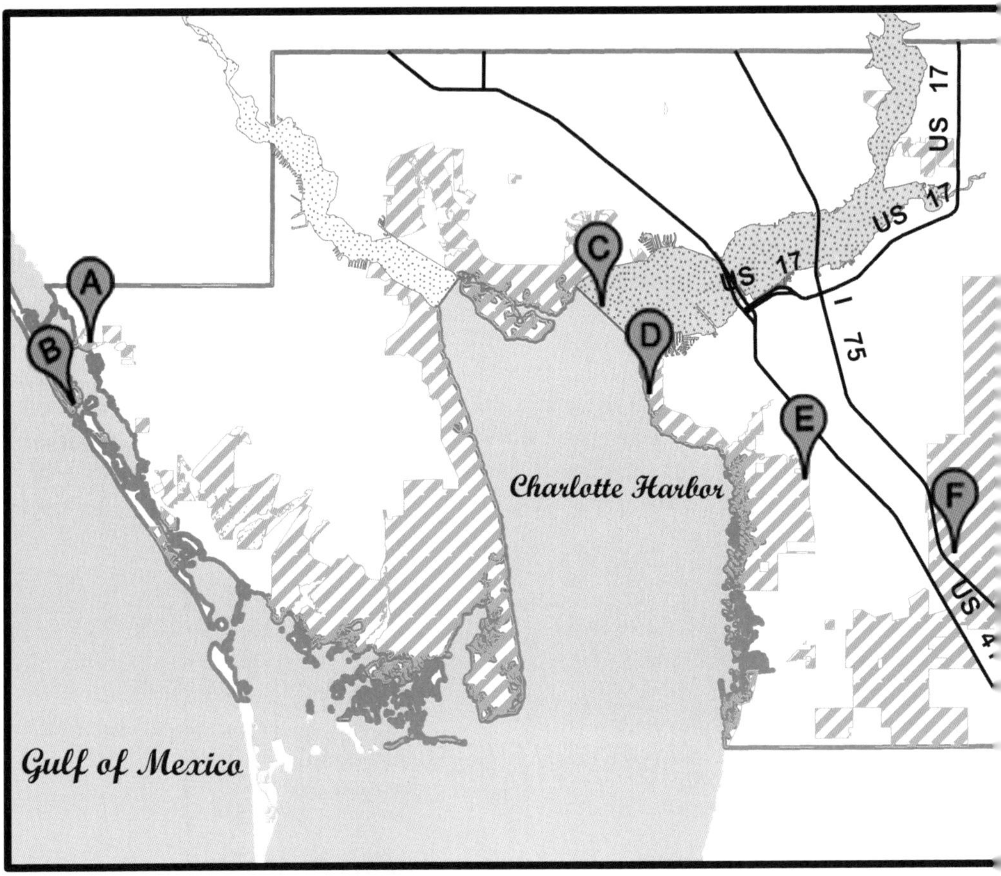

A. Cedar Point Environmental Park
B. Stump Pass Beach State Park
C. The Peace River
D. Peace River Wildlife Center
E. Alligator Creek Preserve/Charlotte Harbor Environmental Center (CHEC)
F. Babcock Webb WMA
G. The Babcock Ranch

CONSERVANCY
Of Southwest Florida
www.conservancy.org

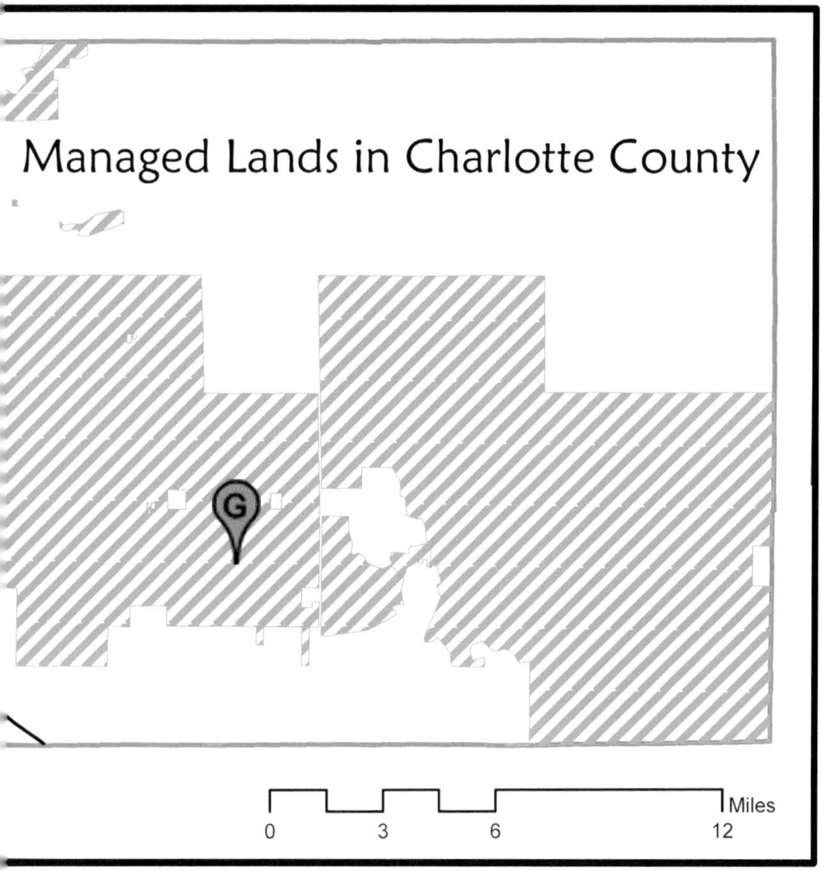

Managed Lands in Southwest Florida

Charlotte County
444,160 Acres
175,534 Acres Managed
40%

❒ ______ A. Cedar Point Environmental Park

Location: 2300 Placida Road, Englewood, FL 34224 / Phone: 941-764-4360 / Fax: 941-575-5497 / Website: www.checflorida.org / E-mail: on Website / 115 acres / Admission is free.

The interpretative center at Cedar Point © Charles Sobczak

Owned by Charlotte County and operated by the Charlotte Harbor Environmental Center (CHEC), the same parent organization that runs the Alligator Creek Preserve in Punta Gorda, the Cedar Point Environmental Park is a much smaller but equally compelling property. Like a handful of other destinations in *The Living Gulf Coast*, Cedar Point is situated on an extremely valuable piece of real estate. The point juts into Lemon Bay and has a 1,000-plus feet of shoreline. A wide trail, called the Jeep Trail, takes you to the Mangrove Trail, which ends at the edge of Lemon Bay, a distance of about a half-mile from the environmental center on this property. A dock at the end of the trail leads down into the grass flats beyond. Because this section of Lemon Bay is very shallow, it is a popular wading area for visitors.

On these healthy grass flats look for horseshoe and blue crabs, seahorses, finger mullet, wading birds of every possible variety, pinfish, and immature fish fry of every species imaginable, from snook to juvenile amberjack. The plants in the bay consist of turtle and shoal grasses, along with any number of species of drift algae. Also look for lightning whelks, king's crowns, and bay scallops.

While walking down to the grass flats, be sure to stop at the solitary cement bench located on the north side of the trail. From there you can look southeast

Swallowtail butterfly © Dick Fortune & Sara Lopez

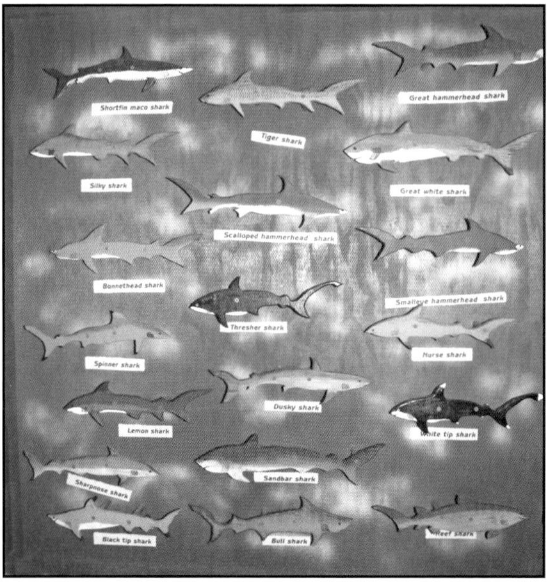

The shark identification board © Charles Sobczak

to spot one of the largest eagle nests imaginable, jammed into the crook of a large slash pine. Like most eagle nests, it has been used year after year by a family of bald eagles, so be sure not to get too close as you may disturb the eaglets that call Cedar Point home. Other common bird sightings include pileated woodpeckers, migrating warblers, and an occasional scrub jay. The park has several other trails totaling 2.6 miles. If that isn't enough of a hike, then head directly across the street to Oyster Creek Regional Park, which has an additional 3.75 miles of hiking trails.

The large modern-looking environmental center situated on this property has lots of displays, artifacts, and information about Charlotte County and Lemon Bay. Items displayed include gopher tortoise shells, sea turtle skulls, shark's teeth, local shells and insects, rattlesnake skins, and otter, bobcat, and owl mounts. During the winter months the facility is used for teaching local students.

From mangroves to pine flatwoods to a well-stocked learning center, Cedar Point Environmental Park is an excellent example of just how much can be done with a relatively small piece of real estate. Children and adults alike will enjoy a visit to this great outreach facility.

❒ ______ B. Stump Pass Beach State Park

Location: Manasota Key, Englewood, FL 34223 / (941) 964-0375 / www.floridastateparks.org/stumppass / E-mail: on website / 245 acres / Parking fee charged.

Located in the northwest corner of Charlotte County on the southern tip of Manasota Key, this mile-long stretch of sand is a combination of a great sunbathing beach and a fascinating hike into a natural dune ecosystem. Most visitors to Stump Pass Beach State Park tend to stay close to the parking lot, which is on the north end of the park just past the entrance. While this is ideal for playing in the surf, near-shore snorkeling, and hunting for fossilized shark's teeth, the real beauty of this park lies farther to the south.

Severe beach erosion at Stump Pass Beach © Charles Sobczak

Roughly halfway into the park the beachgoers and fishermen begin to thin out, and an interior hiking trail begins. The next half-mile of trail runs along stretches of Lemon Bay and winds through buttonwood and red mangrove forests. There are five distinct natural communities found along the trail. During high tide, sections of this path may be flooded.

This area of the park is known for its bird life. Sightings might include red-breasted mergansers, wood storks, and great blue herons, as well as semi-palmated, piping, wilson's, and black-bellied plovers. During the spring and fall migrations you might expect to see red knots, ruddy turnstones, magnificent frigatebirds, and migratory warblers.

You might see an occasional squirrel or an errant raccoon, but also be on the lookout for gopher tortoises, indigo snakes, and green anoles. During the summer months, ask about the ranger-led sea turtle patrols. This secluded beach is a popular nesting site for loggerheads. On the bay side of the park, you might spot a manatee searching for an underwater pasture of turtle grass.

The fishing throughout the park is excellent. Anglers working the beach side will be reeling in whiting, flounder, snook, seatrout, and sheepshead, while the bay side is a good place to catch minnows, black-striped mullet, and redfish. Snorkeling, both on the bay and beach sides, is a popular activity at the park in large part because of the exceptional water quality. Canoeing and kayaking the inside waters of Lemon Bay is a favorite pastime for park visitors, though care should be taken as this long, straight stretch of water is popular with powerboats and water skiers. There are no on-site canoe or kayak rentals.

Snorkelers take in the grass beds along the bay side © Charles Sobczak

Seaside Gentians bloom along the trial © Charles Sobczak

One of the more interesting features of Stump Pass Beach Park is the severe beach erosion occurring on the gulf side. Here you can witness what may eventually happen to barrier islands throughout Florida as a result of rising sea levels. At high tide the waves coming in from the gulf break directly against a two- to four-foot ledge. The beach disappears beneath the sea and the erosion creates a sheer bluff. While this is hardly what the park rangers like to see, these bluffs afford an interesting window into the root systems of beach-stabilizing plants such as sea oats and buttonwood trees. Take a moment to study these exposed root systems to understand why these plants are protected by state law.

Stump Pass Beach State Park was purchased by the state of Florida in 1971. Today it offers picnic tables, rinse-off showers, restrooms, a pleasant pavilion, and boardwalks.

The stumps that gave the park its name can still be found along the southern edge of the pass. Most of these are the remains of Australian pines that probably broke in half during tropical storms and hurricanes. With its shell- and shark's teeth-laden beach, still backwaters, and great fishing, Stump Pass Beach State Park is an excellent destination to take in while in northern Charlotte County.

❒ ______ C. The Peace River

Location: Canoe Outpost-Peace River, 2816 NW County Road 661, Arcadia, FL 34226 / Phone: 863-494-1215 / Toll free: 800-268-0083 / Fax: 863-494-4391 / Website: www. canoeoutpost.com / E-mail: peacepaddler@canoeoutpost.com / Admission to the river is free but canoe rentals and guided tours are fee based.

By the time the Peace River finds its way to Charlotte County it has already traveled more than 100 miles from its beginning on the southern end of Lake Hancock in Polk County. The total length of the Peace River has been estimated at 133 miles, with the river basin encompassing some 2,400 square miles of drainage area. It is considered by many paddlers, kayakers, and naturalists to be one of the finest rivers to navigate in all of Florida.

Canoeing down the Peace
Courtesy Visit Florida

Although it is possible during periods of high water to run the entire length of the river, most outfitters and paddlers avoid the 15-mile stretch from Lake Hancock to Ft. Meade. This section can be extremely shallow, and coupled with numerous snags and windfalls, it is more trouble than it is worth. From the put-in at the Ft. Meade Outdoor Recreation Area to the takeout at DeSoto County Park on the outskirts of Arcadia, the river is 57 miles long. Just south of the Ft. Meade put-in, where Bowlegs Creek joins the Peace River, the water levels are generally high enough to traverse the rest of its length throughout the year. Because of the distance involved, it is impossible to paddle this section in a single day. Numerous campsites and takeouts are accessible along the way. For day-trippers, one of the most popular legs of the river is from the put-in just west of the town of Gardner to the DeSoto County Park, is an easy distance of 13.5 miles.

Kayakers at the mouth of the river Courtesy Charlotte County VCB

South of Arcadia the Peace River widens considerably and the current diminishes. Roughly 10 miles downstream, near Ft. Ogden, the river is influenced as much by the rising and falling of the tides as it is by its freshwater outflow, and canoeists can easily find themselves paddling upstream against an incoming tide. Approximately seven miles south of Ft. Ogden the Peace River widens considerably before entering Charlotte Harbor. When it passes under I-75 it is close to a mile wide, and care should be taken to avoid being caught in summer thunderstorms or winter cold fronts as the wind can be quite treacherous.

There are several outfitters that are more than willing to help you plan your trip, from a one-day leg to a weeklong journey down this spectacular stream. The upper stretches of the Peace River have very little development as the river winds through

Fossilized shark's tooth found in the river Courtesy Visit Florida

pastureland and lush riverine forests. Ancient live oaks spread out over the stream, and alligators and fish thrive in the freshwater. Although it is popular to swim in the Peace River, care should be taken since alligators occupy its entire length. Fishing is a popular in the river; bass and bream populate the upper sections, and snook and redfish are found farther down as the river approaches Punta Gorda.

Fossil hunting is also a popular activity along the Peace River. The best time to find fossils is during periods of low water, which means you might have to drag your canoe or kayak on occasion, but the lower water exposes the best sites for screening for shark's teeth, camel and mammoth teeth, and a host of other finds. The fossils found here date to the Pleistocene period. All you need is a simple kitchen sifter or a large square screen (12 inches square is sufficient) and a shovel. It's much like panning for gold: you dig up a scoop of sand, mud, and gravel, drop it into the sifter and wash out everything but the larger sediments, then comb through what's left looking for mastodon teeth or bone fragments.

The Peace River does not have an official designation such as a wilderness river, and because of its length and size it is not a state or regional park. It is more of an amalgamation of various county parks, bridge ramps, and recreational areas that work together in making this an easy place to spend a day, a weekend, or a week. The website at www. canoeoutpost.com/peace includes pertinent information such as current water levels, recent snags or downfalls that might hamper navigation, links to maps of the river, popular put-in locations, and more.

One of the nicest things about the Peace River is its slow but steady flowing water and sublime scenery. The river valley cuts through the surrounding limestone. Sightings along the banks of the Peace include white-tailed deer, otters, turtles, and a multitude of birds from bald eagles to great blue herons.

The Peace River suffers from some pollution issues arising from the phosphate mines located near the river valley north of Wauchula, and though troublesome, they are not to the point where they have seriously impacted the river. The permitting of future mines upstream has become more restrictive, and hopefully these issues will be resolved in a manner that will never make the Peace River anything less than what it is today—a true Florida treasure.

❒ ______ D. The Peace River Wildlife Center

Location: 3400 Ponce de Leon Parkway, Punta Gorda, FL 33950 / Phone: 941-637-3830 / Fax: 941-637-3857 / Website: www.peaceriverwildlifecenter.com / E-mail: peaceriverwildlife@yahoo.com / 10 acres / Admission is free but donations are appreciated.

Situated along the northern edge of Ponce de Leon Park, the Peace River Wildlife Center offers a close-up encounter with 120 resident birds, turtles, and mammals. The 10-acre park itself sits along the eastern shoreline of Charlotte Harbor, which is one of the healthiest and largest estuaries left along the west coast of Florida. The view across the harbor stretches across miles of open water, and the mangrove-lined buffer of the Charlotte Harbor Preserve State Park on the other shore makes it seem as if you are the first to discover this treasure.

The park has picnic tables, a covered picnic area, restrooms, and a small boat ramp. A boardwalk loop trail takes you through a red and black mangrove forest, where informative placards point out different animal and plant species. One stretch of the boardwalk doubles as a fishing pier. Look for mangrove and fiddler crabs in the trees and blue crabs in the tidal creek that borders the park to the south.

An injured red-tailed hawk

© Charles Sobczak

The Wildlife Center, though fairly small, handled 1,395 orphaned or injured animals in 2009. As the urbanization of Southwest Florida increases, so too do the patient admissions at the Wildlife Center. More subdivisions mean more roads, and more cars mean more accidents involving wildlife. The majority of the birds, mammals, and reptiles admitted to the center are treated, mended, and released into the wild. A handful can be mended but their injuries are too severe to allow them to be returned to the wild. These either remain in the care of the Wildlife Center and are added to their displays of local fauna or are sent to other Florida facilities for public exhibit or long-term care.

The injured pelican enclosure at the hospital © Charles Sobczak

Birds on display at the Wildlife Center include yellow- and black-crowned night herons, bald eagles, and a truly spectacular red-tailed hawk. There are also gopher tortoises, and the center is adding a mammal display area.

Volunteers take visitors through the center's small zoo of injured animals, pointing out the different species and answering questions about the raptors, wading birds, and other animals kept there. This is a great opportunity to see these animals very close up. Feedings are especially interesting to watch as the hungry pelicans and larger wading birds line up for lunch. Several wild great blue herons, white ibis, and an endangered local wood stork are sometimes spotted in the Wildlife Center's open-air enclosure. They were never patients but have come to appreciate the free lunch of glass minnows and threadfin herring.

Entrance into the Wildlife Center is free but donations are welcome to help cover the considerable expense of the veterinary staff, medications, and fish for feeding the hungry birds. One of the major funding sources is through recycling aluminum cans and other items. The center has teamed up with Allied Recycling Inc. and has four large containers by the back gate for locals to deposit their aluminum cans or larger recycled items. The gift shop offers an assortment of T-shirts, gifts, and books for sale, all of which help to fund the mission of helping injured wildlife.

The beach area overlooking Charlotte Harbor

© Charles Sobczak

The combination of the Wildlife Center and the Ponce de Leon Park, with its lovely beach and huge tidal flats to explore, makes this an unusually attractive eco-destination. The birds and wildlife on display constantly change, and there is always something new to see at the Peace River Wildlife Center.

❐ ________ E. Alligator Creek Preserve/Charlotte Harbor Environmental Center (CHEC)

Location: 10941 Burnt Store Road, Punta Gorda, FL 33955 / Phone: 941-575-5435 / Fax: 941-575-5497 / Website: www.checflorida.org / E-mail: on Website / 30,000+ acres / Admission is free.

Located on Burnt Store Road in Punta Gorda, the Alligator Creek Preserve is the most well-known and visited park managed by the non-profit Charlotte Harbor Environmental Center (CHEC), which provides environmental education, research, recreation, and land management services in Charlotte County. The preserve encompasses more than 30,000 acres of state-owned land buffering Charlotte Harbor, a portion of which CHEC leases and manages. (CHEC also manages the county's Cedar Point Environmental Park, also described in this section.)

Interpretive signs are posted along the trails © Charles Sobczak

Among Alligator Creek's highlights is its more than four miles of well-groomed hiking trails. The preserve's network of trails connects with others in the area, including the Old Datsun Trail located a mile south at the entrance to Charlotte Harbor State Park. An experienced hiker could easily cover 10 miles of backwoods

Pine flatwoods flourish beside the trail © Charles Sobczak

trails in a single day here. (Note that like many trails in Southwest Florida, those at Alligator Creek can be very wet during the summer.)

Many of the trails have clearly marked numbers that correspond to a trail map, making it easy for amateur naturalists to take a self-guided stroll through the preserve's various ecosystems and learn about everything from black mangroves to beauty berry. Pine flatwoods is the prevailing habitat found along Burnt Store Road to the northern edge of Cape Coral. Other habitats include salt marshes, mangrove forests, and oak/cabbage palm hammocks. Although the property does have some Brazilian pepper, for the most part it has been kept free of invasive plants, and the native flora dominates the landscape.

Wildlife thrives along the Alligator Creek's trails. Expect to see osprey and wading birds in the various freshwater lakes found in the preserve, where more than 124 species of birds have been documented. Alligators, bobcats, and even an occasional black bear have been sighted here. In fact, more than 22 species of mammals and 59 reptiles and amphibians have been identified in and around the 3,000 acres traversed by the trails. During the spring and fall migrations, the surrounding woods, wetlands, and shrubs abound with warblers, cedar waxwings, and catbirds.

The spacious Charles E. Caniff Visitor's Center, named in honor of the visionary environmentalist who helped establish CHEC and the Alligator Creek Preserve in 1987, features an incredible hand-carved wooden mobile with life-size pelicans, herons, and other regional birds suspended from the ceiling. A mounted adult bald eagle sits on a simulated nest with a

The Caniff Visitor's Center © Charles Sobczak

hatchling. There are other displays on wildlife and Native American Indians, a film, lecture, and educational area, a bookstore and gift shop, and children's play area. A nearby screened picnic pavilion is available for use, though reservations are required.

CHEC also provides guided tours of the preserve and the surrounding estuary (see the website for a schedule). During the winter months it offers a voyage of discovery across Charlotte Harbor aboard a 29-foot tri-pontoon boat, the *Miss Charlotte*, departing out of Cape Haze Marina. These trips sometimes involve shallow-water wading and exploration stops that allow participants to net the seahorses, minnows, lightning whelks, and horseshoe crabs that thrive in one of the largest and healthiest marine estuaries in the state. During the school year the center works with the regional school district to take children through the preserve.

With its proximity to Cape Coral, Punta Gorda, Port Charlotte, and Ft. Myers, the Alligator Creek Preserve is an easy drive away from these population centers to a more natural side of Southwest Florida. A stroll through these lovely forests or a look around the elevated visitor's center with its well-stocked gift shop and friendly staff, makes this a great destination for anyone looking to experience more of what the real Florida is all about. So check out its website, put on your hiking shoes, and get outside.

❐ _____ F. Babcock/Webb Wildlife Management Area

Location: Tuckers Grade, I-75 Exit 158, turn east into the WMA / Phone: Florida Fish and Wildlife Conservation Commission: 863-648-3200 / Fax: n/a / Website: www.myfwc.com/Recreation/WMASites_BabcockWebb / E-mail: on website / 80,335 acres / Admission fee is charged.

Old tote roads criss-cross the WMA
© Charles Sobczak

Visiting the Babcock/Webb Wildlife Management Area (WMA) is a change of pace from state parks, tourist attractions, or wildlife preserves. WMAs are less developed than parks or preserves and are operated and overseen by the Florida Fish and Wildlife Conservation Commission (FWC). That being said, they still offer many recreational opportunities. Because they are designed to manage wildlife, seasonal hunting is not only allowed on most WMAs in Florida, but in some cases actively encouraged. At the Babcock/Webb WMA the hog-hunting season helps to control the feral pig population, which left unchecked would overrun not only the WMA, but the surrounding natural areas and preserves as well.

The expansive landscapes found at Babcock-Webb © Charles Sobczak

Although the 80,335-acre Babcock/Webb WMA seems impressive in size, it ranks only seventh in acreage among all WMAs in the state. The entire system of WMAs consists of more than 4.4 million acres or 6,875 square miles—an area considerably larger than the state of Connecticut. In Southwest Florida, Hendry County has two smaller WMAs—Spirit-of-the Wild and Dinner Island Ranch—and Glades County is home to the Fisheating Creek WMA.

The Babcock/Webb WMA is on property once owned by E.V. Babcock of Ashtola, Pennsylvania. In 1914 he purchased 156,000 acres in south central Florida for use as a hunting preserve and cattle ranch. His son, F. C. Babcock, transferred 65,000 acres of this land to the state of Florida in the 1940s. Cecil M. Webb was the commissioner of the precursor to FWC at the time of the acquisition, and the WMA was renamed to honor both men in 1995. Since that time Charlotte Harbor Flatwoods and the Yucca Pens Unit were added to the management area, increasing the property to its current size. In 1968 the state leased 1,280 acres of the Babcock/Webb WMA to the Boy Scouts of America (BSA). Since then the BSA has invested $3.2 million in campground facilities located along the northeastern corner of the parcel.

The Babcock/Webb WMA is a part of the Great Florida Birding Trail and is a popular destination for spotting two of Florida's most elusive species: Bachman's sparrow and the red-cockaded woodpecker. As this book is published, there are more than 27 colonies of the endangered red-cockaded woodpecker found within the WMA's boundaries. Their cavity trees are clearly marked with a white-painted ring. The website has an extensive list of the birds that have been sighted at the Babcock/Webb. Because the terrain is mostly wet flatwoods, it is not prime habitat for wild turkeys, but it is a popular site for hunting and spotting the northern bobwhite quail.

Two other rare animals found in the Babcock/Webb WMA are the Sherman's fox squirrel and the Florida bonneted bat, which is the largest native bat in Florida. Other mammals you are likely to see here include white-tailed deer, black bear, bobcats, coyotes, otters, armadillos, opossums, gray squirrels, and cottontail rabbits.

Because the area is so immense, biking the many elevated trails is a popular activity, especially during the drier winter months. Fishing, canoeing, boating, and kayaking are popular on the manmade 395-acre Webb Lake where anglers may catch huge freshwater snook, largemouth bass, and bluegills.

Visitors to Babcock/Webb may be surprised to hear the constant crack of firearms emanating from the WMA's shooting range. Located a few miles down Tuckers Grade on the north side of the road, the range is open to the public. It offers two rifle ranges, a separate area for pistol fire, and a skeet-shooting facility for shotgun users. Wildlife officers are on hand to make certain everyone adheres to safe firearm practices, and no rapid-fire or burst firearm usage is allowed (meaning no AK-47s and the like). Within a few miles of the range, the sound of the gunshots fade away, leaving the naturalist with only the sound of the wind in the slash pines.

A hunter practicing on the gun range © Charles Sobczak

While many naturalists might not appreciate the role hunters play in the conservation of wildlife, it is important to note that hunters and fishermen have a vested interest in preserving and protecting wildlife and have proven time and again to be useful allies in the fight against development, mining, and other industries damaging to wildlife habitat. The federal Duck Stamp program alone, required of waterfowl hunters, is responsible for purchasing and protecting millions of acres of wetlands from being drained and turned to farmland. Although the sound of gunshots in the distance can be disconcerting, it's important to understand that if left unchecked, wild pigs and white-tailed deer populations can skyrocket to levels that are harmful to the overall environment.

Whether viewing wildlife through a pair of binoculars or a rifle scope, we all have a vested interest in making sure there will always be places such as the Babcock/Webb WMA left untamed so that wildlife can have a place to call home.

❒ _______ G. Babcock Ranch

Location: 8000 SR 31, Punta Gorda, FL 33982 / Phone: 800-500-5583 / Fax: 941-637-4611 / Website: www. babcockwilderness.com / E-mail: touroffice@ babcockranchpreserve.org / 90,000 acres / Admission fee charged.

A swamp buggy ride through telegraph swamp Courtesy Charlotte County

Babcock Ranch is a working ranch that offers a 90-minute bus ride it calls *Babcock Wilderness Adventures—Swamp Buggy Eco-Tours.* While that may look good on a brochure, it is a bit misleading. Most of the trip is on a stripped-down, diesel-powered school bus. There is minimal walking involved, and no trails are open to hiking or biking if you want to venture off on your own.

This may be a classic case of mis-marketing, since this is more of a historic than an ecological tour. Historically speaking, this 90,000-acre property is a treasure trove of "olde" Florida. One of the first things you see on your "Wilderness Adventure" hasn't been found in the wild for almost 100 years: the herds of cracker cattle grazing on the pastureland the tour bus passes through. These cattle are direct descendants of the original Spanish cattle that escaped from St. Augustine and Ponce de Leon's 1521 visit to the southwest coast of Florida. Spanish cattle at that time were a mixed breed of Celtic domestic cattle and the indigenous wild cattle of prehistoric Europe, the Aurochs. They have long sprawling horns similar in style to Texas longhorns and still have an aura of wildness to them. Anyone who has read Patrick Smith's classic novel of early Florida settlers, *A Land Remembered*, will enjoy seeing these colorfully patterned animals.

The museum on the Babcock Ranch property is nothing out of the ordinary. Most of the displays are jammed into a replica cracker cabin that was built for the movie set for *Just Cause*, a 1995 film starring Sean Connery. The museum's displays include old logging tools, historical photos, and miscellaneous saddles. Another display features the venomous snakes found on the ranch, including coral snakes, dusky and eastern diamondback rattlers, and water moccasins. In keeping with its "roadside attraction" feel, there is also the mounted head of Lulu, a freak three-horned cow.

The eco-tour bus ride provides a glimpse of life on a working ranch. The tour guides are fun and very knowledgeable about the Crescent "B" Ranch, which over the years has won several environmental awards for its land stewardship. The bus tour begins with a trip through the small town of Rouxville, where ranch hands and cowboys still live and work. The old commissary, cattle corrals, and converted boxcars that serve as homes for the cowhands all beg for more exploration, but the bus moves on. Next the tour enters Telegraph Swamp, which has plenty of wading birds, alligators, and wild turkeys to see. Flocks of Osceola turkeys trot about in the oak and pinewood forests, and wild hogs are common sightings. White-tailed deer are found everywhere, especially in the morning.

Cracker cattle can still be found on the ranch

© Blake Sobczak

After crossing the swamp a second time, with the bus wheels almost three feet deep in flowing water, the vehicle comes to a dry field where everyone gets off to walk down a block-long boardwalk to see the fenced-in Florida panthers. Their pen is large enough and so similar to the surrounding habitat that it feels as if you are seeing these panthers in the wild. Many a Florida panther photograph has been shot at Babcock Ranch, since spotting a truly wild Florida panther is all but impossible.

During the winter months the ranch opens its Gator Shack restaurant, featuring pulled pork and ranch-style cuisine. A large cabin called Cypress Lodge can be rented for small corporate retreats or family get-togethers.

Babcock Ranch was sold in 2006, and 17,000 acres in its southwestern section are slated to become the world's first solar-powered, self-sustaining city in the next 25 years. The balance of the ranch, some 73,000 acres, will remain a preserve and a working operation. Ironically, the city of Babcock Ranch plans to put in extensive hiking and biking trails, which would be a welcome addition to the current Babcock experience. While not exactly an eco-tour, a visit to the Babcock Ranch is still a good value, especially for families with younger children or older adults who might find the bus ride both entertaining and easy. Although far from perfect, this destination gives you a unique window into Florida's "cracker" past.

A fledgling great blue heron

© Gareth Pinckard

Birding along the boardwalk Courtesy Lee County VCB

Additional Charlotte County Parks, Preserves, and Eco-destinations

❒ ________ Octagon Wildlife Sanctuary

Location: 41600 Horseshoe Road, Punta Gorda, FL 33982 / Phone: 239-543-1130 / Fax: n/a / Website: www. octagonwildlife.org / E-mail: support @octagonwildlife.org / Admission fee charged.

Octagon Wildlife Sanctuary is a nonprofit organization that rescues animals such as mountain lions, leopards, primates, bears, and reptiles that were abandoned, abused, or confiscated by Fish and Wildlife as illegal imports. It is not a zoo but a sanctuary for these orphaned animals. Donations as well as volunteers help to keep the doors open on this noble enterprise. Pete Caron, who passed away in 2006, founded Octagon 30 years ago. His widow, Lauri Caron, keeps the dream alive today.

❒ ________ Worden Farms

Location: 34900 Bermont Road, Punta Gorda, FL 33982 / Phone: 941-637-4874 / Fax: n/a / Website: www. wordenfarm.com / E-mail: office @wordenfarm.com / Admission fees vary depending on the different workshops being offered.

Worden Farms is an 85-acre certified organic farming operation located 10 miles northeast of Punta Gorda. The farm produces more than 50 varieties of vegetables, fruits, herbs, and flowers that are then sold through farm memberships, farmers' markets, and other outlets across the region. Workshops cover topics such as cheese making, cooking, gardening, sustainable agriculture, and growing, as well as eating, local foods. Go to the website for specifics on tours, workshops, and other scheduled events.

❒ _______ Punta Gorda Historic Railroad Depot

Location: 1009 Taylor Road, Punta Gorda, FL 33950 / Phone: 941-639-6774 / Fax: n/a / Website: www. puntagordavisitor.info / E-mail: n/a / Admission is free.

The 1928 Punta Gorda Train Depot presents historic displays mixed in with an antique mall, providing an interesting combination of history and antique shopping. The depot displays segregated "colored" and "white" waiting rooms. Exhibits include photos and memorabilia relating to Punta Gorda's fishing fleets, the railroad industry, and the Punta Gorda Army Air Field.

❒ _______ A. C. Freeman House

Location: 311 West Retta Esplanade, Punta Gorda, FL 33951 / Phone: 941-639-639-6774 / Fax: n/a / Website: www. puntagordavisitor.info / E-mail: n/a / Admission is free.

Built in 1903, this stunning Victorian house is the only remaining example of residential Victorian architecture in Charlotte County. Free guided walking tours are open to the public. Call the Historical Society for an updated schedule of tours.

❒ _______ History Park, Punta Gorda

Location: 501 Shreve Street, Punta Gorda, FL 33951 / Phone: 941-639-6774 / Fax: n/a / Website: www. puntagordavisitor.info / E-mail: n/a / Admission is free.

This small but fascinating park contains several historic buildings, all within easy walking distance from each other. They include the Cigar Cottage, Trabue (one of Punta Gorda's original town names) Law & Land Sales Office, the Gilchrist House, and the Calaboose, an early Punta Gorda jail. Contact the Historical Society for more information about the park and its hours of operation.

❒ _____ Blanchard House Museum of African-American History

Location: 406 Martin Luther King Blvd., Punta Gorda, FL 33951 / Phone: 941-575-7518 / Fax: n/a / Website: www. puntagordavisitor.info / E-mail: n/a / Admission is free.

This house was built in 1925 for Joseph Blanchard, a black sea captain and key member of Punta Gorda's early business community. It was later purchased by Bernice Russell, who converted it into an open-access educational institute devoted to the preservation, study, and display of artifacts and materials related to the history, culture, and contributions of African-Americans in Charlotte County.

❒ ________ Charlotte Harbor Preserve State Park

Location: 12301 Burnt Store Road, Punta Gorda, FL 33995 / Phone: 941-575-5861 / Fax: n/a / Website: www. floridastateparks.org/charlotteharbor / E-mail: n/a / 42,000 acres / Admission is free.

This preserve is available only via boat, canoe, or kayak. It protects 70 miles of shoreline rimming Charlotte Harbor. You can pick up brochures about the park at the Burnt Store Road headquarters. The Old Datsun Trail, begins here and connects with the trail system of the nearby Charlotte Harbor Environmental Center (CHEC) covered earlier in this section. The North Cape Flats Trail is located 11 miles down Burnt Store Road.

❒ ________ Don Pedro Island State Park

Location: Office is at 880 Belcher Road, Boca Grande, FL 33921 / Phone: 941-964-0375 / Fax: n/a / Website: www. floridastateparks.org/donpedroisland / E-mail: teresa.l.foster @dep.state.fl.us / 330 acres / Admission fee charged.

Accessible only by boat or private ferry (grandetours.com / 941-697-8825), this park consists of 230 acres on Don Pedro Island and another 100 acres at the launch site on the Cape Haze Peninsula. On the island there are picnic areas and hiking trails. Activities include fishing, canoeing, kayaking, snorkeling, and scuba diving. The ferry runs on an irregular schedule so be sure to call Grande Tours to verify availability.

❒ ________ Island Bay National Wildlife Refuge

Location: The southern tip of Cape Haze along Charlotte Harbor. GPS: 26E77'38.13"N / 082E18'03.00"W / Phone: 239-472-4100 / Fax: 239-472-4061 / Website: www. fws.gov/dingdarling / E-mail: dingdarling @fws.gov / 20 acres / Accessible only by watercraft.

The smallest wildlife refuge in the entire 109-million-acre federal system, Island Bay consists of five scattered rookeries and nesting areas along a deserted stretch of mangroves near Turtle Bay. Originally declared a wildlife preserve by Theodore Roosevelt in 1908, these rookeries came under the jurisdiction of the J.N. "Ding" Darling National Wildlife Refuge in 1970. There is no public access because disturbing these critical areas can interfere with breeding and nesting. Boats should remain 200 feet from the refuge at all times. With binoculars or a good telephoto lens, however, the birding is outstanding.

Brown Pelican in Boca Grande Pass just outside Charlotte Harbor

Courtesy Florida State Parks

❒ ________ Tippecanoe Environmental Park

Location: 2400 El Jobean Road, Port Charlotte, FL 33948 / Phone: 941-613-3220 / Fax: n/a / Website: www. charlottecountyfl.com/Community Services/NaturalResources/EnvironmentalLands / E-mail: AndyStevens@ charlottefl.com / 380 acres / Admission is free.

This preserve consists mostly of oak scrub, scrubby flatwoods, pine flatwoods, salt marshes, and mangrove swamp. Both Florida scrub jays and gopher tortoises can be found here. Nearly seven miles of well-marked trails transect the preserve. Trail guides, trailheads, and additional downloads are available on the Charlotte County website.

❒ ________ Tippecanoe II Mitigation Area

Location: 16259 Joppa Avenue, Port Charlotte, FL 33948 / Phone: 941-613-3220 / Fax: n/a / Website: www. charlottecountyfl.com/Community Services/NaturalResources/EnvironmentalLands / E-mail: AndyStevens@ charlottefl.com / 182 acres / Admission is free.

This property was purchased to offset (mitigate) the impact of two Charlotte County projects. It is made up of oak scrub, scrubby flatwoods, and hydric and xeric hammocks. The parcel now provides habitat for two family groups of Florida scrub jays. Other common sightings include six-lined racerunners, screech owls, and bald eagles. The mitigation area has a .27-mile ADA-accessible trail along with a 1.7-mile hiking trail.

❒ ________ Amberjack Environmental Park

Location: 6450 Gasparilla Pines Blvd., Rotonda, FL 34224 / Phone: 941-613-3220 / Fax: n/a / Website: www. charlottecountyfl.com/Community Services/NaturalResources/EnvironmentalLands / E-mail: AndyStevens@ charlottefl.com / 225 acres / Admission is free.

A total of 5.55 miles of hiking trails crisscross this interesting property. It includes Lemon Lake and several seasonal wetlands. Boardwalks and observation platforms allow visitors to spot glossy ibis, roseate spoonbills, and great and snowy egrets. This is a great site for avid birders and wildflower enthusiasts, as a wet prairie blooms wildflowers in this preserve year-round.

❐ ________ Charlotte Flatwoods Environmental Park

Location: 15801 Tamiami Trail, Punta Gorda, FL 33955 / Phone: 941-613-3220 / Fax: n/a / Website: www. charlottecountyfl.com/Community Services/ NaturalResources/EnvironmentalLands / E-mail: AndyStevens@ charlottefl.com / 487 acres / Admission is free.

Consisting of mature pine flatwoods, dry prairies, marsh wetlands, and freshwater ponds, this environmental park is primarily upland in nature. Common sightings include bald eagles, bobcats, great horned owls, and several species of reptiles and amphibians. More than seven miles of well-marked trails traverse the park.

❐ ________ Oyster Creek Regional Park

Location: 6791 San Casa Drive, Englewood, FL 34224 / Phone: 941-613-3220 / Fax: n/a / Website: www. charlottecountyfl.com/Community Services/ NaturalResources/EnvironmentalLands / E-mail: AndyStevens@ charlottefl. com / 250 acres / Admission is free, though fees are charged to rent some of the facilities.

The 3.75 miles of nature trails at Oyster Creek Regional Park are only a small part of this multiuse facility. Other amenities include a dog park, football and soccer fields, basketball courts, a skate park, and swimming pool. There are also several amenities rarely found in any park such as a cricket court, a diving well, and pavilion rentals. Oyster Creek is located directly across the street from Cedar Point Environmental Park.

❐ ________ Buck Creek Preserve

Location: 5350 Placida Road, Englewood, FL 34224 / Phone: 941-613-3220 / Fax: n/a / Website: www. charlottecountyfl.com/Community Services/ NaturalResources/EnvironmentalLands / E-mail: AndyStevens@ charlottefl.com / 80+ acres / Admission is free.

Located along a section of Buck Creek, this preserve's landscape is dominated by scrubby and mesic flatwoods. Common sightings include bald eagles and gopher tortoises. The acquisition of this property is a part of the Conservation Charlotte program.

❒ ________ Deep Creek Property

Location: 28000 Sandhill Blvd., Punta Gorda, FL 33983 / Phone: 941-613-3220 / Fax: n/a / Website: www. charlottecountyfl.com/Community Services/NaturalResources/EnvironmentalLands / E-mail: AndyStevens@ charlottefl.com / 450 acres / Admission is free.

This preserve, which is almost a square mile in size, protects lands that abut the Peace River, as well as Deep Creek. Wading birds and the elusive Florida scrub jay can be found along the preserve's .67-mile hiking trail.

❒ ________ Prairie Creek Preserve

Location: 1900 Duncan Road, Punta Gorda, FL 33982 / Phone: 941-613-3220 / Fax: n/a / Website: www. charlottecountyfl.com/Community Services/NaturalResources/EnvironmentalLands / E-mail: AndyStevens@ charlottefl.com / 1,600 acres / Admission is free.

The small but free-flowing Prairie Creek cuts through this preserve, which is home to bobcats, scrub jays, deer, and many varieties of reptiles and amphibians. Approximately 1.7 miles of hiking trails are available to explore.

❒ ________ Shell Creek Preserve

Location: 4334 Nellis Lane, Punta Gorda, FL 33982 / Phone: 941-613-3220 / Fax: n/a / Website: www. charlottecountyfl.com/Community Services/NaturalResources/EnvironmentalLands / E-mail: AndyStevens@ charlottefl.com / 370 acres / Admission is free.

This preserve runs adjacent to Shell Creek, which is a tributary of the Peace River, entering the river roughly two miles north of the I-75 bridge. It includes not only rare stands of longleaf pine, but also bald and pond cypress along with seasonal wetlands. The trail system here is approximately 2.5 miles long. The banks along the creek rise as much as 10 feet. The creek is a popular destination for canoeing and kayaking. A canoe-kayak launch is still in the planning stages but the creek can be accessed in Hathaway Park, farther to the west.

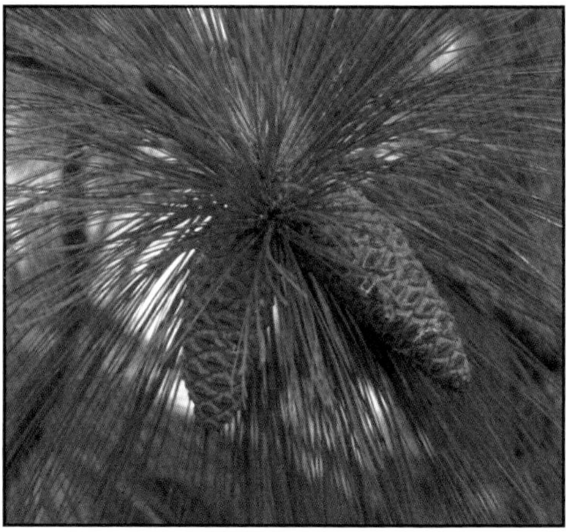

Longleaf pine needles and cones
By Erich G. Vallery, USDA Forest Service, Courtesy Wikipedia Commons

❒ ________ Hathaway Park

Location: 35461 Washington Loop Road, Punta Gorda, FL 33982 / Phone: 941-505-8686 / Fax: n/a / Website: www. charlottecountyfl.com/Community Services/ParkPages/hathaway / E-mail: AndyStevens@ charlottefl.com / 29 acres / Admission is free.

An excellent access point onto Shell Creek and the Peace River, this put-in is approximately nine miles from where the two rivers meet near the top of Charlotte Harbor. Other amenities include horse trails, nature trails, and restrooms. Heading upriver is another option, though Shell Creek starts to shallow up as you head east.

❒ ________ Ainger Creek Park

Location: 2011 Placida Road, Englewood, FL 34224 / Phone: 941-681-3742 / Fax: n/a / Website: www. charlottecountyfl.com/Community Services/ParkPages/aingercreek. / E-mail: AndyStevens@ charlottefl.com / 1.93 acres / Admission fee charged for parking.

This small park is essentially a boat ramp. It's a great place to launch a canoe or kayak to explore Ainger Creek. Look for wading birds along the creek and osprey and eagles overhead.

❒ ________ Audubon-Pennington Nature Park

Location: 1153 Alton Road, Port Charlotte, FL 33948 / Phone: 941-625-7529 / Fax: n/a / Website: www. charlottecountyfl.com/Community Services/ParkPages/audubonpark. / E-mail: AndyStevens@ charlottefl.com / 31.26 acres / Admission is free.

Managed by the Peace River Audubon Society, this park includes nature trails and offers excellent birding throughout the year.

❒ ________ Bayshore Live Oak Park

Location: 23157 Bayshore Road, Port Charlotte, FL 33980 / Phone: 941-629-7278 / Fax: n/a / Website: www. charlottecountyfl.com/Community Services/ParkPages/bayshorepark / E-mail: AndyStevens@ charlottefl.com / 10.32 acres / Admission is free.

This fair-sized park offers birding, fishing, historic features, hiking trails, and picnicking. It is located just south of U.S. 41 along the northern edge of Charlotte Harbor.

Florida Mud Snake
© Kenneth L. Krysko, UF

❒ ______ Cape Haze Pioneer Trail Park

Location: 1688 Gasparilla Road, Rotonda, FL 33981 / Phone: 941-625-7529 / Fax: n/a / Website: www. charlottecountyfl.com/Community Services/ParkPages/capehaze / E-mail: AndyStevens@ charlottefl.com / 67.6 acres / Admission is free.

Known as a great off-road biking destination, this park also includes nature trails, good birding, and picnic grounds.

❒ ________ North Charlotte Regional Park

Location: 1185 O'Donnell Blvd., Port Charlotte, FL 33948 / Phone: 941-627-1074 / Fax: n/a / Website: www. charlottecountyfl.com/Community Services/ParkPages/NorthCarlotteRegionalPark / E-mail: AndyStevens@ charlottefl.com / 103.3 acres / Admission is free.

This is a large regional park with amenities such as baseball, soccer and softball fields, and hiking and nature trails. It also has a Frisbee golf course, which is fun for everyone.

❒ ________ Ollie's Pond Park

Location: 18235 Avon Avenue, Port Charlotte, FL 33948 / Phone: 941-625-7529 / Fax: n/a / Website: www.charlottecountyfl.com/Community Services/ParkPages/ollies / E-mail: AndyStevens@ charlottefl.com / 41.18 acres / Admission is free.

This pond and surrounding wetlands area is a place to view wading birds, along with migratory warblers, raptors, and other mammals and amphibians.

❒ ________ Placida Park

Location: 6499 Gasparilla Road, Placida, FL 33946 / Phone: 941-681-3742 / Fax: n/a / Website: www. charlottecountyfl.com/Community Services/ParkPages/placidapark / E-mail: AndyStevens@ charlottefl.com / 5.62 acres / Admission is charged for parking.

This is primarily a boat ramp, allowing access to the backwaters of Charlotte Harbor and beyond.

❒ ________ Port Charlotte Beach Park

Location: 4500 Harbor Blvd., Port Charlotte, FL 33952 / Phone: 941-627-1628 / Pool phone: 941-629-0170 / Fax: n/a / Website: www. charlottecountyfl.com/Community Services/ParkPages/PortCharlotteBeach / E-mail: AndyStevens@ charlottefl.com / 16.08 acres / Admission fee charged.

A wide array of amenities awaits you at this good-sized park, including a small beach, community pool, and a canoe-kayak rental facility. This is an excellent launch site into the greater Charlotte Harbor preserve.

❒ ________ Riverside Park

Location: 8320 Riverside Drive, Punta Gorda, FL 33982 / Phone: 941-505-8686 / Fax: n/a / Website: www. charlottecountyfl.com/Community Services/ParkPages/riversidepark / E-mail: AndyStevens@ charlottefl.com / .56 acres / Admission is free.

This is essentially a boat ramp and access area for canoeists and kayakers to explore both Shell Creek and the Peace River to the west.

❒ ________ Rotonda Park

Location: 100 Rotonda Blvd., Rotonda West, FL 33947 / Phone: 941-681-3742 / Fax: n/a / Website: www. charlottecountyfl.com/Community Services/ParkPages/rotondacommunity / E-mail: AndyStevens@ charlottefl.com / 32.13 acres / Admission is free.

Located in the very center of the wagon-wheel-shaped Rotonda West subdivision, this park offers biking and hiking trails, a playground, and several tennis courts.

❒ ________ Spring Lake Park

Location: 3520 Lakeview Blvd., Port Charlotte, FL 33946 / Phone: 941-627-1074 / Fax: n/a / Website: www. charlottecountyfl.com/Community Services/ParkPages/springlakepark / E-mail: AndyStevens@ charlottefl.com / 8.11 acres / Admission is free.

Situated on Spring Lake, this park has canoeing, kayaking, fishing, and a pleasant nature walk.

❒ ________ Sunrise Park

Location: 20499 Edgewater Drive, Port Charlotte, FL 33952 / Phone: 941-627-1047 / Fax: n/a / Website: www.charlottecountyfl.com/Community Services/ParkPages/sunrisepark / E-mail: AndyStevens@ charlottefl.com / 40.28 acres / Admission is free.

Although Sunrise Park is only 40 acres in size, it abuts a part of the Charlotte Harbor State Reserve, which is an additional 114 acres in size. This is a great place for canoeing and kayaking.

Sunrise © Dick Fortune & Sara Lopez

Nirvana in the rough

Lee County

Named in honor of the Confederate general, Robert E. Lee, Lee County was formally established May 12, 1887. It was originally much larger than it is today, encompassing all of Collier and Hendry counties before being split apart in 1923. Today, it is 1,212 square miles—two-thirds land and mangroves, and one-third water. The water portion consists of the vast, shallow tidal flats of San Carlos Bay, Pine Island Sound, and the southern edge of Charlotte Harbor, as well as the Caloosahatchee River, which transects a corner of the county from northeast to southwest.

This immense estuarine system of Lee County once flourished with bay scallops, blue crabs, fin fish, and other sea life. During the height of the Calusa empire at the time of the European invasion in 1513, the waters surrounding Mound Key, Pineland, Cabbage Key, and Useppa, among many other Calusa villages, supported tens of thousands of Native Americans. Shellfish such as lightning whelk, oysters, scallops, and conchs formed a large part of their diet. They were also known to take shark, snook, mullet, manatee, and deer, which were far more abundant than they are today.

Sadly, the estuary is struggling beneath the onslaught of development that the county has experienced in recent decades. In 1960 Lee County had a population of 54,539; according to the projected 2010 census, the county now has a population of 615,124—more than a tenfold increase in 50 years. The cost has been a continuous degradation of water quality from urban runoff, deteriorating septic systems, inadequate sewage treatment plants, and boat traffic.

The Caloosahatchee River has also been a conduit of pollution, as freshwater is released from Lake Okeechobee and travels down the river to the estuary. Originally the river received overflow water from Lake Okeechobee only when the lake was at extremely high levels and water seeped west through marshes and lakes. All that changed in 1881 when Hamilton Disston struck a deal with the governor of Florida to purchase 4 million acres from the state with the understanding that half the land be drained and deeded to him. He created a channel between Lake Okeechobee and the head of the river at Ft. Thompson, two miles east of present-day LaBelle. After the ravaging hurricanes of 1926 and 1928, the channel was widened, deepened, and straightened by the Army Corps of Engineers and is now formally called the C-43 canal. During periods of high rainfall in the Kissimmee Valley in central Florida, the locks at Moore Haven are opened and the estuary 43 miles to the west is soon overwhelmed with the nutrient-rich freshwater, resulting in further degradation of its marine ecosystem. Recent fertilizer ordinances along with better sewage treatment and storm runoff regulations are helping to restore Pine Island Sound, but set against the backdrop of continued urban growth it may be a long time before the conflicts are resolved.

Lee County is blessed with a profusion of islands. The most famous are the barrier islands: Lovers Key, Estero, Sanibel, Captiva, North Captiva, Cayo Costa, and Gasparilla stretch just offshore from southeast to northwest. Inside of these beach-bordered isles are the mangrove-lined islands such as Cabbage Key, Mound Key, Useppa Island, and Pine Island, as well as the smaller Panther Key, Chino

Two lovers walk on Lovers Key Courtesy Florida State Parks

Island, York Island, and dozens of unnamed islets. The Great Calusa Blueway, which is covered in this section, is an ingenious set of marked paddling trails that provides paddlers with a roadmap to these watery Lee County treasures.

Lee County is unusual in that it has six state parks (Lovers Key, Mound Key, Koreshan State Historic Site, Cayo Costa, Estero Bay Preserve and Gasparilla Island State Park), three National Wildlife Refuges—the most famous being the J.N. "Ding" Darling National Wildlife Refuge on Sanibel Island—and a host of other amazing regional and local parks and preserves. Although the entire land mass of Lee County is about the same size as the Big Cypress National Preserve to the south, it has a great diversity of habitats and eco-destinations. From the historic interest of both the Koreshan State Historic Site and the Edison & Ford Estates to the manmade wetlands of Harn's Marsh in Lehigh Acres, there is something for every sightseer, birder, and naturalist. The Conservancy of Southwest Florida puts the total portion of managed lands in Lee County at 17 percent, while Lee County administrators claim to have 21 percent managed in parks and preserves. The 4 percent difference is possibly a result of the way the area of mangrove islands and tidal wetlands is calculated.

Hopefully, the residents and guests of Lee County will come to understand that preserving this environment is far more important in the long term than promoting the type of growth that can only add to its degradation. Singer-songwriter Joni Mitchell could not have said it better when she wrote that famous line, "*They paved paradise, and put up a parking lot.*" Lee County must heed her warning and stand fast in promoting clean energy, reducing urban sprawl, and keeping its waters free from fertilizers and urban runoff. In the meantime, get out and take advantage of these glorious destinations and rejoice in the fact that you are about to discover some of the most beautiful places on the planet.

Lee County Eco-Destinations

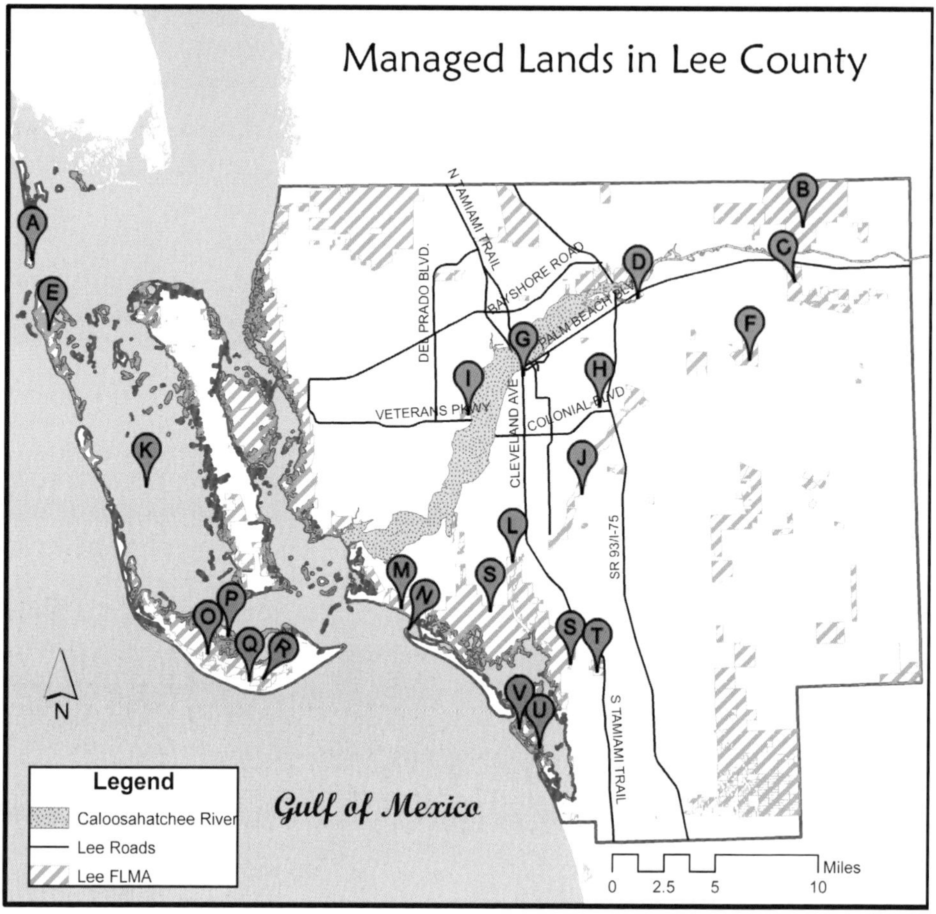

A. Gasparilla Island State Park
B. Caloosahatchee Regional Park
C. Hickey Creek Mitigation Park
D. Manatee Park
E. Cayo Costa State Park
F. Harn's Marsh Preserve
G. Edison & Ford Winter Estates
H. Calusa Nature Center & Planetarium
I. Four Mile Cove Ecological Park
J. Six Mile Cypress Slough Preserve
K. The Great Calusa Blueway (marked as Pine Island Sound)
L. Lakes Regional Park
M. Bunche Beach
N. Bowditch Point Regional Park
O. CROW Wildlife Clinic
P. J.N. "Ding" Darling National Wildlife Refuge
Q. Sanibel-Captiva Conservation Foundation
R. Bailey-Matthews Shell Museum
S. Estero Bay Preserve State Park
T. Koreshan State Historic Site
U. Mound Key and the Estero River
V. Lover's Key State Park

CONSERVANCY
Of Southwest Florida
www.conservancy.org

Managed Lands in Southwest Florida

Lee County
514,560 Acres
87,611 Acres Managed
17%

❒ _______ A. Gasparilla Island State Park

Location: 880 Belcher Road, Boca Grande, FL 33921 / Phone: 941-964-0375 / Fax: n/a / Website: www.floridastateparks.org/gasparillaisland / E-mail: teresa.l.foster@dep.state.fl.us / 144 acres / Admission fee charged.

Located on the southern tip of Gasparilla Island, this 144-acre point of land is one of the most valuable pieces of undeveloped real estate in the entire Florida state park system. A short distance north of the park lie the walled gulf-front estates of members of the du Pont family, as well as movie stars such as Kathleen Turner. Boca Grande Pass is a favorite fishing spot for the Bush family, with both former Presidents George W. and George H. Bush visiting the island to wet a line.

Gasparilla Island State Park fronts on Boca Grande Pass, which translates to "wide mouth" in Spanish and separates Gasparilla Island from the island of Cayo Costa to the south. The deep-water pass is world famous for the schools of tarpon that arrive every spring around late April and depart near the end of summer. If you visit the park during these months, with a good set of binoculars you can actually see these 100-pound "silver kings" from the observation deck surrounding the historic Boca Grande Lighthouse. Tarpon have a primitive lung allowing them to take in oxygen from the air when the surrounding water is too warm to hold enough suspended oxygen for fish this large to survive. When they surface they roll and kick up their tails. On a calm day it is not difficult to spot these fish, some of which are six feet or more in length.

Tarpon have been caught in the pass for decades

Courtesy Sanibel Historical Museum

The fishing here is spectacular. Almost every game and sport fish found along the west coast of Florida can be caught in and around the Boca Grande Pass. Farther north along the beach and well away from the pass are a number of artificial reefs positioned a few hundred feet offshore. One of these reefs is within snorkeling distance, located just off the range light approximately a mile north of the park in twelve feet of water.

Gasparilla lighthouse Courtesy Florida State Parks

Common catches in and around the pass include gag grouper, mangrove snapper, snook, goliath grouper, flounder, sea trout, and large jack crevalle. The world-record all-tackle hammerhead shark was caught just offshore of the pass in 2006. That fish was 14-feet long and weighed an astonishing 1,280 pounds.

The presence of numerous sharks, along with strong rip currents, makes swimming in Boca Grande Pass extremely dangerous. The rip currents are created by the immense tides that wash in and out of the pass, feeding into Charlotte Harbor, one of the largest estuaries on the west coast of Florida. Swimming along the beaches, at least a quarter mile from the pass, is considered safe.

Gasparilla Island State Park has much to offer. The central attraction is the restored lighthouse, built in 1890. Its museum and interpretive center shed light on the history of the abandoned phosphate docks and the legendary captains, who, over the ages, have plied the pass for the elusive silver kings. Also on display are Calusa artifacts, sea turtle shells, and an assortment of fish mounts. The bookstore and gift shop offer an array of products that focus on the sea and the surrounding area.

Hiking and biking are popular activities in and around the park. Gasparilla Island itself has a Rails-to-Trails bike path that runs north/south throughout most of the island. The numerous quaint streets and backroads of the old town of Boca Grande are also popular for walking and biking. The Gasparilla Island State Park has covered picnic areas, and an old, historic chapel on the grounds which is available to rent for weddings, special events and family get-togethers.

For bird watchers, the park attracts a steady stream of shorebirds and seabirds, including black skimmers, snowy plovers, magnificent frigate birds, and even rare sightings of northern gannets and parasitic jaegers. Migratory warblers mingle with raptors such as red-shouldered hawks and osprey as the sun sets over the gulf.

While the shelling isn't as good as it is on Sanibel and Captiva, there are still plenty of fine shells to be found while beachcombing the shoreline of Gasparilla Island. Spectacular sunsets present the perfect opportunity to take a break and watch the world go by. From snorkeling to fishing to just kicking your shoes off and relaxing, Gasparilla Island State Park beckons visitors to stop by and enjoy. It's that easy to do.

❒ ________ B. Caloosahatchee Regional State Park

Location: 18500 North River Road, Alva, FL 33920 / Phone: 239-694-0398 / Fax: 239-485-2300 / Website: www.leeparks.org / E-mail: leeparks@leegov.com / 768 acres / Admission is free, parking and camping fees charged.

With its riverfront setting and wide array of habitats—pine flatwoods, scrub oak, cypress swamps, and oak hammocks—the 1.2-square-mile Caloosahatchee Regional Park (CRP) is a rare find. Here you will discover more than 20 miles of hiking, biking, and horse trails, as well as kayak rentals allowing you to explore the area by water.

The main entrance to Caloosahatchee Regional Park
© Charles Sobczak

The park property, located along the Caloosahatchee River in Alva, was originally purchased by the state of Florida in 1960. The park is bisected by North River Road. Much of the land north of River Road is artificially elevated because it was used as a spoil site when the Caloosahatchee was repeatedly dredged for commerce from the 1920s through the late 1950s. Lee County entered into a lease agreement with the state in 1989 to provide public recreation along the river, and opened CRP in 1999.

Two private organizations had a hand in making the park happen, and today, in an example of a healthy public/private partnership, these groups help maintain the trails. The approximately six miles of horse trails and two equestrian campsites are kept up by the Caloosa Saddle Club. The bike trails, totaling 10.2 miles, are maintained by the Florida Mudcutters, an off-road biking club that is part of the International Mountain Bicycling Association. Volunteers clear away the ever-encroaching bushes and trees and keep the trails from getting too rutted to maneuver. CRP has the only official off-road mountain bike trail in Lee County.

If your preference is to get out on the water, CRP has much to offer. Hickey Creek, which is ideal for canoeing and kayaking, is a short paddle from the boat launch in the park. CRP is part of the Great Calusa Blueway and offers the only place along the Caloosahatchee where dedicated kayakers can camp. The park has a total of 28 campsites, including the two equestrian sites and one designated for handicap use

The Caloosa lodge © Charles Sobczak

Overlooking the beautiful Caloosahatchee © Charles Sobczak

only. The campsites are spread out over the park's acreage, making each one very private. Automobiles are not allowed around the campsite circle; access is via large pull-carts. There are cold-water shower stations located throughout the campgrounds, as well as restrooms, an amphitheater, and a roomy lodge that is available for daily rentals. The lodge can handle groups of up to 80 people and offers a small kitchen and private restrooms.

Although swimming is not advisable in the Caloosahatchee, fishing is encouraged. There is a fishing pier where anglers can catch an assortment of freshwater species including bream, bass, and several exotics such as peacock bass and tilapia. You can also be assured that there are plenty of birds to discover at CRP, including osprey, eagles, common moorhens, and warblers.

Most of the park's programs take place during the winter season. These include guided walks, kayak tours, teen odyssey, and a number of programs for pre-K children about animal homes, butterflies, and trees and leaves.

Annual events at CRP include the River, Roots and Ruts Trail Run every January and the XTERRA Caloosahatchee, a half-triathlon event in mid-April. The park is used several times a year by the School District of Lee County for cross-country races and other special events.

The trails along the river are stunning, with wide-open views of the Caloosahatchee, while shaded beneath cypress trees, live oaks, and palms. With its spacious campsites, hiking and mountain-bike trails, kayak and canoe rentals, and a mixture of programs and guided tours, CRP will not disappoint anyone who takes an afternoon to get out and enjoy this beautiful park.

❒ ________ C. Hickey's Creek Mitigation Park

Location: 17980 Palm Beach Blvd., Alva, FL 33920 / Phone: 239-694-0398 / Fax: 239-485-2300 / Website: www.leeparks.org/pdf/Hickeys_Creek / E-mail: leeparks@leegov.com / 862 acres / Admission is free, parking fee charged.

Kayaking Hickey's Creek Courtesy Lee County VC Bureau

While hardly poetic in name, the mitigation park program administered by the Florida Fish & Wildlife Commission (FWC) is an intriguing study in conservation management. To better understand it, let's start with a fictitious shopping center called Sprawl-Mart.

The developers of this new superstore have chosen a 30-acre site on the outskirts of Shoreside (a fictitious town), Florida. When the developers do an environmental impact study they are surprised to learn that there are seven thriving gopher tortoise burrows and three Florida scrub jay nests on the site. In the past they may well have tried to work around these burrows and nests using "on-site preservation." In the end, with all but three acres paved over, neither the jays nor the tortoises would likely survive.

The FWC created the "mitigation program" to resolve the issue. Under this arrangement the Sprawl-Mart developers and FWC come to a monetary settlement over the cost to offset the impact of the loss of this 30-acre site to these two threatened species. Those funds are then channeled into the mitigation park program, and with the help of local, state, and federal agencies, a search begins for similar acreage that can be purchased as replacement habitat for the displaced jays and gopher tortoises. To date, the program had received more than $33 million from developers and has purchased in excess of 9,700 acres consisting of nine different

The fishing pier on Hickey's Creek Courtesy Lee County Parks

mitigation sites throughout Florida. The result is that instead of three useless acres in the corner of some parking lot, you have 1,000 acres that can be kept free of exotics, have controlled burns, and provide ample forage areas for wildlife. This is essentially the history of Hickey's Creek Mitigation Park.

Using funds from the Mitigation Bank, Lee County's Environmentally Sensitive Lands Program and Florida Communities Trust purchased 770 acres surrounding Hickey's Creek in 1998. Over the years that followed additional lands were purchased through Lee County's Conservation 20/20 Program, resulting in a total of 862 acres. Hickey's Creek Mitigation Park officially opened its doors to the public April 20, 2002. The park's primary mitigation is for the threatened gopher tortoise and Florida scrub jay.

The good news is that it works. This treasure of a site is home to many gopher tortoises, easily spotted hiking its five miles of well-marked trails. The Florida scrub jays are much more difficult to spot, but they can sometimes be seen along the southern portion of the 2.2-mile Palmetto Pines Trail. The park trails also include the 1.8-mile Hickey's Creek Trail and 1.0-mile North Marsh Trail.

The park has a fishing pier, canoe/kayak launch, picnic areas, shelters, restrooms, amphitheater, quaint bridges, and overlooks. The canoe/kayak launch, located nearly a half-mile from the parking lot, is difficult to access without a hand-pulled trailer. A better way to get to the water is via the public launch one mile down the Caloosahatchee River at the Franklin Locks.

The focus of this park is Hickey's Creek, a lovely freshwater stream that flows north into the Caloosahatchee. It is draped in ancient live oaks and lined by saw palmetto. It is home to alligators, gar, bass, bream, and water snakes, such as the Florida banded water snake and venomous cottonmouth.

The largely uplands habitat in the park consists primarily of pine flatwoods, scrubby flatwoods, freshwater marshes, cypress swamps, oak hammocks, and oak-palm forests. It is a great place to find many Florida snakes, including the threatened indigo, the Eastern coachwhip, black racers, Eastern diamondback, and pygmy rattlesnakes. Other sightings may include black bear, bobcats, river otters, and squirrels.

Hickey's Creek Mitigation Park is a part of both the Calusa Blueway and the Great Florida Birding Trail. It is a well-known location for sightings of migratory warblers during their spring and winter journeys, and the marshes are frequented by herons and egrets. Located only 8.6 miles east of I-75 off of exit 141 on State Road 80, it is an easy park to find and a true joy to discover.

❒ ________ D. Manatee County Park

Location: 10901 Palm Beach Blvd., Ft. Myers, FL 33905 / Phone: 239-432-2004 / Fax: 239-485-2300 / Website: www.leeparks.org/facility-info / E-mail: dbergstresser@leegov.com / 17 acres / Admission fee charged.

A typical manatee sighting at the park © Dick Fortune & Sara Lopez

Originally opened in 1996, this 17-acre regional park is *the* place to go in Lee County for manatee viewing, especially from November through March when hundreds of these widely adored marine mammals congregate here. In a curious symbiotic relationship, the manatees have learned to migrate up the Orange River during the coldest months of the year, seeking the warm-water outflow from the adjacent Florida Power and Light power plant. Unlike seals, whales, and many other marine mammals, West Indian manatees do not have thick insulating layers of blubber to protect them from cold water and hypothermia. As a subtropical species, they would normally seek out warm freshwater springs when the water temperature dips below 70 degrees, but coastal development has dried up many of these natural springs, making it difficult for these animals to survive the winter.

Soon after the power plant was constructed in 1957 a handful of manatees appeared at the junction of the discharge canal and the Orange River. Over time, the number of manatees migrating to the outflow increased to the large numbers seen today. How this power-plant memo about survival behavior made it around the manatee world remains a fascinating mystery.

However the information was relayed, the regional manatee populations of both Lee and Charlotte counties now make Manatee Park their winter home. In 2010, when Southwest Florida experienced one of the coldest winters in the past 100 years, as many as 300 manatees were counted in and around the park. A kayak or canoe trip down the Orange River between the outflow of the power plant and the nearby Caloosahatchee River is sure to result in many manatee sightings, but paddlers should be well advised that having a 14-foot-long manatee suddenly surface beside your boat can be quite unnerving. Harassing these animals in any way is strictly forbidden. They are experiencing cold stress and are essentially in a state of quasi-hibernation. Manatees cannot digest the sea grasses they feed on once the water temperature dips below 68 degrees. Dogs are not allowed in the park since their presence can frighten the manatees.

The canoe launch off the Orange River
Courtesy Lee County Parks

Manatee County Park has a small fishing pier, picnic tables, an ethno-botany trail, butterfly garden, authentic Seminole chickee hut, gift shop, and canoe/kayak rentals. For a nominal fee, visitors can launch their own canoes or kayaks. Photographing the manatees is a favorite pastime, but because the water is stained dark brown by the tannic acid coming off the nearby mangroves, a polarized filter is advised. Sadly, you will notice that many of the larger animals have boat propeller scars across their backs and large dorsal fins. Programs about the manatees are presented daily at the Live Oak Amphitheater during the winter months at 2 p.m. (check the website as program schedules are subject to change). Park rangers lead guided tours on weekends, taking visitors through the numerous walking trails and explaining how the park evolved. Manatee Park is unusual in that the land it rests on is owned by Florida Power and Light, though the park is staffed and operated by Lee County Parks Department.

Although the manatees are far more abundant from mid-October through mid-April, they are sometimes seen in the park during the other months of the year as well, though not in any great numbers.

Manatee County Park is small, but it presents a big opportunity to view these endangered mammals. Because of this, attendance at the park has been steadily increasing. It is well worth the stop and a wonderful place to visit during the cooler, winter months.

Leave nothing but your footprints © Charles Sobczak

❐ __________ E. Cayo Costa State Park

Location: Northern end of Cayo Costa Key, Lee County, FL / Office address: 880 Belcher Road, Boca Grande, FL 33921 / Phone: 941-964-0375 / Fax: n/a / Website: www.floridastateparks.org/cayocosta / E-mail: n/a / Admission fee charged. / Ferry information: Tropic Star Ferries of Pine Island, Pineland Marina, 13921 Waterfront Drive, Pineland, FL 33945 / Tropic Star phone: 239-283-0015 / Fax: 239-283-7255 / Website: www.tropicstarcruises.com / E-mail: tropiccruz@aol.com.

Cayo Costa State Park is one of just six of Florida's 160 state parks that are accessible only by water. It is one of only three that offer camping to the maritime visitor, and it is the only park with permanent cabins available for overnight use. Separated by Boca Grande Pass from Gasparilla Island, this barrier-island park is a pristine treasure that has been miraculously spared from the high-rises, strip malls, and parking lots that have transformed most of the islands along Florida's coastline.

Unspoiled is the best word to describe what awaits travelers unloading their picnic or camping gear at the boat docks on the landward (eastern) side of the island. The largely untouched beaches harbor fantastic shelling and sightings that include mole crabs, ghost crabs, and birds such as ruddy turnstones, black-bellied plovers, and dowitchers. Along the 5.5 miles of interior hiking trails you can expect to

A rental cabin being enjoyed by some island campers
© Charles Sobczak

see warblers (seasonal), osprey, and a variety of snakes including eastern coachwhip, the endangered indigo, and both yellow and red rat snakes. Alligators thrive in a number of small ponds and a large freshwater lagoon that lies deep within the interior of the island. The waters that surround the tip of the island abound with manatee, bottlenosed dolphin, tarpon, shark, and numerous surf fish including whiting, crevalle jack, and snook. Special care should be taken when visiting during the sea turtle nesting season (May through September), as Cayo Costa is a prime nesting site.

The name "Cayo Costa" translates to "Key by the Coast," which in this case could really be "Key to Paradise Lost." The 2,426-acre park has nine miles of white sand beaches without a single home or condominium to be found. The island was a fishing camp for the Calusa Indians and earlier tribes for 4,000 years before the arrival of the Spanish. In the 1800s Cayo Costa became a favorite haunt for Cuban "fishing ranchos" where fish were caught, dried, and salted before shipping to the markets of Havana. A walk down Cemetery Trail will take you to the grave of Captain Nelson, whose tombstone reads, "After Life's Fitful Fever He Sleeps Well." Another popular hike is along Quarantine Trail, which brings you to the old dock where around the turn of the 20th century the U.S. military inspected fishermen and sailors for yellow fever and other communicable diseases before allowing them to head to mainland Florida to sell their catch.

An afternoon at the beach on Cayo Costa
© Charles Sobczak

Although the park is a part of the Great Calusa Blueway, getting there by canoe or kayak is not advisable for inexperienced paddlers. Crossing Boca Grande Pass, with its strong currents and winds, can be treacherous, and the nearest launches on Pine Island to the east are precariously far away. Best access is via small powerboat; a scheduled ferry service (www.tropicstarcruises.com) departs from Pineland in the northwest corner of Pine Island. Larger parties can arrange for a private water taxi.

A truck-pulled passenger tram ferries visitors between the bay and the beach side of the island, a distance of one mile. A small concession on the island offers kayak and bicycle rentals, stocks frozen bait, and sells drinks and snacks. The cabins are basic and rustic, but the demand for them is such that reservations should be made months in advance. Drinking water, ice by the scoop, and cold showers are all available in the park.

Cayo Costa is ideal for snorkeling, beach scuba diving, kayaking, hiking, biking, beachcombing, fishing, swimming, shelling, and picnicking. During the peak winter season on-site park rangers present programs on the island's history, as well as its flora and fauna.

The park suffered a direct hit in 2004 from Hurricane Charley whose winds toppled every Australian pine on the island, forever changing the look of the campsites and cabin areas. Since the storm the park has been extensively replanted with native trees, but the shade canopy once provided by the tall pines is gone. Beach umbrellas or small shade tents are recommended since there is little respite from the Florida sun.

Cayo Costa, while a bit more difficult than most parks to get to, is well worth the effort. It opens a window into what the entire coast of Florida looked like a thousand years ago.

❒ ________ F. Harn's Marsh Preserve

Location: 3399 38th Street West, Lehigh Acres, FL 33971 / Phone: 239-533-7275 / Fax: 239-485-2300 / Website: www.leeparks.org / E-mail: leeparks@leegov.com / 578 acres / Admission is free.

Harns Marsh, a storm-water retention facility located at the headwaters of the Orange River in Lehigh Acres, is an unlikely destination for naturalists and birders. It is not included in the South Florida Birding Trail, though no one has informed the countless birds that frequent this large freshwater marsh of that omission. It offers no amenities, no interpretive center, not even any signs directing visitors to the marsh. Now under the jurisdiction of the East County Water Control District, Harns Marsh is slated to become a Lee County regional park, which will bring restrooms, picnic tables, and other amenities to this undiscovered treasure, possibly within the next few years.

Ever elusive snail kite
© Judd Patterson, JuddPatterson.com

The site is roughly one square mile (578 acres). In 2007, some 182 acres along the north marsh were dredged and cleared of invasive plants,

Bass and bream thrive in the deeper water © Charles Sobczak

which improved water quality and wildlife viewing. Hiking and bicycling, but no motorized vehicles, are allowed on the four-mile sandy impoundment road encircling the marsh.

Scores of birds, snakes, snails, and small mammals are found here. Two species of particular interest are the snail kite (aka the Everglades kite) and the limpkin. Birders who might spend years trying to catch a glimpse of either of these species can cut their search short with a single visit to Harn's Marsh. These hard-to-find birds are attracted by the tens of thousands of snails that live in the marsh, including both the native apple snail and the invasive island apple snail. The island apple snail (*Pomacea insularum*) is from South America and has, through accidental releases, invaded many of Florida's freshwater marshes. These enormous snails, many as large as a small apple, litter the edge of the marsh. Snail kites and limpkins are adapting to dining on these foreigners, which have also become an important source of food for turtles, great blue herons, alligators, and other animals.

Other sightings at Harn's Marsh, especially during the winter months, might include redwing blackbirds, cowbirds, various migratory duck species, and sparrows. Sightings of sandhill cranes are common along the western edge of the marsh. Visiting the marsh is best just after dawn and before sunset. Be sure to bring bug spray and a hat, since areas of shade are in short supply. Harn's Marsh is an undiscovered treasure in Lee County that hopefully, once made into a park, will get the recognition it deserves.

The Edison/Ford Estates banyan tree
© Alan Maltz

❒ ______ G. Edison & Ford Winter Estates

Location: 2350 McGregor Blvd., Ft. Myers, FL 33901 / Phone: 239-334-7419 / Fax: n/a / Website: www.efwefla.org / E-mail: info@efwefla.org / 20 acres / Admission fee charged.

The Edison and Ford estates

Courtesy Lee County VC Bureau

The adventure of visiting this 20-acre property encompassing the former estates of Thomas Alva Edison and his close friend, Henry Ford, begins in the parking lot. This is where, in 1925, Edison chose to plant a four-foot cutting taken from the Great Banyan in the Indian Botanical Gardens of Howrah, India, a tree estimated to be between 200 and 250 years old and covering more than four acres. In less than 100 years, Edison's cutting, a gift from his friend Harvey Firestone, has grown into a banyan tree that already covers an acre on the northern fringe of the parking lot. If left unchecked, the Edison banyan would undoubtedly have overtaken the entire parking lot by now. It is an amazing specimen of *Ficus benghalensis* and a marvel to see.

The planting of the banyan tree was part of an effort by Edison, Ford, and Firestone to find another source for rubber because of the rising costs of raw rubber after World War I. In fact, many of the plants found on the grounds of the Edison & Ford Estates were originally brought to Ft. Myers in this search for a replacement to the rubber tree (*Ficus elastica)*, of particular importance to the owners of a car company and a tire company.

Today, Edison's experimental garden is enhanced by hundreds of orchids, mango trees, roses, and flowering frangipani trees, to name just a few. Many of these ornamentals were installed on the grounds by his wife, Mina Miller Edison. Over the years she became an avid gardener, and her love of flowering plants helped to make this the perfect winter home for the growing Edison family.

There are more than 1,417 different species of plants on the combined estates. These include nearly 50 palms, 121 trees, 20 cycads (the ancient predecessor of the palm family), and 11 different kinds of bamboo. It's believed that the original bamboo stands, planted by the properties' former owner, Jacob Summerlin, helped convince Edison to buy the land in 1885. At that time Ft. Myers was little more than an outpost in what was essentially an untamed wilderness. Some of the seeds Edison used to plant the majestic royal palms along McGregor Blvd. are thought to have been purchased from the Seminole Indians still living in the Everglades at the time.

Of course, there is much more to the Edison & Ford Estates than the vegetation. Overlooking the Caloosahatchee River, Seminole Lodge, which was the Edison family's main residence, is open to the public and is an exquisite example of the architecture of the age before air conditioning. Its wide French doors allow for excellent cross ventilation, while its high ceilings trap the rising heat. The furnishings, appointments, and expansive outdoor verandas all take the visitor back to a bygone era where the winters were spent fishing, swimming in the pool (the first in Lee County), and reading. The Ford Estate, with its more traditional olde Florida look, is equally compelling.

The fascinating Edison lab

Courtesy Lee County VC Bureau

Across McGregor Blvd. from the house is a large museum that abuts Edison's working office and an impressive laboratory where he and his staff worked for years on various projects, including the search for a new source of rubber. The museum exhibits many of Edison's most famous inventions. With 1,093 patents to his name, Edison was involved in everything from ticker tapes to electric cars. Some of the most compelling exhibits are collections of his early phonographs and Kinetoscopes. Other exhibits show his lesser-known inventions such as printing telegraph machines and huge DC current generators, all of which have succumbed to better technologies over the years.

Henry Ford is also represented in the museum. Best known as the father of the assembly line, Ford worked closely with Edison and Firestone on the Botanic Research Lab. Walking through the old lab, which closed in the 1930s, is like walking through time, with its rows of glass beakers, flasks and gas burners.

During the holiday season the Estates are decked out in almost 1 million Christmas lights, and the grounds are open for evening tours. Two unique gift shops are located on the property, one near the Ford home (The Ford Cottage Shoppe) along the Caloosahatchee River, and the other adjacent to the museum (The Museum Store). Both offer any number of Edison and Ford biographies, various gifts, and memorabilia pertaining to these two influential businessmen who helped create the America we know today. The true genius of Thomas Alva Edison is best stated in his famous quote, "Genius is one percent inspiration, ninety-nine percent perspiration." A visit to the Edison & Ford Winter Estates is an inspiration to young and old alike.

❐ ______ H. Calusa Nature Center and Planetarium

Location: 3450 Ortiz Avenue, Ft. Myers, FL 33905 / Phone: 239-275-3435 / Fax: 239-275-9016 / Website: www.calusanature.com / E-mail: jennifer@calusanature.org / 105 acres / Admission fee charged.

The boardwalk through the pine flatwoods

© Charles Sobczak

Describing itself as "The Eco Place with Outer Space," the Calusa Nature Center and Planetarium combines the only full-scale planetarium between Bradenton and Miami with a 105-acre preserve and nature center. Established in 1970, the Nature Center is known for its Living Museum. Inside the air-conditioned main building is an extensive collection of live snakes, including venomous species such as the eastern diamondback rattlesnake, cottonmouth, and pygmy rattlesnake. The collection also includes king snakes and the endangered eastern indigo snake. A recent addition to the snake collection is a large Burmese python, the invasive species that is wreaking havoc in the Everglades. The Living Museum also has Florida box turtles and gopher tortoises. Several good-sized aquarium tanks hold eels, sirens, and mosquitofish; saltwater tanks are filled with many of the fish found in the local estuaries, including pinfish, grunts, and sheepshead. Plans are under way to put together an indigenous tree frog exhibit to complement the current frog and toad collection.

The Living Museum collection continues outside and below the main exhibit building where several aviaries are housed. Most of the birds here have sustained injuries that prevent them from returning to the wild. One enclosure has injured brown pelicans, and a circular aviary contains an assortment of regional birds of prey, including great horned and barred owls, red-shouldered and red-tailed hawks, bald eagles, and the elusive crested cara cara. Turkey and black-headed vultures are also on display. The mammal collection includes striped skunks, a bobcat, raccoons, opossum, gray fox, and several pigs. One of the most impressive animals kept at the Calusa Nature Center is a seriously large bull alligator that has to be close to 400 pounds. A lovely butterfly house abounds with local species and is always a favorite with the younger children.

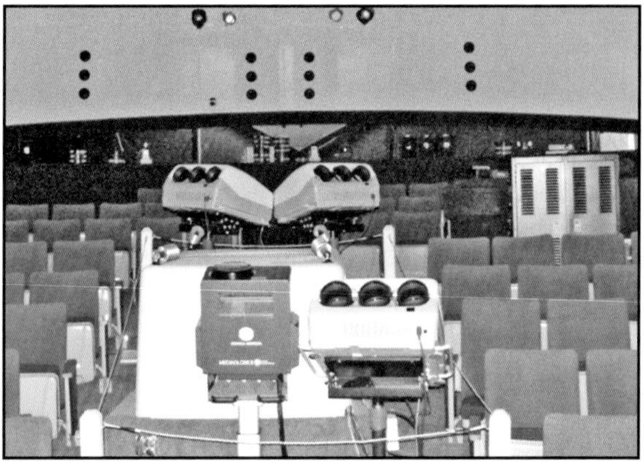

The state of the art equipment in the Planetarium

© Charles Sobczak

The planetarium part of the center consists of the 82-seat, 360-degree Calusa Dome Theater featuring a state-of-the-art Media Globe II projector with a Konica/Minolta fisheye lens that is considered the closest thing to 3D you can have without 3D technology. It is comparable to an IMAX theater experience. The planetarium's shows include trips to the surface of the moon, flying through the rings of Saturn, and down into black holes. The Planetarium Theater also offers laser-light shows, various feature films, and a multimedia presentation called Manatee Encounters. Check the website for a monthly program schedule.

The grounds at the Calusa Nature Center and Planetarium include three well-marked hiking trails that total 2.2 miles. The half-mile Big Cypress Swamp trail takes you along a boardwalk to a native cypress dome. The Pine Loop Trail is another half-mile hike through a beautiful example of pine flatwoods. For the more adventurous, there is a 1.2-mile perimeter trail around the entire grounds, abutting the public Eastwood Golf Course to the north. A staff naturalist leads a guided tour every Tuesday and Friday at 9:30 a.m. throughout the year.

The Calusa Nature Center is known for its outreach programs where the staff takes some of the snakes and iguanas to teach local schoolchildren about the wildlife found across Southwest Florida. The center also conducts a number of in-house programs and special events. One of the most popular is the Haunted Walk held every Halloween season. Other popular programs include Creepie Crawlie, which focuses on edible insects; Behind the Scenes, which takes a small group into some of the enclosures for a closer look at the animals; and Night at the Museum, which includes an overnight camping trip inside the museum for groups numbering up to 25.

Jennifer Cleary, the Director of the Center, with a Burmese python and the author's book

© Charles Sobczak

From stargazing to learning about the flora and fauna of the region to yoga classes and laser-light shows, there is always something happening at the Calusa Nature Center and Planetarium. Its kid-friendly atmosphere makes it a great destination for families looking for a way to spend a fun-filled afternoon.

❐ ______ I. Four Mile Cove Ecological Preserve

Location: Four Mile Cove Ecological Preserve, East End of SE 23rd Terrace, Cape Coral, FL, 33990 / Phone: 239-549-4606 / Kayak Rentals (seasonal): 239-574-7395 / Fax: 239-573-3129 / E-mail: ccpks@capecoral.net / Website: www.capecoral.net/FourMileCoverEcologicalPreserve / 365 acres / Admission is free.

Veterans War Memorial © Charles Sobczak

A true natural treasure in the midst of the sprawling city of Cape Coral, Four Mile Cove Ecological Preserve offers hikers and kayakers a welcome reprieve from the urban surroundings. Most of the park's 365 acres are dedicated to mangrove forests and estuarine environments. A small section known as the Veterans Memorial features a replica statue of the famous flag raising during the battle of Iwo Jima in World War II, as well as a memorial to the soldiers who fought during the Vietnam War. Veterans Parkway runs directly adjacent to the park, which can be distracting at times because of the constant road noise. Next to the parking lot is a small visitor center that has a number of displays such as indigo snake skins and gopher tortoise shells.

Once you leave the parking area and start walking the 1.2 miles of hiking trails, the sound of the traffic and the urban landscape quickly fade into the mangrove habitat—mostly red mangroves, but with several stretches of white, buttonwood, and even a few areas of black mangroves as well. A raised boardwalk allows visitors access through the unending tangle of mangrove roots and periods of high tide when the entire area is under water. While on the boardwalk be on the lookout for yellow-crowned night herons, great egrets, and green anoles. The boardwalk trail is well kept and features two overlooks on the edge of the Caloosahatchee River where the views are spectacular.

An even better way to see the park is by water. Just before the parking area a road turns north to a kayak/canoe launch and small kayak/canoe rental concession that operates seasonally on weekends from October to May. The attraction here is the labyrinth of waterways formed by Alligator Creek. This tidal creek twists and

The kayak shelter on the Caloosahatchee © Charles Sobczak

turns through the interior of the preserve and is renowned for its excellent fishing and wildlife sightings. There is an 800-foot portage that requires some effort along the trail, so keep this in mind before setting out. Three floating kayak shelters on the river allow paddlers a place to relax, have a picnic, or get out of the rain.

While in Cape Coral you may want to spend some time looking for the threatened burrowing owls. The Cape is home to more than 1,000 nesting pairs of these adorable birds. City Hall, Cape Coral Library, and Veteran's Park are among the sites of established nests. There is even a live webcam at one of the nests (www.capecoralburrowingowls.com). Burrowing owls are covered in the bird section of this book.

❐ ______ J. Six Mile Cypress Slough Preserve

Location: 7751 Penzance Blvd., Ft. Myers, FL 33966 / Phone: 239-533-7550 / Fax: 239-936-2543 / Website: www.leeparks.org/sixmile / E-mail: hgienapp@leegov.com / 2,500 acres / Admission is free, parking fee charged.

Although the Six Mile Cypress Slough Preserve covers more than 2,500 acres, the actual park and boardwalk area encompass only about 40 acres. Situated just on the outskirts of the city limits of Ft. Myers, this preserve on the east side of Six Mile Cypress Parkway is a beautiful oasis of wildlife amidst the heavily developed landscapes of Lee County. The park offers an interpretive center, restrooms, picnic tables, and a 1.2-mile boardwalk that leads you through a variety of habitats. Several short spurs with overlooks take you to Gator, Wood Duck, Otter, and Pop Ash ponds. The interpretive center is housed in the area's first certified public "green building," which opened in April 2008. It features various displays about the preserve and a small gift shop.

The history of saving this slough is a fascinating story of citizen activism. In 1976, a group of Lee County students were studying the role of wetlands in Florida when they became alarmed at how rapidly these systems were being drained off and disappearing under a barrage of subdivisions and shopping centers. Calling themselves "The Monday Group," they launched a grassroots campaign to stop the logging and channeling of the Six Mile Cypress Slough that was slated for more development. Lee County voters responded overwhelmingly by increasing their own taxes to purchase the privately held land and convert the slough to a preserve.

Over the next 15 years both Lee County and the South Florida Water Management District struggled to keep the watershed that feeds the slough safe from upstream development that would pollute the system or divert the preserve's precious water sources. That battle continues today, but with the establishment of the park in 1991 and the addition of the state-of-the-art interpretive center, the slough's long-term health is more secure.

Today the slough is a goldmine of flora and fauna. Begin your journey by picking up a copy of the "Explorer's Companion," available near the entrance of the boardwalk (also available on the website in a downloadable format). The 24-page color guide walks both the experienced and novice naturalist through the various ecosystems found along the boardwalk, including pine flatwoods, flag ponds, cypress sloughs, and freshwater ponds. Plants found here include slash pines, pond and bald cypress, wax myrtle, and the swamp, resurrection, and threatened strap fern.

Peninsula cooters in Gator Pond

© Charles Sobczak

Because most of the boardwalk traverses wetlands and overlooks ponds, sightings of amphibians, reptiles, and fish abound. While strolling slowly and quietly along the trail, be on the lookout for alligators, peninsula cooters, and redbelly and Florida softshell turtles. Pig frogs and green tree frogs can be spotted, along with Florida banded water snakes, black racers, ribbon snakes, and the venomous cottonmouth. Mammals include river otters, marsh rabbits, armadillos, white-tailed deer, and the introduced wild hogs.

The birding is equally impressive. During the spring and fall the slough is home to dozens of species of migratory birds including warblers, nuthatches, and waterfowl

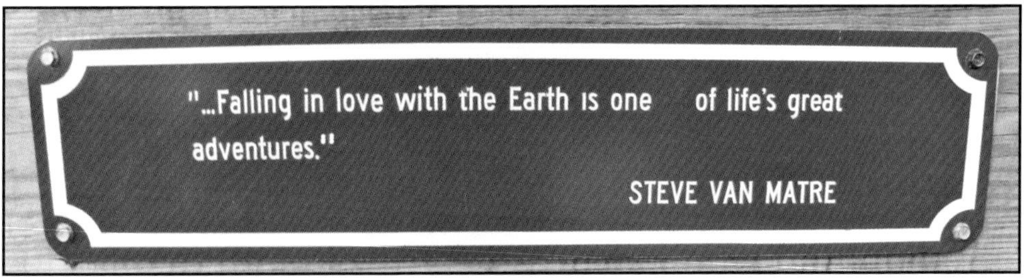

"...Falling in love with the Earth is one of life's great adventures."
STEVE VAN MATRE

One of many similar signs along the boardwalk © Charles Sobczak

such as the pied-billed grebe, and a variety of ducks. Common sightings include anhingas, red-shouldered hawks, barred owls, pileated woodpeckers, and various wading birds.

One of the most amazing aspects of this preserve is that it has so much wildlife compacted into such a small area. It is almost like having a nature preserve built in a tiny glass bottle, and then having the bottle in a readily accessible location. Once beneath the cool canopy of cypress trees, you will feel the world seem to fade away, and all you are left with is the slow-flowing water beneath the boardwalk and the sound of the songbirds foraging in the ferns and plants beside you. Remember to thank "The Monday Group" as you leave.

❐ ______ K. Great Calusa Blueway (*marked as Pine Island Sound*)

Location: Dozens of launches throughout Lee County / Administration office: 6490 South Pointe Blvd., Ft. Myers, FL 33919 / Phone: 239-433-3855 / Fax: 239-485-2300 / Website: www.calusablueway.com / E-mail: paddletrail@leegov.com / 190 miles of GPS-marked trails / Admission fee charged on some launches, others are free.

In May 2010, the annual Great Calusa Blueway Paddling Festival was included as one of the top 20 events and festivals by the Atlanta-based Southeast Tourism Society (STS). With more than 1,000 events and festivals in 12 states competing for this award, winning it is no small achievement. This unique paddling trail, covering more than 190 miles of creeks, estuaries, back bays, and rivers throughout Lee County, originated in 2003 as a joint venture between the Lee County Visitor & Convention Bureau and Lee County Parks and Recreation Department. The first Paddling Festival was held in June 2006. This annual event is now held every fall from the last weekend of October through the first weekend of November.

Blueway trail access at Lover's Key State Park
Courtesy Lee County VC Bureau

The Great Calusa Blueway is divided into three geographical sections: Estero Bay; Pine Island Sound/ Matlacha Pass; and the Caloosahatchee River and its tributaries. The Estero Bay zone begins at Bunche Beach to the northwest and ends in the southeast corner of Lee County at the headwaters of the Imperial River. This is the most protected of the three legs of the Blueway and includes Hurricane Bay, Hell Peckney Bay, much of the Estero Bay Aquatic Preserve, and both the Estero and Imperial rivers. While there are several channel crossings and open-water stretches in this section, most of the Blueway paddling trail hug the mangrove-lined shore, and the open-water stretches are seldom more than a mile in length. Intermittent trail markers along the way also help to make this section the best bet for the less experienced paddler. Stops include Mound Key, Lovers Key State Park, Matanzas Pass Preserve, and Koreshan State Historical Site.

Blueway trail at marker #79
Courtesy Lee County VC Bureau

The second section stretches from Bunche Beach northwest to Cayo Costa State Park, with a branch going to the Charlotte Harbor Preserve State Park to the northeast. Covering this large area would take an average kayaker four to five days, and there are numerous islands and parks where the overnight adventurer can find a safe place to pitch a tent or sleep under the stars. Places to visit along the way include Picnic Island, J.N. "Ding" Darling National Wildlife Refuge, Cabbage Key, Pine Island Flatwoods Preserve, and Buck Key. While there are Blueway trail markers throughout much of this section, they are sometimes too far apart to be spotted visually, so a handheld GPS is recommended for longer trips. Most of these trails wind through the protected waters of Matlacha Pass Aquatic Preserve, but open-water paddling is required to get to the Charlotte Harbor Preserve and Cayo Costa State Park. Care should be taken when crossing the Intracoastal Waterway near Punta Rassa and between Useppa Island and Cabbage Key since it is heavily traveled by large cruising vessels.

The third Blueway section runs parallel to the Intracoastal Waterway, beginning at the Punta Rassa boat ramp and continuing east down the Caloosahatchee

Kayaking at dawn in Pine Island Sound Courtesy Lee County VC Bureau

beyond the Franklin Locks in Alva. While there are plenty of safe havens such as Shell Creek, Whiskey Creek, Yellow Fever Creek, and the Orange River, paddling the broad, heavily trafficked Caloosahatchee can be best managed by staying along one shoreline or the other. There are some great places to explore in this section including Manatee Park, Four Mile Ecological Preserve, Hickey's Creek Mitigation Park, and Caloosahatchee Regional Park.

The Great Calusa Blueway has much to offer the novice and experienced paddler alike. Along the way you are going to see scores of birds, manatees, dolphins, and possibly even alligators. The fishing is fabulous and ranges from snook and mangrove snapper to largemouth bass in the freshwater sections near Alva. Because this expansive trail covers so much territory (encompassing many of the same preserves and parks identified in this book), the best way to get a handle on it before taking your first stroke is to visit its comprehensive website. The many places to stay, restaurants to enjoy, launches, rest stops, and more than 100 trail markers and GPS coordinates to upload will help you grasp the enormity of the Great Calusa Blueway. The website has a list of 20 canoe and kayak vendors who participate in the program, as well as identifying a half-dozen paddlecraft-friendly lodges that will help make your journey more comfortable.

The Great Calusa Blueway is such a refreshing and novel concept that it well deserves the accolades bestowed upon it by the Southern Tourism Society. While motoring across the back bays and estuaries of Lee County might get you there faster, the slow, steady pace of a sea kayak or canoe allows you to slow down and see the watery world of the Calusa Indians much as they did 1,000 years ago in their dugout canoes. Watching the mullet jump, the blue crabs scurry along beneath you, and the frigate birds hover above makes it all worthwhile.

❐ ______ L. Lakes Regional Park

Location: 7330 Gladiolus Drive, Ft. Myers, FL 33908 / Phone: 239-432-2000 / Fax: 239-485-2300 / Website: www.leeparks.org/facility-info / E-mail: leeparks@leegov.com / 279 acres / Admission fee charged.

Amidst the pizzas, ice cream, hot dogs, and surrey rentals, a naturalist might be quick to dismiss Lakes Regional Park as more of a family recreational park than a place to commune with nature. The truth is, plenty of nature is to be found along the many trails that wind through this attractive park. The wide variety of wildlife and bird species that inhabit this 279-acre oasis have earned it a place on the Florida Fish and Wildlife's South Florida Birding Trail.

Fragrance garden blossom

© Charles Sobczak

The park is situated on land that was a large gravel and limestone quarry during the 1960s. After the quarry was abandoned, ground and surface water filled in the excavations, creating the 158-acre lake that now gives the park its name. The water depth ranges from a few inches along the shore to more than 20 feet in places. Lee County purchased the site in 1978 and officially opened the park on April 21, 1984. In 1991 the park added a fragrance garden, which over the years has evolved into a botanical garden that includes exotic trees, flowers, and cacti. Butterflies abound in this area of the park, and identification signs help amateur entomologists identify the numerous species found throughout the gardens.

Birders will find Lakes Regional Park a surprising treasure of species. Wading birds such as great egrets, herons, and occasionally wood storks congregate along the lakeshore. This is one of the rare places where you can spot three different species of ibis in one day: common white ibis, glossy ibis, and the exotic scarlet ibis (these have escaped from zoos). The fragrance garden attracts dozens of species of migratory warblers, vireos, and assorted sparrows during the spring and fall migrations. Cowbirds, blackbirds, boat-tailed grackles, and other urban species can be found throughout the park year-round. Active rookeries on several of the islands found in the lake present unique opportunities for photographers with good telephoto lenses to shoot hungry nestlings and anxious, feeding parents. The birding is so consistent throughout the year

A panorama of Lakes Park Courtesy Lee County Parks

that Lakes Regional Park has volunteers who participate in bird counts for both the Cornell Lab of Ornithology and the National Audubon Society.

Of course, the recreational value of the park should not be overlooked. The Railroad Museum of South Florida is located here and offers displays of model trains, historical information on the early regional railroads, and much more. The nearby playground has a full-size replica locomotive for the kids to play on, and an eighth-size scale railroad train takes children and parents alike on a 1.4-mile ride along a 7.5-inch-wide track for a nominal fee. A restored Baldwin Locomotive known as the ACL #143 (Atlantic Coast Line) and its coal tender sit across from the museum. The machine was built in Philadelphia in 1905 and officially retired in 1959.

Restored Baldwin Locomotive at Lakes Park
© Maggie May Rogers

Along the northern edge of the property two water parks offer welcome relief from the Florida sun for children of all ages. A rock-climbing wall and several playgrounds also help to keep the youngsters busy throughout the day. Visitors can rent bikes, double surreys, choppers, quad-sports, and scooters. Boat rentals include kayaks, canoes, pedal boats, and hydro-bikes. The park rents out several pavilions of varying sizes for private parties, weddings and special events. Fishing is allowed in the lakes, but a freshwater license is required. Swimming is prohibited because of the alligators that thrive in the lakes.

The 2.5 miles of hiking and biking trails that wind through the backwoods offer a more subdued environment where nature lovers can take in the wildlife or relax under the shade of a sprawling live oak. Most of the exotic vegetation has been removed, and, except for the botanical gardens, the park is well on its way to returning to native vegetation. Lakes Regional Park has a little something for everyone, and in the midst of the nearby Wal-Marts and Lowe's superstores, this park is a welcome respite from the urban landscape that surrounds it.

The inviting water park
© Charles Sobczak

❐ ________ M. Bunche Beach Preserve

Location: 18201 John Morris Road, Ft. Myers, FL 33908 / Phone: 239-765-6784 / Fax: 239-485-2300 / Website: www.leeparks.org / E-mail: leeparks@leegov.com / 719 acres / Admission is free.

Kayaking up Terrapin Creek Courtesy Lee County Visitors Convention Bureau

Named in honor of Dr. Ralph Bunche, the first African American to win the Nobel Peace Prize, Bunche Beach has history that is as fascinating as the wildlife that frequents this undeveloped stretch of sand, salt, and tidal flats. The preserve got its start in the racially segregated South in 1949 when members of the Lee County black community purchased a small half-acre stretch of beach that became the only beach for people of color in all of South Florida. One year later, shortly before Dr. Bunche was awarded the Nobel Prize for his work in negotiating a cease-fire between the Arabs and the new state of Israel, more than 3,000 people attended the dedication ceremony for this small park. Participants came from as far away as Tampa to celebrate this historic event, complete with a barbecue and other festivities.

The privately held acreage surrounding the original Bunche Beach remained undeveloped largely because of its low-lying nature. With monies from Lee County's Conservation 20/20 program and in collaboration with the Florida Communities Trust, an additional 705 acres were added to the half-acre site in 2001. Several other acquisitions and donations have increased the preserve to its current 731 acres. In April 2010, Lee County Parks and Recreation added composting restrooms, two kayak and canoe launches, two fishing piers, and a paved, 52-vehicle parking lot. A planned, future small concession will offer kayak and canoe rentals.

Because of the protected nature of this shoreline, canoeists and kayakers are able to cruise up to a mile off the beach. Several nearby tidal creeks, including Terrapin Creek, are well worth exploring. Fishing is allowed throughout the park, and catches might include mangrove snapper, mullet, sheepshead, snook, and seatrout.

Prelude to a dream, Bunche Beach © Alan Maltz

Aside from the beach, which is more than a mile long, and the long, straight John Morris Road that leads into the preserve, hiking at Bunche Beach is limited. The dry salt flats located along the northern edge of the preserve are interesting areas to explore, but there are no trails and the going is strenuous.

The Bunche Beach Preserve is a part of the South Florida Birding Trail, which notes in its brochure (www. FloridaBirdingTrail.com) that Bunche Beach is known for some of the best shorebird watching in South Florida. Common sightings include the rare Wilson's plover, black-bellied and semipalmated plovers, marbled godwits, and whimbrels. Other birds found at low tide include roseate spoonbills, white ibis, and least terns. Because of the nesting shorebirds, dogs are not allowed at Bunche Beach.

An unusual aspect of this beach is the extended shallows that lie offshore. Even at high tide it is possible to wade out a block or more before finding deeper water, making it a favorite destination for families with small children. Wedged between the popular Ft. Myers Beach and often-crowed public beaches of Sanibel and Captiva, Bunche Beach is seldom busy and is one of Lee County's best-kept secrets.

Welcome to Bunche Beach
Courtesy Lee County Parks

❒ ______ N. Bowditch Point Regional Park

Location: 50 Estero Blvd., Ft. Myers Beach, FL 33931 / Phone: 239-765-6784 / Fax: 239-485-2300 / Website: www.leeparks.org / E-mail: leeparks@leegov.com / 17 acres / Admission is free, parking fee charged.

Reddish egret stalks the beach at Bowditch Point
© Charles Sobczak

The small but amazing Bowditch Point Regional Park compresses a bounty of natural treasures into a compact package. It is named after Nathaniel Bowditch, an American mathematical genius and author of *The New American Practical Navigator*, published in 1802 and still used today.

Somehow, Bowditch Point has been spared from development. In the early 1970s there was a serious attempt to develop the site, but the plans never materialized. In December 1987 Lee County purchased the entire parcel, and the park had its official grand opening in February 1994.

The first thing a visitor notices about the park is its elevation, reaching 22 feet above sea level. Though the park's small hills may look like the Calusa-built mounds on nearby Mound Key, they are nothing more than large spoil mounds created by the continual dredging of Matanzas Pass. The views are impressive from atop these manmade hills, overlooking the Sanibel Lighthouse, the Sanibel Causeway, and the boats traversing San Carlos Bay.

The park is divided into two sections. The seven acres directly south of the 75-car parking lot are built for recreational use. This area has restrooms, a small snack bar, outside showers, decks, grills, picnic tables, butterfly gardens, and a raised boardwalk to the gulf beach. A 10-slip boat dock can handle vessels up to 28 feet. Adjacent to the dock is a sandy canoe/kayak launching area that is part of the Great Calusa Blueway.

The other section of the park consists of 10 acres of trails, observation areas, and bay and gulf beaches. Well-manicured footpaths crisscross the park and take you through several distinct terrains. The park is part of the Great Florida Birding Trail and abounds with osprey, bald eagles, and a host of shorebirds, gulls, and terns.

Paddle boarders prepare to head out on part of the Great Calusa Blueway © Lee County VC Bureau

The channel markers that guide boats through Matanzas Pass and into the back bays of Estero Island border the park. You can easily spend an entire afternoon beside the water watching the comings and goings of powerboats, sailboats, shrimp boats, and Coast Guard cutters. Nearly the entire northern point of the park is surrounded by sandy beaches, making for great sunbathing along the gulf side and fantastic shore fishing along the edge of Matanzas Pass and on the Estero Bay side. Catches include sea trout, snook, mangrove snapper, and shark.

Though Bowditch Point is not exactly what this land may have looked like hundreds of years ago, the park still offers visitors the chance to find a small mangrove forest, some tropical hammock species, and various dune plants and animals amid the otherwise commercialized Times Square section of Ft. Myers Beach. Bowditch Point Regional Park is a welcome respite from the condos and high-rises that dominate the nearby landscape.

❒ ______ O. CROW Wildlife Clinic

Location: 3883 Sanibel Captiva Road, Sanibel, FL 33957 / Phone: 239-472-3644 / Fax: 239-472-8544 / Website: www.crowclinic.org / E-mail: crowclinic@crowclinic.org / Campus: 10 acres / Admission fee charged.

Established in 1968, CROW is one of the leading wildlife rehabilitation centers in the United States. Under the direction of two full-time staff veterinarians, CROW treats 4,000 patients annually, representing 160 different wildlife species. CROW's primary mission is the rescue, care, rehabilitation, and eventual release back into the wild of sick, injured, and orphaned native wildlife. Inherent in this mission is the education of humans to ensure a peaceful coexistence with their wild neighbors.

CROW's entrance sign © Blake Sobczak

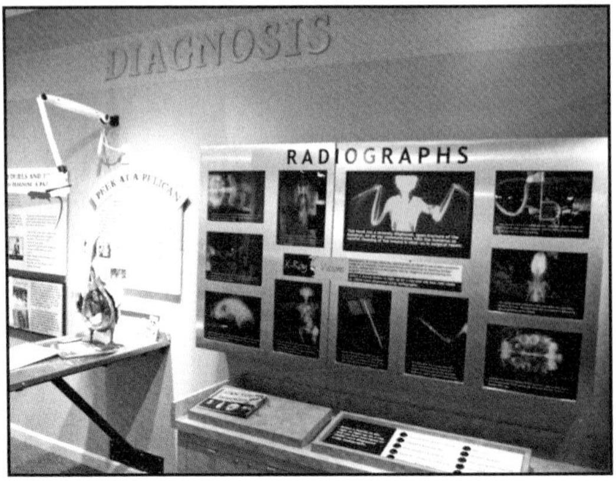

Diagnosis center in the exhibit area

© Blake Sobczak

After a multiyear capital fundraising drive of $3.2 million, with a substantial contribution from the Lee County Visitor and Conventions Bureau, CROW completed a new visitor center and wildlife hospital in 2009. While the hospital is not open to the general public, the Healing Winds Visitor Education Center is one of the most interesting, interactive facilities in the nation.

Designed by Malone Design Fabrication, a firm that has worked with the Smithsonian Institution and the Statue of Liberty National Monument, the visitor center lets you "Be the Vet" and try your hand at diagnosing wildlife injuries, as well as identifying the appropriate treatment options for the injured animal. Other displays include backlit radiographs; a multiscreen television showcase of the various species that have been treated at CROW; case studies that walk visitors through the rescue, treatment, rehabilitation, and release of CROW's numerous patients, many of which are on the endangered species lists; and a televised link to the sea turtle and otter rehabilitation pens. CROW is the only licensed sea turtle facility between Sarasota and Miami. The visitor center also has a unique gift shop.

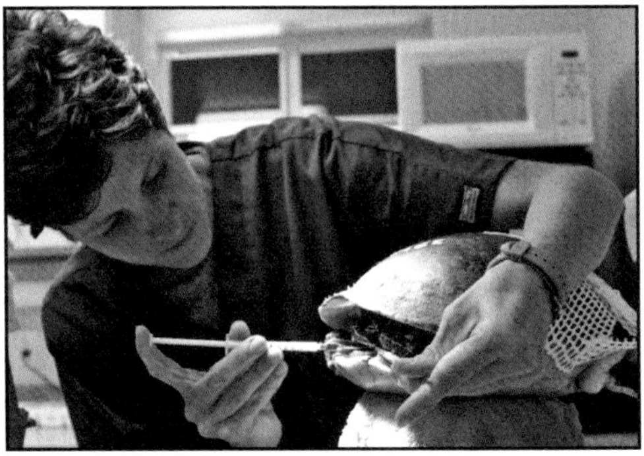

Dr. McNamara injects a cooter

© Brian Johnson

From its humble beginnings operating out of the home of Shirley Walter to today's state-of-the-art hospital and education center, CROW has been an integral part of Sanibel's commitment to living with wildlife. If you chance upon an injured animal, call CROW at 239-472-3644 or go to its website for information about how to capture and transport the animal to the hospital. Be careful, as many birds can inflict painful pecks and scratches, and other animals, such as raccoons and turtles, are capable of vicious bites. To fulfill its mission, CROW needs more than 175 volunteers annually; individuals interested in helping at the clinic should call for more information. CROW is also a teaching wildlife animal hospital, hosting approximately 40 students each year.

A visit to the Healing Winds Visitor Education Center reminds everyone of the impact civilization has had on the native flora and fauna of Southwest Florida. Some of the leading causes of injury for CROW's patients are automobile collisions, entanglements with improperly discarded fishing line, red tide, boat collisions, and orphaned or abandoned immature animals. Wildlife struggles to cope with our ever-encroaching population, and places such as CROW help mitigate our impact.

❒ ________ P. J.N. "Ding" Darling National Wildlife Refuge

Location: 1 Wildlife Drive, Sanibel, FL 33957 / Phone: 239-472-1100 / Fax: 239-472-4061 / Website: www.fws.gov/dingdarling / E-mail: dingdarling@fws.gov / 5,223 acres / Admission is free for the educational center, fee charged for biking or driving through Wildlife Drive.

Replica of Ding's studio in the educational center
© Blake Sobczak

Established in 1945, the J.N. "Ding" Darling National Wildlife Refuge is named in honor of Jay Norwood Darling, one of America's first true environmental activists. A cartoonist from Des Moines, Iowa, he briefly headed the U.S. Biological Survey (now the U.S. Fish and Wildlife Service) in the mid-1930s. While in office he helped establish and coalesce the National Refuge System into the well-managed organization it is today, and, more importantly, in 1934 he proposed and implemented the Federal Duck Stamp program. Revenues generated through the sale of these annual Duck Stamps to hunters and conservationists alike have helped to purchase and preserve millions of acres of crucial wetlands habitat throughout the U.S.

Your visit to this world-renowned refuge should start at the J.N. "Ding" Darling Educational Center, located at the entrance to the 4.2-mile Wildlife Drive. This spacious interpretive center has no admission fee and helps visitors grasp the complex ecology of the mangrove forest, as well as the history of the National Wildlife Refuge system. The center has several art galleries that show the works of various wildlife artists and photographers, and a well-stocked gift shop carries an assortment of field guides, children's nature books, binoculars, spotting scopes, gifts, and memorabilia.

Once on Wildlife Drive, you will quickly see why the "Ding" Darling refuge is one of the most visited in the nation. The road, a converted dike originally constructed to control the spread of saltmarsh mosquitoes, winds through expansive tidal flats. The water on the south side of the impoundment is brackish, while saltier water is found along the northern edge. The optimum time to visit the refuge is during periods of low tide, when the mud-bottom flats are exposed and the wading birds take full advantage of feeding opportunities.

A sunrise over J.N "Ding" Darling

© Dick Fortune & Sara Lopez

A woodstork wading © Dick Fortune and Sara Lopez

There have been an impressive 238 species of birds observed in the "Ding" Darling Refuge. These include the elusive mangrove cuckoo, roseate spoonbills, white pelicans, hooded and red-breasted mergansers, reddish egrets, and wood storks. More than 50 different reptiles and amphibians can be seen in the refuge, including ornate diamondback terrapins, mangrove snakes, alligators, and American crocodiles. Mammals, mollusks, fish, and insects are also plentiful in large part because of the rich productivity of the surrounding mangrove forests.

While the vast majority of "Ding" Darling's 850,000 annual visitors concentrate their refuge experience along Wildlife Drive, the property includes two additional sites on Sanibel that offer unique perspectives on this maze of tidal flats, mangroves, uplands, and spartina marshes. These often-overlooked sections are Tarpon Bay, located two miles before "Ding" Darling's main entrance, and the Bailey Tract, which is located in the central part of Sanibel, a bit south of the entrance into Tarpon Bay on Tarpon Bay Road.

Tarpon Bay is a 950-acre site that offers visitors a chance to get out on the water and experience this pristine mangrove forest first-hand. The concessionaire, Tarpon Bay Explorers (TBE Phone: 239-472-8900 / www.tarponbayexplorers.com), offers canoe, kayak, and bike rentals, pontoon excursions, guided and self-guided tours of the Commodore Canoe Trail in Tarpon Bay, and tram tours along Wildlife Drive. TBE operates a limited-access boat ramp for canoes and kayaks and a shop selling everything from sunglasses to nature-related gifts to Florida postcards. Tarpon Bay is one of the best fishing spots in Lee County, and professional fishing guides can be hired directly through TBE. While canoeing or kayaking Tarpon Bay, be on the lookout for dolphins, manatees, blue crabs, and even the occasional sea turtle.

The Bailey Tract is a 100-acre preserve that is distinctly different from the mangrove forests and wetlands of the larger refuge. Its trails offer visitors almost three miles of hiking opportunities through an assortment of buttonwood forests, spartina marsh, and freshwater ponds. Here you can look for sunning alligators, anhingas, black-necked stilts, osprey, falcons, red-shouldered hawks, and during their annual spring and fall migrations, scores of warblers feeding on the wax myrtle and insects that thrive in this upland habitat.

J.N. "Ding" Darling National Wildlife Refuge offers various programs throughout the year, sponsors a lecture series during the winter months, and hosts the annual "Ding" Days Festival every fall (generally in mid-October). Additional information and detailed maps of the refuge trails are included in the companion book to this work, called *Living Sanibel: A Nature Guide to Sanibel & Captiva Islands.*

❒____ Q. Sanibel-Captiva Conservation Foundation

Location: 3333 Sanibel-Captiva Road, Sanibel, FL 33957 / Phone: 239-472-2329 / Fax: 239-472-6421 / Website: www.sccf.org / E-mail: sccf@sccf.org / 2,000 acres / Admission fee charged.

Gillardia growing along the hiking trails at SCCF © Maggie May Rogers

While the total area under the management of the Sanibel-Captiva Conservation Foundation (SCCF) exceeds 2,000 acres, most of that land is held as actual wildlife preserve and is not accessible to the public. The majority of the hiking trails, along with a small interpretive center, touch tank, and gift shop are located at the headquarters along Sanibel-Captiva Road. There is also a butterfly house and native plant nursery located here. Once a week a staff member takes visitors through a close-up look at the butterfly house, explaining in detail the life cycle of Florida's numerous butterfly species.

The major hiking trails, which total four-plus miles, run directly behind the main building through preserved land known as the Center Tract. Because it abuts other conservation parcels, this area actually feels much larger than its 250 acres. The mowed footpaths lead through corridors of marshes, wetlands, and buttonwood forests. They culminate in a three-story wooden observation tower overlooking a section of the Sanibel River. The view from the top of the tower is extraordinary, in large part because this preserved land exists on what is traditionally some of the most valuable and overdeveloped real estate in Florida—barrier islands complete with beautiful beaches. For more than four decades it has been the primary mission of SCCF to acquire, restore, and protect the lands in and around Sanibel and Captiva and preserve these natural barrier-island habitats for generations to come.

In addition to its Center Tract, SCCF has a number of other holdings that are worth investigating, some on foot and some via canoe or kayak. One popular SCCF hiking trail runs through the Sanibel Gardens Preserve, located directly north of the Bailey Tract of J.N. "Ding" Darling National Wildlife Refuge. The Periwinkle Blue Skies Preserve Trail, whose trailhead begins just across and slightly west of the Sanibel Community Church (1740 Periwinkle Way), takes you through a tropical hardwood hammock. Another interesting short trail, located across from The Sanibel School in the Pick Preserve, takes you back through a series of ancient beach ridges. On all of these trails, because of the freshwater sloughs and ponds found on Sanibel, look for otters, bobcats, marsh rabbits, and a wide array of birds including

The SCCF Nature Center entrance Courtesy SCCF

Cooper's hawks, common moorhens, killdeer, red-bellied woodpeckers, and an assortment of sparrows and warblers during the migratory seasons.

On Captiva, the single largest SCCF holding consists of 47.5-acre Patterson Island and the vast majority of 300-acre Buck Key. While there are no hiking trails on these islands, they can be explored via canoe or kayak. Various watercraft rentals are available on the bay side of Captiva, making it easy to get on the water and take in Roosevelt Channel and the waters surrounding these two mangrove islands.

Beyond the hiking and kayaking, SCCF has several educational programs and guided activities primarily during the winter season. Popular topics include the biology and behavior of sea turtles, bobcats, and alligators, as well as the history of the region, from the days of the Calusa through the incorporation of the city of Sanibel and its ongoing fight against overdevelopment. Other activities include guided tours of the Caloosahatchee River, dolphin and wildlife cruises, and a boat tour of the historic fish houses in Pine Island Sound.

SCCF operates a Marine Lab on Tarpon Bay next to the Tarpon Bay Explorers concession at J.N. "Ding" Darling National Wildlife Refuge. The lab, which is not open to the public, focuses its attention on maintaining water quality in the back bays and estuaries surrounding Sanibel and Captiva, with a special emphasis on the often-harmful freshwater releases from Lake Okeechobee down the Caloosahatchee River.

Captiva turtle nest during the 2010 season Courtesy SCCF

Another important aspect of SCCF's environmental mission is its sea turtle monitoring program. Hundreds of loggerhead, green, Kemp's ridley, and even an occasional leatherback turtle nest are carefully marked and monitored by more than 100 volunteers. During the summer months, protecting the beach nests of the tiny snowy plovers is added to this agenda, keeping the chicks safe from unleashed pets and careless beachcombers. With its hiking trails, interpretive center, native plant nursery and various programs, a stop at SCCF while visiting Sanibel and Captiva will definitely add to your barrier-island experience.

❒ ________ R. Bailey-Matthews Shell Museum

Location: 3075 Sanibel-Captiva Road, Sanibel, FL 33957 / Phone: 239-395-2233 / Toll-free: 888-679-6450 / Fax: 239-395-6706 / Website: www.shellmuseum.org / E-mail: on Website / Campus: 8 acres / Admission fee charged.

The Bailey-Matthews Shell Museum
Courtesy the Bailey-Matthews Shell Museum

The dream of building a shell museum on Sanibel Island, considered one of the premier shelling locations in the world, dates back to 1927 when the first Sanibel Shell Fair was held. The idea got a boost in 1984 with a $10,000 bequest from local shell collector Charlene McMurphy, whose husband, Rolland, put together a committee to explore the formation of a museum. The committee evolved into the Shell Museum and Research Foundation and hired world-renowned shell expert R. Tucker Abbott to lead the effort. It came much closer to reality in 1990 with the donation of an eight-acre site on Sanibel-Captiva Road by the Bailey brothers, John, Francis, and Sam, in memory of their parents, Frank P. Bailey and Annie Matthews. The museum is named in their honor.

The Bailey-Matthews Shell Museum officially opened its doors on November 18, 1995, and has been growing in quality, distinction, and popularity ever since. It achieved accreditation from the American Association of Museums in March 2010. Of the nation's 17,500 museums, only 775 have earned this accreditation, including 48 in Florida.

Junonia
Courtesy Bailey-Matthews Shell Museum

Any visit to the museum should begin with a viewing of one or both of the 30-minute films shown nonstop in the auditorium on the main floor. These films—*Mollusks in Action: The Secret Life of Seashells* and *Trails and Tales of Living Seashells*—provide a good introduction to these fascinating creatures, whose total number of distinct species tops 200,000 worldwide. Then you will want to head into the large octagonal display area and wander through the museum's more than two dozen exhibits.

For people interested in local shelling, one of the most popular displays is called Gifts from the Seas of Sanibel & Captiva. It clearly displays the most common species of seashells found on the beaches and the back bays of the two islands. The museum also offers a free handout with many of these same seashells on it, making it easy to start your own shell collection. Other exhibits include a large display of Florida fossil shells, as well as a life-size model of the original shell people of Southwest Florida—the Calusa Indians.

Children's learning lab at the Bailey-Matthews Shell Museum
© Blake Sobczak

A dazzling display of scallop shells shows an array of color variations rivaling a master painter's palette. The museum showcases the largest horse conch in the world, a massive 23.8-inch univalve that was discovered by Ed Hanley of Sanibel while diving in 130 feet of water in the Gulf of Mexico. Another exhibit, called MMM... Mollusks!, features an interactive touch-screen computer that allows visitors to e-mail shellfish recipes back home, including delicious dishes of oysters, mussels, and scallops.

One of the most popular and unusual displays is Sailors' Valentines. These magnificently crafted octagonal boxes were created in the early 1800s by the women of the Caribbean for sailors to take back home to their sweethearts. Made of thousands of tiny multi-colored shells that are arranged in a form of shell pointillism, these are truly masterpieces of shell folk art. The adjacent display of shell cameos, shell inlay, buttons, and shell bows is also compelling.

The museum has a number of displays and programs designed specifically for younger visitors, including a live-shell display. It also prepares a shell collection kit that it sends across the U.S., Mexico, and Canada to give schoolchildren an opportunity to learn more about the different species of mollusks and the importance they play in the environment; the kit includes sample shells from around the world, a shell identification guide, and teacher's guide.

Upstairs the museum hosts one of the world's largest libraries on shells. Access to this extensive collection of books, scientific journals, and newsletters can be arranged through the Sanibel Public Library or by contacting the museum staff directly. The director of the museum, Dr. José Leal, is the editor of *The Nautilus,* a renowned scientific journal on malacology (the study of shellfish) first published in 1886.

From the giant squid hanging from the ceiling to the well-stocked gift shop featuring a wide assortment of books on shells, shell-related gifts, and artwork, the Bailey-Matthews Shell Museum affords the visitor a first-hand look into the complex and intriguing world of shells. After your trip to the museum, a short drive will take you to the shell-covered beaches of Sanibel, where you can quickly put the knowledge you've gathered at the museum to work. The two closest public beach accesses are Bowman's Beach County Park, located four miles to the west, or at the southern end of Tarpon Bay Road, one mile to the east, then right. Good luck shelling!

❐ ________ S. Estero Bay Preserve Sate Park

Location: Park headquarters: Koreshan State Park, 3800 Corkscrew Road, Estero, FL 33928 / Phone: 239-992-0311 / Fax: n/a / Website: www.floridastateparks.org/esterobay / E-mail: n/a / Admission is free. / Two trailheads: Winkler Point Trailhead is at the southern end of the Winkler Extension off of Summerlin Road. GPS coordinates: 26E28N48.36O—081E53N53.77O / Estero River Scrub Trailhead is on the north side of Broadway West Road off of U.S. 41 next to the Florida Power & Light substation. GPS coordinates: 26E26N31.32O—081E50N10.57O.

The Estero River scrub trail
Courtesy Florida State Parks

The trailhead sign off of Broadway West Road
© Charles Sobczak

The vast majority of this 11,000-acre site consists of sovereign submerged lands and adjacent wetlands that were acquired by the state of Florida to help protect the state's first designated aquatic preserve, Estero Bay. The northern half of the aquatic preserve was established in 1966, and the southern half, running all the way to the Collier County line, was added in 1983.

The Estero Bay Preserve State Park has no real amenities, ranger-guided tours, or designated activities. Two public boat ramps are available: for larger vessels, the boat ramp located on the bay side of Lovers Key State Park is the best choice; for canoeists and kayakers, the smaller launch on the Estero River, located at the Koreshan State Historic Site, is ideal.

Access by land is limited to two systems of hiking trails located on either side of Estero Bay. The larger of these is the Estero River Scrub Trails, accessed by a trailhead near the end of Broadway Avenue West, approximately one mile east of U.S. 41 in Estero. Its 10 miles of trails crisscross through habitats that include pine flatwoods, scrubby flatwoods, salt marshes, salt flats, and mangrove forests. Formerly destined to become a 1,500-unit housing development, the upland

A beautiful view of the upper Estero Bay Courtesy Florida State Parks

section of the park was purchased for preservation by the state of Florida in 2000. The trails accommodate both hikers and off-road bicyclists, but many of the trails become impassable during the summer rainy season.

The other section of trails is located at the very end of the Winkler Road Extension, 3.2 miles south of Summerlin Road (CR 896). Covering just over four miles of flatwoods, salt flats, and tidal marshes, the Winkler Point trails traverse a large area of land that is in the process of reclamation. Once covered in invasive melaleuca and Brazilian pepper, many of the larger trees have been poisoned and now stand in various stages of decay. Among the highlights of these trails are two observation decks overlooking tidal ponds and the vast expanse of salt flats near the southern end of the trail.

Salt flats are non-vegetated zones sometimes called salt barrens or salinas. They are often devoid of any plants or covered by salt-tolerant species such as sea purslane, saltwort, and glasswort. While appearing lifeless and barren, they play a crucial role in habitat for various ground-nesting birds such as black-necked stilts and killdeer. Because they are so different from most of Florida's lush, green environments, the Estero salt flats make for an unusual change of scenery for the curious naturalist.

❒ ________ T. Koreshan State Historic Site

Location: 3800 Corkscrew Road, Estero, FL 33928 / Phone: 239-992-0311 / Fax: n/a / Website: www.floridastateparks.org/koreshan / E-mail: n/a / 100 acres / Admission fee charged.

Without question, the most unique of all the destinations found in *The Living Gulf Coast* is the Koreshan State Historic Site. In fact, it is considered so strange that it is featured in the classic book *Weird Florida* as a place you have to see to believe. Founded by a charismatic leader named Dr. Cyrus R. Teed in 1894, this cult-like community was carved out of the south Florida wilderness by more than

200 dedicated followers of a new religion called Koreshanity.

A historic building at Koreshan State Park © Charles Sobczak

Teed was born in Trout Creek, New York, in 1839, and as a young physician became interested in unconventional beliefs such as alchemy and the newfound science of high-voltage electricity. During an experiment in 1869 Teed was badly shocked. When he came to, he stated that he was visited by a divine spirit during his unconsciousness, and that the spirit had told him he was the new messiah. Teed then vowed to apply his scientific knowledge toward redeeming humanity and changed his name to Koresh, the Hebrew word for Cyrus.

After his electrified rebirth as Koresh, Teed's ideas became increasingly odd. Many now believe the shock he received may have damaged his brain. He began preaching about a unique view of the earth called cellular cosmogony, wherein the earth was located inside a giant sphere, the sun was a battery-operated contraption, and the stars were refractions of its light. As if that weren't enough, he also advocated reincarnation, immortality, celibacy, communism, and a host of other alternative ideas.

When his radical concepts got him chased out of the state of New York, then Chicago, he and his group of followers uprooted and moved to Estero to create his "New Jerusalem." While many of his concepts and beliefs can be dismissed as bizarre, some of his ideas were nothing short of brilliant. During the golden age of the Koreshan community, Teed and his followers had a bakery, printing house, general store, concrete works, and a power plant that supplied electricity to the region decades before it was available anywhere else in Southwest Florida. He steadfastly believed in the equality of women during a time when they did not even have the right to vote in America. He imported scores of exotic trees and vegetation, hoping to find good uses for them in his new utopia. Thomas Edison visited Teed several times in the early 1900s because of their mutual interest in exotic plants and electricity.

One of many interior displays at Koreshan © Charles Sobczak

His eccentric ideas often got Teed into trouble with the locals. It was just

Decorative Bridge at Koreshan © Charles Sobczak

such a dispute that tragically led to his death in 1908 at the age of 69, two years after he was severely pistol whipped by a Ft. Myers town marshal. Convinced that Koresh was going to rise from the dead, his followers put his body in a bathtub and began an around-the-clock vigil, but after several days, local health officials stepped in and forced the burial of his remains. The Koreshan Unity faith Teed founded continued for decades, but by 1961, when the Koreshan property was deeded over to the state of Florida, only four followers of Koreshanity remained alive.

Today the Koreshan State Historic Site is one of the most fascinating 100 acres in Florida. The structures left standing include the generating plant, lecture hall, general store, and workshops, and there are displays showcasing some of this lost religion's beliefs. A video about the history of Koreshanity plays continuously in the Founder's Residence building.

The site has a full-service campground with 60 campsites, 12 of which are designated for tent camping only. The park has a boat ramp on the Estero River, and canoe rentals are available through the ranger station. During the winter months there are ranger-led programs about the Koreshan Unity settlement and interpretive tours of the wide array of plants and animals found on the grounds.

Of particular note is the massive monkey-puzzle tree growing near the Estero River in the sunken gardens section of the park. Originating from southern Chile, this towering tree can grow to more than 130 feet and produces ponderous, edible seed cones that can weigh up to five pounds. Its fallen leaves are two feet long and very sharp. Extensive stands of Chinese bamboo, sausage, and mango trees planted a century ago still grace the grounds.

A short hiking trail runs along the river. The website has a list of the wildlife that can be viewed there. The main attractions of this historic site, however, are the buildings and displays that detail the rise and fall of this New Jerusalem. While almost all of the destinations in this book deal with things natural, this is the only one that includes things supernatural.

❒_____ U. Mound Key Archeological State Park and the Estero River

Location: Boat ramp at Koreshan State Historic Site: 3800 Corkscrew Road, Estero, FL, 33928 / Phone: 239-992-0311 / Fax: n/a / Website: www.floridastateparks.org/koreshan / E-mail: n/a / Mound Key: GPS Coordinates: 26E25'20"N/081E51'55"W / 113 acres / Admission is free but access is by watercraft only.

Located in the heart of the Estero Bay Aquatic Preserve, Mound Key is the ancient home of the Calusa Indians and the highest point of land in Lee County. Today standing at 32 feet above sea level, Mound Key was reported to be nearly twice that height when first encountered by the Spanish in 1513. More than 1,000 Calusans are believed to have lived on Mound Key at that time. Archeological evidence indicates that the Calusa first started inhabiting this 125-acre site around 100 A.D. when it was little more than a mangrove-covered oyster bar. Over the ensuing 1,400 years, as the kingdom of the Calusa grew in stature and power, they built a series of three mounds: one was the home of the Calusan king (*cacique*), one served as the courtyard, and the third held the Calusa temple, which was large enough to hold the entire village under its thatched roof.

Hiking down an ancient Calusa mound

Courtesy Florida State Parks

There is still considerable debate over the origins of the Calusa Indians. Many believe they came from South America and were not closely related to the North American Indians, though with no lineage available for genetic testing, this theory may never be proven. With an average height of 5 feet 8 inches, these Native Americans towered over the Spanish explorers, who stood an average of 5 feet 2 inches. The Calusa were reported to have reddish hair and strong, muscular builds. Although the Spaniards established the New World's first Jesuit mission on Mound Key in 1566, the Calusa, rather than submit to a religion they did not understand, fled Mound Key shortly thereafter, and the mission was abandoned by 1569. The Calusa never lost a battle against the Spanish, nor did they surrender to them. Sadly, largely because of their lack of immunity against European diseases, especially small pox and influenza, the Calusa tribe was wiped out by 1750.

After the Calusa lost control of Mound Key, it was inhabited by pirates, Cuban fishermen, and, eventually, homesteaders. The Koreshan Unity group that lived up the Estero River from Mound Key purchased much of the island and in 1961 donated their holdings to the state of Florida. Nine of the 125 acres of Mound Key are privately held. Mound Key is managed by the park staff at Koreshan State Historical Site.

Kayaking down the Estero River © Charles Sobczak

A half-mile-long hiking trail traverses the island, including a walk through the mangrove-filled former central canal. Unlike almost every other trail described in *The Living Gulf Coast,* this one actually has hills. The view from the top of the highest mound is panoramic. It includes views of Ft. Myers Beach, the Gulf of Mexico, and all of the Estero Bay Aquatic Preserve.

Bird and wildlife sightings, while interesting and diverse, are not the main reason for visiting this site. While hiking up and down these immense shell mounds, one cannot help but wonder what the Calusa kingdom must have looked like 600 years ago. The Calusa were the most powerful tribe in Florida. They lived as hunter-gatherers, and thrived in an ecosystem that teemed with redfish, snook, oysters, shellfish, manatees, and birds. They were a healthy people living in harmony with their surroundings while putting minimal pressures on their environment. Several interesting historical kiosks along the trails will help you get a better grasp of the Calusa culture. Because Mound Key is a designated archeological site, picking up any artifacts or shells, even dead ones, is strictly prohibited.

Getting there is half the fun. For those wishing to visit this archeological treasure by motorboat, the closest launch is the bay-side boat ramp on Lovers Key State Park off of County Road 865. For those who prefer to come by canoe or kayak the easiest way is via the Estero River. The Koreshan State Historic Site rents aluminum canoes for a modest fee; the rangers suggest you begin your six- to seven-hour journey before 9 a.m. to make it back by the 5 p.m. deadline. Another option is to rent a canoe or kayak from Estero River Outfitters (20991 S. Tamiami Trail, just across U.S. 41 from the Koreshan State Historic Site; 239-992-4050; www. esteroriveroutfitters.com). You can also launch your own canoe, kayak, or small powerboat at Koreshan State Park.

Paddling the Estero River to and from Mound Key is a wonderful way to spend the day. The upper section has considerable development, but roughly halfway down the river the houses and condominiums disappear and you find yourself paddling amidst an endless mangrove forest filled with herons, egrets, and osprey. These shallow, estuarine waters are also teeming with sport fish. At the mouth of the river you have to traverse a half-mile of open water to reach Mound Key. The island has two landings: the larger one is on the northwestern edge and is better suited for power craft; the other landing, which is on the southeast side of island, is a better choice for canoes and kayaks. Mosquitoes and no-see-ums can be thick, so be sure to have bug spray with you. There are no facilities on Mound Key.

Accessible only by boat, Mound Key is one of Lee County's most unique destinations. Whether you come by powerboat or under your own paddle power, once atop those 30-foot hills overlooking the Estero Bay Aquatic Preserve, you'll know instantly the journey was worth it.

❐ ________ V. Lovers Key State Park

Location: 8700 Estero Blvd., Ft. Myers Beach, FL 33931 / Phone: 239-463-4588 / Fax: n/a / Website: www.floridastateparks.org/loverskey / E-mail: n/a / 1,616 acres / Admission fee charged.

Consisting of four barrier islands, Lovers Key State Park encompasses 1,616 acres that include a stretch of 2.5 miles of white sandy beaches, 744 acres of mangrove-fringed waterways, and eight miles of hiking and nature trails that thread through the beaches and islands. Originally named after University of Florida engineering graduate Carl E. Johnson, who helped

An aerial view of the pavilion at Lovers Key

Courtesy Lee County VC Bureau

Dolphins in the surf

© Gareth Pinckard

Weddings are popular at Lovers Key © Charles Sobczak

design and build the causeway that connects the park to Bonita Springs along County Road 865, the park is now commonly referred to simply as Lovers Key.

Like many of Florida's state parks, Lovers Key is a day-use-only facility—opening every morning at 8 a.m. and closing at sunset 365 days a year. Because of its strategic location between the urban centers of Naples to the south and Ft. Myers, Ft. Myers Beach and Cape Coral to the north, Lovers Key State Park is one of the most visited parks in the state, topped only by Honeymoon Island in Dunedin, Florida. Although no camping is allowed, the park is a great place for fishing, biking, hiking, sunbathing, picnicking, swimming, and more.

The name Lovers Key dates back to the turn of the last century when it was said that young couples favored the sunsets along the beach that extends between New Pass to the south and Big Carlos Pass to the north. In the early days Lovers Key was accessible only by boat, and the seclusion it offered was a welcome respite from the early Florida land boom of the 1920s. Black Island, which is where a 2.6-mile hiking loop and a five-mile canoe and kayak trail are now located, was slated for a resort-style development in the late 1960s. The island was cleared of all native trees and mangroves and dredged in anticipation of this new subdivision. After a public outcry to halt the development, the state of Florida purchased almost all of the island and added its acreage to what was then the Carl E. Johnson State Park. Since the acquisition by the state, the mangroves and hardwood coastal hammocks have returned, and the land where houses were destined to rise is now covered in palm trees and native plants.

One unique feature of Lovers Key State Park is that it has a nice two-slot boat ramp located on the bay side of County Highway 865 where anglers and boaters can launch their vessels to explore the backwaters of Estero Bay (Florida's first aquatic preserve) and the numerous surrounding passes. There is a $2.00 launch fee per boat. There are also canoe and kayak launches in the park free to all paid park visitors. One section of the park is part of the Great Calusa Blueway.

Another great feature of Lovers Key is the picnic area and children's playground located in the northeast corner of Black Island. Numerous picnic tables and covered kiosks are available for day-trippers for the modest sum of $2.00 per carload. Because of its name and its 100-year-old reputation as a destination for romance, Lovers Key State Park is a particular favorite for beach weddings; a large covered gazebo and tram stop along the beach help to facilitate these events.

The sheer size of the park, coupled with its dredged canals, backwaters, and passes, make it one of the state's top-rated parks for anglers. The south side of the park abutting New Pass is known for producing some of the largest record snook in the state. Other catches include redfish, sea trout, tarpon, and flounder, and visiting anglers are encouraged to try cast-netting for the plentiful black-striped mullet. Wildlife sightings may include roseate spoonbills, least terns, black skimmers, bald eagles, West Indian manatees, bottle-nosed dolphins, and the diminutive marsh rabbit. Because of its location along the coast, Lovers Key has shelling comparable to that found on Sanibel Island.

The free tram at Lovers Key © Charles Sobczak

A free tram ferries the visitors from the parking lot to the beaches and runs daily from the park's opening until 5 p.m. Wildlife tours and presentations are offered during the winter season. Contact the park directly for updates on these events.

The concession company operating in the park offers food, beverages, ice cream, and bike, canoe, and kayak rentals along with an assortment of other amenities including guided sightseeing and fishing tours. The park has been working with Friends of Lovers Key (FOLKS, 239-463-4588) to raise funds to build a visitors center near the main parking lot.

Lovers Key State Park remains nearly as untouched and beautiful today as it was 500 years ago. Several times over the past decade this beach has made it into the top ten in all of Florida, and once you've experienced its white sandy beaches, you'll understand why.

Heading out for a paddle Courtesy Lee County VC Bureau

Additional Parks, Preserves, and Eco-destinations of Lee County

❒ ______ The Shell Factory and Nature Park

Location: 2787 North Tamiami Trail, North Ft. Myers, FL 33903 / Phone: 239-995-2141 / Fax: n/a / Toll-free: 800-282-5805 / Website: www.shellfactory.com / E-mail: questions@shellfactory.com / Admission to the store is free, but an admission fee is charged for the nature park and arcade.

One of the oldest attractions in Southwest Florida, the Shell Factory opened its doors in 1952. Some years later, after a fire destroyed the original building, it relocated to its current site. Today the park offers botanical gardens, an aviary, and a touch and feel center, plus a host of creatures from alligators to pythons to Madagascar hissing cockroaches. An arcade allows the kids to collide on bumper boats, play miniature golf, or try out some video games. Events include dances, singles nights, and an assortment of happenings. This classic Florida roadside attraction has something for everyone.

❐ ________ Everglades Wonder Gardens

Location: 27180 Old U.S. 41, Bonita Springs, FL 34135 / Phone: 239-992-2591 / Fax: n/a / Website: n/a / E-mail: n/a / Admission fee charged.

Originally established in 1936 and still at its initial location along the banks of the Imperial River, this unique roadside attraction is still maintained and operated in much the same way it always was. Offering more than 2,000 species of native wildlife and plants, Wonder Gardens has become host to rescued Florida panthers, alligators, and other injured animals. Attractions include a stuffed crocodile named Big Joe, measuring more than 15 feet long, alligator skulls, and a stuffed cobra and mongoose among other curios. Alligator feedings and guided tours through the lush botanical gardens are among the highlights. This is the way Florida attractions used to be—a far cry from the sterilized versions of the parks now found in and around Orlando. This is the quintessential "roadside attraction."

❐ ________ Imaginarium

Location: 2000 Cranford Avenue, Ft. Myers, FL 33916 / Phone: 239-321-7420 / Fax: 239-334-5915 / Website: www.imaginariumfortmyers.com / E-mail: imag@cityftmyers.com / 4 acres / Admission fee charged.

The Imaginarium is a hands-on museum, aquarium, and learning center for children of all ages. Built in an old water treatment plant, the historic building is now home to a 100-seat theater, aquarium tanks filled with salt and freshwater fish, a television studio, and a host of other fascinating exhibits. Children can experience hurricane-force winds, meet gopher tortoises and iguanas, or spend all afternoon in one of the many hands-on play stations. The Imaginarium is an ideal destination for families with young children with a penchant for exploration.

❐ ________ The Butterfly Estates

Location: 1815 Fowler Street, River District, Ft. Myers, FL 33901 / Phone: 239-690-2359 / Fax: 239-690-2360 / Toll-free: 877-690-2359 / Website: www.thebutterflyestates.com / E-mail: info@butterflyestates.com / Admission fee charged.

This large conservatory holds approximately 800 butterflies and presents the largest collection of native species in Southwest Florida. The Butterfly Estates is a popular site for weddings, corporate retreats, and family get-togethers. The facility also has an ice cream parlor, fudge shop, restaurant, and gift shop. This is a great destination for butterfly lovers.

❒ ______ ECHO (Educational Concerns for Hunger Organization)

Location: 17430 Durrance Road, North Ft. Myers, FL 33917 / Phone: 239-543-3246 / Nursery phone: 239-567-1900 / Fax: n/a / Website: www.echonet.org / E-mail: info@echonet.org / Admission fee charged.

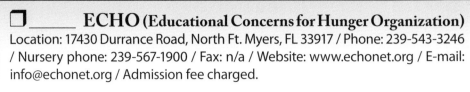

A fascinating organization dedicated to improving the human condition worldwide through better agricultural techniques and the maintenance of a global seed bank. Regularly scheduled 90-minute tours (visit the website for details) take visitors through the campus and explain the mission of ECHO and its multinational outreach programs. The nursery contains an extensive collection of unusual tropical fruit trees, organic fertilizers, and ornamental trees and plants. An on-site bookstore specializes in gardening, cookbooks, and animal husbandry. To visit the bookstore online, go to www.echobooks.org.

❒ ______ Mound House

Location: 289 Connecticut Street, Ft. Myers Beach, FL 33931 / Phone: 239-765-0865 / Fax: 239-765-0841 / Website: www.moundhouse.org / E-mail: moundhouse@fortmyersbeachfl.gov / Admission is free, but fees charged for kayak tours.

Built on an ancient Calusa shell mound, this historic property offers visitors a window into the past. Displays include Calusa tools, history, and artifacts from 100 years B.C. to the present. The grounds include a picnic area and a boat dock.

❒ ______ Southwest Florida Museum of History

Location: 2301 Jackson Street, Ft. Myers, FL 33901 / Phone: 239-321-7430 / Fax: n/a / Website: www.swflmuseumofhistory.com / E-mail: historian@cityftmyers.com / Admission fee charged.

This expansive museum located in downtown Ft. Myers is a great place to learn more about the history of Lee County and the development of Ft. Myers. Exhibits include Paleo Florida, with examples of prehistoric dinosaurs and mammals, Calusa and Seminole Indian artifacts, Spanish explorers, the history of the fort that gives Fort Myers its name, the Esperanza railcar, a vintage cracker house, and the lovely Palm Park. Photography, painting, and other displays are changed seasonally, so go to the museum's website to find out what is being presented currently.

Lightning strikes the Gulf of Mexico

❒ ________ The Sanibel Historical Museum and Village

Location: 950 Dunlop Road, Sanibel, FL 33957 / Phone: 239-472-4648 / Fax: 239-472-2277 / Website: www.sanibelmuseum.org / E-mail: calusa1513@embarqmail.com / Admission fee charged.

This eight-acre site is more of a village than a museum per se. Buildings include the Rutland House, built in 1913, the 1896 East Sanibel School House, the 1898 Burnap Cottage, and the 1926 Miss Charlotta's Tea Room. Artifacts include everything from pre-Columbian Calusa tools to the fully stocked 1927 Bailey's General Store. The museum and village offer a fascinating window into Sanibel's agricultural past.

❒ ______ Cape Coral Historical Museum

Location: 544 Cultural Park Blvd., Cape Coral, FL 33915 / Phone: 239-772-7037 / Fax: 239-573-7518 / Website: www.capecoralhistoricalmuseum.org / E-mail: CcoralMuseum@embarqmail.com / Admission fee charged.

This museum features an excellent collection of aerial maps and photographs of Cape Coral and Lee County, as well as antiques, artifacts, and relics. Another attraction is the Lois Herbert Memorial Rose Garden, adjacent to the museum. Collections on rotation and on loan help to make any trip to this excellent museum a great way to spend a day while visiting Cape Coral.

❒ _______ Randell Research Center

Location: 13810 Waterfront Drive, Pineland, FL 33945 / Phone: 239-283-2062 / Fax: 239-283-2157 / Bookstore: 239-283-2080 / Website: www.flmnh.ufl/RRC / E-mail: randellcenter@comcast.net / 53 acres / Admission fee charged.

A program of the Florida Museum of Natural History, this large site located on Pine Island offers a window into the earliest inhabitants of Southwest Florida. The primary focus of the site is the extinct Calusa Indian people. The Calusa Heritage Trail, a 3,700-foot interpretive walkway, takes visitors through mounds, canals, and other features created by these Native Americans. Colorful signs explain archaeological findings.

Visitors follow trail signs along the Calusa Heritage Trail at the center

Courtesy Randell Research Center

❒ ________ Lighthouse Beach and Fishing Pier

Location: The eastern tip of Sanibel, FL 33957 / GPS coordinates: N26-45-295/ W082-01-426 / Phone: 239-472-3700 / Fax: 239-472-3065 / Website: www.sanibel-captiva.org/play/beaches / E-mail: island@sanibel-captiva.org / 38 acres / Admission is free, fees charged for parking.

This beach gets its name from Sanibel's favorite landmark, the historic Sanibel Lighthouse, built in 1884. Popular not only with sunbathers but also birders, Lighthouse Beach attracts thousands of migratory warblers every spring and fall as they use Sanibel and Captiva as a staging site for their flights across the Gulf of Mexico. Lighthouse Beach is on the Piping Plover cluster of the Great Florida Birding Trail. The fishing pier on the bay side is an ideal location to see the many different species of fish caught in these waters.

❒ ________ Bonita Nature Place

Location: 27601 Kent Road, Bonita Springs, FL 34135 / Phone: 239-992-2556 / Fax: 239-992-1205 / Website: www.bonitaspringsrecreation.org/natureplace / E-mail: n/a / 40 acres / Admission is free.

The newest eco-destination in Lee County, this 40-acre site started with 10 acres in early 2009. While it currently offers some hiking trails, a bat house, an active beehive, and a butterfly garden, plans are under way to increase the length and scope of the hiking trails and to add possible canoe and kayak trips down the nearby Imperial River. A popular location for gopher tortoises, this is one of the best spots in Lee County to spot one of these endangered reptiles.

❒ ________ Caloosahatchee Creek Preserve

Location: Two trailhead locations: 17100 McDowell Drive and 10130 Bayshore Road, North Ft. Myers, FL 33917 / Phone: 239-707-0862 / Fax: 239-485-2300 / Website: www.conservation2020.org/preservedetails / E-mail: jwaller@leegov.com / 1,290 acres / Admission is free on the east side, parking fee charged on the west side.

Divided by Interstate 75, the Caloosahatchee Creek Preserve consists of numerous parcels located along the northern edge of the Caloosahatchee River. There is a 1.5-mile boardwalk on the eastern side of the preserve and a 0.5-mile boardwalk and trail on the western side. The western side also offers a canoe and kayak launch on Popash Creek, which flows into the Caloosahatchee River. Although both sides have to deal with traffic noise, this is nonetheless a lovely preserve to visit.

❒ _______ Popash Creek Preserve

Location: 9451 Nalle Grade Road, North Ft. Myers, FL 33917 / Phone: 239-707-0874 / Fax: 239-485-2300 / Website: www.conservation2020.org/preservedetails / E-mail: lwewerka@leegov.com / 307 acres / Admission is free.

Acquired in 2003, this preserve consists primarily of mesic flatwoods and encompasses a small portion of Popash Creek. Popular with hikers as well as equestrians, a system of trails crisscross the preserve.

❒ _______ Billy Creek Preserve

Location: Woodside Avenue, Ft. Myers, FL 33905 / Phone: 239-707-2206 / Fax: 239-485-2300 / Website: www.conservation2020.org/preservedetails / E-mail: lgreeno@leegov.com / 51 acres / Admission is free.

Still in development, this inner-city preserve will eventually be included in the Great Calusa Blueway. It currently offers hiking and nature trails, a picnic area, and a canoe / kayak launch onto Billy Creek.

❒ _______ Prairie Pines Preserve

Location: 18400 North Tamiami Trail, North Ft. Myers, FL 33903 / Phone: 239-707-2206 / Fax: 239-485-2300 / Website: www.conservation2020.org/preservedetails / E-mail: lgreeno@leegov.com / 2,654 acres / Admission is free.

Prone to flooding during the wet, summer months, this large preserve is located just north of Cape Coral. A large section abuts I-75, but because it is such a big preserve, road noise is not a factor. An abandoned railroad grade traverses the property, which is a popular place for horseback and bicycle riding.

❒ _______ Matanzas Pass Preserve

Location: 307 Nature View Court, Ft. Myers Beach, FL 33931 / Phone: 239-432-2158 / Fax: 239-485-2300 / Website: www.conservation2020.org/preservedetails / E-mail: caintb@leegov.com / 59 acres / Admission is free.

The only remaining stand of maritime oak in Lee County can be found along the 1.25-mile elevated boardwalk in this preserve. A historic cottage and a canoe/kayak launch can also be found on this property.

❒ _______ Pine Island Flatwoods Preserve

Location: 6351 Stringfellow Road, St. James City, FL 33956 / Phone: 239-707-8251 / Fax: 239-485-2300 / Website: www.conservation2020.org/preservedetails / E-mail: janderson@leegov.com / 730 acres / Admission is free.

Several trails take you back into this montage of pine flatwoods, freshwater marshes, tidal swamp, and coastal grassland. Birds include great horned owls, migratory warblers, and pileated woodpeckers. Future plans include a trail all the way to Pine Island Sound.

❒ _______ Big Jim Creek Preserve and Fritts Park

Location: the end of Beach Daisy Lane, Bokeelia, FL 33992 / Phone: 239-392-0090 / Fax: n/a / Website: www.calusalandtrust.org / E-mail: ecalusaed@calusalandtrust.org / 325 acres / Admission is free.

Managed by the Calusa Land Trust, this 325-acre preserve consists largely of red, black, and white mangroves. Well-marked canoe and kayak trails traverse the property, offering more than five miles of paddle trails. The launch is located at Fritts Park.

❒ _______ Bowman's Beach Park

Location: Bowman's Beach Road, Sanibel, FL 33957 / Phone: 239-472-3700 / / Fax: 239-472-3065 / Website: www.sanibel-captiva.org/play/beaches / E-mail: island@sanibel-captiva.org / 170 acres / Admission is free, fee charged for parking.

Voted the most private beach in America by the Huffington Post, this long stretch of sand is truly unique in that it has no visible homes, condos, or other development. The water off of Bowman's Beach is not affected by the runoff of the Caloosahatchee River, so it tends to be clear and excellent for snorkeling and shelling. The beach is wide, and the birding is exceptional.

A shore bird feeds along the beach
© Sara Jane Pinckard

Heron landing

The Everglades Courtesy Collier County VCBureau

Collier County

Collier County is the second-largest county in Florida, surpassed in area only by Palm Beach County. The county has a total of 2,305 square miles: 2,025 on land and 280 in water. Lake Trafford, located entirely within Collier County, is 1,600 acres and one of the largest freshwater lakes in Florida. The county has 16 unincorporated communities, including the recently developed Ave Maria, but only three municipalities: Everglades City, Marco Island, and Naples, which is the county seat.

The county was created in 1923 when it was separated from Lee County. It was named after Barron Collier, a wealthy New York advertising mogul and real estate developer who first came to the region in 1911. In ensuing years he acquired more than 1 million acres in Southwest Florida. He helped construct the Tamiami Trail that crossed the state in what was then the wilderness known as the Everglades. An avid fisherman and early conservationist, Barron Collier left in indelible mark on the county named after him.

More than 68 percent of Collier County is protected from development through the use of easements, public parks, preserves, and national and state parks. The largest of these is the Big Cypress National Preserve, which is 729,000 acres (1,139 square miles), representing more than 40 percent of the entire county (note: portions of Big Cypress are located in Monroe, Dade and Hendry Counties). Other large tracts of protected land include Fakahatchee Strand State Park (85,000 acres), Picayune State Forest (75,000 acres), and Florida Panther National Wildlife Refuge (26,400 acres). While other preserves, such as Rookery Bay (110,000 acres) and the Ten Thousand Islands National Wildlife Refuge (35,000 acres) are even

Zebra Longwing Butterfly
© Charles Sobczak

larger, much of that acreage is brackish or saltwater.

The estimated population of Collier County in 2009 was 333,032 people. During the winter months, the population approaches 400,000, which puts a strain on the services and traffic in the Naples and Marco Island metro region. Tourism is the largest industry in Collier County, which also boasts having the most golfing holes per capita in the continental United States. There are close to 90 golf courses in Collier County.

For the wildlife enthusiast, hiker, and bicyclist, Collier County offers everything from small regional parks such as Eagle Lakes to the immensity of Big Cypress. More than 300 species of birds frequent the area, and tens of thousands of alligators and snakes roam the backwaters and sloughs of the numerous preserves and parks. Though much of the region was logged off in the past 150 years, isolated strands of bald cypress and mature slash pine survived. These can be seen in places such as Audubon Corkscrew Wildlife Sanctuary and Fakahatchee Strand Preserve State Park.

For the canoeist and kayaker Collier County is a watery heaven. From the brackish waters of Halfway Creek in Everglades National Park to the Blackwater River of Collier-Seminole State Park to the launch at Delnor-Wiggins State Park and the headwaters of the Imperial River, there are hundreds of miles of fresh- and saltwater waterways to explore. Add the fact that the fresh and especially the saltwater fishing is world renowned, and you have some of the best paddling found anywhere in the world.

Collier County abounds with wildlife. Its huge preserves serve as the last remaining habitat for the endangered Florida panther; deer, black bear, manatee, dolphins, and dozens of other mammals flourish throughout the region.

For more information about Collier County, go to www.paradisecoast.com or visit Collier County's official website at www.colliergov.net. While there was not enough room in this book to cover all of the 90-plus parks, refuges and preserves in Collier County, the ones included here represent some of the finest eco-destinations you will find anywhere in North America. So choose one of the following sites, grab some water, sunscreen, and maybe a little bug spray just in case, and get outside and start living.

Collier County Eco-Destinations

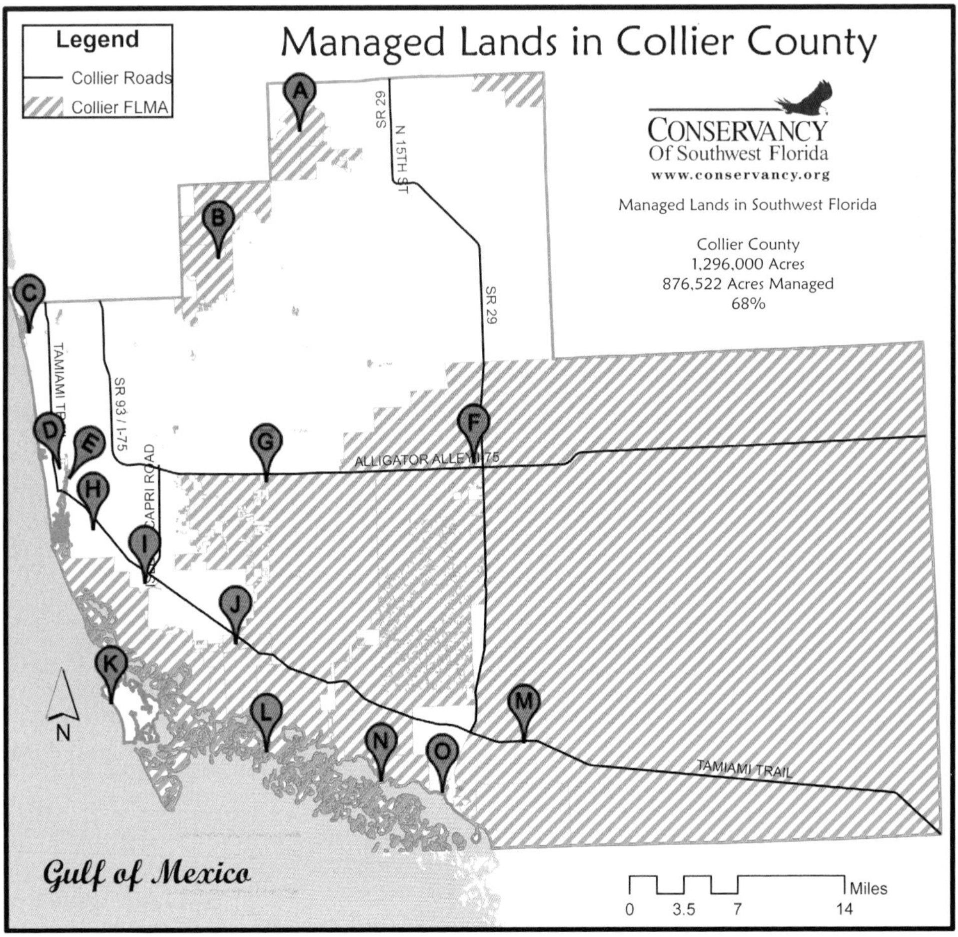

A. CREW Marsh
B. Audubon Corkscrew Swamp Sanctuary
C. Delnor-Wiggins State Park
D. The Naples Zoo at the Caribbean Gardens
E. The Conservancy of Southwest Florida
F. Florida Panther National Wildlife Refuge
G. Picayune Strand State Forest
H. Naples Botanical Garden
I. Rookery Bay National Estuarine Research Reserve
J. Collier-Seminole State Park
K. Tigertail Beach, Marco Island
L. Ten Thousand Islands National Wildlife Refuge
M. Big Cypress National Preserve
N. Fakahatchee Strand Preserve State Park
O. Everglades National Park—Gulf Coast Station

❒ ______ A. CREW Marsh and Cypress Dome Trails

Location: 23998 Corkscrew Road, Estero, FL 33928 / Trailhead address: 4600 County Road 850, Immokalee, FL 34142 / Phone for camping permits: 239-657-2253 / Fax: n/a / E-mail: crewtrust@earthlink.net / Website: www.crewtrust.org / 50,000+ acres / Admission is free, permits required for primitive camping sites.

Located along the southeastern edge of Lee County and the upper northwest corner of Collier County, the CREW Land and Water Trust's Corkscrew Marsh and Cypress Dome trails are part of 60,000 acres of protected watershed managed by the South Florida Water Management District. The unabridged version of CREW is Corkscrew Regional Ecosystem Watershed. Established in the early 1980s and growing under the leadership of Joel Kuperberg, CREW's primary mission is keeping watersheds such as Corkscrew Marsh free from contamination by rock mining and residential or commercial development, which creates drainage ditches, among a host of other potential threats.

CREW Marsh boardwalk © Charles Sobczak

Lying 1,000 feet below the CREW land is the Floridan aquifer, a reservoir of porous rock that contains 90 percent of the drinking water south Floridians need. For these aquifers to be naturally recharged by rainwater, the acreage at the surface has to allow this rainwater to remain captured for months on end, thereby allowing it to seep slowly into the reservoir located deep below. Development diverts the water using drainage ditches and canals that allow rainwater to make its way rapidly into the gulf. By protecting the land that recharges the aquifer, CREW is really protecting the water that comes out of your faucets.

A map of the CREW holdings, which is easy to find on its website (http://www.crewtrust.org/navpage.html), looks like a multicolored jigsaw puzzle. Its holdings include Southwest Florida Regional Airport mitigation lands, conservation easements, and mitigation banks. Much of this land encircles the Audubon Corkscrew Swamp Sanctuary. There are more than 10 miles of trails throughout the CREW property, and more are planned.

The completed trails—known as Corkscrew Marsh and Cypress Dome—are in an area called Corkscrew Marsh, which feeds directly into Corkscrew Swamp. Both trailheads are located on the south side of County Road 850 (Corkscrew Road), approximately 18 miles east of I-75 (Exit 123).

Well-marked trails © Charles Sobczak

Arriving from the west, you first come to the Cypress Dome trails, consisting of several loops and shortcuts. The two main loops are each 1.4 miles in length. Combining the two results in a hike of approximately 2.5 miles and takes about 60 to 90 minutes. Highlighting this series of trails are two cypress dome ecosystems, where you might find swallow-tailed kites, barred owls, and pileated, red-bellied, and downy woodpeckers, as well as feral hogs, black bears, and green anoles. The Cypress Dome trails are open to hiking, biking, and horseback riding (by permit).

Farther up the road you come to the larger Corkscrew Marsh trailhead. Its various trails wind through a variety of habitats including pine flatlands, pop ash sloughs, oak hammocks, and the edge of the 5,000-acre Corkscrew Marsh itself. A tall observation tower overlooks the marsh where you can catch glimpses of distant vultures, red-shouldered hawks, and, possibly, snail kites. The pop ash slough trail takes you across several lengthy boardwalks that are similar in design and feel to the boardwalk at the nearby Corkscrew Swamp Sanctuary. The trails are all mowed and well maintained, and the bold signs make it all but impossible to get lost. Only hiking is permitted on the Marsh trails, which are also dog-friendly.

Observation tower © Charles Sobczak

Because of the numerous birds, including the migratory warblers, that frequent these wetlands, the CREW property is a part of the Great Florida Birding Trail. Open from dawn until dusk, the area has a single Porta-Potty in the parking area and a few benches. Unlike many state parks and other eco-destinations, access to the trails here is free of charge.

For the truly adventurous there is a primitive campsite located some distance off of the main trails. A permit is required to use this facility. Contact the CREW staff to make camping arrangements.

The Corkscrew Marsh and Cypress Dome hiking trails are completely underutilized and a welcome respite from some of the more popular destinations found in this book. When you really feel the need to get away from the crowds and get back in touch with truly unspoiled and unvisited nature, these two trails are the perfect combination.

❒ ______ B. Audubon Corkscrew Swamp Sanctuary

Location: 375 Sanctuary Road West, Naples, FL 34120 / Phone: 239-348-9151 / Fax: 239-348-1522 / E-mail: dlotter@audubon.org / Website: www.corkscrew.audubon.org / 13,000 acres / Admission fee charged.

Woodstork in flight © Blake Sobczak

Established in 1954 to protect some of the last remaining virgin stands of bald and pond cypress trees left in the state of Florida, the Corkscrew Swamp Sanctuary encompasses 13,000 acres. Most of this acreage is not open to the public because it is home to the largest nesting colonies of wood storks in North America. An endangered species, nesting wood storks are very sensitive to any intrusions into their rookeries and have been known to abandon eggs and even chicks if they are disturbed. They nest among the crowns of the 500-year-old bald cypress trees that tower over much of the swamp.

Public access into the swamp is via a 2.25-mile boardwalk that takes visitors through several distinctive habitats. The hike generally takes less than two hours and has to be considered one of the finest nature trails in all of Florida. The boardwalk, originally built in 1955, is today constructed out of Brazilian Ipé (known by the trade name Pau Lope) and is wheelchair accessible. For those who do not want to make the entire walk, a cutoff shortens the trail to one mile.

The Blair Nature Center, located at the beginning of the trail, is situated in a typical upland pine flatwoods forest, as is the old plume hunter's camp, located on a spur off the main trail. This habitat is characterized by Florida slash pine, saw palmetto, cabbage palms, and myriad wildflowers. Wildfires play an important role in keeping this understory open; you can see evidence of this in the burn marks on the trunks of cabbage palms and slash pines along the trail.

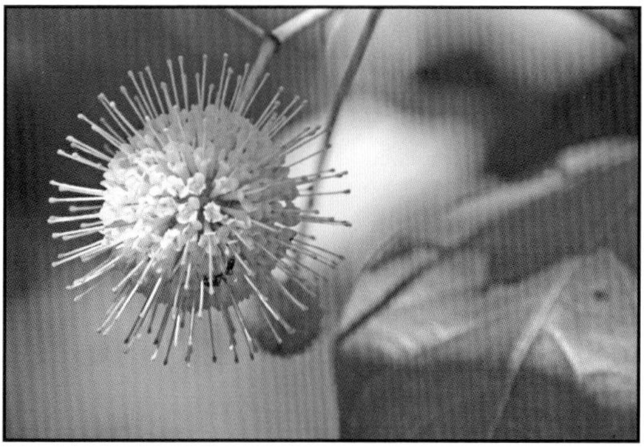

Wildflower © Blake Sobczak

Corkscrew Swamp Board walk

Be sure to take the last spur on your left before entering the wet prairie section of the walk. A suspended bird feeder attracts wintering passerines such as painted buntings, pine warblers, and cedar waxwings. Once into the wide, open wet prairie, look for swamp sparrows, white-tailed deer, and banded water snakes. This habitat is dominated by grasses, sedges, and rushes, with sand cordgrass being the most abundant.

Shortly thereafter you will find yourself in a mature pond cypress forest. These trees are thinner and considerably smaller than the massive bald cypress found deeper in the swamp. The pond cypress forest is home to otters, Florida black bears, common yellowthroats, American bitterns, and white-eyed vireos. Blue flag iris and night-fragrant orchids along with an assortment of bromeliads thrive in the pond cypress forest.

Roughly a mile into the walk you enter the heart and soul of the Corkscrew Swamp: the virgin stand of monumental bald cypress trees. These old-growth trees are centuries old, some reaching heights in excess of 130 feet. The swamp beneath them is laced with strange organic sculptures called cypress knees. These curious-

© R J Wiley

looking protrusions are extensions of the bald cypress root systems and are believed to have evolved to help stabilize the massive trees in the rich, organic peat in which they grow. In the numerous nooks and cavities of these trees look for barred and screech owls, wood ducks, and raccoons, as well as pileated, red-bellied, and downy woodpeckers. This forest is also home to the mythical ghost orchid, which blooms between May and August during the rainy season.

Be sure to take the spur that takes you to the western edge of the boardwalk, overlooking the central marsh. This area is dominated by sawgrass and coastal plain willow. An elevated platform allows you to scope the broad horizon in search of wood stork nests, as well as swallow-tailed kites, vireos, cardinals, and blackbirds. Be careful to watch for native green anoles hiding amidst the similarly colored and shaped coastal plain willow leaves.

Your next stop is in the Lettuce Lakes area of Corkscrew Swamp, and no one should visit here without seeing this unique feature. Here the water is too deep for trees to survive, but the surface of the lake is covered in floating vegetation such as water lettuce, frog's bit, alligator flag, and pickerelweed. Alligators and turtles thrive in these ponds, while the edges are patrolled by limpkins, purple gallinules, and little blue herons. Thirty-nine species of mammals, reptiles, amphibians, and butterflies and more than 108 species of birds have been identified in the swamp.

The boardwalk soon returns to the Blair Audubon Center where you can take in the attractive and well-stocked Nature Store or sit back and have a refreshment and snack in the tearoom. Art shows, often featuring nature photographs that were shot in the swamp, adorn the walls of the center, and a bird feeder just outside the bay window attracts hummingbirds, buntings, and gray squirrels while you enjoy the air conditioning.

An interesting feature of the Blair Center is the Living Machine, a recycling wastewater system that uses sunlight, bacteria, plants, and animals to restore wastewater from the center back into the toilets for reuse again and again. Designed by John Todd of Ocean Arks International, it is the only wastewater treatment plant in Florida that has its own butterfly garden!

Even in the heat of summer, because of the towering canopy provided by the ancient bald cypress found there, Corkscrew Swamp Sanctuary is a joy to visit. The solitude and beauty of a walk through this cathedral of majestic cypress trees is always a welcome and refreshing change of pace. Everyone reading *The Living Gulf Coast* should take a day out of their hurried lives to visit this national treasure.

☐ _______ C. Delnor-Wiggins Pass State Park

Location: 11135 Gulfshore Drive, Naples, FL 34108 / Phone: 239-597-6196 / Fax: n/a / E-mail: n/a / Website: www.floridastateparks.org/delnorwiggins / 166 acres / Admission fee charged.

Afternoon at the Pass © Charles Sobczak

Rare among all the destinations along the southwestern coast of Florida, Delnor-Wiggins Pass State Park offers viable snorkeling and even scuba diving off of its sugar-sand beaches. This is made possible by a remarkable section of hard limestone bottom located roughly 100 yards offshore in approximately 10-12 feet of water. The water clarity is generally good along this stretch of coastline, and with a little effort a snorkeler or diver can swim out to observe snook, sheepshead, mangrove snapper, and an assortment of fish and shellfish species thriving on this hard-bottom reef. Several marker buoys just offshore indicate the location of the reef.

Of course, the beach itself is unimaginably beautiful. Its fine, white sand stretches for more than a mile from the park entrance north to Wiggins Pass. The 166-acre park is perfect for sunbathing, swimming, and enjoying the surf. Fishing is permitted only in and around Wiggins Pass itself. Because of the strong currents and heavy boat traffic, swimming and snorkeling are prohibited at the pass.

The bay side of Delnor-Wiggins Pass State Park lends itself to kayaking and canoeing. A boat ramp to the east accesses Water Turkey Bay, which runs via the South Channel into the Cocohatchee River. A kayak trip up the Cocohatchee winds through mangrove forest and eventually leads east and south to the underpass off of Immokalee Road, approximately three to four miles upriver. Heading north you can explore the backside of Barefoot Beach Preserve all the way to Little Hickory Bay. Although you can paddle south from the ramp, that direction soon puts you into a canal-laced subdivision where boat wakes and the lack of wildlife viewing make for a less enjoyable journey.

The birding at Delnor-Wiggins is fantastic, and the park is part of the Great Florida Birding Trail. Sightings of bald eagles, osprey, and warblers during the spring and fall are common. You will also find scores of shorebirds, plenty of gray squirrels, an occasional raccoon, and any number of reptiles. Be on the lookout for black racers, red and yellow rat snakes, and gopher tortoises. During the summer months, you may come across some sea turtle crawls and nests.

The Beach at Delnor-Wiggins © R J Wiley

Park rangers offer programs throughout the year on topics as diverse as snook fishing, cast-netting lessons, sea turtle discoveries, and native plant walks. Picnic tables, a rentable pavilion, and a concession all help to make a trip to Delnor-Wiggins State Park a day to remember.

❒ _____ D. The Naples Zoo at Caribbean Gardens

Location: 1590 Goodlette Road, Naples, FL 34102 / Phone: 239-262-5409 / Fax: n/a / E-mail: info@napleszoo.org / Website: www.caribbeangardens.com / 43 acres / Admission fee charged.

The long history of the Naples Zoo begins with a deep freeze. In the winter of 1917, Dr. Henry Nehrling, a botanist from Milwaukee, Wisconsin, suffered a devastating loss at his Palm Cottage Gardens located in Gotha, Florida (20 miles west of Orlando) because of an exceptionally cold winter. Looking to find a frost-free climate, he purchased some agricultural acreage in Southwest Florida and began planting thousands of tropical plants. Many of his original plants can still be found on the grounds of Caribbean Gardens today.

Face to Face with a Florida Black Bear
Courtesy The Naples Zoo

The agile fosa from Madagascar Courtesy The Naples Zoo

Sadly, after Dr. Nehrling's death in 1929, his gardens went unattended for years, and many of his prime specimens were lost. Julius Fleischmann, heir to the Fleischmann's Yeast and Standard Brands fortune, discovered what was left of the gardens on his first visit to Naples in 1946. After purchasing the land, he began restoring the gardens in 1952. Two years later Caribbean Gardens, complete with parrot shows, was opened to the public.

In 1967 Col. Lawrence and Nancy Jane Tetzlaff, a colorful couple known in Cedar Point, Ohio, as Jungle Larry and Safari Jane, came to Naples in search of a warmer climate for their private collection of exotic animals. After Julius Fleischmann's death a year later, his heirs contacted the Tetzlaffs to see if they would lease Caribbean Gardens for their animals. The creative merger was renamed Naples Zoo at Caribbean Gardens, and on September 1, 1969, once again was opened to the public. For the next 33 years the zoo continued its mission, which is still exemplified by a 1970 quote by Jungle Larry, "Conservation is the name of the game."

In 2002, the Fleischmann estate decided to put the 43-acre park and 120 surrounding acres on the market. With Naples real estate hitting record highs, the asking price for the property was, at least for the Tetzlaffs, a prohibitive $67.5 million. The Tetzlaff family turned to the city of Naples and Collier County for help. After a public referendum to purchase the property passed with a record 73 percent voter approval, the county purchased all of the land. The Tetzlaffs remained in charge of the operation, and with Jungle Larry's passing in 1984, his two sons, David and Tim, along with a host of zookeepers and staff, keep the vision of the zoo alive and flourishing.

Today, the Naples Zoo is in the top 10 percent of the nation's zoos accredited by the prestigious Association of Zoos and Aquariums. Its grounds are home to many rare and fascinating animals. While the Naples Zoo has long been renowned for its extensive lemur collection (including brown, red-fronted, white-fronted, and ring-tailed), it also hosts the lemur's top predator, the fosa (Cryptoprocta ferox; aka fossa) of Madagascar. This cat-like animal looks like a strange cross between a miniature panther and a jaguarundi.

The zoo has an extensive snake and reptile exhibit, including many venomous snakes such as copperheads, cottonmouths, and canebrake, diamondback,

The giraffes recently arrived Courtesy The Naples Zoo

and Massasauga rattlesnakes. The big cats are represented by the endangered Malayan tigers, African leopards, lions, and ocelots. The recently installed glass observation areas allow you to stand toe to toe with many of these animals, including Florida black bears and pumas, and the experience of being a foot away from these impressive predators is unforgettable. Other exhibits include giraffes, several zebra species, Australian dingoes, hyenas, impalas, and the homely but intriguing red river hogs.

Admission to the Naples Zoo includes any number of daily shows and educational programs. These are aptly named "Planet Predator" (a show on the big cats), "Fangs & Fiction" (pythons and venomous snakes), "Meet the Keeper," and "Alligator Bay," among others. A free primate expedition cruise aboard a pontoon boat runs throughout the day, ferrying visitors to a number of islands where they can observe the lemurs, monkeys, and apes living on them.

The zoo has great outreach programs that extend all the way to Madagascar, where efforts are under way to protect the last remaining wild habitats of endangered lemurs and fosas. The daily event and primate cruise schedules are subject to change, so please check the website or call the zoo before visiting. There is a well-stocked gift shop, restaurant, and a shaded dining and picnic area. What began as a result of an unusual deep freeze near Orlando nearly 100 years ago is now a world-class zoological garden where Dr. Nehrling's botanical specimens are enjoyed by lemurs and gibbons, as well as thousands of hominoid families every year.

❒ ________ E. Conservancy of Southwest Florida

Location: 1450 Merrihue Drive, Naples, FL 34102 / Phone: 239-262-0304 / Wildlife Rehabilitation Center (to report injured wildlife): 239-262-2273 / Fax: 239-262-0672 / E-mail: info@conservancy.org / Website: www.conservancy.org / 21 acres / Admission fee charged.

On Saturday, April 11, 1964, a group of concerned people from all walks of life met on Keewaydin Island to discuss what they viewed as a forthcoming problem. A development group was looking to purchase 2,600 acres of environmentally sensitive land for a subdivision. A road was planned to cut through pristine Rookery Bay and the Henderson Creek region, cross Gordon Pass, and continue into the Ten Thousand Islands. As one of the founders of what was then called the Collier County Conservancy aptly put it, "Keep Naples the gateway to the Ten Thousand Islands, *not* the gateway to the 10,000 lots!"

Troy releasing a recovered sea turtle

Courtesy the Conservancy

Through the concerted efforts of people such as the first conservancy president, Charles Draper, members Nelson and Rachel Sanford, Lester Norris, and Joel Kuperberg, among many others, the monies were raised to cover the $20-per-acre cost, and all 2,600 acres were acquired before the deadline of March 31, 1968. From a single goal—the preservation of Rookery Bay and its surrounding estuaries—the Conservancy of Southwest Florida was born.

Sampling marsh life and doing field work for the Conservancy Courtesy the Conservancy

Times change. Over the ensuing 47 years the mission of the Conservancy of Southwest Florida evolved and broadened from a grassroots land-acquisition organization into one of the region's environmental leaders, protecting the area's water, land, wildlife, and future. It accomplishes this through the integrated efforts of four synergistic teams: environmental education; policy and advocacy; environmental science and research; and a wildlife clinic.

Although relentless growth and development has plagued much of Southwest Florida, the conservancy, through its environmental policy and advocacy team, has time and again been on the front lines of growth management, partnering with like-minded organizations, fighting for habitat protection, striving for better water quality, and at times, opposing developers who have a lack of concern for the long-term well-being of the environment. The Conservancy of Southwest Florida is not an "anti-growth" organization, however. Rather, it uses the influence of its 6,000-plus members to support policies that enhance quality of life, move development to less environmentally sensitive lands, and balance economic vitality with environmental protection.

The Conservancy of Southwest Florida follows a science-based approach to protect the future of the region for the next generation. Its environmental science and research initiatives include one of the longest-running sea turtle monitoring and protection programs in the nation, mangrove protection, western Everglades restoration, native species protection, water-quality programs, and wetlands protection.

Rebecca feeding a fawn at the Conservancy animal hospital Courtesy the Conservancy

The conservancy's wildlife rehabilitation clinic, located at its 21-acre Nature Center, treats more than 2,000 sick or injured animals a year, with more than half successfully returned to the wild.

The environmental education team provides outreach programs to students across several counties, offers award-winning summer camps, and manages the Nature Center and Discovery Center, where tens of thousands of visitors learn about the area's unique ecosystems and why it is important to protect the region for future generations.

The Nature Center's activities and programs, available throughout the year, include a guided electric boat cruise through the mangrove forests and down the Gordon River. These narrated tours open a window into a world of manatees, striped mullet, tarpon, mangrove crabs, and a menagerie of wading birds. More than 140 species of birds have been recorded along the conservancy's nature trails, designated as part of the Great Florida Birding Trail.

The Discovery Center offers interesting dioramas of the various habitats found across Southwest Florida, including live displays of reptiles, invasive species, and a hands-on 500-gallon touch tank where children and adults alike can roll up their sleeves to get the real "feel" of nature's treasures on and under the coastal sands. An interactive "Sounds of the Western Everglades" display allows visitors to learn to differentiate the call of the pig frog from the alligator and more. The spacious store

Children's camp on the electric boat cruise

Courtesy the Conservancy

has one of the area's largest collections of nature books and gifts, including nature-themed games, puzzles, toys, greeting cards, and artwork, most notably original photographs by renowned nature photographer Clyde Butcher.

At this writing, the Conservancy of Southwest Florida is in the midst of a $33 million campaign to raise funds for endowments, land acquisition, core program enhancements, and a $17 million renovation of the Nature Center. Plans include two new buildings—the von Arx Wildlife Rehabilitation Clinic and the Sugden Gomez Environmental Planning Center—and major renovations of the Dalton Discovery Center, the Eaton Conservation Hall, and the Ferguson Interactive Learning Lab. The renovations include moving the entrance from the present location off of 14th Avenue North to Smith Preserve Way, which will be located off Goodlette-Frank Road, a few hundred feet south of the entrance to the Naples Zoo and Caribbean Gardens.

The vision is to achieve Leadership in Energy and Environmental Design (LEED) certification for the Nature Center and its buildings. Initial plans call for the use of passive solar energy for natural lighting and hot water, geothermal heating and cooling, built-in cisterns for water retention and reuse, energy-saving LED lighting and smart-building technologies. The von Arx Wildlife Rehabilitation Center's energy will be sourced from solar panels, and the other buildings will be built as solar-ready for future solar energy applications.

A filter marsh, formerly a dead ditch that drained pollutants from nearby Coastland Mall, is now home to juvenile fish and wading birds, while reducing phosphorus and nitrogen levels flowing into the Gordon River. A second filter marsh, gopher tortoise preserve, and a sustainability courtyard will be added. The entire renovation is expected to be completed in late 2013. The Nature Center remains open to the public during all but the most disruptive renovations.

With its new Nature Center focusing on sustainable buildings and cohabitation with the natural world, the Conservancy of Southwest Florida serves as a shining example of where we all need to be moving toward if we really plan to make tomorrow a better world for not just us, but all living things.

❒ ____ F. Florida Panther National Wildlife Refuge

Location: 3860 Tollgate Blvd., Suite 300, Naples, FL 34114 / Phone: 239-353-8442 / Fax: 239-353-8640 / E-mail: floridapanther@fws.gov / Website: www.fws.gov/floridapanther / 26,400 acres / Admission is free.

Prime Panther Habitat © Charles Sobczak

Until 1989 the vast majority of the Florida Panther National Wildlife Refuge's 26,400 acres was used for private hunting and cattle grazing. Once owned by the Collier family, the property is part of the Big Cypress Basin. The Lee-Tidewater Cypress Company logged most of this area from 1944 to 1957, at about the same time the adjacent Fakahatchee Strand was being logged. By the time U.S. Fish and Wildlife acquired the land in 1989, all of the virgin stands of bald cypress were gone, but there were still expansive stands of slash pine, immature cypress domes, wet prairies, hardwood hammocks, and marshes.

Soon after acquisition, U.S. Fish and Wildlife biologists began a regimen of prescribed burns. Every year several different sites are burned on three- to four-year rotations. The objective of these 5,000- to 7,000-acre burns is twofold: primarily to increase browsing areas for white-tailed deer, which, along with feral hogs, are the primary prey of Florida panthers; second, to rid the forest understory of invasive plants such as Brazilian pepper, melaleuca, cogongrass, and Old World climbing fern.

It is important to understand that the Panther Refuge is not designed with the eco-tourist in mind. This is a true refuge, for not only the endangered panther, but also a host of other wildlife that struggle beneath Florida's unending growth and urban sprawl. These include the threatened indigo snake, wood stork, limpkin, swallowtail kite, snail kite, Big Cypress fox squirrel, Florida black bear, and the very rare Everglades mink. Therefore, access is limited to two short hiking trails located approximately one-quarter mile north of I-75 along the southeastern edge of the refuge.

A Florida Panther
© Dick Fortune & Sara Lopez

A sign directs visitors into the parking lot where two gates lead to the trails. The shorter trail (0.3 mile) is improved and wheelchair accessible. The second trail is 1.3 miles long and takes you through a nice mixture of habitats. After a brief stroll through a

The trails are well maintained © Charles Sobczak

hardwood hammock, you find yourself walking on limestone bedrock beside saw palmetto and vast, open stands of slash pine. The highway noise coming from I-75 is a distraction, but this is probably why this region was chosen for the trails in the first place.

The nearby I-75 underpass, connecting the Florida Panther Refuge to the Fakahatchee Strand to the south, is one of the most frequently used underpasses by panthers. They are definitely around, but only five to 11 radio-collared panthers use the property every month, and given the refuge's immense size, you are not likely to see one during your 30-minute hike. If you are lucky, you might find a panther track left in the mud beside the numerous deer tracks you will see.

Though you probably will not glimpse a panther, you may well see wild turkeys, swallow-tailed kites, northern parula warblers, eastern diamondback rattlesnakes, and white-tailed deer along the trail. A total of 126 bird species, 46 reptile and amphibian species, 22 mammal species, dozens of fish species, and more than 700 plant species inhabit the preserve. The drainage ditches found on either side of State Highway 29 on the eastern border of the refuge abound with wading birds, alligators, and freshwater fish.

The drive along Highway 29, heading north from I-75, is an example of how far Floridians are willing to go to protect panthers. A 12-foot-high security fence straddles both sides of this roadway, which is considered the world's deadliest stretch of highway for Florida panthers. Expensive underpasses allow the animals to cross safely between the refuge and Big Cypress National Preserve to the east and Fakahatchee to the south.

The optimum time to visit the Panther Refuge is during the winter (insect spray is recommended at any time of the year). An excellent 20-page brochure about the refuge is available on its website (http://www.fws.gov/floridapanther/). Although you can traverse only a tiny section of this sanctuary, it is a hike you will never forget.

❒ ________ G. Picayune Strand State Preserve

Location: 2121 52nd Avenue SE, Naples, FL 34117 / Phone: 239-348-7557 / Fax: n/a / E-mail: ihleg@doacs.state.fl.us / Website: www.fl-dof.com/state_forest/picayune_strand / 76,000+ acres / Admission is free, fees charged for overnight camping.

Janes Memorial Drive entrance to the Picayune Strand
© Charles Sobczak

Driving down Everglades Blvd. in the very heart of the Picayune Strand is a bit like being in a chapter of *The World Without Us,* Alan Weisman's book on what the planet would be like if humans suddenly disappeared. There are no homes, no gas stations, no telephone poles, or any sign of civilization except for empty roads that appear to take you nowhere. Once called Southern Golden Gates Estates, this undeveloped subdivision, along with the adjacent Belle Meade subdivision to the west, were once destined to be the two largest developments in all of Florida.

They were the brainchild of Jack and Leonard Rosen, the brothers who purchased the land from the Lee-Tidewater Cypress Company after it had logged off all of the virgin cypress timber in the late 1950s. The Rosens' Gulf American Land Corporation is considered by many to have originated the "swampland in Florida" sales scheme, selling 1.25-acre parcels to unsuspecting investors up north. Unbeknownst to these buyers, during the rainy season most of these two subdivisions were underwater. Gulf American built 227 miles of road and dug 83 miles of drainage ditches here before the state of Florida shut down the entire operation because of fraudulent and misleading sales practices.

In 1985 Florida began an ambitious plan to buy back all the individually owned parcels, numbering 17,000, and reclaim the 85 square miles of developed land included in the Picayune Strand. Most of the lot owners received only pennies on the dollar for their worthless investments, but by 1998 the majority of the land was owned by the state. The state has begun ripping up roads and filling in canals, but the entire project to restore the land to a more natural state is expected to take decades to complete.

The Picayune Strand State Forest totals more than 78,615 acres (118 square miles). To the east lies the Fakahatchee Strand and beyond that the enormous Big Cypress National Preserve. Together with Everglades National Park and the Florida Panther National Wildlife Refuge, along with tens of thousands of acres of private land, this vast region forms the backbone for the survival of the Florida panther, the only remnant population of wild pumas left in the eastern U.S. The area has a large deer and wild hog population, making it prime panther habitat.

Other wildlife sightings might include the elusive red-cockaded woodpecker, black bear, bald eagles, wood storks, and Big Cypress fox squirrels. The preserve has two primary trails for recreational use, both located in the western Belle Meade tract. The longer trail, 22 miles in length, is part of Florida's State Forest Trailtrotter Program, which is designed to get visitors out on horseback to enjoy the state forests and preserves. It includes an equestrian camping area and 10 paddocks. The other trail, known as the Sabal Palm hiking trail, is 3.2 miles long and wanders through a forest of cypress trees that were left uncut in the 1950s. This short trail provides a glimpse into what the original forest must have once looked like. Be advised that the trail can be very wet during the rainy season. Visitors can also wander down some of the empty roadbeds in search of wading birds and other wildlife. These are not marked hiking trails, however, so care should be taken not to get lost in this maze of endless deserted streets.

One of the many canals to be filled in the Picayune

© Charles Sobczak

Over time the Picayune Strand will regain its former glory. As part of the Big Cypress drainage basin, its roads and canals will eventually disappear, and the gigantic sheet flows that once covered the land will return. This ambitious restoration project is part of the federal Comprehensive Everglades Restoration Project (CERP). More information about the strand and its future restoration can be found at www. evergladesfoundation.org.

❒ ________ H. Naples Botanical Garden

Location: 4820 Bayshore Drive, Naples, FL 34112 / Phone: 239-643-7275 / Toll-free: 877-433-1874 / Fax: 239-649-7306 / E-mail: info@naplesgarden.org / Website: www.naplesgarden.org / 170 acres / Admission fee charged.

The Naples Botanical Garden is the newest eco-destination in *The Living Gulf Coast.* Fifteen years of careful planning culminated on November 14, 2009, when this beautifully designed garden first opened its doors to the plant-loving public. The 80-acre botanical garden is now the second largest in the state, behind the 83-acre Fairchild Tropical Botanic Garden in Coral Gables. (The Naples Botanical Garden property actually encompasses 170 acres, but more than half has been set aside as a nature preserve.) By contrast, Marie Selby Botanical Gardens

The treehouse and waterfall at the Children's Garden Courtesy Naples Botanical Garden

in Sarasota has recently expanded to 13 acres.

When completed, the Naples Botanical Garden will consist of six distinct gardens situated between the two 26th degrees of latitude, both north and south of the equator; hence the subtitle: Gardens with Latitude. Within this band of the planet lie some of the richest and most diverse rainforests and plant life on earth.

The first of the Naples Botanical Gardens' six sections is the Children's Garden, a celebration of Florida, with half serving as an exploration of native habitats and the other half demonstrating the important agricultural heritage of the state. Here children can lose themselves in a natural wonderland of flowers, vegetables, a butterfly house, a water fountain that the young visitors can play in, tree houses, and a babbling stream.

Next is the Hidden Garden, where flowers sprout from shoes, purses, sinks, and even an old, clogged toilet. A walkway winds down a sloping hillside through various Florida ecosystems, from a tropical hardwood hammock to red mangrove forest. Because the trees and plants—from bald cypress to leather fern—are all identified with easy-to-read placards, this is a great place to get a quick overview of the state's diverse native species.

The Brazilian Garden is an amazing collection of the plants and trees of that country. It is designed by Raymond Jungles, a student and friend of world-renowned landscape architect Roberto Burle Marx, in whose honor he created this space. A large ceramic mural designed by Marx is the centerpiece of the garden. It overlooks a series of cascading waterfalls amidst a shallow pool filled with a number of species of blooming water lilies. Countless specimen trees and plants taken from the Brazilian rainforest, one of the most biodiverse environments on earth, make this a fascinating and striking section of the Naples Botanical Gardens.

The Caribbean Garden is a colorful array of plants from the diverse landscapes of the Caribbean islands. These range from the many cactus and shrub species found on some of the arid Caribbean islands to the lush, flowering plants that thrive along the mountaintop rainforests of Hispaniola and Jamaica. This section includes a plantation garden, citrus garden, and coconut grove, all containing plants that indicate the important economic value of Caribbean vegetation. The Caribbean Garden is highlighted by a replica turquoise chattel house set among fields of pineapples.

Spending a lovely day at the Naples Botanical Gardens Courtesy Naples Botanical Gardens

The Florida Garden focuses on native plantings and helps people determine which plants and trees are best suited for the local environment; the central focus here is the Great Circle, a circular planting of sabal palms, surrounded by silver palmettos and underplanted with purple bougainvillea and swaths of Florida's most beautiful native grasses and wild flowers.

The Asian Garden displays that region's plant and tree species, including some of the more important food and timber crops, such as bamboo and fruiting trees from Thailand, Bali, Java, and Vietnam. Finally, in the heart of the Naples Botanical Garden is the Water Garden, hosting a variety of stunning aquatics such as papyrus and lotus flowers.

If you want to explore natural habitats, a well-kept walking trail whisks you off into the 90-acre nature sanctuary where you can discover towering Florida slash pines, cypress trees, unspoiled marshes, and hundreds of species of animals. More than 50 threatened gopher tortoises make their home in the preserve, and more than 130 species of birds have already been identified here. The removal of thousands of invasive melaleuca and Brazilian pepper trees, along with the replanting of native grasses, sedges, rushes, and ferns, have helped to make this expansive preserve come back to life. A visit to the birding tower is a highlight of the nature walk.

Although many of the trees are still young and the Naples Botanical Garden is in its infancy, it is well worth a visit. From a humble beginning as a dream of eight Naples residents in 1993, the Naples Botanical Garden already has much to offer. This nonprofit group has invested more than $30 million into the project, including a $10 million donation by one family alone. The gardens also open their facility to weddings, luncheons, seminars, and corporate events. Although two major frosts during the winter of 2010 impeded the tropical growth for a short time, the Naples Botanical Garden will assuredly take root and flower into a beautiful place for all Floridians and visitors to enjoy.

Laughing Gulls

❒ ____ I. Rookery Bay National Estuarine Research Reserve

Location: 300 Tower Road, Naples, FL 34113 / Phone: 239-417-6310 / Fax: 239-417-6315 / E-mail: info@rookerybay.org / Website: www.rookerybay.org / 110,000 acres / Admission fee charged.

Aerial of Rookery Bay near the canoe/kayak launch

© Katie Laakkonen

The establishment of Rookery Bay National Estuarine Preserve dates back to the mid-1960s when the Collier County Conservancy, now the Conservancy of Southwest Florida, was formed. This 110,000-acre aquatic preserve became its own entity in 1978, and in 2003 was expanded to its current size. The Rookery Bay preserve is unusual in that the majority (70,000 acres) is water, while the remaining acreage consists of mangroves, marshes, and upland habitats.

Rookery Bay itself, along with the Ten Thousand Islands, is one of Florida's most pristine estuarine environments. These estuaries are identified as shallow mixing grounds where the freshwater flowing down from the Big Cypress Preserve and the Everglades National Park meets the saltwater of the Gulf of Mexico. The average depth of the entire preserve is only one meter. This ever-changing dynamic of brackish water, coupled with the constant nutrient loading produced by the red, black, and white mangrove detritus, is considered one of the richest ecosystems on earth, rivaled only by coral reefs and tropical rainforests. The estuaries in and around Rookery Bay are home to scores of fish species. The area is considered by many to be the world's best juvenile habitat for the endangered goliath grouper, as well as juvenile nurse, bonnethead, and bull sharks.

Any visit to Rookery Bay should begin with a trip to the learning center, located on Tower Road just south of U.S. 41 on County Road 951. Completed in 2004, this 16,500-square-foot facility is the ideal place to get a better understanding of the size of the preserve, as well as the research that is being conducted there. Exhibits

One of many fine displays at Rookery Bay
© Charles Sobczak

include a 2,300-gallon aquarium teeming with a variety of fish species found within the preserve. A short film displays the natural beauty of the region and shows research biologists at work in the backwaters. There are displays on the effects of global warming and the history of the estuary dating back to the Calusa Indians, as well as some interactive exhibits. While at the learning center be sure to take a journey over the Henderson Creek pedestrian bridge, leading to a half-mile nature walk through pine flatwoods. The view overlooking the tidal Henderson Creek is amazing. Look for striped mullet, snook, tarpon, and manatees, all of which frequent this stretch of the creek.

Of course, the best way to see a preserve that is mostly water is to get out on Rookery Bay itself. A number of guided kayak tours are offered during the winter months, and a sandy boat ramp is located just a few miles south of the learning center off of Shell Island Road. From there you can reach the well-marked Shell Point Canoe Trail, which takes you through a water maze of mangrove tunnels, mudflats, oyster beds, and rookery islands inhabited by ibis, pelicans, and other species. Don't forget to bring a pair of polarized sunglasses, allowing you to see beneath the glare and into the tidal flats and oyster bars beneath you. The world just below the surface is alive with pastures of manatee, shoal, and turtle grasses. Blue crabs and bottom-feeding horseshoe crabs search for food, while passing shoals of minnows dance across the surface.

Be on the lookout for mangrove tree crabs, hermit and stone crabs, as well as the dozens of bird species that nest and live in the surrounding red mangrove forest. These might include the elusive mangrove cuckoo, anhinga, belted kingfisher, magnificent frigatebird, osprey, roseate spoonbill, and the yellow-crowned night heron. Mammals also enjoy the estuarine environment. The most commonly seen are bottle-nosed dolphins, manatees, and the ever-present raccoons that scour the tangled mangrove forest in search of coon oysters, bird eggs, and crabs. Fishing is allowed throughout the entire preserve, but remember, anglers must comply with all local, state, and federal laws.

Another boaters-only access point within the preserve is Keewaydin Island. Stretching for eight miles along the coastline, this barrier island has long been a popular destination for boaters. Today, more than 85 percent of the 1,300-acre island is preserved. State and federal grants have allowed the removal of much of the non-native Australian pine, Brazilian pepper, and melaleuca trees. The island has a small primitive camping area, but most people simply anchor up their boats, wade ashore, and enjoy Florida the way it was 1,000 years ago.

Rookery Bay has partnerships with several important groups such as the Gulf of Mexico Alliance, Greenscape Alliance, and various universities. Student programs encouraging better stewardship and appreciation of marine estuaries are offered throughout the year for middle and high schools. With its state-of-the-art interpretive center and nature and canoe trails, Rookery Bay is an ideal place for naturalists who don't mind getting their feet wet.

❒ ________ J. Collier-Seminole State Park

Location: 20200 E. Tamiami Trail, Naples, FL 34114 / Phone: 239-394-3397 / Reservations: 800-326-3521 / Fax: n/a / E-mail: n/a / Website: www. floridstateparks/collierseminole / 6,430 acres / Admission fee charged.

Located along the western fringe of the Ten Thousand Islands, Collier-Seminole State Park is a stepping stone into the labyrinth of one of the largest remaining mangrove forests in the world. The real wilderness here is discovered by kayak, canoe, or small powerboat with an excursion down Blackwater River. A 13.6-mile canoe and kayak trail takes you through the park to Mud Bay and out to the edge of the Gulf of Mexico. The park has a large square boat basin complete with a ramp from which you can launch small to medium-size watercraft.

J. Collier-Seminole State Park Courtesy Florida State Parks

Unlike most Florida rivers, Blackwater shows barely a sign of human habitation. Other than a primitive campsite for the more adventurous, located nine miles from the boat basin, and aside from fellow canoeists and an occasional fisherman casting from a flats boat out of nearby Goodland, all you will see along the river are countless fiddler crabs, ibis, and night herons and miles upon miles of red, black, and white mangrove forest. Sightings of black bear, Big Cypress fox squirrel, and the rare red-cockaded woodpecker occur near the nature trails.

Camping at Collier-Seminole State Park Courtesy Collier County VC Bureau

One of the most fascinating things to do in Collier-Seminole is to get out of your canoe and wade in the endless grass flats found in the expansive estuary at the mouth of the Blackwater River. The water is clear and the sea grasses largely untouched from the way they were when the Seminole Indians retreated into this region 150 years ago. Here you can find immature blue crab, foot-long nurse sharks, schools of striped mullet, and a variety of living shellfish. The fishing is excellent, with catches including snook, redfish, mullet, and juvenile tarpon.

The park encompasses 7,271 acres. The entrance is located 17 miles from Naples and approximately 10 miles from Marco Island. It was originally a county park established in 1923 as a gift from pioneer county developer Barron Collier, then donated to the state of Florida in 1947. Its primary purpose was to preserve one of only three stands of native Florida royal palms found in the state. Originally believed to be a separate species, the Florida royal palm is now known to be a subspecies of the Cuban royal palm and has been reclassified as such. These trees are located along the 6.5-mile hiking trail that takes you through pine flatwoods and cypress swamps. There is also a .9-mile self-guided tour featuring a boardwalk and observation platform overlooking a salt marsh. Additional exhibits of native plants and animals may be seen in the park's interpretive center. Bicycling in the park is difficult, but there is an interesting ride along the historic San-Marco Road (County Road 92) leading to the small fishing village of Goodland.

A 120-unit campsite in the park accommodates everything from tents to motor homes. During the winter months park rangers host campfire circles and offer slide shows about various topics, including black bears, Seminole history, and the construction of the Tamiami Trail in the 1920s. In fact, the world's last remaining walking dredge, used in the construction of U.S. 41 across the Everglades, is now a National Historic Mechanical Engineering Landmark displayed near the park entrance.

Bear in mind that because of all the similar-looking terrain, it is extremely easy to get lost in the Ten Thousand Islands, so visitors need to take care not to wander too far from the navigational markers located along the Blackwater River; a handheld GPS device is a good idea. Tidal flow can also be quite dramatic in the park, and paddling back to the boat basin against a flowing tide can be very strenuous. Swimming near the headwaters of the river is not recommended because of the numerous alligators found there.

Mosquitoes are also a concern for anyone visiting Collier-Seminole State Park during the wetter summer months. Head-netting and ample bug spray may be well advised. Staying away from the mangrove edges while traveling down the Blackwater River also seems to help.

The International Union for the Conservation of Nature and Natural Resources (IUCN) has listed Collier-Seminole State Park as a designated wilderness area. Paddling along the pristine Blackwater River, you will find miles upon miles of untouched mangrove islands and oyster bars—a true wilderness experience located mere miles from civilization.

❐ ______ K. Tigertail Beach, Marco Island

Location: 490 Hernando Drive, Marco Island, FL 34145 / Phone: 239-389-8414 / Fax: n/a / E-mail: moreinfo@cyberisle.com / Website: www.marco-island-florida.com / 79 acres / Admission fee charged.

A decade ago the lagoon that stretches more than a mile along the northwest corner of Marco Island was bordered by a large sandbar. Today, that sandbar is called Sand Dollar Island and is an excellent example of the dynamic nature of Florida's barrier islands. With its emergence from the sea and its low, brushy vegetation, this newly born island has quickly become a favorite nesting site for black skimmers, least terns, and other shorebirds looking for solitude amidst the towering high-rise condominiums that lie less than a mile south of Tigertail Beach.

A family wades across the bayou towards the beach

© Charles Sobczak

With 210 parking spaces, a restaurant, bathhouse, beach concession, volleyball court, playground, restrooms, and picnic areas, you might think that the birds would avoid this crowded retreat. The good news is that the birds have learned to live with the hustle and bustle of this busy stretch of sand. In fact, according to the literature found in the Great Florida Birding Trail series, Tigertail

Beach is "one of the best all-around birding spots in southwest Florida."

Sightings along the beach include Wilson's, piping and snowy plovers; black skimmers; Forster's, sandwich, and least terns; red knots, peregrine falcons, bald eagles, and a myriad of wading birds such as reddish egrets, great egrets, and great blue herons. While the beach is the main attraction for the wintering tourists, the real birding lies along either shoreline of the expansive saltwater lagoon. Here, during certain times of the year, tens of thousands of fiddler crabs dance along the edge of the exposed mudflats, feeding on the detritus and nutrients found there. Mangrove crabs, sea lice, and hundreds of king's crown shellfish work the same tidal flats.

Aerial of Tigertail Beach © Katie Laakkonen

The shallow lagoon abounds with striped mullet, mojarra, pinfish, and schools of various minnow species that include the fry of seatrout, snook, and redfish. Larger, predatory adults enter the lagoon to feed during periods of high tide. A short walk down either edge of the lagoon will reveal a wealth of sea life and shorebirds, though care should be taken not to disturb nesting birds.

Tens of thousands of fiddler crabs live on the edge of the bayou © Charles Sobczak

There is a small parking fee at Tigertail, and the beach closes every evening at sunset. For the dedicated birder, Tigertail Beach is a true oasis of nature in the otherwise, heavily urbanized landscape of Marco Island. For the general nature lover, the beach itself is nothing short of spectacular, and the paddleboats, blue and white cabanas, and amenities make it just another perfect day in paradise.

❒ ________ L. Ten Thousand Islands National Wildlife Refuge

Location: 3860 Tollgate Blvd., Suite 300, Naples, FL 34114 / Phone: 239-353-8442 / Fax: 239-353-8640 / E-mail: floridapanther@fws.gov / Website: www.fws.gov/floridapanther/TenThousandIsland / 35,000 acres / Admission is free.

Mangrove Isle at Dusk © Judd Patterson, JuddPatterson.com

While Ten Thousand Islands National Wildlife Refuge encompasses more than 35,000 acres, most of that acreage is either saltwater or uninhabitable and untraversable mangrove forest. This immense refuge is part of the largest unbroken mangrove forest in North America, bordered to the west by the 110,000-acre Rookery Bay and to the east by the 1.5-million-acre Everglades National Park. This forest is predominantly red mangroves, or "the walking trees" as they are sometimes called, but also has black, white, and buttonwood mangroves. All of these trees have the capacity to flourish in brackish or saltwater environments.

The best way to see this watery expanse of mangrove forest is by canoe or kayak. Primitive camping is allowed on Panther Key and Round Key but not on any of the other beaches and keys found along the southern fringe of the refuge. There are multiple accesses to this maze of tidal creeks, mangrove islands, and

Well marked canoe trails
© Charles Sobczak

islets: via the boat launch at Goodland, the nearby Collier-Seminole State Park, the Port of the Islands Marina located at the top end of the long, straight manmade Faka Union Canal, Everglades City, and several stops along U.S. 41.

The only way to see any of the refuge on foot is via the Marsh Trail, which lies approximately 2½ miles east of where County Road 92 (aka San Marco Road) enters U.S. 41 from the south. A round-trip hike on this trail is 2.2 miles. Roughly three-tenths of a mile from the spacious parking lot is an observation tower that overlooks this grand expanse of tiny mangrove islets and brackish waters. Look for schools of finger mullet dancing across the surface, wading birds such as little green herons, tri-colored herons, and great egrets. Alligators can also be spotted along the way, as can raptors such as osprey, bald eagles, and red-shouldered hawks. The trail itself is an abandoned oil-well road and is high and dry even during the summer rainy season. It is also an excellent biking trail. There are four marked canoe trails in the immediate region. A small canoe/kayak launch is located just off the parking area.

Hiking the short Marsh Trail, then continuing east roughly five miles and hiking the Big Cypress Bend boardwalk into the Fakahatchee Strand State Preserve provides an interesting study in contrasting ecosystems. The mangroves of the Ten Thousand Islands rarely reach 35 feet in height, while the ancient bald cypress in the Fakahatchee top 100 feet and tower over the boardwalk. The Marsh Trail is open and the views endless, while the Big Cypress Bend boardwalk cuts through a dense swamp of pond apple, strangler fig, and bald cypress trees. Seeing the difference back to back is a great way to spend a sunlit morning.

If you plan to head into some of the tidal rivers in this area, it's a good idea to carry a reliable hand-held GPS for navigation, as well as plenty of fresh water, insect spray, and rain gear. After a while every mangrove island and mangrove-covered point looks exactly the same as the last one, and finding your way out might turn out to be a lot harder than finding your way in, even for experienced paddlers.

If you come prepared, however, you will find a treasure of wildlife in the mangrove forests of the Ten Thousand Islands National Wildlife Refuge. More than 200 species of fish and 189 species of birds live here. During the summer, as many as 10,000 wading birds roost on a small island in Pumpkin Bay. The only hunting allowed is for duck and coot at designated sites and times, so conflict with nature lovers is kept at a minimum. Other sightings might include alligators, American crocodiles, manatee, and bottle-nosed dolphin. So grab your binoculars and your camera and start paddling: there are 10,000 islands left to explore.

Cypress Fogbow

❐ ________ M. Big Cypress National Preserve

Location: Oasis Visitor Center, 33100 Tamiami Trail East, Ochopee, FL 34141 / Phone: 239-695-1201 / Fax: 239-695-3901 / E-mail: on Website / Website: www.nps.gov/bicy / 729,000 acres / Admission is free, camping and access fees are charged.

To understand the sheer size of Big Cypress National Preserve—729,000 acres, or 1,139 square miles—you first have to appreciate the immense size of Collier County itself. With a total of 2,305 square miles, Collier County is larger than Rhode Island (1,545 square miles) and almost as large as Delaware (2,489 square miles).

Big Cypress National Preserve was created in 1974 as one of the first two preserves in the U.S. National Park System. It was originally slated to be a part of Everglades National Park in 1947 but too much of the land was held privately at that time to do so. Over the ensuing 27 years, the government purchased most of that land, and Big Cypress was born.

Big Cypress Swamp © Katie Laakkonen

The preserve is primarily in Collier County, with small portions located in Miami-Dade and Monroe counties. Bordered to the west by Fakahatchee Strand, to the north by the Big Cypress Indian Reservation, and to the south by Everglades National Park, Big Cypress and its neighboring parks and preserves have become the prime remaining habitat for the endangered Florida panther. Other large animals that reside here include the Florida black bear, white-tailed deer, wild hogs, alligators, and, unfortunately, the invasive Burmese python.

Big Cypress has numerous campgrounds, miles of hiking trails, and an estimated 400 miles of official off-road vehicle trails. Any visit to the preserve should start

Alligators abound in the Oasis Center Slough © Charles Sobczak

with a stop at either the Big Cypress Swamp Welcome Center (opened in spring 2010) on the western edge or the Oasis Visitor Center near the eastern edge of the preserve on U.S. 41 (Tamiami Trail). The Oasis facility has a short boardwalk overlooking a freshwater slough that is teeming with alligators, gar, bream, and exotic fish such as tilapia, peacock bass, and oscar. The welcome center has a similar short boardwalk where manatees often congregate during the cooler winter months.

Kayaking or canoeing on the Turner River Canoe Trail is a popular adventure, as is the shorter Halfway Creek Canoe Trail located along Seagrape Drive near the very western edge of the park on U.S. 41. If you prefer to stay dry and on land, try the Turner River/Upper Wagonwheel/Birdon Road Loop Drive. This 16.4-mile drive takes you off the heavily traveled Tamiami Trail through some of the more remote backcountry. Flora sightings along the way include pond and bald cypress trees, coastal plain willows, wild orchids, a wide array of bromeliads, and yellow tickseed. Birds are plentiful along the drainage canals and numerous swamps and marshes, and could include wood storks, snail kites, herons, purple gallinules, and egrets. Alligators, turtles, and snakes, including the venomous eastern diamondback and water moccasin, thrive throughout Big Cypress, so care should be taken whenever you wade into the marshes or swamps in pursuit of the elusive ghost orchid.

Another popular tour is the scenic loop drive (County Road 94) that exits U.S. 41 at Monroe Station and rejoins the highway at the Forty-mile Bend. The 23-mile drive takes you through swamps, hammocks, pinelands, and prairies. Halfway down that road is the start of the Florida National Scenic Trail, a 1,400-mile footpath running from Big Cypress to the Gulf Islands National Seashore in the far western Florida Panhandle. Approximately 45.4 miles of this trail runs through Big Cypress. The first leg, starting from County Road 94 and continuing up to U.S. 41, is approximately 8.3 miles long and can be easily hiked in one day. The trail continues north into the backcountry of the preserve. The length of this section requires overnight backpacking and camping, and should not be attempted by inexperienced hikers.

Many short and readily accessible trails are located throughout the preserve. The 2.5-mile Fire Prairie Trail is in the northwest corner of the preserve on County Road 839. The Kirby Storter Roadside Park is 14.1 miles east of U.S. 29 and offers a half-mile boardwalk into a variety of habitats, ending in a swamp where alligators and snakes are readily observed. This short boardwalk offers an easy way to enjoy the vegetation and wildlife found in Big Cypress without getting your feet wet.

The preserve offers numerous ranger-led activities throughout the winter months. These range from swamp stomps to kayak outings to bicycle rides. Consult the preserve's website (http:// www.nps.gov/bicy/index.htm) prior to visiting to see if any of these guided adventures can fit into your schedule.

During the wetter summer season many of the preserve's campgrounds shut down; the Midway campground near the Oasis Visitor Center is among the few that remain open all year. Mosquitoes and thunderstorms make Big Cypress more difficult to experience in the summer months, though shorter morning excursions are still enjoyable.

With its immense size and wide assortment of habitats and wildlife, Big Cypress National Preserve offers a window into the nature of the Everglades and the cypress ecosystems. It is a definite addition to any naturalist's life list of great places visited.

☐ _____ N. Fakahatchee Strand Preserve State Park

Location: 137 Coastline Drive, Copeland, FL 34137 / Phone: 239-695-4593 / Canoe trip and swamp walk reservations: 239-695-1023 / Fax: n/a / E-mail: islandgirlm@msn.com / Website: www.floridastateparks.org/fakahatcheestrand / 85,000 acres / Admission is free, fees charges for guided swamp walks and canoe trips.

The lamentable history of Fakahatchee Strand Preserve dates back to 1913 when the Lee-Tidewater Cypress Company purchased the land for $1.4 million with the sole intention of logging off all of the virgin stands of ancient bald cypress. Before that could be accomplished, the company needed to dig drainage ditches and canals to remove standing water. Those plans were delayed initially because of World War I, then the collapse of the 1920s land boom, and once again because of World War II. Major logging of the strand did not get under way until 1947. When the company finally closed its logging operations 10 years later, more than 1 million board-feet of cypress were taken out every year. In the end, 36,000 railcar loads of cypress came out of the Fakahatchee Strand.

In 1966 Lee-Tidewater sold 75,000 acres of the logged-off strand to brothers Leonard and Julius "Jack" Rosen, founders of the Gulf American Land Corporation.

Ghost Orchids © R J Wiley

Already wealthy from the successful development of Cape Coral in Lee County, they set their sights on selling off this new subdivision called Golden Gate Estates. Their high-pressure sales techniques included slick, colorful brochures, free steak dinners, and even "free" trips to Florida for prospective purchasers. Home sites were actually given away on television shows such as *The Price is Right.* Salesmen often failed to mention, however, that many of the lots would be completely underwater during the wet, summer months.

In 1967 the state of Florida charged the Gulf American Land Corporation with using false, misleading, deceptive, and other unfair practices to sell the land. The developers pleaded guilty to the charges and filed for bankruptcy soon after. In the end, much of the company's land was forfeited to the state. By this time, the Fakahatchee Strand was a green nightmare of dense understory, deserted logging roads, and sinkholes. But even then, in the late 1960s, the region was known for harboring one of the rarest flowering plants on earth, the ghost orchid.

In 1972 Florida passed the Land Conservation Act, which led in 1974 to the purchase of tracts abutting the forfeited Gulf American holdings. Today, the Fakahatchee Strand State Preserve encompasses nearly 70,000 acres. There remain close to 17,000 additional acres to secure. While it may take 200 years or more

Fakahatchee Strand swamp walk © Collier County VC Bureau

Janes Scenic Highway speed bump © Charles Sobczak

for the majestic bald cypress trees once again to tower above the scrub, the strand will hopefully recover from the double threat of logging and development.

Because it is a preserve, the Fakahatchee does not offer the same kinds of amenities found in nearby Collier-Seminole State Park. There are no campgrounds or interpretive centers; the only amenities are two Porta-Potty units situated at the beginning of the Big Cypress Bend Boardwalk on U.S. 41.

That 1.2-mile boardwalk and the 11-mile Janes Scenic Drive are the two main access points in the preserve. The boardwalk takes you back into a tiny slice of the original cypress forest that was miraculously spared from logging. These ancient bald cypress trees are three feet in diameter. Their canopies are often covered in bromeliads and their trunks wrapped by aspiring strangler figs. Other trees include the stately royal palm, sabal palm, pop ash, and pond apple. In the freshwater marshes along the boardwalk you can find pickerelweed and alligator flag. At the end of the boardwalk lies a beautiful pond where you will often find alligators, sometimes including females and their broods. Be on the lookout for bald eagles, pileated woodpeckers, barred owls, Florida banded watersnakes, and water moccasins.

To access the Janes Scenic Drive, travel north on State Highway 29 and turn into the small village of Copeland. Turning sharply north, you are soon driving on the unpaved Janes Scenic Drive, 11 miles of pothole-laced roadway that ends in an even more unlikely preserve called the Picayune Strand. Take care not to hit basking alligators along the way, as they serve as unwanted speed bumps during the heat of the midday sun. The wet, dark forests along the drive are where people such as photographer Clyde Butcher and resident park biologist Mike Owen go for swamp stomps. Sometimes up to their chests in swamp water, they traverse this inhospitable world in search of wild orchids, air plants, and exotic ferns.

While the Fakahatchee Strand State Preserve is certainly not for everyone, it is an amazing window into Florida's tarnished real estate history. The boardwalk at Big Cypress Bend, located next to an Indian village seven miles east of State Highway 29, is accessible to all, but beyond that, a swamp walk or any other venture into this watery wilderness should be undertaken only with an experienced ranger or guide. Tours can be arranged through the park or by visiting the Friends of the Fakahatchee website (www. friendsoffakahatchee.org).

❐ ____ O. Everglades National Park — Gulf Coast Visitor Center

Location: 815 Oysterbar Lane, Everglades City, FL 34139 / Phone: 239-695-3311 / Camping reservations: 877-444-6777 / Fax: 305-242-7711 / E-mail: on Website / Website: www.nps.gov/ever / 1.5 million acres / Admission fees charged for camping etc., though admission is free to the Gulf Coast Visitor Center.

The Visitor's Center in Everglades City

© Charles Sobczak

Considered the gateway to the Ten Thousand Islands, the Gulf Coast Visitor Center is a charming outpost on the western edge of Everglades National Park. Established in 1934, Everglades National Park, encompassing 1.5 million acres, is the third largest park in the United States, exceeded only by Death Valley (3.36 million acres) and Yellowstone (2.22 million acres). It has been declared an International Biosphere Reserve, a World Heritage Site, and a Wetland of International Importance.

There are no hiking trails located in the vicinity of the Gulf Coast Visitor Center except those accessible by watercraft. Outdoor recreational activity in this area is focused on the surrounding waterways, including freshwater rivers, brackish estuaries, and the Gulf of Mexico. The western end of the Wilderness Waterway Trail is here. The trail itself runs 99 miles to Flamingo Station on the eastern edge of the Everglades and can take more than a week for the average canoeist or kayaker to complete. Because of the bewildering maze-like nature of the mangrove forest and the Ten Thousand Islands, this journey is not recommended for novice paddlers. It is easy to get lost in the backwaters of the Everglades, and mosquitoes, a lack of freshwater, and a host of other challenges can turn an ill-planned adventure into a potential nightmare.

Plenty of shorter paddling trips are recommended for the less adventurous visitors, including a paddle up the Turner River, through Halfway Creek, the East River Canoe Route, or a journey to and from nearby Sandfly Island. The Sandfly Island trip takes approximately 2.5 hours and can be combined with a one-hour hiking trail on Sandfly Island. The only concern a paddler might have on this trip is traversing the open waters of Chokoloskee Bay, which can be rough during winter cold fronts and summer thunderstorms. Canoes and kayaks are available for rent at the Gulf Coast Visitor Center.

The Manatee II does near shore tours © Charles Sobczak

One popular way to see the area is a guided tour aboard one of several boats operating as independent concessionaires out of the visitor center. On the Mangrove Wilderness Tour visitors spend just under two hours on a 24-foot Carolina Skiff, heading deep into the mangroves where they might see alligators, American crocodiles, mangrove and fiddler crabs, eagles, osprey, ibis, herons, and egrets. The Ten Thousand Islands Tour takes visitors on a 42-foot catamaran through the maze of islands and channels that make up the outside edge of the Everglades. On this 1.5-hour tour you might expect to see bottlenose dolphins, striped mullet, osprey, eagle rays, stingrays, and possibly even manatees. Both tours are narrated by trained naturalists and offer an inexpensive and safe way into the tangled mangrove forests.

The visitor center features a number of interesting displays about the region. One of these includes important information about catching, measuring, and releasing smalltooth sawfish, a critically endangered species once common throughout the estuary. Other displays include various animal skulls, several interpretive movies, interactive computer learning centers, and more. The gift shop handles a wide array of nature books on local flora and fauna and any number of Everglades Park souvenirs.

Fishing is a popular activity in the park and for good reason. The nearshore waters abound with record-breaking snook, redfish, sharks, tarpon, goliath and gag grouper, mangrove snapper, sheepshead, seatrout, and dozens of other species. Ranger-guided programs are available during the winter season; check the park's website for schedules and topics (http:// www.nps.gov/ever/planyourvisit/things2do.htm). Other ranger-led activities include evening canoe trips, bike tours, and guided nature walks around the grounds of the visitor center itself, helping people to identify the various plants and creatures that make the Everglades their home.

In addition to the Gulf Coast Visitor Center, the park has several other visitor centers. The largest is in Flamingo 38 miles to the south of the main park entrance. It has educational displays and nearby hiking and canoe trails. Also popular is the Shark Valley Visitor Center, on U.S. 41 about 70 miles east of Naples. Here you can enjoy a 15-mile bike ride through the famous "River of Grass" or take a guided tram tour.

With its immense size and amazing array of wildlife, Everglades National Park is a destination that is hard to overlook while visiting Florida's southwest coast.

Paradise Coast sunset Courtesy Collier County VC Bureau

Additional Collier County Parks, Preserves & Eco-Attractions

❒ ________ Eagle Lakes Community Park

Location: 11566 Tamiami Trail, Naples, FL 34112 / Phone: 239-793-4414 / Fax: n/a / E-mail: parksandrecreation@colliergov.net / Website: www.colliergov.net / 32 acres / Admission is free

Noted in the South Florida Birding Trail, Eagle Lakes Park has several expanses of wetlands that provide habitat for a great number of wading and migratory birds. More than 158 species have been identified at this site. It also offers a 2.5-mile nature trail.

❒ ________ Freedom Park

Location: 1515 Golden Gate Parkway, Naples, FL 34105 / Phone: 239-252-4000 / Fax: n/a / E-mail: parksandrecreation@colliergov.net / Website: www.colliergov.net / 50 acres / Admission is free.

This 50-acre water retention area, opened in 2009, is becoming a local hot spot for birders and nature lovers. A 2,500-square-foot nature center, plus a self-guided nature walk more than two-thirds of a mile long add to this exciting new Collier County park.

❒ ________ Clam Pass Beach Park

Location: 410 Seagate Drive, Naples, FL 34103 / Phone: 239-252-4000 / Fax: n/a / E-mail: parksandrecreation@colliergov.net / Website: www.colliergov.net / 35 acres / Admission fee charged.

With approximately 3,200 feet of beachfront, this park is an excellent location for spotting shorebirds, as well as for sunbathing, fishing, and swimming. A free tram takes you three-quarters of a mile back and forth to the beach through a thriving mangrove forest. The same roadway is an excellent hiking trail.

❒ ________ Sugden Regional Park

Location: 4284 Avalon Drive, Naples, FL 34112 / Phone: 239-252-4000 / Fax: n/a / E-mail: parksandrecreation@colliergov.net / Website: www.colliergov.net / 60 acres / Admission is free.

This lakefront park is a popular destination for freshwater swimming, paddleboats, canoes and kayaks, power boating, and sailing. A walking trail around the lake offers a chance to discover wading birds, red-winged blackbirds, migratory shorebirds, and warblers.

❒ ________ Collier County Museum

Location: 3301 Tamiami Trail East, Naples, FL 34112 / Phone: 239-252-8476 / Fax: n/a / E-mail: curator11@att.net / Website: www.colliermuseums.com / Campus: 5 acres / Admission is free, but donations are appreciated.

A diverse and fascinating assortment of historical exhibits are on hand on this five-acre site located in the county government center in Naples. Inside, the exhibition hall offers everything from mastodon tusks, through the rise and fall of the Calusa Indians, the Seminole Wars, and Barron Collier's vision for the county named after him. Outside, take in the historic Naples Cottage, logging locomotive, George G. Huntoon Gallery, the restored Craighead Laboratory, orchid house, and native Florida garden displaying more than 150 varieties of native trees, plants, and flowers. An authentic Seminole chickee hut and re-created Calusa camp are showcased on the grounds. Be sure to check the website for the current traveling exhibits and programs, as these vary seasonally.

❒ ________ Museum of the Everglades

Location: 105 West Broadway, Everglades City, FL 34139 / Phone: 239-695-0008 / Fax: n/a / E-mail: curator11@att.net / Website: www.colliermuseums.com / Admission is free, but donations are appreciated.

Until 1962, Everglades City was the Collier County seat. In the 1920s Barron Collier purchased most of the property in and around the Everglades City and turned it into a company town. The Museum of the Everglades has a permanent exhibit on the local history, from the time of the pre-Columbian Calusa to the present. Other exhibits vary seasonally and include the works of regional photographers, painters, and artists.

❒ _____ Immokalee Pioneer Museum at Roberts Ranch

Location: 1215 Roberts Avenue, Immokalee, FL 34143 / Phone: 239-658-2466 / Cellular: 239-734-0359 / E-mail: curator11@att.net / Website: www.colliermuseums.com / 15 acres / Admission is free, but donations are appreciated.

The Immokalee Pioneer Museum is located on the site of the old Robert Roberts Ranch, a cattle ranch from the early 1900s. The museum's displays and 20 restored buildings give visitors a window into the hardships of life back when the surrounding land was untamed wilderness. It is listed on the National Register of Historic Places.

❒ ________ Historic Smallwood Store

Location: , P.O. Box 367, 360 Mamie Street, Chokoloskee, FL 33925 / Phone: 239-695-2989 / Fax: 239-695-4454 / E-mail: on website / Website: www.smallwoodstore.com / Admission fee charged.

This old Indian trading post and general store is a fascinating glimpse into the life and times of Ted Smallwood, who opened it in 1906. The store, which was placed on the National Registry of Historic Places in 1974, was turned into a museum by Smallwood's granddaughter and features artifacts and goods that were originally sold there. This was the site of the killing of the legendary outlaw Edgar Watson, a story fictionalized by Peter Matthiessen in *Killing Mister Watson.*

❐ _______ The Rod and Gun Club

Location: 200 Riverside Drive, Everglades City, FL 34130 / Phone: 239-695-2101 / E-mail: n/a / Website: www.evergladesrodandgun.com / Admission is free.

A living museum, the Rod and Gun Club has been in operation since the original foundation was built in 1864. The lobby, veranda, and grounds abound with historic photographs, authentic alligator skins, and various taxidermy mounts. The facility offers lodging, a full bar, restaurant, and marina. The Everglades City playground is located directly across the street.

❐ _______ Cocohatchee Creek Preserve

Location: 1880 Veteran's Park Drive, North Naples, FL 34112 / Phone: 239-252-2961 / Fax: 239-793-3795 / E-mail: ConservationCollier@Colliergov.net / Website: www.colliergov.net/conservationcollier / 3.64 acres / Admission is free.

This preserve protects a rare stand of riverine oaks. It is also known for its gopher tortoise population. A 700-foot trail takes you through pine flatwoods, wetlands, and laurel oaks. A brochure for the park is downloadable at the website. Parking is available at nearby Veteran's Park.

❐ _______ Logan Woods Preserve

Location: 831 Logan Blvd., Naples, FL, 34119 / Phone: 239-252-2961 / Fax: 239-793-3795 / E-mail: ConservationCollier@Colliergov.net / Website: www.colliergov.net/conservationcollier / 6.8 acres / Admission is free.

This small preserve has a short hiking trail through pine flatwoods. With the removal of exotics such as Brazilian pepper and melaleuca, the trail is a welcome stretch of green space in a heavily developed area of Naples.

❒ _______ Otter Mound Preserve

Location: 1831 Addison Court, Marco Island, FL 34145 / Phone: 239-252-2961 / Fax: 239-793-3795 / E-mail: ConservationCollier@Colliergov.net / Website: www.colliergov.net/conservationcollier / 2.45 acres / Admission is free.

Built on an ancient Calusa shell mound, this small but amazing park is part of the Caxambas Point archaeological site. The former owners, Mr. and Mrs. Ernest Otter, used native Calusa whelk shells to build the terracing seen throughout the preserve. The elevated land has resulted in a plant community called tropical hardwood hammock. It is a haven for migratory and resident bird species.

❒ _______ Pepper Ranch Preserve

Location: 6315 Pepper Ranch Road, Immokalee, FL 34142 / Phone: 239-252-2961 / Fax: 239-793-3795 / E-mail: ConservationCollier@Colliergov.net / Website: www.colliergov.net/conservationcollier / 2,612 acres / Admission is free.

This large tract of land was acquired by the Conservation Collier Program in February 2009 at a cost of more than $32 million. The ranch has historic significance that dates back to the time of the Calusa. Several artifacts, including ancient canoes, have been found here. With frontage on Lake Trafford and thousands of acres to work with, the Pepper Ranch Preserve is still in its infancy. Look for this site to continue to grow into a great Collier County environmental destination in the years to come.

❒ _______ Limpkin Marsh Preserve

Location: 1330 Limpkin Road, Big Corkscrew Island, FL 34142 / Phone: 239-252-2961 / Fax: 239-793-3795 / E-mail: ConservationCollier@Colliergov.net / Website: www.colliergov.net/conservationcollier / 9.26 acres / Admission is free.

A combination of seasonal wetlands and mesic pine flatwoods make this preserve an interesting place to visit. Located near Immokalee and not far from the Audubon Corkscrew Swamp Sanctuary, the preserve has a single trail leading hikers through a sawgrass marsh and a forest of saw palmetto and slash pines. Limpkins frequent the wetlands area, and the surrounding forest is popular with migratory warblers. Parking is limited to three cars.

❒ ________ Alligator Flag Preserve

Location: 7875 Immokalee Road, Naples, FL 34142 / Phone: 239-252-2961 / Fax: 239-793-3795 / E-mail: ConservationCollier@Colliergov.net / Website: www.colliergov.net/conservationcollier / 18.46 acres / Admission is free.

A single loop trail takes you through this cypress/pine/cabbage palm community. The trails are virtually impassible during the rainy summer season but are interesting to hike or bike during the winter months. Home to fox squirrels, black bear, and various snakes, the preserve is a part of the larger Corkscrew Swamp Sanctuary Wood Stork Core Foraging Area. There is no parking at the trailhead.

❒ ________ Railhead Scrub Preserve

Location: Veterans Memorial Blvd., Naples, FL 34112 / Phone: 239-252-2961 / Fax: 239-793-3795 / E-mail: ConservationCollier@Colliergov.net / Website: www.colliergov.net/conservationcollier / 132 acres / Admission is free.

This large tract of land has limited parking and a one-mile hiking and biking trail into the heart of the preserve. Made up primarily of flooded cypress, hyric flatwoods, and xeric oak scrub, it represents some of the last remaining sections of xeric oak scrub left in Collier County. More that 409 species of native plants can be found here, along with a host of reptiles, mammals, and birds.

Sunrise over the Florida Panther National Wildlife Refuge © Dick Fortune & Sarah Lopez

Anhinga in Flight

© Sarah Pinckard

Eastern Indigo Snake © Kenneth L. Krysko, UF

Glades and Hendry Counties

Once away from the heavily populated and developed coast, the interior sections of Southwest Florida give way to sprawling cattle ranches, fields of sugarcane, and expansive stretches of sloughs, swamps, and wetlands. Because of the rural and predominantly agricultural nature of both Glades and Hendry counties, the attractions here move away from those that rely on a steady stream of patrons and require considerable infrastructure such as Mote Marine Laboratory and Aquarium, the Naples Zoo, and the Edison & Ford Winter Estates, and instead tend to be truly wild places. The OK Slough and the Fisheating Creek Water Management Area are perfect examples. When heading inland to explore natural Florida, you are also heading back in time.

Glades County was established in 1921 and named after the Florida Everglades. The county seat is Moore Haven, located on the Caloosahatchee River. The total area of the county is 986 square miles, 773 of which are land and 213 water, mostly the western portion of Lake Okeechobee.

The estimated 2010 population of Glades County is 11,092. The population of the county in 2000 was 10,576, indicating that this county has experienced little of the rapid growth that has so dramatically impacted the coastal communities to the west. The population density of Glades County—14 people per square mile—is the lowest of the six counties covered in this book. Glades' density pales in comparison to Lee County's 765 and Sarasota's 678 per square mile. Lacking any major urban developments, Glades is likely to continue this low and stable population trend. Whereas Lee County's population has increased more than tenfold since 1960, Glades County's has not even tripled (the 1960 census was 2,950).

Hendry County, although slightly more populated, follows suit when it comes to recent growth trends. The county has a total of 1,190 square miles, all of which are land except for 37 square miles of Lake Okeechobee. The estimated 2010 population of the county was 40,298 people, with a density of 35 people per square mile, double that of Glades but well below the coastal population centers. The county was named after Major Francis A. Hendry, one of the earliest settlers in the region. The county seat is LaBelle. Major Hendry not only platted out the town of LaBelle, but also named it for his two daughters, Laura and Belle.

Because so much of the land is still being actively ranched and/or farmed, neither county has as much managed land as do the coastal counties. Glades has 70,419 acres set aside as parks or preserves (14 percent), and Hendry has 94,404 acres of protected space (13 percent). Much of the remaining land is undeveloped pastureland, as well as numerous swamps, marshes, and wetlands that cannot be cultivated, so the actual acreage of potential wildlife habitat is far greater than these numbers reflect. This becomes obvious when you consider that there is not a single house or building to be found along the entire 52 miles of Fisheating Creek.

Glades and Hendry have water-quality and development issues, though they are of a different nature from those of the coastal counties. Cattle ranchers and farmers are being pressured into implementing best management practices to help control excess fertilizer and cattle manure runoff. Phosphate mining, especially in Glades County, is also an ongoing issue. The runoff from these mines can leach into the local creeks and rivers and wreak havoc on nutrient levels. For the most part, however, neither of these counties is plagued by the same kinds of issues that have left much of coastal Florida an unbroken series of strip malls and asphalt.

In fact, two of the most amazing destinations in this book are located in Glades and Hendry County, respectively. The Fisheating Creek Water Management Area is without question one of the most beautiful stretches of undeveloped property in all of Florida. A kayak or canoe trip down this pristine stream is like floating down a dreamscape. Likewise, the expansive Okaloacoochee Slough State Forest, better known as the OK Slough, is just as compelling to the dedicated naturalist. Miles upon miles of untraveled roads take you through some of the most compelling landscapes in Southwest Florida. There is even a primitive campsite on the property where the quiet of true wilderness can still be found.

Down the road, if we can put enough pressure on the South Florida Water Management District, perhaps we can get the newly created STA 5 reservoir opened up for general public access. There is something to be said for being able to visit a place where a single day's bird count can top 40,000 birds and hundreds of different species. You can read more about STA 5 at the end of this chapter.

Between Lake Okeechobee and the coast lies some of the emptiest land in all of Florida. Inhabited by rare species such as wood storks, swallow-tailed and snail kites, as well as the fascinating crested caracara, these remote destinations offer us a place to get away from the crowds and discover another side of Florida.

Glades County Eco-Destinations

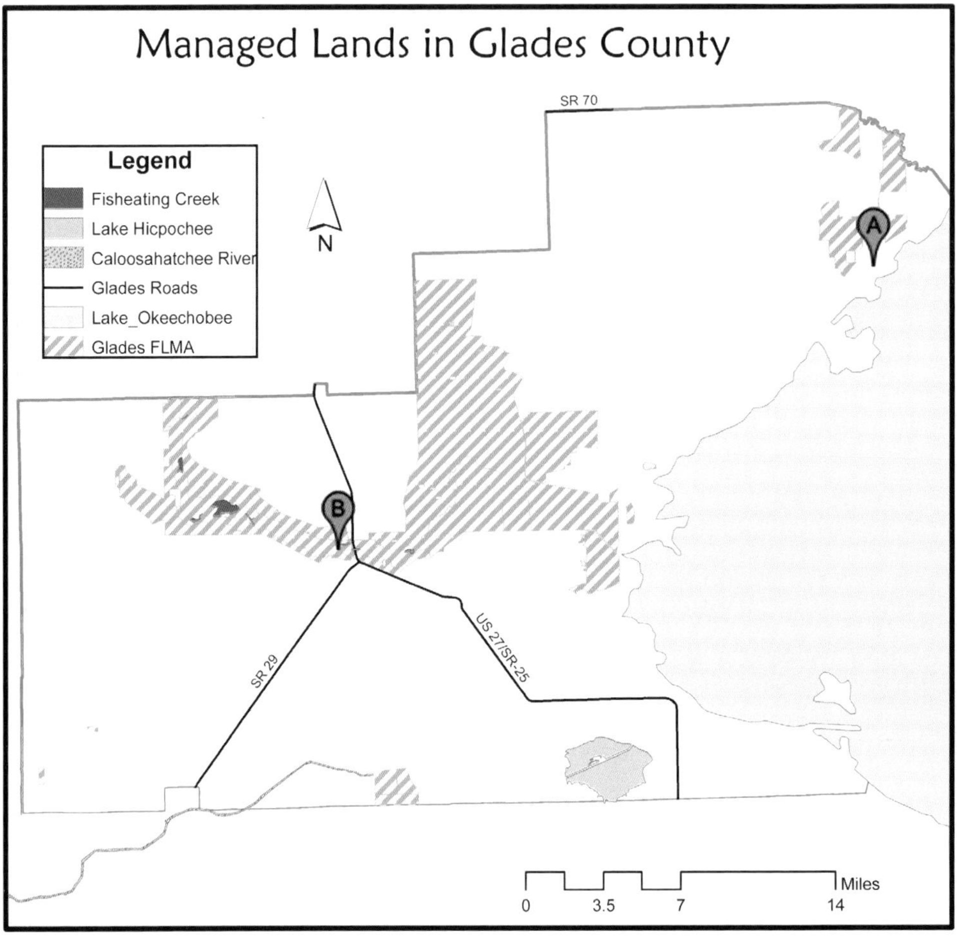

A. LOST Trail
B. Fisheating Creek WMA

CONSERVANCY
Of Southwest Florida
www.conservancy.org

Managed Lands in Southwest Florida

Glades County
494,720 Acres
175,534 Acres Managed
40%

Hendry County Eco-Destinations

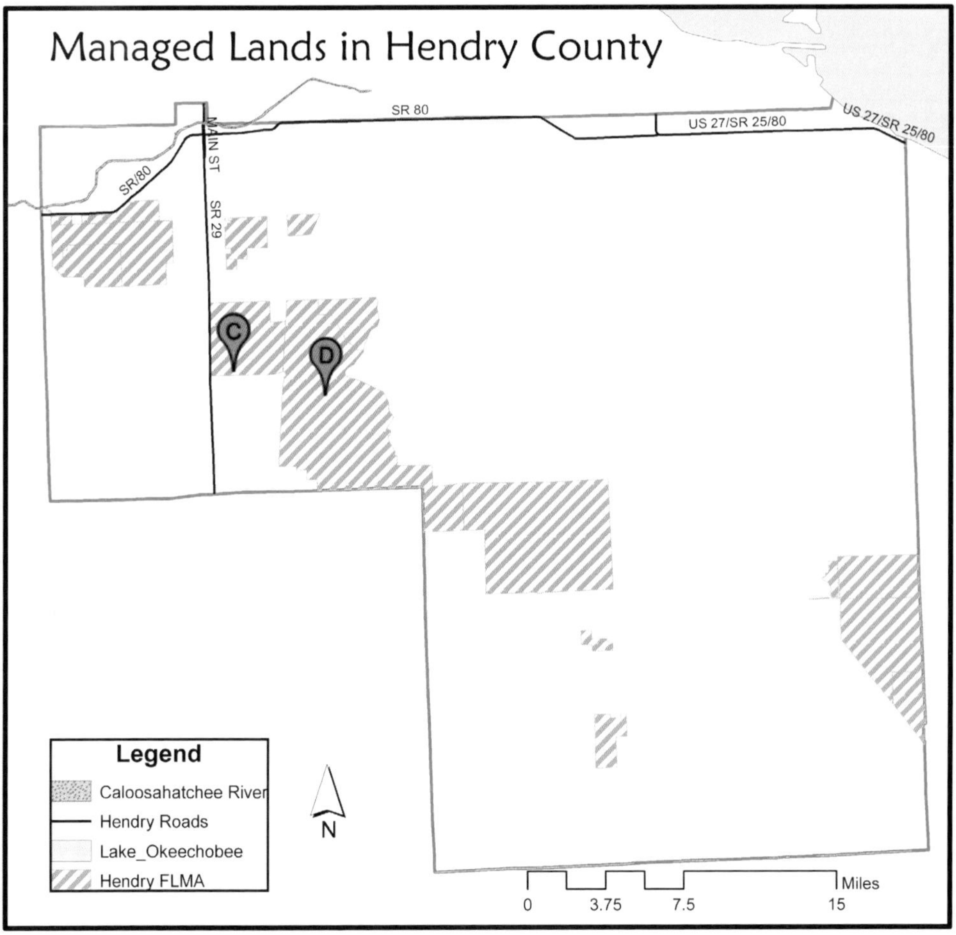

C. Spirit of the Wild
D. OK Slough

CONSERVANCY
Of Southwest Florida
www.conservancy.org

Managed Lands in Southwest Florida

Hendry County
737,920 Acres
94,404 Acres Managed
13%

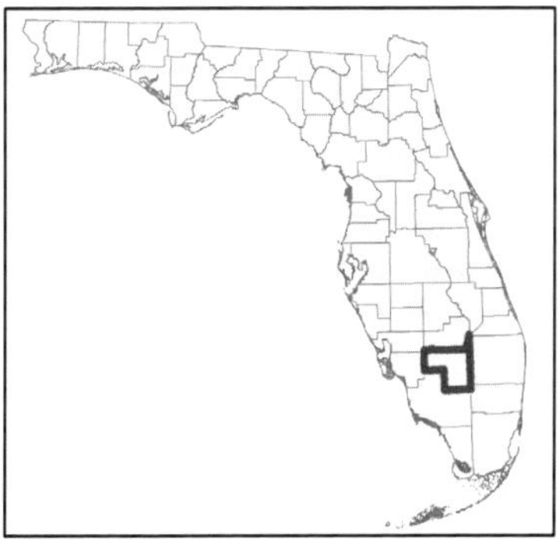

The views from the top can be stunning

❐ ________ A. The LOST Trail

Location: Numerous access points throughout the 110-mile-long trail / Phone: 850-245-2052 / Fax: 850-245-2128 / Website: www.dep.state.fl.us/gwt/state/lakeotrail / E-mail: carol.sheppard@deb.state.fl.us / Admission is free.

The 110-mile Lake Okeechobee Scenic Trail, popularly known as the LOST Trail, encircles the second-largest freshwater lake in the continental United States (Lake Michigan being the largest). The LOST Trail crosses five Florida counties—Hendry, Glades, Okeechobee, Martin, and Palm Beach. Most of the trail runs atop the Herbert Hoover Dike surrounding the lake, but long stretches have to be traversed along state and county highways. The long-range plan is to continue the LOST Trail entirely atop the 35-foot-high dike, but erosion repairs, locks, and rivers and canals entering the Big "O" at different places make this a daunting task. It will likely be decades before that dream comes to fruition.

A limpkin feeds on an island apple snail
© Charles Sobczak

The LOST trail is part of the Great Cross-Florida Hiking Trail (www.floridatrail.org) that runs from the Big Cypress National Preserve in southern Collier County to the Gulf Islands National Seashore in Pensacola. The best route for hikers is along the eastern

© Charles Sobczak

shoreline of the lake, which avoids the 30-mile stretch in Glades County where access to the dike is impossible. Here the trail runs along State Highway 78, where the shoulder is wide enough, but the traffic, though never heavy, is fast.

A family heads out for a bike ride © Charles Sobczak

The best way to experience the LOST Trail is by bicycle. The paved sections of the trail are long and straight and ideal for road bikers who like to pick up some speed, while the unpaved sections offer riders a challenge. A good interactive map is available from Palm Beach Bike Tours (www.Palmbeachbiketours.com/lake-okeechobee-scenic-trail-lost-map) and helps peddlers get a better understanding of what riding this trail involves.

A good section for beginners to bike runs 6.7 miles from the Moore Haven Locks to Liberty Point. The only problem with this section is the Western Swamp, which extends into the Big "O" and makes any view of open water impossible. The next leg of that trip, heading east from Liberty Point to the town of Clewiston (5.17 miles) provides some nice views of the lake. An even better stretch for seeing the Big "O" is the run between Clewiston and Rita Village (4.47 miles).

Because much of the LOST Trail segment in Glades County is along State Road 78, a better stretch of the trail begins when you cross the county line into Okeechobee County where you can access the dike at the Okeetanta Trailhead. Continuing north, the trail runs on top of the dike all the way to Port Mayaca in southern Martin County.

The views from atop the dike are the bicyclist's reward. On one side is the rim canal, which surrounds much of the perimeter of Lake Okeechobee. Seldom more than 50 feet wide, the rim canal abounds with numerous limpkins, herons, egrets, ducks, alligators,

Airboats are popular in and around the Big O
© Charles Sobczak

gar, bass, bream, and dozens of different species of passerines such as red-winged blackbirds, warblers, and boat-tailed grackles. On the Lake "O" side of the dike, the views can be stunning. The lake is so wide that you cannot see across to the other side. Its shoreline abounds with birds and animals, including armadillos, raccoons, and river otters. Of course, there are also airboats, pontoon boats, bass boats, and everything in between roaring up and down the rim canal and the lake, accompanied by plenty of noise.

Small shaded shelters and portable toilets are placed sporadically along the trail atop the dike. Primitive campsites are situated at various spots around the lake, but bicyclists may also choose to overnight in local motels found in towns such as Okeechobee, Clewiston, Pahokee, and Moore Haven. There are also plenty of small, local eateries along the way.

The LOST Trail isn't for everyone. If you, or your children, lose control of your bike, it's not all that hard to wind up heading down a steep embankment toward the rim canal or the lake. There are no shade trees anywhere, and the wind blows unabated once you are up on the dike. A tailwind can be a biker's dream come true, but the odds are always 50/50 that it could be a stiff headwind instead. Applying plenty of sunscreen is a must, and a hat is also recommended. Remember to bring bug repellent if you plan to ride at dawn or dusk, as the mosquitoes can be fearsome. Biking in the dark along the rim is not recommended.

For the avid bicyclist, the LOST Trail is well worth the effort. It is unlike any other bike path in the state in that you are riding above your surroundings, be it rundown trailer parks, busy marinas, or endless fields of sugarcane. *Unique* best describes a bike path that runs for miles on end atop one of the largest man-made structures on earth—the Herbert Hoover Dike—built by the Army Corp of Engineers in the 1930s after the devastating hurricane of 1928. The storm surge overwhelmed a much smaller dike and flooded the towns of Clewiston and Okeechobee, killing more than 2,500 people. A mass grave at the Port Mayaca Cemetery contains the bodies of 1,600 victims of that terrible storm.

Today the dike is somewhat controversial. The huge agricultural interests that farm sugarcane along much of the southern sections of the lake also prevent the natural sheet flow of water from the Big "O" and as a result, starve the Everglades of freshwater. The two outlets for the constant inflow of water from the Kissimmee River basin—the Caloosahatchee River to the west and the St. Lucie Canal to the east—wreak havoc on the estuaries located along the coast with far more freshwater than these systems can handle. The Southwest Florida Water Management District is under pressure to purchase some of this agricultural land back from U.S. Sugar and other corporations in an effort to save the Everglades. The issues are complex and solutions difficult. Like other water projects across the world, the Herbert Hoover Dike may well be an engineering marvel, but its environmental impact is closer to catastrophic than marvelous.

Sandhill crane

❐___ B. Fisheating Creek Wildlife Management Area

Location: 7555 U.S. Highway 27 North, Palmdale, FL 33944 / Phone: 863-675-5999 / Fax: n/a / Website: www.fisheatingcreekoutpost.com / E-mail: info@fisheatingcreekoutpost.com / 18,272 acres / Admission is free, fees charged for launching canoes and camping.

Getting ready to put out on Fisheating Creek © Charles Sobczak

The most attractive feature of Fisheating Creek is the complete absence of houses, cabins, or any substantial development along its 52 miles of navigable waterway. Aside from a few private roads leading down to the water and the train trestle next to the Highway 27 overpass near the town of Palmdale, Fisheating Creek is a true wilderness waterway.

Ancient bald cypress trees tower over this free-flowing stream, while immense alligators bask on small patches of sandy shoreline. The creek teems with bream, bass, and crappie. On the higher ridges massive live oak branches reach out over the water, their limbs covered with resurrection fern and bromeliads. Deer, wild boar, and wild turkeys can often be spotted along the shoreline, and swallowtail kites and crested caracaras hover overhead. Cypress knees appear to spring up everywhere, sometimes catching the keel of the canoe and making for some unexpected bumps and spins for the inexperienced paddler. The water is stained almost black by the tannic acid coming off the roots of the cypress and oak forests, and it runs deep and steady through these untouched remnants of what much of Florida must have looked like 500 years ago.

Bald Cypress line the banks of the creek © Charles Sobczak

The headquarters for much of the activity on the creek is the Fisheating Creek Outpost, which is located on the west side of U.S. Highway 27 about a mile north of where State Road 29 enters the highway. The campground, renovated in 2010, is operated by Patty and Allen Register, who also run the nearby roadside attraction, Gatorama. It has 120 campsites, ranging from primitive tent sites right along the creek to 52 RV sites, most with hook-ups for water, electricity, and sewer. Several of the primitive tent sites sit along the shoreline of Depot Lake, which is kept free of alligators and a popular swimming hole during the warmer months of the year. Every campsite has a picnic table and a fire pit, and the communal bathhouses offer hot showers and restrooms. Firewood is available at the nearby camp store.

The history of the creek is a fascinating study in riparian rights and the power of a community committed to preserving a beautiful piece of wilderness. Almost all of the land abutting the creek was owned by the Lykes Brothers, who were, and in many ways still are, the local land barons for much of this section of Glades County. The land, some 300,000 acres, was purchased by Dr. Howell Tyson Lykes in the 1880s and inherited

A perfect campsite at the creek © Charles Sobczak

by his seven sons. At one point the family owned 76 percent of Glades County. The Lykes Brothers Company became the largest cattle producer and biggest meatpacking firm in Florida.

In 1989 the family decided to close the campground and canoe concession located in Palmdale (the same location where the Outpost is today) and seal off the entire creek to the general public. The citizens of Glades County were outraged by the sudden and unexpected closure of one of the most popular fishing and outdoor destinations in their county. Under U.S. law, any navigable body of water is open to use by the public. The question was this: Was Fisheating Creek a navigable body of water?

Within months paddlers, campers, fishermen, and hunters, as well as the local Sierra Club and the Calusa Group came together to form a nonprofit organization called Save Our Creeks. The group was a unique combination of environmentalists, hunters, and fishermen who felt they were about to lose access to this pristine stretch of water. The lawsuit over these riparian rights continued for 10 years until, on Feb. 19, 1998, Judge Charles Carlton ruled that Fisheating Creek was navigable, and by the laws and statutes pertaining to these rights, it belonged not to Lykes Brothers, but to the people. Lykes Brothers immediately appealed the judge's decision. To put an end to the court battle, the parties agreed to a settlement calling for the state of Florida to purchase a corridor along the creek under the auspices of CARL (Conservation and Recreation Lands Program) and using funds from the Florida Forever Act. The state purchased 18,272 acres, which became known as the Fisheating Creek Wildlife Management Area. The settlement came with stipulations that prohibit the use of motorized vehicles, airboats, and personal watercraft, along with some specific hunting regulations, which are posted on the website.

Today Save Our Creeks is embroiled in a battle to connect Fisheating Creek to Lake Okeechobee. Although it comes within nine miles of the lake, the creek eventually widens out into a massive swamp known as Cowbone Marsh. Thick floating vegetation and a newly built weir prevent paddlers from making it all the way to the Big "O." Although most of Fisheating Creek itself is protected, there is always more work to be done to preserve and protect these wild waterways.

❐ __ C. Spirit-of-the-Wild Wildlife Management Area

Location: Entrance is on the north side of County Road 832, approximately one mile east of State Road 29. GPS Coordinates: 26E59'61.97"N / 081E40'69.91"W / Phone: 850-488-4676 / Fax: n/a / Website: www.myfwc.com/recreation/WMASites_SpiritoftheWild / E-mail: n/a / 7,487 acres / Admission fee charged.

The entrance sign on county road 832 © Charles Sobczak

The name says it all at the 7,487-acre Spirit-of-the-Wild WMA. Originally a ranch, sod operation, and vegetable farm, the property was purchased by the state of Florida in 2002, which turned it over to the Florida Fish and Wildlife Conservation Commission (FWC) to oversee as a wildlife management area (WMA). It is near the much larger Okaloacoochee (OK) Slough, and together the two properties form close to 40,000 acres of wilderness preserve in Hendry County.

As is often the case with these purchases by the state, the former owner of the property leased it back for cattle grazing. That lease ran out in 2007, and

Wild Boar in mud © Richard Bartz, Courtesy Wikipedia Commons

FWC, in collaboration with the state, are filling in many of the drainage ditches and canals, removing the old pastures of Bahia grass (remnants of the former sod farm), and replanting the acreage with native trees, shrubs, and grasses. Owing to the immensity of the property, this will likely take decades to complete.

Like all wildlife management areas, Spirit-of-the-Wild permits recreational hunting, as well as birding, bicycling, and horseback riding. Archery hunting of the local feral pigs is a popular activity. Gun season generally is open in late

The kiosk and brochure box at Spirit of the Wild WMA © Charles Sobczak

October and November. Small game, turkey, and dove seasons also occur at Spirit-of-the-Wild.

The entrance to this wildlife management area is on the north side of County Road 832 about 1½ miles east of State Road 29 north of Immokalee. The main road is called Canoe Road, though the property has no navigable waterway. Just up the road is a game check-in station staffed by FWC. Canoe Road continues north until it becomes the Albritton Loop Road, then crosses Robert's Canal and becomes Thomas Road, returning seven miles later to County Road 832. Five hiking trails head east off of Canoe Road. These old farm roads are also used by all-terrain vehicles and can be quite chewed up because of it.

The terrain is mostly pine flatwoods, oak hammocks, and seasonal wetlands typical of this part of interior Florida. Birding is fantastic here. The region has eastern meadowlarks, swallowtail kites, snail kites, loggerhead shrikes, wood ducks, and northern harriers. The FWC website has a complete list of birds found at Spirit-of-the-Wild.

The preserve is home to many Eastern diamondback rattlesnakes and water moccasins, so care should be taken when leaving the main path and heading into the saw palmetto thickets or marshes. If you take a scenic drive or head out on a short hike along its four-plus miles of trails, you might also come across some of the wild hogs, deer, and wild turkeys that frequent the area.

Although this wildlife management area is well on its way to becoming a first-class eco-destination, it is still a work in progress. If you are on your way to the nearby OK Slough, however, a short side trip to Spirit-of-the-Wild is well worth the time.

Eastern Diamondback Rattlesnake
© Ryan E. Poplin, Courtesy Wikipedia Commons

The Okaloacoochee Slough State Forest

❒ ________ D. Okaloacoochee Slough State Forest

Location: Division of Forestry Office, 6265 County Road 832, Felda, FL 33930 / Phone: 863-612-0776 / Fax: n/a / Website: www.fl-dof.com/state_forests/okaloacoochee / E-mail: schmiec@doacs.state.fl.us / 32,039 acres / Admission fee charged.

With a name that is derived from the Creek Indians and is all but impossible to pronounce, everyone, including the Florida Division of Forestry staff, simply calls this state forest the OK Slough. Okaloacoochee was coined by the Seminoles and is a combination of several Creek words that describe "dark, shallow waters." That description holds true today since the freshwater found throughout the slough has a dark tint produced by the tannic acid from the roots of the surrounding vegetation.

These 32,039 acres of state forest were purchased between 1996 and 2000 under the Conservation and Recreation Land (CARL) program using a combination of Preservation 2000 and Save Our River funds. The slough itself is 13,382 acres, a wide-open expanse of sedges, cattails, and marsh grasses, with cypress domes rising in the distance. A hiking trail, with an elevated boardwalk and overlook, gives visitors a first-hand view of its expanse. Because the slough is so shallow, canoeing and kayaking are not recommended.

The slough drains slowly to the south, eventually feeding the waters of Corkscrew Swamp, then down through the Fakahatchee Strand and out through the Ten Thousand Islands to the Gulf of Mexico. It is an important wetlands and the state of Florida must be lauded for having the foresight to save this stretch of pristine wilderness.

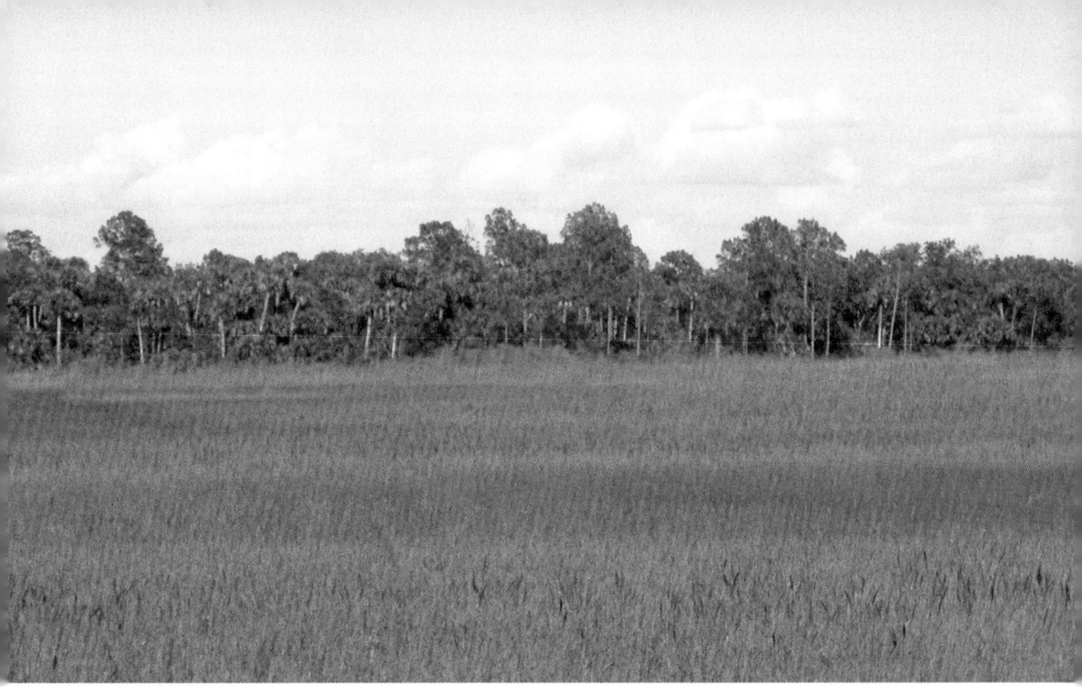

© Charles Sobczak

This wasn't always the case. In the early 1900s, slash pines, bald cypress, and other viable timber were logged off primarily for use as railroad ties. By the 1930s, with most of the lumber gone, the land was converted to ranching and agricultural purposes, though the slough itself was left untouched.

Today the old logging roads, with names such as Wildcow Grade, North Loop West, and Twin Mills Grade, are one of the greatest assets of the OK Slough. These old roads and trails, totaling 39 miles, wind through expansive dry prairies of saw palmetto and slash pine, giving visitors open, unobstructed views. While a few of them require a high-center truck or a four-wheel-drive vehicle to navigate, most are high and dry, especially in the winter season. They also present an unparalleled off-road biking opportunity. Though not paved, they are fairly hard packed and are an easy pedal for most crossover or trail bikes.

Access to the various logging roads is by inexpensive self-pay stations. Trail maps and bird checklists are often available at these stations, though you would be well advised to print these out from the website before coming, just in case the stations are out.

Beyond the old logging trails are numerous hiking paths that branch off of the main roads for the adventurous to explore. There are several primitive campsites in the park, available on a first-come, first-served basis. There is no potable water. Care should be taken when visiting during

A primitive campsite at the OK Slough © Charles Sobczak

The new overlook with stunning views © Charles Sobczak

hunting seasons, since wild pig, turkey, and dove hunting is allowed throughout the forest.

The wildlife, from mammals to reptiles to birds, is unbelievable. Birders can often sight the elusive crested caracara. Other common sightings include wild turkey, swallow-tailed and snail kites, barred owls, tufted titmouse, warblers, ducks, and more. The website includes a downloadable OK Slough checklist of 85 different species. The slough is a part of the Great Florida Birding Trail.

Because of its remoteness and sheer size, the OK Slough State Forest is home to many larger animals such as wild hogs, white-tailed deer, Florida black bears, and on rare occasions, the Florida panther. Reptiles include gopher tortoises and large alligators that roam the immense wetlands.

If you ask most people about the Okaloacoochee Slough, they will say they've never heard of it. That will change, however, because the OK Slough is far, far better than just OK. It is one of the few places north of the Everglades where you can see what pre-Columbian Florida looked like—an undiscovered treasure within a short day's drive from almost anywhere along Florida's southwest coast. It is better than OK, it is simply great!

Crested caracaras are common at the OK Slough
© Joseph Blanda, M.D.

Additional Hendry and Glades County Parks, Preserves, and Eco-destinations

❒ ________ Gatorama

Location: 6180 U.S. Highway 27, Palmdale, FL 33994 / Phone: 863-675-0623 / Fax: n/a / Website: www. gatorama.com / E-mail: Patty @gatorama.com / 15 acres / Admission fee charged.

Established in the 1950s by Cecil Clemons, Gatorama prides itself on being one of the few remaining "roadside attractions" in Florida. Today it is run by Allen and Patty Register, who also operate the nearby Fisheating Creek Outpost concession for Florida Fish and Wildlife Conservation Commission. Gatorama features daily alligator feedings and a 1,000-foot boardwalk over ponds filled with various species of crocodiles, including the endangered American crocodile. Gatorama hosts an annual Alligator Hatching Festival in late August. It also specializes in selling alligator meat, hides, and other products at its on-site gift shop.

❒ ________ Billie Swamp Safari

Location: 30000 Gator Tail Trail, Clewiston, FL 33440 / Phone: 863-983-9396 / Fax: 863-983-9396 / Website: www. swampsafari.com / E-mail: safari @semtribe.com / 2,000 acres / Admission fee charged.

Run by the Seminole Tribe of Florida, Billie Swamp Safari includes a host of touristy activities such as airboat rides, crocodile pits, animal exhibits, and swamp buggy rides. Located on a large tract of land, this chickee-hut-themed park offers some good bird, deer, and other wildlife viewing on any of its "safaris." The annual Big Cypress Shootout reenactment each February celebrates the fact that the Seminoles were the only undefeated Indian tribe in the United States. The Ah-Tah-Thi-Ki Museum, displaying the historic tools and artifacts of the tribe, is located on-site.

❒ ________ Clewiston Museum

Location: 109 Central Avenue, Clewiston, FL 33440 / Phone: 863-983-2870 / Fax: n/a / Website: www. clewistonmuseum.org / E-mail: clewistonmuseum @ embarqmail.com / Admission fee charged.

Located in the original home of The Clewiston News, this regional museum focuses on Native Americans, Seminoles, and more recently, the Number 5 British Flying Training School that was housed just outside of Clewiston during World War II. Other exhibits include saber-toothed tiger skulls, mastodon remains, and photographic archives of the history of Clewiston and the sugarcane industry.

An alligator at Dinner Island WMA © Charles Sobczak

❒ ________ LaBelle Heritage Museum

Location: 150 South Lee Street, LaBelle, FL 33935 / Phone: 863-674-0034 / Fax: n/a / Website: www. asp.naples.net / E-mail: labelleheritagemuseum@ comcast. net / Admission fee charged.

Focusing on the history and development of western Hendry County, the LaBelle Heritage Museum offers a cornucopia of old photographs, artifacts, and stories about the formation of the county. Primarily cattle country, LaBelle has also had a long-term relationship with the Caloosahatchee River, which runs along the north end of the town.

❒ ________ Alva Historical Museum

Location: 21420 East Pearl Street, Alva, FL 33920 / Phone: n/a / Fax: n/a / Website: www. myfloridahistory.org / E-mail: n/a / Admission is free.

Located in the old library building, this small regional museum focuses on what life was like in 1887 when the city was established. It is open only on Saturdays from 2-4 p.m.

❒ ________ Glades County Courthouse

Location: 500 Avenue J, Moore Haven, FL 33471 / Phone: 863-946-6010 / Fax: n/a / Website: www. mygladescounty.com / E-mail: n/a / Admission is free.

Built in 1928 in the Classical Revival style, this impressive structure has been noted in several books and numerous magazine articles. It was designed by the American architect Edward Columbus Hosford. You can tour the courthouse during business hours.

❒ _______ LaBelle Nature Park

Location: 414 Fraser Avenue, LaBelle, FL 33935 / Phone: 863-675-2872 / Fax: n/a / Website: www. labellenaturepark.net / E-mail: phil @labellenaturepark.net / 9 acres / Admission is free.

Situated on the southern shoreline of the Caloosahatchee River, the LaBelle Nature Park is already a great destination for birders and naturalists, but plans are under way to add an interpretive center, canoe and kayak launch, and a host of other amenities.

❒ _______ Ortona Lock Campground

Location: 4330 Dalton Lane SW, Moore Haven, FL 33477 / Phone: 863-675-8400 / Fax: n/a / Website: www. visitglades.com/ortona-lock-campground / Admission is free, but fees are charged for camping.

Located at the Ortona Lock along the Caloosahatchee River approximately 10 miles east of LaBelle, off of State Road 80, this campground has 51 campsites, a fishing pier, restrooms, and showers. The facility is operated by the U.S. Army Corps of Engineers as Ortona South and is open year-round.

❒ _______ Ortona Indian Mound Park

Location: North side of State Road 78 between US 27 and State Road 29 just to the west of the old Ortona Cemetery. GPS Coordinates: 26E81'59.61"N / 081E30'53.51"W / Phone: 863-946-0300 / Fax: n/a / Website: www. visitglades. com / E-mail: on Website / 30 acres / Admission is free.

The ancient mounds at Ortona Indian Mound Park date back to 200 A.D. and were built by tribes related to the Calusa Indians. The highest of the mounds, at 22 feet, is also the highest point in all of Glades County. Several ancient Native America canals are located nearby, as are a small picnic area and pavilion.

Nesting wood storks

© Gareth Pinckard

❐ ________ Moore Haven Riverwalk

Location: At the intersection of Avenue J and Riverside Drive in Moore Haven, GPS Coordinates: 26E83'18.35"N / 081E09'03.24"W / Phone: 863-946-0300 / Fax: n/a / Website: www. visitglades.com / E-mail: on Website / Admission is free.

Starting at a tree called The Lone Cypress that is now considered a historic site, this attractive linear park follows the Caloosahatchee River through Moore Haven. The Lone Cypress was once a familiar navigational marker for sailors going between Lake Okeechobee and the Gulf of Mexico.

❐ ________ Fort Center

Location: The trailhead that takes you back to Fort Center is located on State Road 78 approximately eight miles north of Moore Haven, GPS Coordinates: 26E95'16.06"N / 081E12'20.17"W / Phone: 863-946-0300 / Fax: n/a / Website: www. visitglades.com / E-mail: on Website / Admission is free.

Fort Center is located within the Fisheating Creek Water Management Area and is one of the oldest known Native American archaeological sites in the Lake Okeechobee region. A long walking trail takes you to the site, which is still being explored. It is thought to be the first place in North America where maize was cultivated.

❐ ________ STA 5 (Storage Treatment Area 5)

Location: Proceed south out of Clewiston on County Road 835 (Evercane Road). Turn left onto Blumberg Road for nine miles until you reach the STA 5 gravel turnoff road. STA 5 is 2.5 miles down that road. GPS Coordinates: 26E46'13.52"N / 080E91'53.37"W / Phone: Margaret England 863-674-0695 / Fax: n/a / Website: www. audobonswfl.org / E-mail: sta5birding@ earthlink.net / 7,680 acres / Admission is by special arrangement only.

Operated by the South Florida Water Management District as a public small-game hunting area, this 11-square-mile manmade wetlands has coincidentally become one of the premier birding locations in the state. It is a haven for literally tens of thousands of birds. In the 2008 Great Backyard Bird Count, Clewiston and STA 5 counted 143,748 birds, placing it in the top 10 localities in all of North America. One of STA 5's daily counts alone exceeded 43,000 birds. Tours are made by special arrangement with the Hendry-Glades Audubon Society at www. orgsites.com/fl/hgaudubon or by calling Margaret England.

About the Author

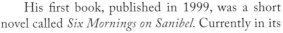

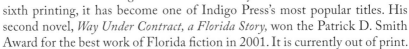

Charles Sobczak is an award-winning author who lives and writes on Sanibel Island. In 2010 he released *Living Sanibel—A Nature Guide to Sanibel & Captiva Islands*, which gone on to become one of the best-selling books on the islands and has received critical acclaim throughout Southwest Florida.

His first book, published in 1999, was a short novel called *Six Mornings on Sanibel.* Currently in its sixth printing, it has become one of Indigo Press's most popular titles. His second novel, *Way Under Contract, a Florida Story,* won the Patrick D. Smith Award for the best work of Florida fiction in 2001. It is currently out of print.

Following his second novel, Sobczak published *Rhythm of the Tides,* a collection of his most popular essays, short stories, and poetry. His third novel, *A Choice of Angels*, was a departure from his previous books. Set in Atlanta, Georgia, and Istanbul, Turkey, it tells the story of a forbidden romance between the son of a Baptist minister and the daughter of an Islamic family. It received a starred review in *Booklist*, the official publication of the American Library Association. His most recent novel, *Chain of Fools*, is set in northern Minnesota and is based on his father's dysfunctional family.

His first nonfiction title was *Alligators, Sharks and Panthers: Deadly Encounters with Florida's Top Predator—Man.* It won several awards, including the best regional non-fiction of 2007. To read Sobczak's award-winning essays or excerpts from any of his books, go to www.indigopress.net.

Sobczak has two sons: Logan, a student at the University of Florida, and Blake, who is studying at Northwestern University. He is happily married to Molly Heuer, and both enjoy hiking, biking, and kayaking throughout the region. Sobczak is past president of the Sanibel Island Fishing Club, current president of Lee Reefs (Lee County's artificial reef organization), a lifetime member of the Sanibel-Captiva Conservation Foundation, and an avid offshore fisherman.

A portion of the proceeds of the sale of *The Living Gulf Coast* will go toward the author's continued support of organizations such as the Natural Resources Defense Council, Sierra Club, Audubon Society, World Wildlife Fund, and other groups dedicated to regional and worldwide conservation projects. To contact Sobczak via e-mail regarding any of his writings, or to arrange a speaking engagement, you can contact him via e-mail at livingsanibel@gmail.com or by calling Indigo Press at 239-472-0491.

Bibliography

To save paper and make it easier to link to the numerous research websites used in this book, the bibliography of this work is online. Go to www.indigopress.net and look for the link on the *Living Gulf Coast* web page.

Contributors

Dick Fortune and Sara Lopez /www.throughthelensgallery.com / Dick Fortune and Sara Lopez share a deep understanding and love of nature that is reflected in their exquisite wildlife images. Both artistically unique and technically astounding, their photographs truly honor the wildlife they represent. Dick and Sara promote positive photographic practices that respect and protect the wildlife that has become so dear to them by discouraging harassment, feeding, or provocation of any kind. To view more of their work please visit their website.

Judd Patterson / www.Birdsinfocus.com / www.juddpatterson.com / Judd Patterson's photos have appeared in a variety of publications including *Audubon Magazine* and *The Nature Conservancy*. His work has been shown at Everglades National Park and the Tallgrass Prairie National Preserve. He continues to pursue nature photography to promote environmental education/conservation and for the sheer joy of being in the wild. Judd was also a major contributor to *Living Sanibel—A Nature Guide to Sanibel & Captiva Islands.*

David Seibel / www.davidseibel.com / www.birdsinfocus.com / David Seibel not only is a lifelong birder and outstanding wildlife photographer, but also holds a Ph.D. in ornithology from the University of Kansas and is a biology professor at Johnson County Community College. He is a poet, popular lecturer, and co-author of an upcoming book, *Birds of Kansas*, to be published in May 2011. More of his work can be seen at his two websites.

Bob Gress / www.birdsinfocus.com / Bob Gress has photographed wildlife for an array of publications for more than 30 years. He has co-authored *The Guide to Kansas Birds and Birding Hot Spots* and *Faces of the Great Plains: Prairie Wildlife.* He is the director of the Great Plains Nature Center in Wichita, Kansas, and is one of the three collaborators on the Birds in Focus website, which, to date, features more than 3,900 images and 747 species.

Alan S. Maltz / www.alanmaltz.com / Alan Maltz has been designated the "Official Fine Art Photographer for the State of Florida" by Visit Florida and "The Official Wildlife Photographer of Florida" by the Wildlife Foundation of Florida. His work has been published in numerous national publications such as *The New Yorker, Publishers Weekly, Philadelphia Inquirer, New York Post,* and *O, The Oprah Magazine.* Alan published a photography book focusing on Lee County, titled *Visions of Beauty—Ft. Myers, Sanibel and Beyond,* and is working on a similar book defining the natural beauty of Collier County. His work can be seen at his gallery located at 1210 Duval Street, Key West, Florida and on his website.

Heather Green / www.heathergreenphoto.com / Heather Green has had a lifelong passion for photography. She specializes in portraits, equine photography, nature, and landscapes. Her lens captures the essence of her subjects, which she enjoys photographing outdoors, as well as in her studio. Based in Ft. Myers, Florida, Heather has photographed many local parks and preserves, as well as their wild inhabitants. To see more of her work visit her website or her larger gallery on Flickr.com.

Blake Sobczak / www.blakesobczak.com / Blake Sobczak is currently studying photojournalism and Arabic studies at Northwestern University in Evanston, Illinois. His recent scholastic work has taken him to Qatar, Morocco, and Egypt, where his camera focused on the people and places in these faraway lands. His photos can be viewed on his website or visit his blog at **www.the195.com/northwestern.**

Clair Postmus / An award-winning photographer for more than 40 years, Clair Postmus's works have appeared in many books including Don and Lillian Stokes's *Beginner's Guide to Shorebirds,* Dennis Paulson's *Shorebirds of North America,* and *Living Sanibel.* He resides in Arizona with his lovely and talented wife, Bev Postmus, and continues to photograph the flora and fauna of that region.

Gareth and Sarah-Jane Pinckard / www.manxphoto.com / With their home base on the Isle of Man in Great Britain, this dynamic couple makes frequent visits to Southwest Florida with two cameras in hand. They have captured the essence of subjects such as butterflies, dolphins, birds, and insects and continue shooting the birds, people, and places of their native country. Please visit their website to see additional photos of Florida and Great Britain.

Maggie May Rogers / www.maggiemaydesignsphotos.shutterfly.com / Maggie May Rogers is an award-winning book designer, as well as an experienced nature and wildlife photographer. She collaborated with the Sanibel-Captiva Conservation Foundation staff in putting together *A Natural Course, the 35th Anniversary of the Sanibel-Captiva Conservation Foundation* in 2005. She also contributed to and designed *Living Sanibel — A Nature Guide to Sanibel & Captiva Islands* and *Alligators, Sharks & Panthers,* both by Sanibel author Charles Sobczak. She resides in central Kentucky and can be contacted via Facebook at MaggieMay Designs.

Dr. Kenneth L. Krysko, UF / www. flmnh.ufl.edu/directory/cvs/kennyk_cv / With a Ph.D. in wildlife ecology and conservation, Dr. Kenny Krysko is head of collections of herpetology at the University of Florida, Gainesville. His writings have appeared in a number of scientific journals including *Florida Scientist, Southeastern Naturalist,* and *Applied Herpetology.* His interests include photographing the native snakes and lizards and exotic non-native species found throughout Florida.

David Irving / www. flickr.com/people/dave_irving / A world-traveled professional, David Irving has shot wildlife, people, and landscapes in dozens of countries across North and South America, Africa, Asia, and Australia. His work has appeared in *Smithsonian Magazine, Sport Fishing Magazine,* and *Subtropic* (Australia). He has also been published on numerous websites and has had his work included in several nature books including the *Atlas of Florida's Natural Places* and *Morelet's Crocodile.* Thousands of his photographs are posted on Flickr.com and include such diverse subjects as African wild dogs, koala bears, and the waterfalls of Iguazú, Argentina.

Additional contributors include:

Katie Fuhr Laakkonen / Environmental Science Specialist, Naples, Florida
Al Tuttle / Nature Photographer / www.flickr.com/people/al-ien
Susie Holly / Copy Editor / www.macintoshbooks.com
Mary Harper / Indexing / www.accesspointsindexing.com
Hung V. Do / Naturalist, Miami Zoo / www.flickr.com/photos/roninstudio
Rob Pailes / Realtor & Nature Photographer / www.santiva-images.com
John James Audubon / Courtesy Wikipedia Commons
Joseph Blanda, MD / Nature Photographer
Ken Haley / Nature Photographer
Mark Kenderdine / Nature Photographer www.flickr.com/photos/67809251@N00
Sara Yunsoo Kim / Nature Photographer / www.flickr.com/people/kphoto
Jennifer Beltran / Nature Photographer / www.floridabats.org
Brian Johnson /Realtor, Photographer, and Publisher / www.islandscenes.com
Sarasota Visitors and Convention Bureau / www.sarasotafl.org
Charlotte County Visitors and Convention Bureau / www.charlotteharbortravel.com
Martha Robinson / Florida State Parks / www.floridastateparks.org
Lee County Visitors and Convention Bureau / www.leevcb.com
Kenneth Mills / Lee County Parks and Recreation / www.leeparks.org
Collier County Visitors and Convention Bureau / www.paradisecoast.com
Alex Warner / Sanibel Historical Museum / www.sanibelmuseum.org
Nature Conservancy of Southwest Florida / www.conservancy.org
Sanibel-Captiva Conservation Foundation / www.sccf.org
Bailey-Matthews Shell Museum / www.shellmuseum.org
Randell Research Center / www.flmnh.ufl.edu/rrc/
Naples Zoo at the Caribbean Gardens / www.carribeangardens.com
Naples Botanical Garden / www.naplesgarden.org
Mote Marine Lab and Aquarium / www.mote.org
Sarasota County Parks and Recreation / www.scgov.net/parksandrecreation
Visit Florida / www.visitflorida.com
U.S. Geological Survey / www.usgs.gov
U.S. Fish & Wildlife / www.fws.gov
Georgia Fish & Wildlife / www.georgiawildlife.com
National Oceanic and Atmospheric Administration / www.noaa.gov
Wikipedia Commons and all the photographers who contribute to this important site / www.wikipedia.org

INDEX

A

B

C

D

G

H

I

J

K

L

M

T